Pacifying the Homeland

Pacifying the Homeland

Intelligence Fusion and Mass Supervision

BRENDAN McQUADE

University of California Press

University of California Press, one of the most distinguished university presses in the United States, enriches lives around the world by advancing scholarship in the humanities, social sciences, and natural sciences. Its activities are supported by the UC Press Foundation and by philanthropic contributions from individuals and institutions. For more information, visit www.ucpress.edu.

University of California Press
Oakland, California

Library of Congress Cataloging-in-Publication Data

Names: McQuade, Brendan, author.
Title: Pacifying the homeland : intelligence fusion and mass supervision / Brendan McQuade.
Description: Oakland, California : University of California Press, [2019] | Includes bibliographical references and index. |
Identifiers: LCCN 2019004170 (print) | LCCN 2019006629 (ebook) | ISBN 9780520971349 (ebook) | ISBN 9780520299740 (cloth : alk. paper) | ISBN 9780520299757 (pbk. : alk. paper)
Subjects: LCSH: Terrorism—United States—Prevention—Information services. | National security—United States—Information services. | Intelligence service—United States—Information services. | Interagency coordination—United States.
Classification: LCC HV6432 (ebook) | LCC HV6432 .M38 2019 (print) | DDC 363.325/170973—dc23
LC record available at https://lccn.loc.gov/2019004170

Manufactured in the United States of America

26 25 24 23 22 21 20 19
10 9 8 7 6 5 4 3 2 1

For Silas and Eliot

Contents

Acknowledgments

While my name is on the cover of this book, a project like this one is never a solitary endeavor. It took me six years to research and write this book. Data collection took me all over New York and New Jersey. The analysis and writing occurred at three different universities. Over the years, many people helped me make this project possible. With this in mind, these acknowledgments should be read as the first draft of a long and extended thank you.

The first thanks must go to my wife, Alison Eromin, who has done so much, big and small, to make my scholarly career possible. The next thank you belongs to my parents, Michael and Diane McQuade, who have always supported and encouraged all my efforts. I also must acknowledge my oldest friends. My way of thinking has certainly been shaped by many conversations with Winslow Behney, Mike Horrigan, Tristan Kading, Chris Morrissey, and Sean Wimpfheimer.

Over these six years, many colleagues and friends have read drafts, provided useful comments at conferences, talked through the various arguments in the book, created opportunities for me to refine my work, and otherwise contributed to this endeavor. Thank you to Apurva, Samantha Applin, Toivo Asheeke, Michael Ashkin, Walden Bello, Matt Birkhold, Raymond Baldino, Carrie Brietbach, Simone Brown, Kade Crockford, Stephen Danley, John Eason, Lynn Eden, Cassie Follett, Samantha Fox, Colandus "Kelly" Francis, Leslie Gates, Zeynep Gönen, Shawn Gude, Darnell Hardwick, Herbert Haines, Euan Hague, Kevin Haggerty, Kevan Harris, Terrence Hoffman, Tim Holland, Will Jackson, George Joseph, Charlotte Kading, Nikolay Karkov, Rafael Khachaturian, Zhandarka Kurti, Jonghwa Kwon, Latoya Lee, Travis Linnemann, Walter Luers, Shiera Malik, William Martin, Alfred McCoy, Michael McIntyre, Reuben Miller, Xhercis Méndez,

Jeffrey Monaghan, Torin Monahan, Mark Neocleous, Denis O'Hearn, Roberto Ortiz, Gulden Ozcan, Will Parrish, Brian Perkins, Andrew Pragacz, Joshua Price, Priscilla Regen, George Rigakos, Kevin Revier, Kelvin Santiago-Valles, Esra Sarioglu, Judah Schept, Stuart Schrader, Micol Seigel, Guillermina Seri, Meg Stalcup, Lisa Stampnitzky, Nicholas Walrath, Tyler Wall, Kristian Williams, and Alex Vitale. Out this group, the contributions of William Martin and Leslie Gates warrant an extra mention. Thank you, Bill, for the tireless commitment to your students. I wouldn't have an academic career without your guidance. Thank you to Leslie for reading every word of every draft of this book. Our writing group improved this book immeasurably and accelerated its passage to publication.

While researching and writing this book I was working with a variety of social movement organizations. My involvement in New York Students Rising, Binghamton Justice Projects, We Charge Genocide, Decarcerate Tompkins County, and the Ithaca chapter of the Democratic Socialists of America did much to shape my thinking. Of my many comrades and friends, a few conversations with Mariame Kaba were especially helpful in getting me to think through some of the wider implications of this study.

Although human subject protection prevents me from thanking them by name, I am also indebted to the many police officers, intelligence analysts, and others who agreed to be interviewed for this project and referred me to others. I am grateful to Gary Hamel, Kate Hoffman, Sabrina Robleh, Nicholle Robertson, Maura Roessner, and Madison Wetzell and all the staff at University of California Press for their professionalism and support. I'm particularly thankful for the faith Maura Roessner showed in me. She believed in this project from day one, when I, a no-name, non-tenure-track professor, first pitched it to her in the summer of 2015. When I finally delivered something substantial to Maura two years later, her enthusiasm had not waned.

Prologue: Policing Camden's Crisis

Intelligence Fusion, Pacification,
and the Fabrication of Social Order

The creation of the Department of Homeland Security (DHS) and the Office of the Director of National Intelligence was the largest reorganization of the federal government since the reforms following World War II. Since these reforms sought to improve intelligence sharing, they did not remain limited to federal agencies. Not only did state governments set up their own homeland security agencies and offices, they also worked with federal agencies, professional associations, and private companies to build a series of interagency intelligence centers: what is now called the National Network of Fusion Centers. At these secure and secretive government facilities, teams of analysts do the work of "intelligence fusion," mining disparate data sources and "fusing" them together to create useful information or "intelligence." In 2004, a year after DHS officially opened its doors, the department recognized eighteen fusion centers. Two years later, that number increased to thirty-seven. Now there are seventy-nine DHS-recognized fusion centers.[1]

The first fusion center I visited was the New Jersey Regional Operations Intelligence Center (ROIC, pronounced "rock"). The center is located at the sprawling New Jersey State Police (NJSP) Headquarters compound in East Ewing Township, an affluent suburb in a state that ranks as one of the wealthiest and most unequal in the Union.[2] Though the building is accessible to the public (the headquarters is also home to the New Jersey State Police Museum and Learning Center), a state trooper greets visitors, inspects their identification, and records their names. The newest addition to the headquarters, the ROIC is in the back of the compound. The building is impressive: a $26.7 million, 65,500-square-foot, two-story structure that can withstand winds of 125 miles per hour and earthquakes measuring 5.5 on the Richter scale. With on-site generators and photovoltaic cells, it can operate off the grid.[3] Inside, a security guard sits in an enclosed booth to take the names and identifications of visitors. After I checked in for the first time, the state trooper tasked with coordinating my visit led me to a main room where the intelligence analysts worked, swiping his key card to access the elevator and open doors. When we arrived, the fusion center—the secretive intelligence facility I spent months trying to access—looked like any other office: men (and a few women) dressed business casual, a maze of cubicles on the right, a few breakout areas with conference tables on the left.

As the result of a grant-driven federal initiative that stipulates "baseline capabilities" but no binding standards, no two fusion centers are alike. The variation from fusion center to fusion center can be dramatic. The phrase— "If you've seen one fusion center, you've seen one fusion center"—has become clichéd within the fusion center community.[4] Official secrecy obscures fusion centers, so the little public information available on a particular fusion center rarely details its unique profile. For these reasons, I arrived at the ROIC with a series of basic questions that could not be answered from the outside. *What data are available and how are they used?* Fusion centers do not store most of the data available to them. Instead, they negotiate agreements that allow remote access to existing databases. These partnerships are not limited to law enforcement agencies; fusion centers also make agreements with other agencies, such as the Department of Motor Vehicles or private operators of "critical infrastructure," for example, an electric utility or freight rail operators. They will work around privacy protections and buy access to the private databases of firms like Accurnit or Choicepoint, which provide a plethora of information on individuals with no criminal record. Analysts crunch this data with specialized software that produces individual "pattern-of-life analyses" or tries to divine the future by finding "predictive" correlations among these massive datasets.

Who works at fusion centers and how are they managed? Who receives their intelligence products? While fusion centers are managed by state or municipal police, they are staffed by personnel from many agencies. Some fusion center analysts focus on criminal intelligence and produce regular analyses of crime trends, while also providing case support, which can include extended involvement in an investigation. Others concentrate on "counterterrorism" and produce regular threat reports as well as more focused briefings on particular security issues such as threat assessments for large public gatherings. Task specialization is not the only factor influencing the focus of fusion center staff. Agency representatives assigned to fusion centers work for two superiors, the police officers managing the fusion center and their home agency supervisor. This arrangement can exacerbate jurisdictional rivalries and cause confusion. The public mission is information sharing, but, underneath, there is often a bureaucratic battle to control the resources accessible through the fusion center and the work that it does. On the outside, a diverse group of "stakeholders"—including many in the private sector—receive fusion center intelligence. The interests of all the parties do not necessarily converge. These competing demands complicate the work of fusion centers and muddle lines of authority.[5]

The difficulty of research alone does not explain why these questions remain largely unanswered. Most discussions of fusion centers do not include detailed assessments of any given fusion center. Instead, the abiding concern is the effectiveness of counterterrorism policy and its consequences for civil liberties. With so much attention on how fusion centers ought to work, few have examined their concrete effects or systemic connections to other institutions (such as the wider criminal legal system) and other domains of the social world (such as politics or economics). Consider the expert conversation in trade publications, academic journals, and policy reports. Police officers, professionals in homeland security and intelligence, criminologists, and others discuss the finer points of intelligence fusion, often as part of larger conversations on counterterrorism and intelligence-led policing. Some journalists, the American Civil Liberties Union (ACLU), and other policy advocates make "critical" interventions in this expert conversation, but their impact is much the same: to stake a position in an elite debate about how to set up, regulate, or otherwise refine the work of intelligence fusion. While there are some scholarly studies on fusion centers, the majority of this work remains oriented toward administrative concerns of policy implementation.

Starting with these basic questions concerning the concrete characteristics of a particular fusion center provides the perspective to ask more important, foundational questions that are often ignored in favor of seemingly more pragmatic concerns: What is the work of actually existing fusion centers? How does the institutionalization of intelligence fusion change police agencies, the criminal legal system, and the wider institutional apparatus of the United States? How does it influence political life and the practices of government? How has the rise of fusion centers been shaped by other developments such as the Great Recession? How do fusion centers inform related shifts in policy such as the declaration of the "War on Terror" or the recent efforts to reduce America's prison population? These questions expand the scope of analysis beyond the confines of policy refinement and civil liberties protection. They highlight concerns erased by the security discourses that pervade discussions of fusion centers. Rather than accepting the assumptions that the world is dangerous, terrorism is an existential threat to world order, and new security measures—including intelligence programs like fusion centers—are required to combat this exceptional danger, this study examines how fusion centers emerged and with what effects. Rather than asking how fusion centers can be more effective or more sensitive to the limits of law, this study examines what "threats" fusion centers monitor and whose "security" they preserve.

This approach reveals that many claims about fusion centers are correct but incomplete. Professionals and practitioners can point to real improvements in interagency intelligence sharing and operational collaboration. At the same time, government auditors have good reason to call fusion centers ineffective and a wasted public investment. The fears of civil libertarians are not unfounded. Fusion centers are involved in civil liberties violations, including political policing, although not in the ways often imagined. All these claims offer glimpses into the operation of fusion centers, but they miss the main target of intelligence fusion: dispossessed and criminalized surplus populations. Now numbering in the billions globally, surplus populations are the economically redundant mass of humanity that is no longer needed as either workers or consumers and, as such, no longer protected as citizens.[6] The growth of surplus populations is the product of global restructuring since the 1970s: the deindustrialization of the old capitalist core and the collapse of its welfare states in the face of a truly global and ruthlessly competitive world-economy. During this period, the United States built the largest prison system on the planet to warehouse surplus populations and otherwise manage the violent, wrenching social transformations caused by dramatic social change.[7] While much attention has rightly focused on mass incarceration, a complementary set of arrangements, sometimes called mass supervision, also developed to manage "problem populations"—the poor; racial, religious, and sexual minorities; and formerly incarcerated and otherwise criminalized people—outside of the prison.[8] In the more recent period bookended by the dotcom crash of 2001 and the Great Recession of 2008, intelligence fusion has gone from an unacknowledged feature of these punitive shifts in criminal justice to the central component of an increasingly visible system of mass supervision.

Placed in this context, fusion centers provide missing perspective on the current moment of ambiguous change in the US criminal legal system. Nationwide, the prison population is declining, in some states quite dramatically. Yet there has not been a clear return to the rehabilitative ethos of "penal-welfarism" that defined the criminal legal system for much of the twentieth century.[9] Instead, contemporary changes center on a series of "alternatives" to incarceration that are not true alternatives but rather supplements to imprisonment. The recent round of reforms has reduced the incarceration of "non-serious, non-violent, non-sexual offenders" by expanding—and often privatizing—prisoner reentry and community supervision, establishing specialized courts that defer prosecution pending successful completion of court-supervised programs or simply reducing sentences to a year or less and shifting the burden of incarceration down to county jails.[10]

As prison populations continue to contract, mass supervision becomes both more visible and important. The result, however, is not a simple and straightforward substitution of incarceration for community supervision. Indeed, the use of probation and parole has not increased in every state with decreasing prison populations.[11] The intelligence capacities of state and local law enforcement, however, have expanded across the country. Today, there are DHS-recognized fusion centers in every state of the Union as well as Washington, D.C.; Puerto Rico; Guam; and the US Virgin Islands. The National Network of Fusion Centers, moreover, is just the newest addition in a series of police intelligence centers and other information-sharing arrangements that date back to the early 1970s. In this context, *mass supervision*, an outgrowth and extension of mass incarceration, helps maintain the stark—and starkly racialized—inequalities that characterize the United States. Through intensive surveillance, intelligence gathering, and policing, fusion centers help transform entire communities into open-air prisons. Although this concern is absent in the literature on fusion centers, this reality confronted me in stark fashion the first time I entered the ROIC.

. . .

One of the first interviews I conducted at the ROIC was with an officer who managed the fusion center's computer systems while also overseeing the intelligence analysts working on violent crime. He was portly, jovial, and a bit eccentric. While many of his coworkers kept Spartan cubicles, his was decorated with posters and knickknacks, including a *High Times* magazine–style centerfold of a lush marijuana plant—I did not comment on that adornment—and a parody "Greetings from Camden" postcard, which mocked the city's economic decline and outsized crime rate. During our interview, he showed me large social network analyses of drug networks. These sprawling link charts mapped out a web of relations: lines of authority in the distribution network extending outward to the kinship and friendship relationships and property (businesses, automobiles, guns) of the individuals in the chart. He was going back and forth between two charts, one that concerned a Camden-based network and another in nearby Bridgeton. While explaining how analysts made these charts and what value these intelligence products provided for investigators, he got them mixed up.

"I think that's the Camden one," I said.

"Oh yeah, you're right. It doesn't really matter, though. Look at them. They're all the same element." I looked at the black and brown faces on the charts and then back to him. I must have given him an expression of shock or dismay because he immediately started backpedaling. He laughed awkwardly. "After seventeen years on this job, you see a lot and you get cynical. It all starts to look the same. A lot of the cities here have serious problems, and Camden's the worst."[12]

The detective sergeant was right. Camden does have serious problems, and while these problems are more pronounced than most cities, they are not uncommon. Camden's decline is an extreme example of larger processes: the deindustrialization of the United States, the rollback of the welfare state, and the increasing use of the criminal legal system to contain complex social problems. It took half a century for the industrial center that Walt Whitman once called the "city invincible" to become a poster—or parody postcard?—child of intractable urban decay. In the mid-twentieth century, Camden was home to 365 different industries that employed fifty-one thousand people—industries such as shipbuilding (the once famous Camden Shipyards of New York Shipbuilding), electronics manufacturing (RCA Victor), and food processing (Campbell Soup Company, which is still headquartered in the city but only employs a fifth of its former workforce of fifty-six hundred).[13] By the early 1980s, the city had lost nearly thirty-two thousand jobs, including twenty-eight thousand seven hundred in manufacturing.[14] Population collapse accompanied the economic woes, with a 40 percent decrease from its 1950 peak of one hundred twenty-five thousand. As the population declined, its complexion darkened. By the 2010 census, this beleaguered city of seventy-seven thousand was 48 percent black and 47 percent Hispanic. Over a third of residents lived below the poverty line. The median household income was a mere $26,000—compared to over $50,000 nationally and $71,000 in New Jersey.[15]

As the legal economy abandoned Camden, the drug trade filled the vacuum. In 2012, there were an estimated 175 open-air drug markets, or one drug market for every 440 residents.[16] Of course, these markets did not supply the locals. "The suburbanites are generally the lifeblood to our open air drug market problem," Camden's police chief told a reporter.[17] Several police officers I interviewed claimed the heroin trade in the Northeast US begins in Camden. "Camden has some of the purest heroin in the country," one administrator told me. "That means we're likely at the starting point, or one of the starting points for the heroin trade." He went on: "It's unbelievable who you'll see. I've seen enough professionals in BMWs in the worst parts of Camden looking for heroin that I wouldn't be surprised to see my own grandmother show up."[18] The Camden-based drug trade brings in an estimated $250 million yearly and, according to the same trooper, an individual "drug set" or a distribution team can easily make $20,000 in a day moving narcotics.[19] This clandestine and criminalized trade is necessarily regulated by violence. In 2012, the crime rate topped out at 2,566 violent crimes for every 100,000 people, the highest in the country and 560 percent higher than the national average.[20]

New Jersey responded to Camden's problems with market-based reforms in all policy areas, including policing. In recent decades, the city's tax base collapsed under the combined pressures of deindustrialization and white flight. In 2002, New Jersey governor Jim McGreevey (D, 2002–2004) signed the Municipal Recovery and Economic Recovery Act, which eliminated t he authority of Camden's mayor and city council in exchange for $150 million in city rehabilitation projects. Camden County added $50 million and assumed control of the city's parks, 911 emergency call system, and sewage. Governor Jon Corzine (D, 2006–2010) extended the government takeover until 2010. At the time, it was the largest municipal takeover in US history.[21] The city manager envisioned a recovery based on public-private partnerships, including more development in the city's downtown waterfront: Campbell's Field, a minor league ballpark; Susquehanna Bank Center, a concert venue; and some luxury housing with views of Philadelphia. The New Jersey State Aquarium, the centerpiece of an earlier urban renewal project, was expanded, renovated, and privatized. Now called the Adventure Aquarium, the state funded the project to the tune of $25 million.[22]

The state takeover failed. In 2010, the state restored municipal government in Camden, but the city still lacked the tax base to fund basic services. In the 2013 fiscal year, the city had an operating budget of $151 million, but collected just $39 million in taxes.[23] The median income and crime rates had not changed significantly. The state committed public resources for private development, but the expected private investment did not follow. The takeover and redevelopment created a small middle-class enclave between Rutgers-Camden and the waterfront, but redevelopment was weakly felt elsewhere in the city. Five million dollars in public funds did go to The

Camden Home Improvement Program, which provided money to remodel and restore homes anywhere in the city, but this investment was far less than the $24 million demanded during protests organized by the Camden Churches Organized for People in 2005. Two hundred homes were remodeled, and five hundred more remained on the waiting list when the program's budget ran out.[24] As Howard Gillette, the chief chronicler of the city's travails, explains, "Recovery came to mean, as it has elsewhere in the county, an investment in physical structures over a commitment to people in need."[25]

Upon assuming office, New Jersey's governor, Chris Christie (R, 2010–2018) declared that "the taxpayers of New Jersey aren't going to pay any more for Camden's excesses" and cut $445 million in state aid to the city. The city immediately laid off 168 of its 368 police officers. The remaining cops responded by "calling in sick in record numbers, with absenteeism rates rising as high as 30 percent over the rest of 2011." The next year, a record sixty-seven homicides officially gave Camden the highest murder rate in the country. The state's withdrawal of funds was part of Christie's larger effort to break the back of public sector unions and, where possible, privatize public services. While these efforts met stiff resistance in the education system, the gambit succeeded in law enforcement. In May 2013, the city disbanded the municipal police and replaced them with reformed Camden County Police, which, despite its name, only has jurisdiction in the City of Camden. While reformers envisioned consolidation, none of the surrounding suburban municipalities merged with the new "county" force. Even without consolidation, the reform accomplished its goal. It cut the average cost per officer from $182,168 to $99,605, reductions achieved through a 65 percent cut to "fringe pay," which included pensions and health care. Camden County estimated it would save the city between $14 million and $16 million. By August 2013, Christie was holding up the Camden County Police Force as "a model" and calling on Trenton and Mercer County to follow suit.[26]

While Camden struggled with fiscal shock therapy, the NJSP sent a "surge" of troopers to join a contingent that had been deployed to the city since the 2002 state takeover.[27] The surge included the deployment of the fusion center's Intelligence Collection Cell, a small team of state troopers that, in the words of the senior supervisor at the ROIC, "are in the midst of daily operations and sort of embed[ded] . . . with these folks. . . . We're actually going to ride along with you and, when you lock up somebody in Camden, we're going to debrief them and interview them."[28] These increased efforts to collect "human intelligence"—information gleaned from interpersonal relations—took place in a city transformed by surveillance systems: 121 cameras watching "virtually every inch of sidewalk"; thirty-five SpotShotter microphones to detect gunshots; new scanners to read license plates; and SkyPatrol, a mobile observation post that can scan six square blocks with thermal-imaging equipment.[29]

At the time, much of this data was filtered back to the ROIC to the analysts working under the portly detective sergeant. While I was doing interviews at the ROIC, they had recently finished work on Operation Padlock. After nine months of investigative and analytic work, the ROIC provided the beleaguered Camden Police Department, NJSP and Camden County Prosecutor with the intelligence to launch a series of police operations targeting Camden's prodigious drug economy. In seven weeks in August and September of 2012, the multiagency group undertook ninety-three targeted operations, resulting in 535 arrests for offenses including drug possession, weapons possession, and active warrants. The operation also led to the confiscation of $35,535 in cash and drugs with a street value of $44,300, the towing of nearly seventy vehicles, and the closure of a Chinese restaurant for health code violations.[30]

This early interview with the detective sergeant offered a glimpse into a different reality that was not acknowledged in varied conversations on fusion centers. My original questions concerning surveillance, civil liberties, and public-private partnerships felt quaint. It recast "privacy" as a pedantic concern, an abstract formalism. I wanted to understand how massive investment in the name of security and counterterrorism produced a system of ubiquitous surveillance and aggressive policing that managed the social problems expressed so dramatically in Camden's crisis. The intelligence gathering and related policing practices that were remaking Camden were not simply enforcing law and order. They were attempting to create a new city. The police operation and wider government austerity project were complementary state strategies to manage the long-term decline of Camden—and places like it. Making sense of this situation required a broader perspective that could hold policing, poverty, and political authority within one frame of vision.

PACIFICATION AND ITS PROSE

I conceptualize intelligence fusion and related practices as an example of what Mark Neocleous, George Rigakos, and other scholars call *pacification*, or the systemic fabrication of capitalist forms of order. The volatility and dynamism that define capitalism creates much insecurity: the vulnerability of the ever-growing masses of proletarianized workers (like the redundant, racially devalued labor warehoused in Camden); the vicissitudes of politics (revolt from below, machinations of elite factions); market shifts (the ebb and flow of business cycles, the movement of capital); and, most importantly, the fundamental structural precariousness of capitalist social relations (the silent compulsion of the market, which privatizes the means of subsistence and inscribes "insecurity" into commodified social relations with the demand that one must sell their labor for their life). The order of capital must be secured against these various risks. As an effort to critique security, Neocleous concludes that the modern world is an "order of social *insecurity*," which "gives rise to a *politics of security*."[31]

"Security" is a euphemism that obscures the political work of organizing and maintaining a social reality based on individualism, market relations, and the commodity form in the face of the "insecurities" produced by capital accumulation. It is, crudely, the way the routine work of policing maintains particular social property relations, even in the context of the most absurd inequalities. In Camden, for example, 15 percent of all buildings, some thirty-five hundred structures, are vacant. Meanwhile, there are nearly six hundred homeless people in the city.[32] The plainly obvious solution—providing the surplus housing to homeless people—is politically impossible, unimaginable even. Instead, our self-evident norm is to use the most basic power of the state, bodies of armed men, to prevent unofficial access to private property. These perverse arrangements can only be naturalized as "common sense" because, as Rigakos contends, "security is hegemony," or as Marx wrote in 1844, "Security is the highest social concept of civil society, the concept of police, expressing the fact that the whole of society exists only in order to guarantee to each of its members the preservation of his person, his rights, and his property."[33]

The critique of security is the effort to unsettle this hegemony and analyze security without being subsumed by it. In his reading of classic liberals, Neocleous notes that the "liberty" that is said to define liberalism presupposes security:

> We are often and rightly told that security is intimately associated with the rise of the modern state. But we also need to note that it is equally intimately bound up with the rise of bourgeois property rights. . . . [L]iberalism's conception of security was intimately connected to its vision of political subjectivity centred on the self-contained and property-owning individual. The reason liberty is wrapped in the concept of security, then, is because security is simultaneously wrapped in the question of property, giving us a triad of concepts which are usually run so close together that they are almost conflated ("liberty,

security, property"), a triad found in Smith, Blackstone, Paine, the French Declaration of the Rights of Man, and in various other formulations elsewhere. Thus as liberalism generated a new conception of "the economy" as its founding political act, a conception which integrated the wealth of nations, the world market and the labour of the population, its notion of liberty necessitated a particular vision of security: the ideological guarantee of the egoism of the independent and self-interested pursuit of property. It is for this reason Marx calls security "the supreme concept of bourgeois society."

Simply put, the "liberty" engendered within historical capitalism is contingent on the *security* of private property. On this basis, the critique of security, like Marx's critique of political economy, begins with a deep engagement with existing security ideology and its social context, "simultaneously unmasking ideas and rooting them within the context of class society and the commodity form."[34]

A central part of this project is the reappropriation of the term *pacification* from military jargon to analyze practical and historical connections among policing, warfare, and social policy as processes of order making. Pacification connotes the systematic fabrication of capitalist social relations. While security discourses rest on assumption of risk and mutual hostility (a war of one against all, waged among both individuals and nations), the critique of security invites to us consider what relations produce these conflicts and how they have been managed. Considering Camden from this perspective reconfigures this moment as the latest chapter in the broader transformation of the United States, as social formation, in the last forty to fifty years. How did Camden come to be afflicted by such insecurities as poverty and crime? What is the role of policing in pacifying—and possibly producing—these insecurities? What history informs the contemporary organization of pacification? What balance of social forces does it reflect?

Pacification is also a project with a world-historical resonance, something that is not lost on managers of state violence. In 2012, when Camden's sixty-seven homicides gave it a murder rate 560 times higher than the national average, Police Chief Scott Thomson was sardonic, telling a reporter that the city's violence fell "somewhere between Honduras and Somalia." Reflecting on the situation, Chuck Wexler of the Police Executive Research Forum, a police professional association, evoked similar imagery: "If Camden was overseas, we'd have sent troops and foreign aid."[35] Implicitly, these police officials describe Camden as a pocket of state failure enmeshed within the wealthiest and most advanced society in human history, a little piece of Mogadishu tucked away in a neglected corner of the Northeast Megalopolis that stretches from Boston to Washington, D.C.

These comparisons are points of entry into what I call *the prose of pacification*: the shared discourses, forms of expertise, and practices that tie together the indeterminable wars on drugs (Honduras), crime/poverty (Camden), and terror (Somalia), boundless wars on vaguely defined social problems that do much to define contemporary political life the world over. The language used to define problems is also a productive force shaping social reality. The varied security discourses understood as examples of pacification—policing, military strategy, and social policy in general—share common historical origins in the creation of the capitalist world-economy and the consolidation of a social order organized around individualism, market relations, and the commodity form. When police executives evoke the language of the war on crime, they are unconsciously drawing upon deep histories of capitalist order making that color their perception of what the problems are and orient their action within a likely range of responses.

The deep roots of the pacification reveal the immense historical force evoked by security discourses and their formative power to shape present realities. Neocleous, for example, traces the genealogy of "pacification" far beyond its strong associations with counterinsurgency campaigns of the Vietnam War to the formative moments of the modern world. The term was first used in the sixteenth century to describe the necessity of governing "in peace." It was used in two contexts: (1) the Edicts of Pacification, which brought an end to the French Wars of Religion; and (2) the "pacification" of Spain's colonial possessions in the Americas. These events "are important because they are deep into the period of early global accumulation and the history of capital. . . . [T]hey are the point of departure for the period in which the insecurity of bourgeois order had to be secured." Hence, the "peace" created by these pacifications was a particular type of peace. The Edicts of Pacification, in part, put an end to the decentralized violence that characterized medieval sovereignty and began the slow centralization of power and violence that defines the modern state. The pacification of New Spain, similarly, was a formative moment in the emergence of the capitalist world-economy. It marks a shift from naked plunder to a different practice of rule centered on "gathering information about the population, the teaching of trades, education, welfare provision, ideological indoctrination, and most importantly, the construction of a market."[36]

The pacification of the nascent capitalist world-economy was a continuous process. As Europe, the Americas, and West Africa became linked in a global division of labor, it created new commercial cities—new problems of urban insecurity: vice, crime, blasphemy, and the general disorder associated with the itinerant poor. These problems of poverty led the centralizing states of early modern Europe to undertake massive pacification projects, understood and organized in terms of the largely forgotten "police science" or *polizeiwissenschaft* of the seventeenth to early nineteenth centuries. This pre-disciplinary discourse united English liberals and Continental philosophers in a shared project to construct what Patrick Colquhoun called "a general police system" to promote commerce and manage poverty. In this nascent science of social order, the critique of security has found the origins of public law, administrative science, political economy, public health, and urban planning.[37] By end of the nineteenth century, however, the meaning of "police" contracted to "*the* police," the uniformed officers "enforcing the law." This narrowed meaning reflected the growing influence of liberalism, in which the individual and the market supplanted the sovereign and the state as the theoretical wellspring of social order. These philosophical shifts masked capital's reliance on the state to *fabricate* social relations, but it did not end the structural necessity of such work. In this context, police science gave way to criminology, public health, urban planning, and varied administrative discourses, which sought to regulate different domains of social life in a manner consonant with the class biases of the old "police science." In this sense, the different genres of social policy are also and always police discourses. They are examples of the prose of pacification.[38]

The concept of pacification highlights these systemic interconnections.[39] Echoes of Colquhoun's "general police system" are evident in the example of Camden, where police reform and economic development—today discussed as separate domains of public policy—are part of a common pacification project. Analytically and methodologically, the "prose of pacification" draws the conceptual and practical link between my primary research and the larger histories and processes that surround fusion centers. The prose of pacification is the productive integument of power and practice that links the aforementioned "wars" on drugs (Honduras), crime (Camden), and terror (Somalia). For example, one of the main security discourses animating fusion center is intelligence-led policing (ILP), which connects these wars through the circulation of ideas, people, and technologies. The chief proponent of ILP is Jerry Ratcliffe. A former officer with the London Metropolitan Police, Ratcliffe literally "wrote the book" on ILP.[40] He's also involved in its implementation. In the mid-2000s, he advised the NJSP on reorganizing their Investigations Branch, adopting ILP, and creating the ROIC.[41] A few years later, Ratcliffe was working at the behest of the US State Department's Institute for Narcotics and Law Enforcement on a program to introduce Honduran National Police to ILP. This meant a shift from the old tactic of military sweeps—that is, mass arrests—to more individual targeting. To facilitate this transition, "the government of Honduras has developed a central intelligence center," trained more SWAT teams, and created a national interagency task force led by the Honduran military with participation of the police, the Attorney General's Office, and intelligence agencies.[42]

Thinking of pacification as both a structured set of relations *and* prose to be spoken or practice to be enacted breaks the tendency to assume that particular discourses neatly and necessarily produce the orderly social relations envisioned by their authors. Instead, considering pacification as prose identifies the production, performance, and reception of "security" as an important moment to be considered on its own terms. Most security discourses do not describe reality as much as they help structure it through the redefinition or erasure of class struggle. The "prose of pacification" is a deliberate nod to Ranajit Guha's "prose of counterinsurgency," rhetoric that "serves a blinding function that renders ... subaltern struggles ... illegible, deemed 'spontaneous'" and not the results of "motivated and conscious undertaking on the part of the ... masses."[43] In *Incarcerating the Crisis*, a study of the political origins of mass incarceration, Jordan Camp recently invoked Guha to show how the "suffering that motivates rebellions, insurrections, and uprisings against police violence and mass criminalization are often poorly translated."[44] To return to the anecdote that introduces this book, the crime afflicting Camden is not the product of an indistinguishable and unscrupulous "criminal element" but the product of social insecurity and an expression of class struggle.

In this way, the prose of pacification centers the fact that *pacification presupposes politics*: the resistance of active agents and the oft-obscured class content of routine state administration. Hence, in 2012, when Camden was reeling from Governor Christie's withdrawal of aid and struggling to manage a spectacular crescendo of violence, the city spent $77,000 on overtime for officers to provide "security" at the Susquehanna Center, a concert venue and one of the main anchors of the middle-class enclave between Rutgers-Camden and the waterfront. While the so-called criminal element died in the street, the police made what the mayor's spokesperson called a "deployment decision" to secure a large capital investment and the well-being of those who came to Camden as consumers.[45] By centering the normally mystified class politics—including the inchoate expressions of class struggle we call "crime"—entailed in "security," pacification brings together all security practices as examples of "a proactive, organized, and systematic war strategy targeting domestic and foreign enemies and as a process that actively shapes and fabricates a social order in which capitalist accumulation can function."[46]

This approach moves the analysis of fusion centers beyond the limiting confines of the policy debate. It reveals the broader meaning of Operation Padlock and the massive intelligence system upon which such police actions are predicated. The DHS-recognized National Network of Fusion Centers and the broader institutionalization of intelligence fusion in the United States is not a narrow topic with implications only for counterterrorism and security policy. Nor is it a legalistic matter of civil liberties and privacy protection. Instead, it offers insights into the changing administrative strategies that states use to pacify class struggle, administer poverty, and fabricate social order. While pacification highlights the issues obscured by other approaches, my research establishes the specificities of the current historical moment. The seventy-nine fusion centers recognized by DHS and the broader institutionalization of intelligence fusion are central, constitutive components of an increasingly prominent strategy of mass supervision. While mass supervision has long been an unacknowledged complement to mass incarceration, the dramatic expansion of the intelligence capacities of state and local police—during a time of falling prison populations—places empowered policing and ubiquitous surveillance at the center of mass supervision.

Mass supervision is an outgrowth and extension of the administrative strategies that constituted the state during the period of neoliberal globalization. This utopian project to radically remake world order largely succeeded, perhaps even pushing capitalism to its ecological and social limits. In the United States, many scholars and activists concluded that these changes produced either a *workfare state*, which imposed a new accord between labor and capital, or *carceral state*, which warehoused surplus workers, mostly racial minorities, who were left out of the new economic order. In today's emergent post-neoliberal world defined by low growth, soaring inequality, and ever-expanding surplus populations, mass supervision helps shore up this workfare-carceral state and consolidate life organized around radical dependence on the market during a period of acute structural crisis. As the central component of mass supervision, the process of intelligence fusion mobilizes the decentralized surveillance capacities of state and private powers to render the complexity of social life legible as "intelligence." The result is a potentially more supple system of social regulation that couples decentralized control with increased inter-institutional coordination across the state and private sector. In the short term, the institutionalization of intelligence fusion in the United States enables decarceration and an apparent rollback of the carceral state without addressing the underlying social problems at the root of mass incarceration. In the long term, it may be a novel strategy to pacify social unrest, necessary for a lasting reconfiguration of the state.

In the coming chapters, I will employ and elaborate the idea of pacification and its prose to confirm and clarify the central contention of this book: fusion centers and the broader institutionalization of intelligence fusion are a central component of mass supervision, a state strategy to pacify surplus populations in our nascent post-neoliberal world of low growth and soaring inequality. *Pacifying the Homeland* is divided into three parts, each of which is comprised of two chapters. The first part critiques security discourses and existing research that animate or otherwise make claims on fusion centers, while situating *Pacifying the Homeland* within conversations on surplus populations, the workfare state, and the carceral state. The first chapter, "Connecting the Dots beyond Counterterrorism and Seeing Past Organizational Failure," shows how seemingly self-evident explanations for the spread of fusion centers—terrorism and counterterrorism—obscure more about intelligence fusion than they illuminate. Building on the introductory comments on the prose of pacification, the chapter shows how the concerns about counterterrorism, organizational dysfunction, and privacy miss the broader consequences of the long-term institutionalization of intelligence fusion. Instead, these administrative discourses are productive investments in fusion centers that shape the practice of intelligence fusion as much as they explain it. To this end, the chapter develops materialist methodology that recuperates the poststructural approach of discourse analysis to situate and analyze the relevant literature on fusion centers. This critical literature review clears the way for a different kind of comparative study, one that "incorporates" the comparison within historical time to illuminate the larger processes currently remaking the United States. The institutionalization of intelligence fusion in New York and New Jersey are not distinct "cases" that can be abstracted out of their time and space. Instead, they are mutually constituting "instances" that can illuminate the larger whole that other approaches tend to obscure.

To fully appreciate these changes, the next chapter, "The Rise and Present Demise of the Workfare-Carceral State," synthesizes scholarship on the emergence of the carceral state—which largely ignores labor-formation and capital accumulation—with the literature on the workfare state, which is mostly silent on questions of incarceration, policing, and racial-formation. More specifically, this chapter theoretically develops the critique of security by demonstrating how processes of labor-formation, racial-formation, state-formation, and pacification interact to produce specific state-forms, developing this framework through an account of the emergence of the *herrenvolk*-welfare state and its transformation into the workfare-carceral state. This historical analysis provides the wider context to situate fusion centers within their constitutive conjuncture, a wider historical moment informed by decarceration, the politicization of "police-involved killings," economic crises, and austerity. Understood within these parameters, it is possible to ask what the broader rise of intelligence fusion means for contemporary patterns of political order.

From here, parts 2 and 3 present the original research that provides the book's core contribution. Part 2 deals with the way the institutionalization of intelligence fusion has transformed the state. The third chapter, "The Institutionalization of Intelligence Fusion," details the exact mechanisms that undermine the dream of a seamless information-sharing environment and, instead, produce discontinuous pockets of increased intelligence cooperation and operational coordination. This uneven and conflictive intelligence system should not be simply dismissed as a "failure," nor should it be understood as a natural outcome of the layered US federal government. Rather, it is a complex outgrowth of the workfarist emphasis on structural competitiveness and commitment to punitive criminal justice policies that produced mass incarceration. Following the comparative logic detailed in the first chapter, New York and New Jersey are not "cases." They are formative moments that shaped the wider institutionalization of intelligence fusion. In the 1990s, New York City pioneered policing practices that would inform the eventual construction of the DHS-recognized National Network of Fusion Centers. The subsequent spread of intelligence fusion, however, did not occur in a vacuum. The experience of New York City shows the iterative nature of state-formation. Social struggles within and apart from the state produced intelligence fusion as a coherent state strategy. The apparent success of this strategy, as evidenced in the transformation of New York City from a blighted city of high crime and postindustrial decline to a dynamic cultural and economic center, created a structural predisposition toward the further spread of intelligence fusion. At the same time, intelligence fusion did not simply diffuse out from New York City. The institutional apparatus of the state mediates these changes in ways that produced complex and uneven results.

The fourth chapter, "Policing Decarceration," focuses on a series of now-commonplace "intelligence-led manhunts." These ILP operations emerged organically from a shifting composition of social forces: chronic unemployment, and deepening austerity that reduces the prison system and elevates a less labor-intensive form of policing. Both New York and New Jersey are leaders in criminal justice reform, having reduced their state prison populations by at least one-quarter in the last decade. This apparent decarceration, however, has not been complemented by a renewed emphasis on rehabilitation or any reinvestment in criminalized communities. Instead, the contracting prison is supplemented by intelligence fusion, which enables punitive forms of decarceration. These changes are making mass supervision an increasingly salient and important state strategy. The central focus on imprisonment, which defined mass incarceration, is giving way to a more surveillance- and police-intensive mode of regulation. Specifically, warrant sweeps, compliance checks, chronic-offender initiatives, and saturation patrols supplement contracting prisons with expansive policing in an effort to pacify criminalized surplus populations. Even as aggressive policing complements reduced prison populations to produce a punitive version of decarceration, the commitment to workfare remains and in some ways deepens, as seen in the restructuring of the police agencies.

The third and final part of the book concerns the fabrication of social order, showing the novel reconfiguration of political policing effected by fusion centers and detailing the varied ways fusion centers and related ILP operations regulate surplus populations *beyond incarceration.* "Beyond COINTELRPO," the fifth chapter, examines the contention that fusion centers are involved in political policing. While activists on the far right and far left both allege that fusion centers are the centerpiece of a new crackdown on dissent, a massive collection of released documents and my own interviews and observations reveal that there is no federally coordinated project to repress political activity along the lines of the earlier COINTELPRO program. Instead, political policing today operates through overlapping interagency intelligence networks, including the DHS-recognized National Network of Fusion Centers. Reflecting the decentralized and competitive nature of this state-form, these intelligence networks are subject to a diverse set of political pressures, such as the external forces that shaped the divergent responses to different Occupy encampments or the internal struggles within the state that complicate the relations between the security apparatus and far-right movements. This patchwork of political policing is a complex and convoluted arrangement. Enhanced coordination creates organic opportunities for plausible deniability. It is hard to discern the leading actors and exact sequence of events. It also muddles command hierarchies. This lack of clarity is only partially caused by secrecy and the proximity of events. Increased political indeterminacy is built into the very structure of the workfare-carceral state. The current patchwork of political policing is much harder to expose and redress than COINTELPRO. If these arrangements can withstand their own internal contradictions, they may be a more effective means to contain class struggle.

The sixth chapter, "Pacifying Poverty," reveals the way fusion centers and related police operations produce capitalist forms of social order. While activists fear government persecution, reformers bemoan waste and mission failures, and watchdogs fret about civil liberties, intelligence fusion subjects entire populations to constant surveillance and, often, aggressive ILP operations. These activities continue with little to no controversy because they target a group with almost no formal political power—the surplus populations warehoused in hyper-ghettoized communities, doubly segregated by race and class. This situation reflects the basic mandate of police power: to regulate poverty and fabricate capitalist forms of order. This conclusion becomes clear in light of a series of ILP operations that share a common convergence in the criminalization of "the moral economies of poverty," the ill-understood survival strategies of those struggling at the bottom of the crushing inequalities that define capitalist societies. These police projects attempt to reorganize social relations on terms that support capital accumulation. Much of this work centers on the drug economy. Today, intelligence fusion helps police launch multiagency investigations into drug-related criminal networks. These operations attempt to regulate and, through asset forfeiture laws, tax the criminalized labor at the core of moral economies of poverty. When successful, they push the drug economy off the street and indoors. Here, landlord training, trespass affidavit, and narcotics eviction programs enlist non-state actors in the work of pacification, compelling landlords to police the survival strategies and quotidian behaviors of surplus populations. Finally, secondhand dealer laws provide police new tools to not only monitor and manage the market in stolen goods but also (re)produce the market and reaffirm the power of capital. These efforts continually (re)produce capitalist social relations by subsuming threatening forms of labor within the criminal legal system, enforcing legal forms of subjectivity, and constructing administratively legible market relations.

Pacifying the Homeland concludes with a reflection on contemporary movements and returns to Camden, New Jersey. The Black Lives Matter (BLM) movement formed after the 2012 Trayvon Martin shooting and exploded into American consciousness following the 2014 death of Mike Brown and the subsequent rebellion in Ferguson, Missouri. The mounting deaths and continuing protests created a crisis of legitimacy in policing and the wider criminal legal system. In response, President Obama convened the President's Task Force on 21st Century Policing, bringing together police administrators, academics, and police advocates to articulate a vision for police reform. Moderate elements of BLM, such as Campaign Zero, endorsed the commission's eventual findings. When President Obama announced the proposed reforms, he traveled to Camden, New Jersey, to use the city as a backdrop. By 2015, crime rates in Camden had fallen considerably from their 2012 crescendo. The president attributed the success to their community policing programs *and* their use of intelligence.

While BLM moderates have endorsed these reforms, more radical organizations have rejected them as an effort not to police with the community but police *through the community*, selectively deputizing certain individuals to act as intelligence collectors and unofficial apparatchiks of the carceral state. Indeed, when President Obama traveled to Chicago to promote his reforms to the annual meeting of the International Associations of Chiefs of Police, he was met by street demonstrations and civil disobedience. A few days after, a group of grassroots organizations released *The Counter-CAPS Report: The Community Engagement Arm of the Police State*, an independent study of Chicago's community policing programs that sought to recast the debate around police reform and challenge the reemergence of community policing. These battle lines have only sharpened during the Trump administration. The effort to co-opt and mollify BLM moderates and repair the public image of police with the media-friendly optics of community policing seems to be on hold, if not completely collapsed. Meanwhile, a new law-and-order offensive promises to reverse the modest reforms that began under the Obama administration. While these polarized politics have raised the stakes, they have also increased the stature of BLM radicals, a nascent socialist movement, and autonomous grassroots organizations who are working to abolish the workfare-carceral state and replace it with real alternatives that seek to transcend police power and capital.

1. Connecting the Dots beyond Counterterrorism and Seeing Past Organizational Failure

The Critique of Security and the Prose of Pacification

On September 9, 2001, a Maryland state trooper stopped Ziad Jarrah for a traffic violation. Having no reason to do otherwise, the trooper sent Jarrah on his way. Two days later, he was the hijacker-pilot of Flight 93, which crashed in rural Pennsylvania. Citing incidents like this stop, the 9/11 Commission found that the intelligence community had failed to "connect the dots."[1] In response, the new Department of Homeland Security (DHS) promised to link the entirety of domestic intelligence—from municipal police departments to the federal intelligence community—with a new National Network of Fusion Centers. At the same time, the spread of intelligence-led policing (ILP) complemented the rise of these networked intelligence hubs with a "smarter" approach that uses intelligence to preempt threats.

The resultant process of intelligence fusion starts with information: massive databases decades in the making; open-source data gleaned from the web and social media; and streams of information created by new surveillance systems like automated license plate readers. To "fuse" data into useful information, analysts often use powerful computers and specialized software to "connect the dots" and, in theory, draw out the signal from the noise of data. Different tools offer different insights. With specialized software, analysts can turn unintelligible and interminably long lists of phone calls into a pattern of use, and, from there, a social network analysis. They can map unwieldy agglomerations of information—such as geospatial data drawn from police files, the census, and other public records—to create "predictive" heat maps to anticipate where the next shooting is likely to occur. Intelligence fusion also "connects the dots" in simpler ways. Often, fusion centers operate as data brokers, providing investigative support to law enforcement partners. Data brokerage can also mean doing even less: in so-called "pass-throughs," fusion centers simply disseminate another agency's intelligence reports.

For the most ardent proponents, the intelligence fusion never really ends. Traditionally, there is an iterative tendency built into intelligence: a cycle in which decision-makers demand information, officers collect information, and analysts process the data into intelligence. The feedback executives provide helps orient the next turn of the intelligence cycle. Intelligence-led policing tries to transcend this reactive model with a proactive approach. It collapses intelligence collection and analysis into a conjoined and continuous activity. Intelligence producers strive to maintain the situational awareness necessary to preempt and disrupt behaviors deemed criminal and disorderly.[2] Hence, their ever-creeping reach: first, government records and private data brokers; next, the integration of old surveillance systems like closed-circuit TV cameras and new ones like automated license plate readers; and, most recently, wholesale data-mining of social media and other forms of open-source intelligence.

Intelligence-led policing is also an administrative philosophy. The goal is efficiency. About three decades ago, police executives started using crime mapping to manage police departments. With crime hot spots identified, they knew where to direct patrols and investigators and which middle manager to hold accountable. Today, ILP strives for proactive crime control with increasingly individual targeting, a shift from "hot spots" to "hot people." Under this pressure, officers target "chronic offenders." Detectives try to refine leads out of data. Analysts work to stay ahead of events and otherwise divine the future. They collaborate with police on long-term investigations, providing a variety of services from simple database searches, to routine crime analysis and mapping, to in-depth criminal profiles and social network analyses.[3] In theory, intelligence fusion and ILP will produce more proficient policing.

One decade and upwards of a billion dollars later, the results are unimpressive. In October 2012, the US Senate excoriated fusion centers. After two years of investigation, they could not identify any "reporting which uncovered a terrorist threat ... [or any] contribution such fusion center reporting made to disrupt an active terrorist plot."[4] The report brought uncomfortable national attention to fusion centers. "DHS 'fusion centers' portrayed as pools of ineptitude and civil liberties intrusions" read the *Washington Post*'s headline.[5] The *New York Times* had a more subdued title but opened with an equally damaging assessment: "One of the nation's biggest domestic counterterrorism programs has failed to provide virtually any useful intelligence."[6] "It's brutal," one federal official involved in funding and management of fusion centers later told me. "It's one-sided. Definitely. But it's not totally wrong. We have some problems to work out."[7] Seven months later, the Senate's findings were confirmed in spectacular fashion by the Boston Marathon bombing. In the preceding two years, the FBI and CIA had neglected to share information about Tamerlan Tsarnaev, the elder brother implicated in the attack, with the Boston Regional Intelligence Center. Even if they had, Boston's fusion center was preoccupied with other matters: spying on Occupy Boston.[8]

The wider conversation on fusion centers reflects the major themes of the Senate report: dysfunction, mission failure, and abuse. From the very start in 2004, when DHS began encouraging state and local governments to create fusion centers, journalists criticized the new program for its ineffectiveness, the potential for mission creep, and civil liberties violations.[9] By 2008, government researchers and auditors identified the factors contributing to these problems: an ill-defined, vague mission, poor coordination, over-classification, and incompatible information systems.[10] Policy advocates repeated many of these concerns and recommended reform. Liberal organizations like the American Civil Liberties Union (ACLU) and the Brennan Center for Justice focused on protecting civil liberties and recommended greater oversight, while conservative groups like the American Enterprise Institute argued that centralization could reduce costs and increase information sharing.[11] Only practitioners in law enforcement and a later report from the House of Representatives found that fusion centers were an effective and worthwhile addition to law enforcement.[12] Some journalists, activists and civil liberties groups inverted this stance, charging that fusion centers are effective, not at counterterrorism, but at suppressing dissent.[13]

Despite all the criticism and bad press, neither politicians nor the public have subjected fusion centers to meaningful oversight or sustained scrutiny. Not only did all of the DHS-recognized fusion centers survive the public sector austerity that followed the Great Recession, the network expanded, increasing from seventy-two centers in 2009 to seventy-nine in 2018. The funds continue to flow: state governments increased their investment in intelligence fusion, and federal support, although reduced, has not stopped.[14] Surely, there is more to the story than organizational failure? Even the sharply critical Senate report acknowledged that "[f]usion centers may provide valuable services in fields other than terrorism, such as contributions to traditional criminal investigations, public safety, or disaster response and recovery efforts."[15] Perhaps fusion centers are effective, just not at counterterrorism? Even if fusion centers have failed, it begs the question: what are the unintended consequences of this apparent institutional failure?

A wider view brings more urgency to these questions. The DHS-recognized National Network of Fusion Centers is only part of the story. In 2013, the Government Accountability Office (GAO) identified five kinds of "field-based information-sharing entities" totaling up to 268 interagency intelligence taskforces in the United States, including the then seventy-two fusion centers recognized by DHS and predecessor intelligence centers like the thirty-two investigative support centers set up under the High Intensity Drug Trafficking Program as well as the six multistate Regional Intelligence Sharing Centers administered by the Bureau of Justice Statistics. This count only includes federally funded initiatives, which leaves out, for example, at least thirteen county intelligence centers in New York State alone. The history of fusion centers, then, extends beyond DHS and the "War on Terror." The first intelligence-sharing operation that could be labeled a "fusion center," the Drug Enforcement Administration's El Paso Intelligence Center, was founded in 1974. Furthermore, counterterrorism is not the mission of all these interagency intelligence centers.[16] The mission of most DHS-recognized fusion centers quickly crept from a narrow focus on counterterrorism to a broader "all crimes, all threats, all hazards" mission.[17] Altogether, the institutionalization of intelligence fusion cannot be explained by 9/11 and the increased emphasis on counterterrorism. The scathing Senate report should not be the final word on the subject.

Fusion centers and the related rise of ILP, I contend, provide a window into larger changes, the scope and consequences of which are obscured by the fear of terrorism, the immediate focus on policy implementation, and the apparent failure of fusion centers. To appreciate the full significance of fusion centers, it is essential to connect the dots beyond counterterrorism and see past the discourse of organizational failure. The hyperbolic concerns with terrorism and the perpetual efforts to reform fusion centers are examples of the prose of pacification—that is, the productive play of discourse that organizes and animates the state apparatus. While immediate policy questions are usually determined within these domains, these administrative discourses do not adequately explain how intelligence fusion and ILP are changing the criminal legal system and reshaping the social world. The prose of pacification obscures the materiality of power—the concrete social relations that tie the haves and have-nots together in historically enduring systems of domination and exploitation.

Quieting all this sound and fury requires some theoretical reflection on the power of language to shape social reality. To this end, this chapter first considers the meaning of the term *terrorism* in order to elaborate the concept of the prose of pacification, which was introduced in the prologue.

From here, I demonstrate how concerns about counterterrorism, organizational dysfunction, and privacy miss the broader consequences of the long-term institutionalization of intelligence fusion. Instead, these administrative concerns are productive investments in fusion centers that shape the practice of intelligence fusion as much as they explain it. In this way, this chapter situates the larger study within the relevant literature on fusion centers while also advancing a materialist methodology that recuperates the poststructural approach of discourse analysis and explains the overarching comparative logic of this study. This approach incorporates the comparison within its constitutive historical moment. The goal is to construct a larger whole—in this case, the processes remaking the United States—not deduce causal relations (the factors that enhance information sharing at fusion centers, for example). Traditional comparative approaches define the systemic totality out of existence. It becomes a mess of complicating details to be "abstracted" away. "Incorporating" the comparison means that institutionalization of intelligence fusion in New York and New Jersey are not distinct "cases" that can be abstracted out of their time and space. Instead, they are interrelated "instances" that form and are also formed within a greater whole: our contemporary historical moment and, more specifically, the US state apparatus. This approach is less likely to lead to fraught entanglements with the prose of pacification because it focuses analysis on the larger questions other approaches tend to avoid.

THE MEANING OF *TERRORISM* AND THE PROSE OF PACIFICATION

The language used to define reality also shapes it. Consider the term *terrorism*. Critical terrorism scholars like Richard Jackson and Lee Jarvis show that labeling political opponents "terrorists" places them beyond politics and beyond understanding, creating a dichotomy between irrational, barbarous "terrorists" and virtuous, civilized states. Incidents labeled "terrorism" are also defined as exceptional acts outside the normal confines of war and beyond any historical or social context. Hence, the "War on Terror" became a timeless struggle between good and evil.[18] This kind of rhetoric is not just limited to public proclamations of politicians. Lisa Stampnitzky finds that the expert conversation is "continually hybridized by the moral discourse of the public sphere, in which terrorism is conceived as a problem of evil and pathology." Instead of a "rational" and "scientific" debate, "the language of evil creates 'a black box' around terrorism, which creates its own explanation: terrorists commit terrorism because they are evil."[19]

anding shapes the response to terrorism. Evil cannot be rec-
be defeated. After 9/11, George W. Bush proclaimed, "No
otiate with terrorists." A decade and a half earlier Ronald
d, "America will never make concessions to terrorism." In
ce, the then national security advisor for the Obama administration, repeated the mantra, "We don't negotiate with terrorists."[20] With
diplomacy off the table, the United States has engaged in a boundless, borderless, ceaseless "War on Terror." After nearly two decades, an untold
number of military operations in at least seventy-six countries, and some
$7.6 trillion spent on a global pacification project, a grim accounting of the
costs shows an immense human toll: nearly a million dead from fighting
and the related predations of war and over ten million more displaced in
Iraq, Afghanistan, and Pakistan, to say nothing of other affected regions.[21]
Importantly, this immense violence has not ended terrorism. Instead, foreign interventions have devastated Afghanistan, Iraq, Libya, Syria, and
Yemen, creating the conditions for intensified conflict and more terrorism.
For the United States, this massive investment in security has led to loose
monetary policy, and increased indebtedness. It has diverted resources from
pressing social problems like health care and infrastructure, helping to create the conditions for the Great Recession. As economists Joseph Stiglitz
and Linda Bilmes explain, "With more spending at home, and without the
need for such low interest rates and such soft regulation to keep the economy going in its absence, the bubble would have been smaller, and the
consequences of its breaking therefore less severe."[22] This situation created
the political opportunity to direct economic anxieties toward refugees. The
resulting dynamics are destabilizing both the United States and Europe,
where the far-right, including its paramilitary fringe, is ascendant. Despite
the failure of the "War on Terror," security remains *the* solution to the
problem of terrorism. Why?

Critical terrorism scholars would say it is because the discourse of the
"War on Terror" supports "power." Hence, the aforementioned studies by
Jackson and Jarvis analyzed the contemporary political rhetoric to reveal
how the language of the "War on Terror" is, in Jackson's words, "a carefully
constructed *discourse* . . . designed to achieve a number of key political
goals." By "denaturalizing" the discourse of the "War on Terror," these
scholars make a vital contribution. They show that the "War on Terror" is
not "an objective or neutral reflection of reality." However, these studies
cannot explain why the "War on Terror" advances such "key political goals"
like "normalis[ing] and legitimis[ing] the current counter-terrorism
approach" or "disciplin[ing] domestic society by marginalising dissent or

protest." In short, they can show that the discourse of the "War on Terror" is "an exercise of power" but they cannot define what is specific about that "power."[23]

Getting at the particularities of "power" requires a different approach. Much of "critical terrorism studies" takes the work of Michel Foucault as its methodological and theoretical point of departure.[24] Foucault famously upended the study of "power," which he reconceptualized not as a thing that could be wielded by individuals or institutions but as a diffuse effect of social relations. In this conception, power is a productive force that resides in discourses, practices, and forms of knowledge. Hence, in his influential work on the prison, asylum, and hospital, Foucault analyzed the discursive construction of criminality, madness, and disease.[25] He argued these power apparatuses developed in tandem with systems of knowledge, creating "heterogeneous ensemble[s] consisting of discourses, institutions, architectural forms, regulatory decisions, laws, administrative measures, scientific statements, philosophical, moral and philanthropic propositions." These *dispositifs* are unique assemblages of heterogonous elements. They cannot be reduced to or derived from material relationships.[26]

In his efforts to decenter the analysis of power, however, Foucault failed to give due weight to the historically produced differences in power among institutions and peoples. Nicos Poulantzas, the first Marxist to take Foucault seriously, noted that his "metaphysical and mystical" conception of power "dilutes and scatters power among innumerable microsituations." Hence, Poulantzas concluded that, "for Foucault, the power relation never has any other basis than itself: it becomes a pure 'situation' in which power is always immanent."[27] As a theoretical intervention, the critique of security continues Poulantzas's work and completes a Marxist recuperation of the poststructural theory of "power." Hence, Neocleous, while working his way from Poulantzas to the critique of security, noted that Foucault's great contribution—the focus "on the networks of *administrative* power mechanisms that operate in the ordering of capitalist society"—is lost to fuzzy theorization, where "the state is dissolved into power, in turn dissolved into the social." As a result, Foucault—and, particularly, his poststructural followers who have canonized his work in an ever-proliferating number of academic subfields—are unable to see "the significant differences between different forms, modalities, institutions and exercises of power, most obviously the difference between the power of the state in relation to civil society and the relative power of individuals and groups within civil society." This ill-defined, ahistorical theorization of "power" is evident in a "spurious materialism" that replaces legal subjects with "bodies," reduces law and sovereignty to mere repression, and denies the "wider constitutive, regulative, and policing functions" of the state. Indeed, "not all legal subjects are human beings and therefore cannot be treated as 'bodies.'"[28] The approach often fails to acknowledge, let alone analyze, the stark power differentials between individual workers and the massive multinational corporations with which they sign employment contracts or—more germane to this study—the "drug pusher" and the police.

Returning to Poulantzas's critique of Foucault centers analysis squarely on the materiality of power relations, as expressed in the historically specific relationships among capital, state, and class struggle. Here, it is important to note that Poulantzas's work was more than "a first shot at a materialist appropriation of Foucault."[29] In many ways, Poulantzas *anticipated* Foucault on the relational and productive nature of power, and the relation between power and knowledge, among other points.[30] However, where Foucault developed a suggestive but ultimately ambiguous theory of micropowers that lacked any clear connection to actually existing social relations, Poulantzas tried to reinvigorate historical materialism. He developed his own conception of the productive and relational nature of power, reconceptualizing state institutions as "organically present in the generation of class powers." The state plays a *productive* role in the reproduction of a social formation through the maintenance of production relations and the management of class conflict by varied means (repression, material concessions, institutional incorporation of subordinate classes and class fragments, and ideological and cultural production). At the same time, the state is neither an autonomous actor nor the subject of a greater locus of (economic) power. Instead, it is the "specific material condensation of a given relationship of forces."[31] The state does not wield power. Instead, it is the structural effect of the cacophony of competing class powers, defined as the capacity to realize historically specific material interests. In this way, Poulantzas conceptualized a relational "field of class practices," where class interests could not be deduced from an "objective" position within the relations of production. Instead, class interests are historically specific outcomes formed through the subjective *experience* of individual and collective class relations.[32]

The critique of security extends and elaborates Poulantzas's state theory. The notion of pacification and the broader conception of policing derived from the critical read of police science add further specificity by identifying the key class strategies that have organized and animated state administration. In contrast to Foucaultian categories like discipline and biopower, which de-emphasize the state as "nothing more than the mobile effect of a regime of multiple governmentalities," the idea of pacification brings together a variety of social regulatory mechanisms—the coercive power of police and military agencies, the light touch of surveillance, and social policy more broadly—into a holistic and integrative account of the productive power of capitalist states to shape the societies they govern.[33]

The critique of security also continues Poulantzas's polemics toward Foucault and extends it to contemporary debates. In this way, the critique of security represents an alternative research agenda to largely Foucaultian subfields like critical terrorism studies, surveillance studies, or securitization theory. Consonant with Poulantzas's remarks on Foucault, these fields also advance a self-referential theorization of "power": the discourse and practices of counterterrorism, surveillance, and security are freestanding processes grounded in themselves. In contrast, the critique of security considers these discourses and practices in relation to social relations expressed in given moments of the world-economy and specific instances of state-formation.[34] As a project of critique, it begins with deep engagement with the histories and constitutive ideas that produced—and are produced within—the capitalist world-economy and the modern administrative state.

To advance this project, I read the relevant literature and my primary research as examples of *the prose of pacification*, or the discourses and performances that provide practical logic and functional coherence to the state apparatus. Pacification is both an administrative strategy to manage class struggle and a prose, a loosely connected but still coherent body of ideas, practices, and performances that animate and organize the provisioning of "security." In contrast to the now well-known notion of discourse, my effort to highlight the discursive aspect of pacification is a deliberate attempt to avoid poststructuralism's drift toward idealism. Rather than a free-floating idea of discourse, which can often be seen as *the* productive nexus of social relations, as in Foucault's ambiguous and self-referential conception of power, the prose of pacification centers the discursive aspects of administration in the historically specific and changing relations among capital, the state, and class struggle. In this way, the prose of pacification is a reformulation of what Poultanzas called "a state discourse." "[B]roken into segments and fragments according to lines intersecting the strategy of power," these "discourses of organization" are "elements of state knowledge to be used for the purposes of political strategy."[35] The prose of pacification, while productive of social relations, is also produced by historically enduring relations that cannot be reduced, in a circular fashion, to the effects of discourse. The relationship is dialectic and nonlinear. Hence, "the state is not aware of its own strategy in advance and cannot formulate it at the level of discourse." Rather, what I term the prose of pacification "constitutes the state

ـgic field by giving expression to class interests in a selective man- ـ
ـistent with the social relations of forces."[36]

ـe following two sections, I consider the counterterrorism intelligence ـ ـced at fusion centers and the related concerns about dysfunction and civil liberties voiced by criminologists, civil libertarians, and surveillance scholars. As examples of the prose of pacification, these expert debates provide voice and consistency to different classes and class fragments vying to control the state apparatus and dictate its dominant strategies. In the case of counterterrorism, police officers, intelligence analysts, and other security professionals speak the language of counterterrorism to claim authority over the definition of "threats" and, in so doing, assert control over distribution of resources within the state apparatus. Criminologists, surveillance scholars, and civil libertarians engage in similar struggle but at a distance from the state. They position themselves as experts capable of remedying the dysfunction and redressing the civil liberties violations associated with fusion centers. Insofar as criminologists form an essential part of what might be thought of as the law-and-order lobby, surveillance scholars and civil libertarians get caught up in traditional reformist politics; both of these expert conversations are constructive contributions to the institutionalization of intelligence fusion that do more to refine and perpetuate fusion centers than explain or analyze them.

CONNECTING THE DOTS BEYOND COUNTERTERRORISM

Concerns about their poor performance fail to acknowledge the actual work done at fusion centers. The politically inconvenient reality is that the threat from political violence is insufficient to warrant the amount of resources invested in counterterrorism. Since 9/11, there have been few fatalities from terrorism in the United States. According to the Global Terrorism Database, a comprehensive collection of open-source data on all attacks deemed "terrorism," these incidents of political violence have killed 197 people in the United States from 9/11 to the end of 2016.[37] In other words, the threat of terrorism is exceedingly remote. The chance of dying from terrorism in the United States is one in twenty million. These odds pale in comparison to other, more mundane threats like heart disease and cancer (one in seven); the flu, pneumonia, and emphysema (one in twenty-eight); suicide (one in a hundred); motor vehicle accidents (1 in 112); falling (1 in 144); assault by firearms (1 in 358); and even a host of exceedingly remote causes of death such as accidental suffocation during sleep (1 in 5,721), bee stings (1 in 55,764), or lightning strikes (1 in 164,968).[38]

While the threat of terrorism is statistically unlikely, mounting fears cannot be simply discounted. However, terrorism must be placed in a wider political context, beyond the hyperbolic rhetoric of security professionals, politicians, and terrorism experts. Acts labeled "terrorism" are forms of political violence that most often emerge from the breakdown of social order: civil war, revolution, and state failure or collapse. As such, most terrorism takes place in destabilized regions beset by armed conflict. In 2016, for example, most incidents of terrorism occurred in Iraq, Afghanistan, Pakistan, Nigeria and Syria.[39] The weakening of these states and surrounding regions, moreover, cannot be fully explained without considering military interventions and covert operations of Western states and, particularly, the United States. The current crisis is a day of reckoning that has been long in the making. It extends beyond the aggressive attempt to remake the Greater Middle East during the "War on Terror" to the long history of Western support for dictatorial regimes that constrained politics in much of the formerly colonized world during the Cold War. Such sober public policy data and broader historical context notwithstanding, the federal government has poured at least a trillion dollars into DHS, including, by some counts, over a billion dollars into fusion centers.[40]

There is also little evidence to show that these counterterrorism programs actually prevent terrorism. Many of the highest-profile attempted terrorist attacks since 9/11—the "shoe bomber" in 2001, the "underwear bomber" in 2009, and the "subway bomber" in 2010—were not foiled by counterterrorism programs. Instead, bystanders observed alarming behavior and responded accordingly.[41] These incidents fit within a general trend. In 2012, the US Senate concluded that "fusion center success stories" related to counterterrorism were fraudulent. They were "unable to confirm that the fusion centers' contributions were as significant as DHS portrayed them; were unique to the intelligence and analytical work expected of fusion centers; or would not have occurred absent a fusion center."[42] Most of the terrorism convictions in the last decade, moreover, are either manufactured farces, a product of FBI entrapment operations, or legal artifices— smaller convictions enhanced to appear as counterterrorism coups. As of late August 2018, 864 people have been charged for terrorism in the United States, 569 defendants pleaded guilty, courts found 186 guilty, three have been acquitted and three have seen their charges dropped or dismissed, 365 are in custody with fifty-eight awaiting trial, 314 have been caught in FBI stings, and thirty-four have been cooperating informants who have served little to no prison time. Over half of those charged—453 people—have since been released, often without supervision, suggesting the courts do not

view them as threats. As Trevor Aaronson, the journalist who assembled
and analyzed these data explained, "I could count on one hand the number
of actual terrorists, such as failed New York City subway bomber Najibullah
Zazi, who posed a direct and immediate threat to the United States."[43]

If terrorism is statistically an insignificant threat and intelligence produced at fusion centers cannot be linked to any foiled plots, then, is it correct to repeat the mantra about the misaligned mission and ineffectiveness
of fusion centers? The content of the intelligence reports that the US Senate
dismissed as "problematic and useless" provides some necessary perspective.[44] Given the insignificant threat of terrorism to the United States,
fusion centers cannot report on imminent threats. Instead, they often detail
attacks in places with active armed movements in order to make the case
that law enforcement and the private sector in the United States report
information to fusion centers. This dynamic was evident in both of the
DHS-recognized fusion centers I studied, the New Jersey Regional
Operations Intelligence Center (ROIC) and the New York State Intelligence
Center (NYSIC). In March 2012, the NYSIC, for example, released a threat
assessment on major terrorist attacks on hotels in Afghanistan, Egypt,
Indonesia, India, Iraq, Israel, Jordan, Pakistan, and Somalia. The report contained no information about threats to the United States. It simply asserted
that there was a threat to hotels:

> Radical Islamic groups, including al-Qaeda and al-Qaeda linked groups,
> continue to plan attacks against the West, including the United States
> (US). These groups view civilians as potential targets and will continue
> to use a variety of attack methods. Lack of information pertaining to a
> certain category in this report does not necessarily represent the
> absence of a threat. However, the frequency and tactic of attack
> analyzed in this report may indicate the most common vulnerabilities
> to an attack on the hotel sector.[45]

The ROIC put out a similar report following a June 2012 attack on a hotel
in Afghanistan. Like the NYSIC report, the ROIC's briefing contained no
specific threat information but made similar assertions about the nature of
threat:

> The threat to the hotel industry in New Jersey and the surrounding
> region is high because of frequent attacks domestically [—of which the
> report cites no examples—] and internationally, and the potential threat
> from [homegrown violent extremists] to the hospitality industry. As
> military and government facilities continue to improve their security
> measures, terrorists are likely to target hotels and other facilities that
> are easier to attack. While numerous terrorist groups have expressed

the intent to target the United States, the ROIC is unaware of any group that has specifically mentioned the hotel sector in New Jersey as a potential target. Law enforcement and private-sector security personnel should remain vigilant for suspicious activity that may be indicative of terrorist activity.[46]

Rather than sobering analysis of realistic dangers, these reports construct the threat of terrorism and call on others to gather intelligence.

This type of analysis is common. For example, I collected 163 of the ROIC's reports, which were posted on a publicly accessible Google Group for New Jersey fire chiefs. This collection covers the period from January to July 2014. It includes fifty-seven examples of the "ROIC Intelligence and Analysis Threat Unit Daily Overview." This report is broken into two sections. The first section, "Homeland Security Reporting," includes three subsections: international terrorism reporting, which summarizes news pertaining to political violence abroad or cybersecurity; New Jersey Suspicious Activity Reports, which lists the content of recently vetted Suspicious Activity Reports; and State Threat Posture, which always closes with this disclaimer/ call for vigilance:

> The ROIC has no specific or current information regarding a threat to New Jersey; however, large-scale events may create potential targets of opportunity for international and domestic terrorist groups as well as lone offenders. Individuals or terrorists could attempt to utilize these high-profile/high-visibility events as a stage to make a statement or otherwise further their goals.[47]

During the summer months the language shifted slightly to:

> The ROIC has no specific or current information regarding a threat to New Jersey; however, large scale events during the summer season will likely generate a large amount of national and regional media attention. These events create potential targets of opportunities for terrorist organizations and Homegrown Violent Extremists (HVEs) that recognize highly populated, high-profile events as an opportunity to further their goals.[48]

The second section of the daily threat briefing is titled "International Threat Environment," which covers developments in global conflicts, almost exclusively dominated by events in the Middle East. Clearly, these reports are of dubious analytic value, something both the intelligence analyst tasked to produce them and the law enforcement officers receiving them noted in interviews with me.[49] As examples of the prose of pacification, however, these "problematic and useless" reports communicate a pedagogical mission:

to educate and encourage police officers, and private security to "remain vigilant" and report "suspicious activity."

At both the NYSIC and the ROIC, managers consider this pedagogical mission to be important. As a senior supervisor at the NYISC told me:

> After 9-11, obviously, everybody was on board. Everybody wanted to play their part and prevent the next 9-11 from happening, but, as time goes on, human nature kicks in and less and less do people want to be prevented from doing things in their lives or be inconvenienced in any way. So we fight that all the time, not only with the public but also with law enforcement, to keep people on track and keep this stuff in their mind.[50]

A senior supervisor at the ROIC also echoed these comments:

> It really comes down to our ability to sell our services and educate the people on the importance of the work that we do. We need to get people to understand the threat environment better so they can act or be proactive in the proper manner and do their jobs better. A better-informed public, a better-informed police officer, a better-informed public safety official is somebody that is going to be doing their job at a higher level and, therefore, the safety of the citizens of New Jersey is impacted in a positive manner as a result.[51]

Whether or not fusion centers are effective at counterterrorism, these sentiments and related intelligence products are productive: they organize the work done at fusion centers, while also attempting to construct the threat of terrorism and encouraging others to report information.

This pedagogical mission is also evident in the national programming of DHS and the state-level initiatives of the ROIC and NYSIC. One of DHS's main programs is the "See Something, Say Something Campaign," a nationwide public education campaign "to raise public awareness of indicators of terrorism and terrorism-related crime, and to emphasize the importance of reporting suspicious activity to the proper local law enforcement authorities" and "underscore the concept that homeland security begins with hometown security."[52] The formal goal of the program is to encourage the public to report information to police who will create a "suspicious activity report" that becomes part of a national database, accessible to fusion center analysts and others. The wider effect of this National Suspicious Activity Reporting Initiative, however, is "to encourage and facilitate a new vigilance in peer-to-peer monitoring—in making it as easy and natural as possible for lay individuals to be the 'eyes and ears' that listen to and watch their neighbors, family members, and fellow shoppers, travelers, and sports fans."[53]

The ROIC and the NYSIC also run more focused programs with the same goal to recruit intelligence collectors. The ROIC runs a Fusion Liaison Officer Initiative, which, in the words of the trooper managing it, aims to "recruit folks from law enforcement, public safety and the private sector to attend the training. They would see an overview of about four hours of what fusion center is, what we do, how we process information, privacy and civil liberties, and the parameters we operate under."[54] The NYSIC makes a similar effort with the Field Intelligence Officer program to "provide basic training on intelligence and counterterrorism and familiarize officers with the NYSIC's products and services and also national programs like the National Suspicious Activity Reporting Initiative."[55] Both fusion centers also train private sector security personnel and produce a version of their daily reporting for the private sector.

The NYSIC takes their training even further. Through Operation Red Cell, they covertly assess the effectiveness of their outreach to the private sector. An analyst

> will go out to a specific area and inquire about information that should trigger that business to make a call or otherwise reach out to us. So, it is a way to see if we've been successful or if we need to do more outreach. It tells us what kind of information we've gotten out there and what need to improve upon. It's a test.[56]

The NYSIC also organizes a yearly State-Wide Intelligence Summit to train police executives. It is a "higher-level overview" on terrorism, crime trends, and intelligence tradecraft.[57] An administrator described the goal of the meeting as "getting new people in the fold, making them aware of terrorism, and get them exposed to the other professionals at that level, and then the upper echelon of communication is opened up."[58] In 2012, two hundred police chiefs and sheriffs attended the meeting.[59] For the NYISC, the conference is an opportunity to build their network of intelligence collectors. "We will have people who are unaware of our services. We have a booth set up at the conference and we market the NYSIC. . . . We'll see new departments reaching out to us after the summit."[60]

These counterterrorism products and programs are more than examples of the discourse of terrorism that constructs a terror threat. They are also political acts that assert the professional authority to define "threats" and make collective claims about the appropriate distribution of resources and the direction of state strategy. The massive public investment in the name of counterterrorism is a class project in at least two senses. There is a "law-and-order lobby"—a segment of the capitalist class with allies in government, academia, and popular culture—that has a vested interested in "security."

Homeland security has been a boon for this constituency. For police officers and other security professionals, an assignment at a fusion center can create opportunities for higher-prestige work in and outside of government. For example, the NYSIC catapulted New York State Police Colonel Bart Johnson, its first director, to principal deputy undersecretary for intelligence and analysis at DHS. "He saw an opportunity and made the most of it," one interviewee told me.[61] From here, Johnson moved to the private sector, becoming the executive director of the International Association of Chiefs of Police (IACP), the influential professional association. After IACP, Johnson moved back to government. Today, he is the Transportation Security Administration's federal security director for fifteen upstate New York airports.

Counterterrorism is also a class project in that it is a systemic reorganization of the state, one that recalibrates and intensifies the ability to pacify disturbances in an era of increasingly sharp social polarization. Drawing on Poulantzas, Christos Boukalas contends that DHS and the related rise of counterterrorism policies signals *"the pre-emptive shielding of capitalist rule from anticipated popular struggles against political exclusion and economic dispossession."* Boukalas locates this authoritarian hardening in the reforms of the George W. Bush administration and the related rise of particular capitalist-class fragments—armaments and oil. This important work presents a formal logic of a particular structure of power. He writes:

> In line with the discursive construction of the Enemy as being potentially anyone/anywhere, the scope of surveillance seeks to encompass all: all social interaction, by all individuals. The totality of social activity is the ultimate target of surveillance. Thus, the unified police mechanism, operating in a uniform space, is set to police an homogenised target: all of us.[62]

This provocative argument serves better as a hypothesis, which subsequent chapters explore at length. While a universal, total intelligence state could be activated, this process would be mediated through the previous history of political struggle, which shapes the specific character of the state. In other words, DHS exists to pacify those coded by the prose of pacification as a "threat." As such, it seems more likely that surveillance and police power would operate along historical lines of power. Not only are more vulnerable groups more likely to feel the ill effects of security expansion, dominant groups are more likely to embody the prose of pacification and invest their energy and emotion into "security." In this way, this study builds on Boukalas's contribution to consider some questions: How has the massive investment in intelligence changed the practice of policing? How do these changes affect the criminal legal system and the larger state apparatus? How do they shape politics? These are not the questions taken up by the scholarship on intelligence fusion and ILP.

SEEING PAST THE DISCOURSE OF ORGANIZATIONAL FAILURE

A discourse of organizational failure also surrounds fusion centers and clouds a full accounting of their effects. Virtually all writing on intelligence fusion and ILP is fixated upon shortcomings and recommendations for reform. No doubt, there are real technical problems entailed in the institutionalization of intelligence fusion and the implementation of ILP that could be redressed through study and analysis. This debate, however, is not simply applied study for public administration. Neither should it be understood as straightforward evidence of the failure of fusion centers. What Foucault said of the prison expresses a tendency implicit in every reform effort: "Prison 'reform' is virtually contemporary with the prison itself: it constitutes, as it were, its programme."[63] Similarly, this discourse of failure is not a critical check on the development of fusion centers. Instead, these expert performances are always and unavoidably productive investments in the institution. They are expert interventions in "the problem of fusion centers," which, in producing both the "expert" and "the problem," are incapable of solving the latter (just as criminology will never stop crime or deviance). Instead, these individual enactments of expertise expand the list of problems associated with intelligence and ILP. To the extent that this work contributes to conventional reforms, they get caught up in the play of the prose of pacification.

Here, both criminologists and law enforcement practitioners, on one hand, and surveillance scholars and civil libertarians, on the other, reproduce the same logic of argument, even if their content is very different. For both, the abiding concern, whether consciously articulated or implicit, is administrative: how to refine the operation of fusion centers? The de-politicized and objective tone of criminologists and law enforcement on fusion centers masks a professional project to legitimize, institutionalize, and refine intelligence fusion. Hence, scholars and practitioners identify best practices, such as outreach efforts that have measurably increased intelligence sharing or the best use of specific technologies like geospatial mapping.[64] Others have identified problems—police officers' passive posture toward fusion centers, low-quality intelligence, poor coordination—that impede intelligence fusion and ILP.[65]

This conversation is not disinterested. It happens in forums connected to large political associations of security professionals like *Police Chief*, the IACP's magazine, or the *Journal of Intelligence Analysis*, a peer-reviewed publication of the International Association of Law Enforcement Intelligence Analysts. These organizations are the political arm of security profession-als. They lobby to direct resources to security agencies, promote profes-sional standards, and manage public perceptions of the institution. They are also increasingly involved in policy formation. In the mid-2000s, the young National Fusion Center Association (NFCA)—among older associations like IACP—worked with DHS and the Department of Justice (DOJ) to rec-ommend standards and guidelines that conditioned the consolidation of fusion centers throughout the next decade.[66] For its part, the NFCA also organizes yearly conventions, which, starting in 2013, were independent of DHS or DOJ.[67] Instead, security and technology firms "cosponsor" the annual gathering: older titans like IBM and Thomson Reuters, which both sell data analysis platforms, established firms like Esri, the geographic information system (GIS) mapping juggernaut, and relative upstarts like Dataminr and Geofeedia, the early leaders in social media monitoring. Instead of a discourse of failure, this block of professional and corporate interests is producing the prose of pacification, creating the knowledge and practices that animate and organize intelligence fusion and ILP.

In a more oblique way, even ostensibly "critical" voices like surveillance scholars and civil libertarians get caught up in the prose of pacification. While surveillance scholars provide empirical insights on fusion centers, they have not asked how their findings relate to larger power structures. A case in point is Torin Monahan and Priscilla Regan's survey of thirty-six DHS-recognized fusion centers. They present the bulk of their findings in the same narrow, objective style that characterizes criminology. Hence, they identify the reason the mission of fusion centers has crept from coun-terterrorism to "all hazards." They similarly note the administrative and interagency factors that result in weak accountability at fusion centers. They also examine fusion centers' role in the expansion of suspicious activity reporting.[68] Their most ambitious argument conceptualizes fusion centers as "centers of concatenation" or clearinghouses where "disparate data are drawn together as needed, invested with meaning, communicated to others, and then discarded such that no records exist of such surveil-lance activities."[69] This theorization, however, does not explore the ends of fusion center surveillance. Why is this monitoring happening? Who is surveilled and with what effects? In short, it does not explore systemic connections with the concrete specificities of "power." Since surveillance is—by definition—an exercise of power, ignoring these questions leaves the study unfinished.

Most importantly, the tentative nature of these studies coupled with their objective tone leads surveillance scholars to some fraught conclusions. In an article written with Krista Carven, Monahan and Regan consider what is arguably the most egregious example of political policing connected to fusion centers: the policing of Occupy Wall Street and, particularly, Occupy Phoenix (an incident discussed in chapter 5). They use this example "to better understand" the tension between the claims of security officials that "the public should trust police and intelligence communities not to violate their rights" and the dynamic where "the very act of engaging in secretive surveillance operations erodes public trust in government." While they find that fusion centers are generally "well aware of these dangers and are generally wary of scrutiny by the media or others," they contend that increased public accountability would formalize this tendency. In other words, ostensibly "critical" scholars of surveillance conclude that enhanced regulation may lead to more public legitimacy for law enforcement intelligence centers, which, they note in the first sentence of the article, operate "in direct tension with ideals of democratic governance and accountability."[70]

In this way, the work of surveillance scholars underscores the dilemma of traditional reformist politics. Efforts to ameliorate the excesses of state power often entrench and perpetuate those same abuses. Consider the stance of the premier civil liberties organization, the ACLU, toward fusion centers. In 2008, they identified a series of problems with fusion centers— ambiguous lines of authority, private sector and military participation, and wholesale data mining and excessive secrecy. They recommended that the US Congress and state legislatures work to increase oversight of fusion centers, regulate the flow of information between fusion centers and the private sector, clarify "how and when" military personnel can collect intelligence for law enforcement purposes, and strengthen open records laws.[71] The ACLU did not demand an end to these problematic practices. Instead, they sought to regulate and, thus, codify them. Challenging intelligence fusion on these terms will, at best, produce limited public oversight (an ACLU representative on the fusion center's executive board) and some modest restrictions on intelligence gathering (three-month retention periods for certain kinds of data), which would only be contravened in exceptional circumstances (an emergency warrant or administrative subpoena).

In this way, the analyses of surveillance scholars and the reformist efforts of civil libertarians reify state power. Consider the politics of privacy. Surveillance scholars often focus narrowly on the implementation of privacy policies and their inadequacy.[72] Civil libertarians view privacy as a universal right that can be asserted against the encroachment of outside parties. They position "*the* right to privacy" or "*the* state" as independent entities that stand apart from the social relations and political processes that, historically, created them and still imbue them with meaning. This way of thinking transforms historically specific social relations and the ideas that animate them into abstract "things." The "private" is not natural condition that is always and already in opposition to the state and capital. Instead, "privacy" is a particular claim articulated within a particular context: sixteenth-century liberal theory, a concession that the consolidating administrative state made to "the public." Privacy has no essential essence. It is a shifting boundary with demarcations set and reset by the state. The meaningful foil to the "private" is not the state—the "public"—but the "criminal," or the other activities outside the state but disallowed by the sovereign. Rather than a basis of resistance, privacy is a tool of regulation: privacy as pacification. In a social world already governed by the commodity form and wage relation, privacy

> entrenches the very separations between people presupposed by capitalist social relations that security is used to enforce and maintain. Privacy, then, promises a life apart, a mode of existence separate from others and to this end is presupposed by our appearance as individuals who are autonomous from another and can, therefore, "choose" to be further detached and apart.[73]

The notion of privacy further alienates social relations and fetishizes the processes that define our lives as mystified things.

For this reason, the work of surveillance scholars and civil libertarians often amounts to a moral critique: an appeal to law and a demand, sometimes only implicit, for further state regulation. This moral critique is simultaneously performance of and productive investment in a particular conception of the social world. Insofar as it remains uncritically wedded to privacy, the efforts of surveillance scholars and civil libertarian represent the liberal counterpoint to the law-and-order advocacy of criminologists and law enforcement practitioners. While the former highlights accountability and the latter emphasizes effectiveness, both offer "better" surveillance and policing. In contrast, this study asks how such intensive surveillance and aggressive policing became a common practice in the first place. To meaningfully consider this question, it is necessary to resist conventional understandings of "reform," a subject the conclusion revisits. Instead of trying to fix fusion centers, *Pacifying the Homeland* travels inside the secret world of intelligence fusion to unearth and analyze the intended consequences of an apparent organizational failure.

INSIDE THE WORLD OF INTELLIGENCE FUSION

The world of intelligence fusion is muddled and complex. It entails more than just one type of institution, fusion centers. It encompasses an entire network of actors: the police agencies that manage fusion centers; the intelligence analysts from state homeland security offices; and the representatives from a variety of local, state, and federal agencies that work at fusion centers. There are also more arms-length relationships, such as the government and private sector "partners" that may call the fusion center for support or receive their products. Some of these relationships are more administrative, like those with federal officials involved in the funding and evaluation of fusion centers. Of course, there are also the contractors, both the companies that sell and service information technology systems and subcontractors that work at fusion centers.

The confusion is not just a matter of secrecy. It is also a product of a specific set of institutions, a particular *state-form*. Indeed, when the Senate hammered fusion centers for their ineffectiveness at counterterrorism, the House of Representatives responded that such standardization was never the point. "The strength of the National Network," the House report contended, "lies in the diversity of expertise, individual fusion centers' unique identities, and operational independence from the Federal Government; a cookie-cutter approach would be detrimental to the National Network."[74] This statement is not just a defensive reframing of the Senate's criticism. It also gets at an important truth. Fusion centers are a product of a distinct era of public policy, where efficiency is more important than the standardization. The key policies that shape fusion centers are not binding regulations written by legislators or agency heads. They were drafted as "recommendations" and "baseline capabilities" in large working groups, which included the participation of a wide group of "stakeholders," including the aforementioned police professional associations. "The missions of fusion centers vary based on the environment in which the center operates," as one of these documents explains. "Some capabilities may not need to be housed or performed within a fusion center itself; instead, the center may rely on another fusion center or other operational entity to provide the capability. This approach is particularly appropriate, since one of the founding principles of the *Fusion Center Guidelines* is to leverage existing resources and expertise where possible."[75]

These arrangements reflect a reorganization of political authority, one aptly cast as the workfare state, which, in contrast to the more centralized welfare state, seeks to promote innovation with competition. The next chapter discusses these changes at length. For now, it suffices to note that what most reformers, policy advocates, and academics systematically mis-recognize as signs of failure are more properly understood as the variegated outcomes produced by the decentralized planning and competitiveness baked into the system. To better understand how these outcomes are pro-duced, I examined two very different institutionalizations of intelligence fusion and ILP: the two adjacent states connected by the metro area that was the "ground zero" of 9/11. I compare New York and New Jersey to illustrate a larger structural shift. In both states, police—empowered by the increased emphasis on and investment in intelligence—are enabling a lev-eling-off of the prison population and a shift to more surveillance- and police-intensive pacification practices. The overall context of the workfare state clarifies the cumulative effects of intelligence fusion and ILP, while explaining the institutional differences between New York and New Jersey.

There is also an important historical aspect. The New York Police Department (NYPD) is the largest police department in the world, with great power and influence. It is a trendsetter that pioneered some of the techniques now being exported across the country under the rubric of intel-ligence fusion and ILP. Indeed, as the federal government began to advance fusion centers, New York State's Division of Criminal Justice Services (DCJS), an agency dedicated to supporting and training other criminal jus-tice agencies, launched Operation IMPACT, a grant-driven interagency partnership between DCJS and the major law enforcement agencies in the seventeen counties that, together, account for 80 percent of the crime out-side of New York City. The goal of IMPACT was to export New York City's policing innovations throughout the state, including intelligence-led polic-ing. As a result of IMPACT, New York State has what is likely the most robust state-level intelligence network in the United States: thirteen county crime analysis centers located throughout the state. These miniature fusion centers specialize in criminal intelligence and serve New York's other urban centers. Between the NYPD and IMPACT, New York's DHS-recognized, statewide fusion center, the NYSIC, has to compete for its mission space and niche. It has largely lost this battle. As a result, New York, an early innovator in policing, has a DHS-recognized fusion center that appears to be redundant and dysfunctional. In contrast, the ROIC has little competi-tion and struggles to meet the intelligence needs of a densely populated state with high rates of violent crime.

In this way, the comparison between New York and New Jersey strength-ens this book's central claim that intelligence fusion and ILP are the central components in the reconfiguration of the state. A focus on just DHS-recognized fusion centers would present a false picture, where New Jersey is a model and New York is laggard. A broader focus, however, reveals that the nationwide attempt to institutionalize intelligence fusion through DHS counterterrorism initiatives is part of a larger structural transformation that some of the policing innovations in New York City prefigure. In short, this comparison shows a common outcome produced through different institutional means. It highlights a new configuration of the state's security apparatus, while explaining the complex—and regionally varied—political and institutional transformations through which this change unfolded. It moves the conversation beyond hyperbolic claims about terrorism and a nearsighted obsession with failure and reform.

Instead, this study of intelligence fusion incorporates the comparison of New York and New Jersey into a larger investigation of the development of the state-form. A conventional comparison would produce "objective" knowledge about some abstracted "thing." Consider, for example, Renee Graphia-Joyal's comparison of four fusion centers to determine how interpersonal relationships and trust affect information sharing and collaboration. Each fusion center is taken at face value as a discreet "case" comparable to similar "cases."[76] In contrast, the comparison given in this study does not assume a given fusion center operates as an independent entity, a case that can be isolated and studied. Instead, it constructs a larger totality formed, in part, by different *moments* or *processes* of intelligence fusion. It compares the operation and institutionalization of intelligence fusion in New York and New Jersey *in time*: What resources do these intelligence centers muster? How are they used? How are these fusion centers institutionally situated? How are they connected to other agencies and entities? It also compares their development *through time*: How were these intelligence centers put in place? How have they changed over time? How have they helped define or refine the work of "intelligence fusion"?[77]

These simultaneous synchronic and diachronic comparisons avoid the common problem of abstracted empiricism. In one of the classic texts of sociological methods, C. Wright Mill denounced the "pronounced tendency to confuse whatever is to be studied with the set of methods suggested for its study." Hence, he criticized "public opinion" research for assuming the existence of "the public" and conflating it with the statistical survey. This approach lost sight of the "problem of the public" as it developed during the transformation of Western societies from the collapse of the medieval order through the modern period up to the consolidating "mass societies" of Mills's time. By the late 1950s, the relevant question was not, what does "the public" think? but, does "the public" exist? and, what relevance does its opinion hold when "men at large become 'mass men' each trapped in quite a powerless milieux"?[78]

Similarly, Graphia-Joyal's comparison of fusion centers conflates her object of study with her methods, a four-part case study. The very problem of fusion centers—What is intelligence fusion? How did it develop? How is it institutionalized and with what effects?—is lost to her assumption that fusion centers exist as a "thing" or "case" that needs no explanation or investigation. Graphia-Joyal's problem—like the questions taken up by criminologists, surveillance scholars, and civil libertarians—is much narrower. She asks how to improve information sharing and interagency collaboration at fusion centers. While her answer may help fusion center managers refine their operations, it will do little to advance "public" understanding of intelligence fusion or its consequences. In contrast, incorporating the comparison through history and within the present allows us to consider intelligence fusion as *both* a constitutive component of a state-form *and* a dynamic variable in ongoing processes of state-formation. In other words, this study places intelligence fusion within the broader social and historical context of the crisis of the workfare-carceral state and uses the analytic insights of the comparison to identify a shift in state strategy toward mass supervision, a more surveillance- and police-intensive practice of pacification. The next chapter details the necessary historical background to situate this comparison.

2. The Rise and Present Demise of the Workfare-Carceral State

The Lineages of the United States

Connecting the dots beyond counterterrorism creates a more complicated picture of fusion centers. It reveals that the apparent failure of the fusion centers recognized by the Department of Homeland Security (DHS) is a shortsighted explanation that obscures a deeper history. "The terror attacks of 9/11 have created a kind of amnesia," Jonathan Simon maintains, "wherein a quarter of a century of fearing crime and securing social spaces has been suddenly recognized, but misidentified as a response to an astounding act of terrorism, rather than a generation-long pattern of political and social change."[1] Indeed, the National Network of Fusion Centers may be a dysfunctional counterterrorism program, but they are also the most recent development in a four-decade-long trend. The origins of these "fusion centers" can be traced back to the early days of the "wars" on crime and drugs, when the Johnson and Nixon administrations greatly expanded federal involvement in state and local law enforcement. The story begins with federal support to computerize police records and develop interagency databases of law enforcement information. These efforts led to the creation, in 1974, of what could be retroactively called "the first fusion centers": the Drug Enforcement Administration (DEA)'s El Paso Intelligence Center and the Regional Information Sharing System, a networked series of law enforcement databases created by the Bureau of Justice Assistance and anchored by six multistate intelligence centers.[2]

The late 1960s and early 1970s, of course, was also time of political ferment and economic crisis. Social movements—civil rights, Black Power, second-wave feminism, the New Left and the broader counterculture—challenged the distribution of power in the United States and questioned its place in the world. Simultaneously, the post–World War II economic boom had begun to bust. The grand compromise between labor and capital at the base of the New Deal and Great Society unraveled under the pressure of declining profits, rising unemployment, and runaway inflation. By the 1980s, a new arrangement was taking shape. The reforms that can now be seen as the origins of fusion centers were part of larger changes in the criminal legal system that gave rise to mass incarceration, the excessive use of imprisonment as a strategy "for addressing problems of poverty, inequality, unemployment, racial conflict, citizenship, sexuality, and gender as well as crime."[3] Many of these problems were exacerbated by the new economic order, which empowered capital by removing many of the measures that previously had protected much of the population from the market's worst ravages. In the last quarter of the twentieth century, the United States became a workfare-carceral state.

While most other advanced capitalist states to varying degrees have become workfare states, no other state has built a carceral complex that compares to the United States.[4] With just one-twentieth of the global population, the United States accounts for a quarter of the world's prisoners.[5] The incarceration rate in the United States is seven to ten times higher than the rates of other advanced industrial countries in Europe and East Asia and two to five times higher than high-crime countries like Brazil and South Africa. Even with the declining US prison population since 2008, the 2016 incarceration rate of 660 persons for every 100,000 is still by far the highest in the world.[6] The rates are even higher for racial minorities: 831 per 100,000 Hispanics and 2,306 per 100,000 blacks.[7] The fusion centers and the larger post-9/11 security surge, then, are embedded within the larger problem of mass incarceration and police violence in the United States. To fully reckon with fusion centers, they need to be holistically approached within their historical context and understood as components of a vast security apparatus that took generations to build.

In their efforts to understand this new order, however, most scholars focused on only one part of the workfare-carceral state couplet. The literature on welfare states is a distinct thread of conversation that exists within larger academic and public policy debates about the global economic restructuring that began in the 1970s. While not the first to use the term, President Nixon first introduced "workfare" into discussions of social assistance programs. As workfare went "from a programme of reform *within* the welfare system to a codification of an *alternative to* this system," scholars and activists worked to identify the contours—and contradictions—of a new economic order, explaining how it arose from the decaying welfare state and resolved, at least for a few decades, the economic crisis that afflicted advanced capitalist states in the 1970s.[8] This scholarly conversation on workfare often bleeds into the larger discussion about changes effected by "neoliberalism": the reorganization of production into flexible global networks, the rise of East Asia as a dynamic center of capital accumulation, the increasing power of finance capital, and widening global inequality.[9]

The scholarship on mass incarceration developed as the story of US prisons clearly diverged from the European experience. By the early 1990s, the United States had over a million people caged. At the time, the incarceration rate (426 per 100,000) could only compare with apartheid South Africa (333 per 100,000) and the Soviet Union (236 per 100,000).[10] By the late 1990s, activists and scholars began to use the term *carceral state* to understand how the United States' unprecedented prison boom created a new politics where incarceration and policing managed social problems exacerbated by economic change. This massive expansion of the criminal legal system compounded the problem and destroyed entire communities. Since criminal records "marked" people as unemployable "criminals," already impoverished communities reached new lows. The black middle class left the "communal" ghettos of the Jim Crow era for segregated suburbs, leaving behind "hyperghettos" doubly segregated on the basis of race and class. As the starkest racial disparity (eight to one), incarceration became the central core of a renewed and reorganized edifice of racial inequality around which disparities in unemployment (two to one), nonmarital childbearing (three to one), infant mortality (two to one), and wealth (one to five) revolved.[11]

At the same time, neither the workfare state scholarship nor the literature on mass incarceration can fully explain the precise nature of the United States' unprecedented incarceration rates and levels of police violence. The workfare state literature does not consider the question. For example, Bob Jessop's landmark analysis overlooks the security apparatus altogether: "since [his research agenda] focuses on economic and social policy, there are important aspects of the capitalist state that it ignores. Most notable of these are the military and police apparatuses, their changing forms and functions, the nature of modern warfare, and their overall connections to the broader state system." The omission of prisons and policing is a particularly arbitrary disconnect, as if they have no bearing on "social policy" and no impact on labor markets.[12] The reformation of the United States into a workfare state may help contextualize mass incarceration and police violence as, in part, expressions of a new, harsher relationship between labor and capital, but it cannot explain these phenomena, especially in comparison to other states, which implemented workfare policies without resorting to mass incarceration.

For their part, scholars of mass incarceration have emphasized the enduring power of racism as their explanation of mass incarceration. Hence,

Loïc Wacquant traces the evolution of the United States' "peculiar institutions" from slavery to mass incarceration and Michelle Alexander documents the legal architecture of the new Jim Crow.[13] Other scholars, like Naomi Murakawa and Elizabeth Hinton, have traced the deeper historical roots of mass incarceration to paternal ideas about racial oppression embedded into the War on Poverty and the larger project of "racial liberalism."[14] Some, like Bruce Western and Marc Mauer, simply document the stark racial inequities of the system.[15] All these studies have made important contributions. They all provide needed perspective on the specificities of oppression in the United States. They help answer why black and brown people are incarcerated and killed by police at rates that far exceed their proportional share of the population. They also largely fail to explain why the US criminal justice system incarcerates and kills so many of all races. The current white incarceration rate, 380 per 100,000, still compares unfavorably with other countries. A similar dynamic is evident with "police-involved killings," although the data is incomplete. To the best we know, police in the United States kill between nine hundred and eleven hundred people per year, 40 to 50 percent of whom are white.[16]

Here, a one-dimensional conception of *subjectivity* simplifies the relevant social relations and processes at work. The new Jim Crow thesis, for example, positions mass incarceration as a continuation of racial caste, a system of domination disconnected from political economy. This framing obscures the important differences between Jim Crow, a system that marshaled and mobilized racially devalued labor, and mass incarceration, an arrangement to warehouse superfluous labor. In denying class differences *within* racial groups, it also simplifies the politics of mass incarceration, erasing *both* the support the black elite and middle class provided for mass incarceration *and* the reality that the United States imprisons hundreds of thousands of white people, while police kill hundreds of white people each year.[17] To approach this question, it is necessary to consider the systemic interrelations among race and class. On this point, the literature on workfare states provides an equally one-sided treatment of subjectivity. However, where the mass incarceration scholars simply assume "race" as a self-evident category in a historical narrative, the workfare state literature focuses on a flat and formal class on paper (a class in itself) and pays little attention to the historical formation of particular working classes and their political mobilization as a self-conscious collective subject (a class for itself).[18]

While welfare state literature often leans toward a theoretical formalism that emphasizes systemic tendencies in capital accumulation and ignores the concrete histories and conflicts that shape a social formation, the mass incarceration scholarship has the opposite problem. Most of this work simply describes the historical formation of mass incarceration or provides an empirical assessment of its social impacts. The broader sociological processes informing the rise of mass incarceration and animating its current composition are largely undertheorized. As a result, the scholarship on the subject has largely failed to explain—let alone foresee—contemporary developments. At the end of the twentieth century, most activists and scholars viewed mass incarceration as "an entrenched feature of the social landscape of the country and a central pillar of the post-welfare, neoliberal state. Mass imprisonment, it was widely agreed, had no limits to its future."[19] Indeed, Bruce Western concluded that mass incarceration was "self-sustaining," and "the penal system will remain as it has become, a significant feature on the new landscape of American poverty and race relations."[20] Yet, as Western wrote those words halfway through the first decade of the twenty-first century, an important change was becoming clear: decarceration. By the end of that decade, the total US prison population began its ongoing—however modest—decline. More dramatic drops on the state level account for much of the reduction. In nearly half the country, twenty-four states, prison populations are shrinking, including sharp reductions of over a fifth in New York and New Jersey.[21] While many scholars of mass incarceration welcomed this change, no one anticipated it.

The incommensurable harshness of the US criminal legal system—a complex of issues that includes the institutionalization of intelligence fusion—cannot be fully explained by a focus on one variable, whether race or class, politics or economics. To approach the complexity of the problem of mass incarceration and police violence in the United States, this chapter examines historically unique *state-forms*: the enduring institutions created from the social struggles among different social forces to shift the power differentials between them and institutionalize a favorable balance of forces. Recalling the discussion of Poulantzas in the previous chapter, these state-forms are neither *the* privileged site of power nor autonomous actors in their own right. Neither a subject nor an object, the state-form is the institutional condensation of social relations. It develops in interaction with ongoing conflicts both within the institutional apparatus of the state and apart from it. The United States' excessive use of incarceration, its terrifying levels of police violence, and its expansive security apparatus are best explained in these terms. The most relevant factor is not a single variable but culminating historical processes: the systemic transformation of the United States, as a social formation and state-form, from a *herrenvolk-*welfare state into a workfare-carceral state.

To understand this historical transformation, this chapter considers the systemic interconnections among processes of labor-formation, racial-formation, pacification, and state-formation. Drawing on the humanist and historical currents within Marxism, it explains basic theoretical assumptions about the accumulation of capital, the formation of labor, and the regulation of the social surplus.[22] In these terms, it returns to the critique of security to demonstrate how the threat of revolt from below and the resultant administrative incorporation of the working class has been one of the historical drivers of state-formation. Given the concrete characteristics of the working class in the United States, however, the pacification of labor also entailed its racial differentiation. These intertwined processes of labor-formation, racial-formation, pacification, and state-formation condition the particular ways that the United States has formed and been reformed. The interaction of these processes produced historically specific *state-forms*: the *herrenvolk*-welfare state and the workfare-carceral state. Fusion centers are an important part of the workfare-carceral state. Their increasing prominence—and the larger "post-9/11" security surge associated—is reformulation of state strategy. The ambiguous turn toward a punitive, police-intensive form of decarceration and the further expansion of intelligence fusion, I contend, is an outgrowth of and response to contemporary crisis.

In other words, this chapter considers workfare and mass incarceration as complementary state strategies, parts that constitute the larger processes of *social regulation* that remade the United States during the four decades between 1970 and 2010. Understanding this transformation, in turn, requires historical perspective on the previous struggles that produced contemporary strategies, hence the attention to the earlier *herrenvolk*-welfare state. This attempted synthesis is not a purely synthetic project. Indeed, Poulantzas's work informs the discussions on workfare and mass incarceration. In his final works in the late 1970s, Poulantzas presciently concluded that the internationalization of production, the increased power of finance capital, and the resultant global social "insecurities" forced states into a position of permanent crisis management. The resultant "authoritarian statism" necessitated "growing involvement on the part of the State, so that . . . class hegemony [may be] reproduced." This "growing involvement" required "intensified state control over every sphere of socioeconomic life combined with radical decline of the institutions of political democracy and with draconian and multiform curtailment of so-called 'formal' liberties." The workfare-carceral state, then, is the form that authoritarian statism takes in the United States.

In this way, I synthesize the subsequent scholarship influenced by Poulantzas, namely the critique of security, Jessop's analysis of the workfare state, and the efforts of Stuart Hall and his collaborators to map the coercive "law-and-order" politics of the 1970s. While Hall focused on the United Kingdom, his work informed important analyses of mass incarceration, including Ruth Gilmore's examination of California's prison boom as a way of managing the social surplus, and Jordan Camp's investigation into the relationship between political repression and the formation of the carceral state.[23] This chapter builds on these contributions and draws on their organic connections to the humanist and historical currents within Marxism. This theoretical synthesis avoids any entanglement with the prose of pacification, while providing a perspective that can appreciate the systemic implications of the institutionalization of intelligence fusion.

THE ACCUMULATION OF CAPITAL AND THE REGULATION OF THE SOCIAL SURPLUS

At its core, Marxism asks a deceptively simple question: How is a given social formation reproduced through time? This is not the economic determinism of "orthodox Marxism." The accumulation of capital concerns the production, valorization, and accretion of surplus value, the excess social product after the capitalist has paid wages and covered other costs.[24] The *regulation* of capitalist societies, however, entails the broader management of the social surplus, which connotes three interrelated social products: (1) the surplus value produced as capital; (2) the surplus populations who are not (fully) incorporated within the circuit of capital; and (3) the needs and desires of the population that cannot be (fully) satisfied within the constraints of capitalist social relations.[25] The politics of capitalist societies center on the management of this expanded notion of social surplus. How much capital will be returned to workers as wages? How much will appropriated by the state to fabricate social order? How will excess labor be managed? How will subjectivities—the emotive, aesthetic, and sensuous desires of actually existing populations—be variously articulated, mobilized, fulfilled, and/or repressed? Considering the broader regulation of the social surplus refocuses attention on the expanded notion of social reproduction, which extends beyond the production and circulation of goods in the formal economy.[26] The reproduction and regulation of social formation includes diverse processes such as the ways capital accumulation draws on non-waged sources of labor like the usually feminized labor that fulfills many human needs in the "hidden abode" of households or the broader ideological and political projects that fabricate the social order within "civil society." This latter category includes the discourses and interventions of the administrative state introduced in the preceding chapter as pacification and its prose.

This broader, humanist approach breaks the determinism often associated with Marxism. It reminds us that labor is not just an "abstract" factor of production. It is also "concrete" flesh-and-blood workers: individuals and peoples with "'political passion[s]'... born on the 'permanent and organic' terrain of economic life but which transcend ... it, bringing into play emotions and aspirations in whose incandescent atmosphere even calculations involving the individual human life itself obey different laws from those of individual profit."[27] Capital's inescapable reliance on labor, and the dogged, irrepressible, and incommensurable humanity of "living labor" means that resistance to exploitation is a structural feature of capitalist civilization. Workers' autonomy continually presents itself in the everyday "weapons of the weak"—work slowdowns, insubordination, and disrespect for authority, so-called "petty crimes"—and the threat of politics, the dangerous prospect of collective consciousness and mobilization.[28] This essential antagonism between labor and capital—in addition to the capitalist's imperative to accumulate—also contributes to the constant change and dynamism that characterizes capitalism. As capital flees from and attempts to undermine the victories of working classes, the world is continually remade through "creative destruction": the search for new profitable investments, new technologies to deskill labor and speed up production, new markets to tap, and new behaviors or needs to commodify.

Capital accumulation, then, entails much more than the growth of capital through investment and trade. It also forms and continually reforms the groups and classes that constitute a social formation. In providing the labor power that makes the system move, workers produce their own obsolescence. Put crudely, there is a progressive deskilling: the crafts of artisans and mechanics are transformed from concrete activities of living labor and transmuted into the assembly line, which employs fewer and fewer workers of increasingly less skill until all are replaced by robots and a handful of highly trained technicians. As this process unfolds, the basic *needs* of the population are increasingly separated from their *capacity* to provide them. In previous modes of production, basic needs were often met by the primary producers themselves in some kind of subsistence economy. Under capitalism, however, all accoutrements of life—from the basic necessities of survival to the most vulgar and silly consumer thing—are increasingly provisioned to the population through the market (commodity exchange) and the state (social policy).

Noting the deepening spiral of commodification entailed in capital accumulation, Marx argued that capital accumulation necessarily produces "surplus" workers. The creation of ever-expanding wealth or capital also entailed the production of dispossessed workers or proletarians. As capital grew larger and larger and as technology advanced to make labor increasingly efficient, it produced ever larger working classes and, with them, larger surplus populations:

> The greater the social wealth, the functioning capital, the extent and energy of its growth, and therefore also the greater the absolute mass of the proletariat and the productivity of its labor, the greater is the industrial reserve army. The same causes which develop the expansive power of capital, also develop the labor-power at its disposal. . . . But the greater this reserve army in proportion to the active labor-army, the greater is the mass of a consolidated surplus population, whose misery is in inverse ratio to the amount of torture it has to undergo in the form of labor. The more extensive, finally, the pauperized sections of the working class and the industrial reserve army, the greater is official pauperism.

While Marx noted that this process was "modified in its working by many circumstances," it constituted the culmination of his critique of political economy, what he called "the general law of capital accumulation."[29]

The emphasis Marx placed on this process is well justified. The polarization of wealth and power is the basic conflict that defines capitalist societies, and "surplus populations" are one of the key actors in this struggle. Historically, they are the "masterless men" uprooted from traditional obligations but without place in the constantly changing economic order. The consolidation of "capitalism entailed the taking of land, the criminalizing of the conditions of survival for those thrown off the land, and the violation of criminal laws by people who had no choice but crime for their livelihood."[30] Crime became most strongly associated with a particular subset of surplus populations, what Marx called the lumpenproletariat. Distinguished morally from the proletariat, this "lowest sediment" of society includes vagabonds, criminals, and prostitutes.[31] While other strata of the surplus populations (the so-called "deserving poor") were managed with the gentler hand of social policy such as poor aid, the lumpen became the primary responsibility of the police.[32] Managing these surplus populations spurred the formation of the administrative capacities of the state, while the threat they pose to social order has given rise to many of the security practices and disciplinary institutions that pacify the seeming disorder produced by immiserated surplus populations. The security apparatus and social policy are the iron hand and velvet glove that pacify class struggle. Together, they enforce the rule of capital and private property, maintain the separation of needs and capacities, and fabricate capitalist forms of order.

PACIFICATION AS THE INCORPORATION AND
RACIALIZATION OF THE WORKING CLASS

As capitalism developed into an increasingly totalizing world-system, the "strong" states at the core of the world-economy—that is, the regions that accumulated a disproportionate share of global value—politically incorporated and pacified the working class through the extension of the franchise and collective bargaining rights, the creation of police forces, and the amelioration of misery through social policy. Focusing on the New Poor Law in 1834 and the contemporaneous expansion of the vote, Neocleous argues that growing administrative capacities of the state in the United Kingdom politically incorporated the working class and subsumed class struggle through the legal system:

> Recognizing the power of the working class, the state assumes a
> position as the wedge between needs and capacities, but does so through
> a series of administrative forms. The development of national insurance,
> as one element of the response to the threat of the working class, signals
> the formal recognition of need by the state, a process which consolidates
> the separation of needs and capacities of the working class and yet at the
> same time locks it in a relationship with capital and the state. In return
> the working class is granted increased political rights: individual rights
> of citizenship, such as the right to vote, and the collective rights through
> the legal immunities granted to trade unions.[33]

The political incorporation and legal recognition of the working class—the franchise and collective bargaining—subsumed working-class politics within the state, creating the possibility for peaceful mediation within "civil society."

This process speaks to the unique role of the state as the "part" of the social formation that, as an expression of the "general interest" and legitimate holder of the monopoly on violence, assumes the role as the universal arbiter of social struggle.[34] The state, then, becomes the uneven institutional synthesis of the conflicting demands and competing strategies of different fractions of a social formation.[35] The selective repression, accommodation, and incorporation of social struggle within the institutional apparatus defines the scope and boundaries of a given state-form. Hence, the recognition of collective bargaining rights moves the politics of organized labor from the realm of criminality and revolution—what, in the United States, was called "industrial warfare" before the New Deal—into routine administration—what we now call "labor relations." This is an ambiguous process. On the one hand, labor won real power and used it to the benefit of the working class. By the mid-twentieth century, the labor parties (or parties with unions as a central constituent, like the US Democratic Party) ruled "the West" and built welfare states.[36] On the other hand, the incorporation of labor also mollified it. It entailed a selective process of repression and accommodation that purged the radicals and narrowed the political horizons of organized labor. It subsumed labor within politics that did not challenge capital. As these processes played out in different states, the industrial working class that Marx considered to be the vanguard of the revolution became the "labor aristocracy" later identified by Lenin.[37] The transformation of the proletariat from an exploited mass with "nothing to lose but their chains" to a politically integrated constituency administered by the state pacified the working class.[38]

Of course, the incorporation of different working classes reflects the concrete, historical characteristics of a social formation. Thus, in the United States, the working class was incorporated in a racially differentiated manner. Capital does contain the universal and theoretical ambition to create "a world after its own image," a smooth space where capital can move freely, where all of humanity sells their labor for a wage, and all human activities are organized through the commodity-form and cash nexus.[39] However, capital is also a pragmatic and promiscuous producer of difference. Historically, capital organized and subsumed all forms of labor control—slavery, serfdom, small independent commodity production, and reciprocity—within a global division of labor.[40] The global differentiation and territorial spread of these modes of labor control have forever linked processes of labor- and racial-formation. Historically, capital formed non-white populations as marginalized groups through a process of wholesale, collective proletarianization, what Oliver Cromwell Cox understood as the substantive material force behind modern racism as a social structure.[41] The nascent capitalist world-economy of the sixteenth century was also a global racial regime: slavery for blacks, indentured labor for whites, and "coerced cash crop labour" for the indigenous populations of the Americas. Over time, racialized subjectivities are also enforced from below in ways that are "simultaneously politically calming (learning how to adapt and thereby cope) and radicalizing (learning the nature and source of oppressions)."[42] As Stuart Hall famously put it, "Race is the modality in which class is lived. It is also the medium in which class relations are experienced."[43] The interwoven nature of racial- and labor-formation created an interwoven global structure of racial and class oppression, "the problem color line" that marked the boundary between global poles of wealth and poverty, inclusion and exclusion, exaltation and abnegation.[44]

While the color line set the boundary between Europe and the colonialized world, it ran through the United States and shaped the formation and incorporation of the working class. In what would become the United States, the racialization of the working class preceded the extension of the franchise and the recognition of organized labor. During the early colonial period, ruling mercantile elites relied on two sources of bonded labor: African slaves and the indentured servitude of poor Europeans. In 1676, these two groups joined together in Bacon's Rebellion, a revolt in Virginia spurred by the wretched conditions of bonded laborers, among other issues. After authorities put down the uprising, however, plantation owners and mercantile elites codified racial hierarchy into law, the Virginia Slave Codes of 1705, inventing the white race and dividing the working class with the color line.[45] *The racialization of the working class also affected its pacification.* A formal, legal system of racial control now mediated the organization of labor and the relations among individuals.

The reformulation of the state as an overtly white supremacist entity, however, was not a direct and simple outgrowth of the racist elites. Instead, this transformation of the state is the condensation of a *relationship*. In other words, the formalization of racial conflict after Bacon's Rebellion was a *strategic* response of the ruling class to an unfavorable *relation of forces*, the threat of rebellion from bonded labor. It led to reformulation of the law and the institutional apparatus of the state that formalized racial domination, divided the working class, pacified a revolutionary threat, and strengthened elites by disarticulating the working class. In this way, the state is neither a "Thing-instrument . . . which is so completely manipulated by one class or fraction that it is divested of any autonomy whatsoever," nor a "Subject . . . enjoy[ing] absolute autonomy." Instead, a particular "state-form" arises from the *materiality* of social relations. In this conception, the state is "a *site* and *centre* of the exercise of power but possesses no power of its own."[46] Power is located in the struggles around and within the institutional apparatus of the state. The outcomes of these struggles—the shifting power differentials among groups and their institutionalization—produce a particular state-form, the complex of relations and institutions that organizes capital accumulation and regulates the social surplus. In the United States, the intertwining of racial- and labor-formation means that the state-form is inescapably racialized. Labor, as a whole, did not gain a foothold in the state. Labor racially valued as *white* did. This racialization pacified the working class, limiting the extent and scope of class struggle. Racial politics constrained working-class politics, conditioned the formation of the state, and colored the prose of pacification that animated it.

THE *HERRENVOLK*-WELFARE STATE

This racialized incorporation and pacification of the working class had far-reaching consequences. More than just a specific facet of labor-formation, racialization is also an epistemic process of subject formation that infantilizes, animalizes, and criminalizes racialized populations, rather than humanizing them as rational subjects and human lives with value.[47] In the United States, the intertwined nature of racial- and labor-formation organized life at the most quotidian levels, shaping how people understood themselves, interpreted their world, and interacted with each other. These processes created a fundamentally racialized polity, what some scholars labeled a *herrenvolk* democracy:[48]

> Under this regime, which persisted until the civil rights movement, all whites are political equals while all not-white persons are relegated to an inferior status. The result is a curious mix of democratic government and egalitarian values along with state repression, mob violence, and an ideology, justified by religion and science, of the eternal inequality of humanity.[49]

Herrenvolk democracy pacified social struggles by linking blackness with criminality and creating whiteness as a vessel through which the productive violence of pacification flowed. These arrangements also pacified the working classes in a different way. Race provided an alternative to class identity. The cross-class alliance created by a strongly felt white identity redirected political attention away from capital-labor antagonism and toward contradictions within the working class. As a result, the (white) working class won a weak welfare state within a stark and punitive system of racial order.[50]

While the origins of *herrenvolk* democracy lie in the sixteenth century, this racialized system of social regulation not only survived the disruptions associated with the Civil War, it structured the rise of industrial capitalism in ways that benefited capital. As W. E. B. DuBois famously argued in *Black Reconstruction*, white workers chose the "psychological wage" of white supremacy over proletarian solidarity and abolition democracy.[51] Furthermore, white workers earned their whiteness, in part, by participating in the subjugation of non-whites. Policing played a critical role. During slavery and Jim Crow—the period of overt, legally codified white supremacy—policing was a vehicle through which whiteness was expanded. European ethnics, particularly the Irish and Germans, solidified their claims to whiteness, in part, through working in and eventually seizing political control over police forces.[52] More broadly, the late nineteenth and early twentieth centuries—

a period historians call "the nadir of race relations"—was a time of pro-tracted, "low-intensity" racial terror: thousands lynched, anti-Chinese pogroms, the genocidal end to the "Indian Wars," the imperial incursions in the Caribbean and Pacific. Whiteness solidified in relation to this violence.[53]

The policing of industrializing cities was particularly important. Urbanization created new social worlds with possibilities for interracial socialization, cultural subversion, and political radicalism. The city became a clear site of class struggle. Between 1889 and 1915, an estimated 57,000 strikes mobilized ten million workers. As with the racial terror of the period, private groups like the Pinkerton Detective Agency and the American Legion were major players in the pacification of labor unrest. The conflicts also spurred the modernization of police forces, leading to the formation of the first police intelligence units, Red Squads.[54] Fabricating the new indus-trial order required more than strike breaking, policing also secured the color line. During this period, theories of racism evolved. As Khalil Muhammed shows, "Racial knowledge that had been dominated by anecdo-tal, hereditation and pseudo-biological theories would be gradually trans-formed by new social scientific theories of race and society and new tools of analysis, namely racial statistics and social surveys." Based on "the 1870, 1880, and 1890 census reports," a new seemingly scientific discourse of "black criminality would emerge, alongside disease and intelligence, as fun-damental measure of black inferiority." In this context, black criminality became "crucial to the making of modern urban America. In nearly every sphere of life it impacted how people defined differences between native whites, immigrants and blacks."[55]

The intertwining of racial- and labor-formation also shaped class conflict in ways that facilitated the pacification and administrative subsumption of social struggle. Instead of creating a classless utopia or, even, a robust wel-fare state, the racialized incorporation of the working class produced a split system, a *herrenvolk*-welfare state. As the United States became an indus-trial power after the Civil War, it naturally gave rise to waves of labor mili-tancy: an initial upsurge of mostly railroad workers in the late nineteenth century, a second swell of miners and factory workers in the early twenti-eth century, and the seeming triumph of industrial unionism with the Congress of Industrial Unions in the 1930s, which provided necessary bot-tom-up pressure to push the New Deal in an increasingly pro-labor direc-tion. At the same time, these waves of working-class militancy were under-mined by racism. White workers organized for better wages and working conditions, while also excluding racial monitories from the benefits of the unionized workplace and the welfare state.[56]

Racism mediated the class struggles that produced the New Deal, creating a *herrenvolk*-welfare state. As the black revolutionary autoworker James Boggs explained, the color line was a "horizontal platform, resting on the backs of blacks and holding them down, while on top white workers have been free to move up the social economic ladder of advancing capitalism."[57] Racism undermined the bargaining power of unions, depressed the wages of white and black workers alike, and increased the amounts of surplus value that became capital. These politics limited the New Deal, creating a welfare state that never matched its European counterparts. While measures like recognition of unions, Social Security, unemployment compensation, the minimum wage, and the GI Bill created a white middle class, these policies were implemented in a discriminatory manner. The wealth gap between blacks and whites widened, despite the wartime economic boom that finally ended the Great Depression and decades of prosperity that followed.[58]

While the racialized incorporation of the working class created a weak welfare state, the interaction of *herrenvolk* democracy and industrial capitalism also produced a unique situation where seemingly contradictory systems of punishment coexisted.[59] As the United States became a significant economic and political power, it also became an increasingly important cultural and intellectual center. The Northeast, for example, became the crucible of modernist penology: the Auburn (1816), Philadelphia (1829), and Elmira (1876) penitentiaries punctuated two waves of prison reforms that sought to discipline, rehabilitate, and reintegrate "criminals" into an expanding industrial economy.[60] In the South, in contrast, the convict leasing system was a form of "levying violence" that led "back toward slavery."[61] These different systems coexisted and helped to distribute and manage social surpluses. Not only did this split system maintain the racial divisions within the working class and allow capital to exploit the particularly vulnerable class of workers, it also channeled political energies. Racial fear and conflict muddled class antagonisms. While racism was an important state strategy to pacify and administer class struggle, white workers also enforced racism from below, continually renewing these arrangements.

The racially devalued segments of the working class also formed a disposable class of labor that helped sustain capital accumulation at a higher rate. These dynamics, Boggs realized, counteracted "the fundamental contradiction between constantly advancing technology and the needs to maintain the value of existing plants . . . by collectively and often forcibly restricting blacks to technologically less advanced industries or to what is known as 'common labor.'" As whiteness channeled both the productive violence of pacification and the politics of organized labor, it produced unique political arrangements and subjectivities. Instead of a strong welfare state and a self-conscious, politicized working class, the United States became "a unique Land of Opportunity in which whites climb up the social economic ladder on the backs of blacks," and "the American people have become the most materialistic, the most opportunistic, the most individualistic—in sum, the most politically and socially irresponsible people in the world."[62]

This split system and the subjectivities that it engendered provide the necessary historical and theoretical perspective to approach the incomparable incarceration rates and levels of police violence that exist in the United States today. Rather than focusing just on class struggle or racial conflict, examining the systemic interconnections among labor-formation, racial-formation, pacification, and state-formation reveal how seemingly natural groups and institutions—"elites," "workers," "Americans," "black folks," "the police," "the prison" or "the state"—are formed and reformed through social struggle. The resolution of these conflicts and their institutional condensation produce the specificity of a given state-form. Hence, the history of imprisonment, policing, and pacification in the United States had diverged from the European experience long before the differences in incarceration rates made this reality plain. Indeed, the split systems of punishment—celebrated institutions of modernist penology in the North and convict leasing in the South—are the outcomes of, on the one hand, the particular ways the US working class has been pacified through racialization and, on the other hand, the strategic failure of the US working class form as a collective subject to meaningfully confront capital and effectively seize power in key crises such as Reconstruction or the upsurge in labor militancy that followed World War I. Instead, the US working class, disarticulated and divided by racial strife, became a junior partner to capital: a labor aristocracy committed to preservation of their privileged position and not a revolutionary force out to remake the world. This history was the immediate context informing the emergence of the workfare-carceral state.

THE WORKFARE-CARCERAL STATE

By the mid-twentieth century, the *herrenvolk*-welfare state began to disintegrate under the combined pressure of revolt from below and world-scale changes in the organization of capital accumulation. The civil rights and Black Power movements politicized the color line, contested the criminalization of black and brown Americans, and tried to renew and restore the humanity of all the peoples of the United States. These movements joined a growing struggle against the Vietnam War to produce generalized revolt. The once staid labor movement radicalized. Wild cat strikes proliferated. Cities rebelled and "rioted." Some even took up arms. At moments, it must have felt like a genuine revolutionary situation: a collapse of state authority. Indeed, elsewhere in world—even in places in the advanced capitalist West such as France and in the Socialist Bloc, as in Czechoslovakia—there were no doubts about the scope of the struggle.[63] To pacify this mounting rebellion within the United States, the Johnson Administration's Great Society reforms tried to move beyond New Deal. Instead of a singular focus on economic security, the Great Society brought attention to civil rights, housing, education, and health care. With this broader focus, the Great Society took on systemic racism more directly than any government policy since Radical Reconstruction.[64]

This effort to complete the New Deal, however, came at the moment when the broader political economic arrangements that underpinned welfare states were exhausted. The largest productive expansion in the history of the capitalist world-economy, the post–World War II boom, was petering out. Technological development and increased competition reduced the rate of profit. The compact between labor and capital that had moderated class conflict, managed the boom and busts of business cycles, and formed the core of the welfare state now hindered accumulation. Unemployment and inflation surged, creating the "stagflation" that mired the 1970s. Meanwhile, the Keynesian measures used to manage the world-economy since the 1930s proved inadequate in the face of a new development: the largest financial expansion in the history of the capitalist world-economy. The Bretton Woods system of fixed exchange rates collapsed in 1971, and exchange rates were allowed to float. States deregulated financial, capital, and currency markets. Deindustrialization swept the core zones of the world-economy. Labor was further deskilled, mechanized, and disaggregated. Increasingly complex supply chains scattered production across the globe. Global capital battered down the remaining "Chinese walls,"[65] inaugurating a new era of economic deregulation and empowered markets. With the economic opening of China and India and the collapse of the Soviet Union, the utopia of liberal thinkers—the global market society—became reality. We called it "globalization."[66]

For the advanced economies, these epochal shifts in the world-economy were completed and constituted by transformations of the state-form. A reconfigured compact with labor formed the core of this new workfare state. Where the welfare state valued labor as a source of demand within a national economy, the workfare state reduced labor to a cost of production in an increasingly global economy. With work reconceptualized as an individual responsibility and not a social right, full employment dropped off the policy agenda. Politicians and other elites redefined poverty as a burden imposed by the moral failure of irresponsible individuals and groups. They restricted and conditioned social welfare policies. Stripped of the protections won through collective bargaining and related social struggles, the compacts between labor and capital at the heart of the welfare state either learned to flex or broke. Labor became "precarious": part-time, temporary, continually re-skilled and retrained, and poorly paid. These changes gradually snaked through labor markets. The workfare state subjected education, health, public services, security, and administration to market discipline, whereas these public goods and services had formerly been more insulated by the state. The increasing commodification of knowledge and services effectively proletarianized the middle class. Salaried, pensioned, protected professionals faded away, and "knowledge workers" took over.[67]

In the United States, capital could not be empowered to such a degree without breaking the structural power of labor, defeating social movements, and transforming the state's institutional apparatus. *This process is the vital linkage between the workfare and carceral state literatures.* The "wars" on crime and drugs began, not with Nixon's law-and-order victory in 1968, but with Johnson and another war of pacification.[68] In 1965, the year after signing the Civil Rights Act and the War on Poverty, the Johnson administration launched the "war on crime" with the Law Enforcement Assistance Act, involving the federal government in law enforcement like never before in US history. Two years later, the administration formed the Law Enforcement Assistance Administration (LEAA), which, in its thirteen-year life, funded some eighty thousand crime-control initiatives and doled out $10 billion in grant money.[69] From the very beginning, the war on crime and the subsequent rise of mass incarceration was a bipartisan project, a state strategy advanced by elites to manage mounting social problems.[70]

These wars of pacification against crime and poverty were animated by shared assumptions. "Across political and ideological lines," Hinton explains, "federal policymakers shared a set of assumptions about African Americans, poverty and crime that in time became a causal and consensus-building force in the domestic urban policy following civil rights legislation." Although "their legislative language never evoked race explicitly, policy-makers interpreted black poverty as pathological ... distort[ing] the aims of the War on Poverty and ... also shap[ing] ... the War on Crime."[71] The new order, "colorblind racism," was taking shape. Overt racist rhetoric and legal discrimination became taboo, but racialized inequalities endured. Without a structural intervention like an antiracist capstone to the New Deal, the landmark civil rights legislation paradoxically normalized enduring racialized inequalities of *material* power. With no overtly discriminatory laws, a renewed, post–civil rights faith in liberal meritocracy redefined racial problems as cultural deficiencies of communities, households, and individuals, thereby minimizing the structural bases of racial inequality and erasing the last impact of the *herrenvolk*-era.[72] When coupled with the post–civil rights incorporation of the black elite and middle class—what Keeanga-Yamahtta Taylor criticizes as "black faces in high places"—colorblind racism became even more difficult for antiracists to address. It also encouraged a reaction among whites, who tended to misrecognize their worsening economic positioned as a direct consequence of the new racial order, which tokenized minority elites. Few directed their attention to the real cause, the imposition of workfare.[73]

The reaction to the Attica Prison rebellion exemplified these new revanchist politics. It produced a new prose of pacification, a law-and-order rhetoric that mobilized simmering white resentment with changing racial hierarchies and middle-class anxieties about growing economic uncertainty into a popular support for increased policing, expanded incarceration, and the rollback of the welfare state. In 1971, a multiracial group of prisoners seized hold of Attica State Prison in Upstate New York in support of demands consonant with the radical movements of the period. Despite the explicit politics of the rebellion, media figures and political elites cast the revolt as an apolitical, spontaneous riot that was rooted in the "anger," "hostility" and "alienation" of the largely black participants of the rebellion. In the official discourse, Attica was "analogous," Camp contends, "to the so-called ghetto disturbances of the 1960s . . . chaotic expression of disorder rather than . . . political expression of a multiracial class struggle." New York Governor Nelson Rockefeller responded with a violent crackdown: a state police raid that left forty-three dead and an emergency allocation of $4 million increase security at Attica.[74]

The immediate response to Attica rolled into a wider attack on both the welfare state and social movements. Reversing his previous commitment to rehabilitative measures, the governor gave his name to the Rockefeller Drug Laws, punitive legislation that required mandatory minimum sentences for drug possession. The laws signaled the abandonment of the welfare state's commitment to managing social reproduction. They mark the shift to an ethos of personal responsibility that animates the workfare state. Julilly Kohler-Hausmann explains:

> [The Rockefeller Drug Laws] dramatically revised the subject position
> of the addict, for not only was their welfare no longer at issue in these
> policies but they were also being constructed as emphatically outside of
> "the public." Since the addict/pusher targeted by these laws was almost
> universally understood to be a Black or Puerto Rican man, these
> characterizations had wide political implications at a time when society
> wrestled over Civil Rights activists' demands for full, equal citizenship.
> They positioned addicts as "anti-citizens," the opposite of right-bearing
> citizens. In terms of the dominant medical metaphor of addiction,
> pusher/addicts moved from being considered diseased to being cast as
> the disease. Politicians constructed them as outside of citizenship,
> holding addict/pushers responsible not only for their own condition,
> but also for many of the problems plaguing society, such as crime,
> deteriorating urban infrastructure, and mass social and economic
> insecurity. Locating the cause of these problems outside of the nation
> exonerated American society from culpability and the American state
> from responsibility to ameliorate these conditions—precisely the
> opposite arguments advanced by social movement participants who
> demanded the state redress past and present injustices.[75]

The new politics inaugurated by Attica and the Rockefeller Drug Laws
mobilized lingering racial resentments from the *herrenvolk* era in the new
terms of colorblind racism. Non-white populations, reluctantly admitted to
the polity under the pressure of massive mobilization, were excluded again,
but on the basis of perceived criminality, not overt racism. This new prose
of pacification would sustain the construction of the workfare-carceral state
as a bipartisan project. New York's Rockefeller Laws were a first. By 1994,
every state had instituted mandatory minimums.[76]

This new pacification war empowered police and prosecutors. Signed into
law in 1970, the Racketeer Influenced and Corrupt Organization Act created
secret "special grand juries," permitted courts to hear evidence obtained illegally, allowed police agencies to seize criminal assets, and created new categories of crimes.[77] In practice, the wars on drugs and crime blurred with
COINTELPRO, the FBI's infamous counterintelligence program that sought
to "disrupt and discredit" the social movements of the era.[78] All the while,
LEAA provided millions in grants for police agencies to computerize their
records and link their databases of law enforcement, the first steps in the
institutionalization of intelligence fusion. During the Johnson, Nixon, and
Ford administrations, the LEAA distributed $90 million to state and munic-
ipal police departments for over one hundred computer-driven command
control or data processing systems. In 1968, ten states had automated criminal justice information systems. By 1972, only three states lacked such systems. At the federal level, the FBI created the National Crime Information

Center (NCIC) in 1967. By 1974, the NCIC connected all fifty-five FBI field offices with ninety-four other law enforcement agencies. It contained 4.9 million total entries and four hundred thousand criminal histories. It was accessed one hundred twenty thousand times daily.[79] That same year, the Nixon administration merged two smaller federal antidrug offices into the DEA and, as part of this new agency, created one of the first fusion centers, the aforementioned El-Paso Intelligence Center.

While the direction of US politics remained contested and unclear in the immediate post-Watergate years, the 1980 election and the "Reagan Revolution" finally and decisively resolved the economic and political crises of the 1960s and 1970s in the favor of capital. Although the Carter administration made important moves that helped consolidate the workfare-carceral state (namely the appointment of Paul Volcker as Federal Reserve chairman and the subsequent increase in interest rates to fight inflation, the "Volcker shock"), the Reagan administration made the new political order irreversible in the near term. In 1981, air traffic controllers were striking in support of bold demands, including a thirty-two-hour, four-day work week. Reagan declared the strike a national security risk and ordered air traffic controllers back to work. When the vast majority refused, the president signed an executive order, firing eleven thousand striking air traffic controllers *and* banning them from federal service.[80]

The dramatic confrontation signaled the beginning of a new compact with labor. In 1980, no union would agree to a contract with pay freezes or cuts. By 1982, it was common practice, included in nearly half of new contracts. In subsequent years, the Reagan administration oversaw the liberalization of labor law (the legalization of homework and authorization of contingent labor within government), cuts to social services (significant reductions to welfare, urban development action grants, education block grants, among other programs), and massive tax cuts for the wealthy. Reagan's policies further empowered capital, which increasingly left the United States to exploit labor overseas. Between 1980 and 1985, some 2.3 million manufacturing jobs disappeared for good. The army of surplus populations swelled.[81]

The Reagan administration's efforts to crush labor and empower capital were necessarily complemented by an acceleration of the drug war and the real beginnings of mass incarceration as a strategy to warehouse growing numbers of surplus workers.[82] Passed in 1984 with significant Democratic support, the Comprehensive Crime Control Act was the centerpiece of Reagan's renewed drug war. The most significant federal crime bill since the Johnson administration, the act created preventative pretrial detention for federal defendants, established mandatory minimum sentences, put in place the US Sentencing Commission to formulate harsh sentencing guidelines for federal courts, reinstated the federal death penalty, eliminated federal parole, and expanded the government's power to seize assets from convicted *or accused* drug dealers. Passed at the height of the moral panic with the "crack boom," the 1986 Anti-Drug Abuse Act created the infamous sentencing disparity between crack and powder cocaine. It created stark racial disparities in incarceration. In 1980, black Americans, just 12 percent of the population, accounted for 23 percent of drug arrests. By 1990, there had been no significant demographic changes but now 40 percent of those arrested on drug charges were black. Critics denounced the policy as "apartheid sentencing." Although the drug war had clear racial bias, it also devoured people of all races. In 1985, about eight hundred thousand people were arrested on drug charges. By 1989, the annual number of drug arrests rose to 1.4 million. The prison population swelled from approximately five hundred thousand to nearly one million.[83]

The escalation of the drug war and increasing incarceration rate further consolidated the new workfare regime. Not simply the punitive regulation of surplus populations, Reagan's drug war also reshaped the institutional structure of the state. In 1981, the Reagan administration replaced the centralized LEAA with a network of crime control boards and committees. Unlike the LEAA, which emphasized uniform application of policies, this new arrangement prioritized structural competitiveness. The idea was to decentralize decision-making, empower local authorities rather than federal policy makers, and, as such, insert a market ethos into the administrative state. Although the Reagan administration disbanded the LEAA, money continued to flow from the federal government and down the administrative hierarchy to state and local law enforcement. Now, the FBI, DEA, and the drug interdiction programs of the Defense Department—respectively enriched with $96 million, $14 million, and $33 million dollar budget increases—took over LEAA's role as "the grantmaking arm of the national law enforcement program."[84]

In 1988, the Omnibus Anti-Drug Abuse Act institutionalized these arrangements.[85] The legislation created a new "drug czar" at the head of the Office of National Drug Control Policy (ONDCP), which sat directly under the Executive Office of the President. One of the drug czar's major responsibilities was the High Intensity Drug Trafficking Areas (HIDTA) initiative. The stated goals of HIDTA are "Facilitating cooperation . . . enhancing law enforcement intelligence sharing . . . [and] . . . [s]upporting coordinated law enforcement strategies."[86] The ONDCP provides a yearly budget to twenty-eight HIDTA directors who disperse grants to various anti-drug programs in their area. In 2013, an HIDTA administrator told me that "HIDTA is not an agency. It is an investment fund. We invest in partnerships to reduce crime and drug abuse. We invest in initiatives toward that end."[87] Both in terms of its competitive grant-driven funding model and the programs it funds, HIDTA was an important precursor to and model for the DHS-recognized National Network of Fusion Centers a quarter of a century later. In 1990, HIDTA began funding anti-drug intelligence hubs called Investigative Support Centers. As of 2013, there were thirty-two of these interagency intelligence centers.[88]

Subsequent administrations and congresses—whether controlled by Republicans or Democrats—continued to follow the course set by Reagan. Indeed, the Clinton administration arguably did as much if not more than any Republican president to create the workfare-carceral state. Clinton signed several crime bills. Under his watch, the incarcerated population reached two million and the combined national correctional budget increased eightfold from its 1980 figure to reach a staggering $57 billion per year. The most important contribution of this post–New Deal "New Democrat" to the workfare-carceral state, however, was to "end welfare as we know it" with the Personal Responsibility and Work Opportunity Reconciliation Act of 1996.[89] For Wacquant, one of the few scholars to connect workfare and mass incarceration, the new welfare regime

> was not a reform but a counterrevolutionary measure, since it
> essentially abolished the right to assistance for the country's most
> destitute children, which had required a half-century of struggles to
> fully establish, and replaced it with the obligation of unskilled and
> underpaid wage labor for their mothers in the short run.

These interconnected, gradual transformations in social policy—workfare and mass incarceration—become, for Wacquant, an "*exercise in statecraft aimed at producing—and then adapting to—these very changes . . . like its 'prisonfare' counterpart, the workfare revolution is a specifically political project aimed at remaking not only the market but also and above all, the state itself.*"[90]

Wacquant's insistence on the counterrevolutionary nature of workfare and mass incarceration is well put.[91] The workfare-carceral state was a response to the crisis of the 1960s and 1970s and the related threat of revolutionary transformation. Not only did these changes in the state pacify social movements, they also empowered capital and created the new politics. The stagnation that had characterized both the global and US economy since the early 1970s was addressed in such a way that it produced the belle époque of the 1990s.[92] The social costs of the change were enormous. The Reagan administration engineered a violent, wrenching transformation. The more profitable economy that emerged on the other side was more precarious, unequal, and unstable. In the United States, falling union membership moved along with rising income inequality. From 1970 to 2003, union density halved, falling from 24 to 12 percent. Meanwhile, the share of national income claimed by the top decile rose from 35 to 50 percent in the same period.[93] To manage this growing insecurity, the United States empowered the police and courts to fill the largest prison system in the world. In 2009, the prison population peaked at 2.5 million. Swelling ranks of the supervised joined these forgotten millions in cages. By 2011, 4.8 million—nearly 3 percent of the adult population—were on probation or parole.[94] Colorblind racism held up the cruel edifice of the workfare-carceral state. These revanchist politics rationalized the stark racial selectivity of the system with a renewed faith in liberal meritocracy and obscured the reality that mass incarceration and workfare are ruling-class pacification projects.

THE PRESENT DEMISE OF THE WORKFARE-CARCERAL STATE

In the twenty-first century, the workfare-carceral state—and the larger globalization project—unraveled. The financialized world-economy was more prone to cycles of boom and bust than the highly regulated Keynesian system that preceded it. With the overvaluation of the internet economy and subsequent "dot-com" crash in 2000, the cycle of busts hit the US economy. The panic that followed the 9/11 attacks extended the economic crisis.[95] The crash was significant: $6.4 trillion in financial assets and 1.4 million jobs were lost.[96] This downturn was resolved, in part, by a massive state-led investment in security: another war of pacification against terror and a dramatic expansion of the state's institutional apparatus, the creation of DHS. Between these two interrelated security projects, the United States spent $7.6 trillion in the decade following 9/11.[97] This ersatz investment in security began with the "scattergun acquisition" of $30 billion in security equipment "ranging from airport screeners to anti-hacker software in 2002." In the following years, yearly federal spending on DHS ranged between $31 and $53 billion with a $76 billion outlier in 2006. The sheer "abundance of public money ... caused existing industries to re-orient operations towards homeland security ... from IT to armaments, and from pharmaceuticals to finance." In 2006, when the DHS budget peaked, "IT stocks were performing at almost double ... while security and defence stocks were beating the average by 4:1."[98]

While this security spending did provide some reprieve in the immediate aftermath of the dot-com crash, it could not address the underlying structural problems: the excessive power of capital over labor and declining profitability. With no resolution, another blow hit the world-economy: the mortgage crisis and subsequent "Great Recession." In the United States, households lost an estimated $11 trillion in asset value. Globally, the crisis spiraled out and destroyed $50 trillion in assets. While 2008 was "the mother of all crises," it was also "the culmination of a pattern of financial crises that had become both more frequent and deeper over the years."[99] No doubt, the financed-led, workfarist mode of accumulation is inherently unstable. However, the continued inability of either the old capitalist powers—the United States and the European Union—or the rising contenders—Brazil, Russia, India, China and South Africa, the so-called BRICS—to stabilize global political economy suggests a dark possibility, at least in the near- and medium-term. Economic indicators are equally bleak, the apparent recovery illusory. Profitability has not recovered, investment is low, and debt remains high. The $700 billon bank bailout and "quantitative easing" kept the financial sector afloat but prevented the "creative destruction" that could have restored profitability. For this reason, Marxist economist Michael Roberts argues that the neoliberal period is over and the "Great Recession" is really the opening stage of a Long Depression.[100] In this context of low growth and depressed profits, crisis and plunder are the defining characteristics of capital accumulation.[101]

In strictly economic terms, this hypothesis is supported by the new predatory accumulation strategies, what Saskia Sassen deems expulsions, wherein advanced, thoroughly financialized capitalism preys upon and destroys traditional capitalism. She writes:

> Today, enormous technical and legal complexities are needed to execute what are ultimately elementary extractions. It is, to cite a few cases, the enclosure by financial firms of a country's resources and citizens' taxes, the repositioning of expanding stretches of the world as sites for extraction of resources, and the regearing of government budgets in liberal democracies away from social and workers' needs. . . . The dominant dynamic at work for these populations is, to a good extent, the opposite of the old Keynesian dynamic of valuing people as workers and as consumers. Expulsions from home, land, and job have also had the effect of giving expanded operational space to criminal networks and to the trafficking of people, as well as greater access to land and underground water resources to foreign buyers, whether firms or governments.

She sees this predatory logic at work in the global debt crisis, which destroyed much of the state and industrial capacities built up during the development project and caused large areas of Africa and Latin America to revert to resource extraction, particularly foreign land grabs. The subprime housing crisis is another example. Enormously complex financial instruments transformed the mortgage—a mechanism to provide housing to modest income families—into a means to extract wealth that separates finance from the material entity: the house, and the neighborhood.[102] She compares these predatory formations of capital accumulation "to wanting only the horns of the rhino, and throwing away the rest of the animal, devaluing it, no matter its multiple utilities."[103]

Politically, the emergence of crisis as a mode of accumulation and regulation was further underscored by the political response to the Great Recession. Instead of a paradigm shift, every solution was deferent to capital: the bank bailout in the United States, the European Union's imposition of austerity, and the capitulation of left governments like Syriza in Greece or the French Socialist Party. The Great Recession and subsequent austerity, moreover, did not meaningfully affect security spending. The Homeland Security budget has actually grown from $52 billion in 2009 to $66 billion in 2016.[104] Not only did the Obama administration steadily increase funding to DHS, it also did not reverse or repeal any of its major policies.[105] This continued commitment to an expansive domestic security regime comes, paradoxically, at the same time that the total prison population is decreasing, raising the question of whether the pendulum is shifting back toward rehabilitation. This study seeks to explain this curious conjuncture. Instead of an apparent return to a more welfarist model of penology and policing, the systems put in place in the name of DHS and counterterrorism are enabling a shift in state strategy away from incarceration and toward ubiquitous surveillance and aggressive policing. As subsequent chapters will show, mass supervision is the centerpiece of a nascent pacification project that seeks to manage and contain ever-growing surplus populations in a post-neoliberal world of low growth and soaring inequality.

3. The Institutionalization of Intelligence Fusion

Points of Conflict and Pockets of Intelligence Sharing

In the decade following 9/11, the United States invested $7.6 trillion into the Department of Homeland Security (DHS) and the war on terror. This commitment to "security" seems irreversible. The 2008 market crash, the Great Recession, and the Obama administration have all come and gone. Yet the war on terror still rages, and DHS funding continues to creep up. Recalling chapter 1, fusion centers are no exception to this trend. In 2012, the Senate slammed them for producing "'intelligence' of uneven quality—oftentimes shoddy, rarely timely, sometimes endangering citizens' civil liberties and Privacy Act protections, occasionally taken from already-published public sources, and more often than not unrelated to terrorism."[1] Previous government auditors foreshadowed these problems, advocacy organizations on the both right and left added their own concerns, and journalists amplified the Senate's damning conclusions, yet the National Network of Fusion Centers still stands today, a seemingly permanent fixture of American politics. While many bemoan the apparent failure of fusion centers, few have sought to identify the underlying mechanisms that produce this outcome. Rather than investigate the concrete effects of this massive expansion of intelligence capacities, most making claims upon fusion centers—whether from positions in government, journalism, think tanks, or academia—focus on how fusion centers ought to work. These debates, I contend, are examples of the prose of pacification. They are productive investments in fusion centers, and they do more to animate the work of these intelligence hubs than to explain them.

In contrast, this chapter goes inside the secret world of intelligence fusion. It details the institutionalization of intelligence fusion in New York and New Jersey, identifying the exact mechanisms that undermine the dream of seamless information sharing and, instead, produce discontinuous pockets of increased interagency coordination. This uneven and conflictive intelligence system should not be simply dismissed as a "failure." Rather, it is a complex outgrowth of the workfare-carceral state and, more specifically, the workfarist emphasis on structural competitiveness and the punitive measures that produced mass incarceration. Most importantly, New York and New Jersey are not straightforward "cases" to be compared. Instead, they are formative moments in both the consolidation of intelligence fusion as a state strategy and the addition of fusion centers to the state apparatus. In the 1990s, New York City pioneered policing practices that would later inform the Department of Homeland Security (DHS) recognized National Network of Fusion Centers. The subsequent spread of intelligence fusion, however, did not occur in a vacuum. It was an iterative process of state-formation. Social struggles within and apart from the state produced intelligence fusion as a coherent state strategy. The apparent success of this strategy, as evidenced in the transformation of New York City from a blighted city of high crime and postindustrial decline to a dynamic cultural and economic center, created a structural predisposition toward the further spread of intelligence fusion.

However, intelligence fusion did not simply diffuse out from New York City. Rather, the institutional apparatus of the state mediated these changes in ways that produced complex and uneven results. In New York State, the apparent dysfunction that defines fusion centers is a product of competition between the New York Police Department (NYPD), the New York State Police (NYSP), and the Division of Criminal Justice Services (DCJS). An unusual situation prevails in New York State, where the New York State Intelligence Center (NYSIC)—the statewide fusion center officially recognized by DHS—is largely redundant, even though New York State is one of the crucibles of intelligence fusion. The institutionalization of intelligence fusion in New Jersey produced the opposite problem. The New Jersey Regional Operations Intelligence Center (ROIC) is overextended and struggles to meet the state's demanding criminal intelligence needs. This contrasting outcome needs to be parsed out in detail to show the way a common practice, intelligence fusion, is differentially institutionalized.

NEW YORK CITY AND THE RISE OF THE WORKFARE-CARCERAL STATE

New York is a pioneer of what we can now call intelligence fusion. The story begins not with 9/11 and DHS but with Mayor Rudolph Giuliani and his bellicose promise to clear New York City of "disorder" linked to crime and homelessness. At the center of this effort stood CompStat, the crime-mapping system launched in 1994 by Giuliani's newly appointed NYPD Commissioner Bill Bratton. CompStat is a means to hold local precinct commanders accountable for increases in crime. It is built on four principles: (1) timely and accurate crime data, (2) effective strategies, (3) rapid deployment of police resources and (4) relentless follow up and assessment.[2] Operationally, CompStat maps crime data in order to proactively direct police patrols on crime hotspots. In practice, CompStat is closely related to what is variously called public order, quality of life, or broken-windows policing, which emphasizes the focused application of police power to address so-called quality-of-life issues such has vagrancy, vandalism, and other "anti-social behaviors."[3] The ethos of the workfare state suffuses this policing paradigm. Alex Vitale describes it as a reorientation of "city government away from directly improving the lives of the disenfranchised and toward restoring social order in the city's public spaces . . . [through] a variety of punitive social control practices directed at minor incivilities as the way to restore neighborhood stability."[4] Managerially, CompStat tightened control over police labor. In notorious rituals of public shaming, senior NYPD officials would take precinct commanders to task, aggressively questioning them if crime numbers did not drop on their watch. Bratton replaced over a third of NYPD's precinct commanders in his first year and a half as commissioner.[5]

In the two decades since the NYPD's first CompStat meetings, the model has evolved into a larger policing doctrine: intelligence-led policing (ILP). Where CompStat revolves around crime mapping, ILP emphasizes individual targeting of "chronic offenders" and makes greater use of intelligence to identify and surveil them. Like CompStat, ILP focuses on rapid deployment, but it tries to move beyond "effective strategies" to preventive measures. Where CompStat uses crime mapping to evaluate commanders and hold them accountable, ILP tries to shift the posture of policing toward "a top-down management approach" that "uses crime intelligence to objectively direct police resources decisions." Like CompStat, ILP carries the managerial biases of workfare. Not just a policing strategy, ILP is a "business model and managerial philosophy where data analysis and crime intelligence are pivotal to an objective, decision-making framework that facilitate crime and problem reduction, disruption, and prevention through both strategic management and effective enforcement strategies that target prolific and serious offenders."[6]

By the time DHS and other federal agencies started offering grants to set up the National Network of Fusion Centers, New York City had already built a comprehensive intelligence system. The NYPD's Investigative Support Center (ISC) is "staffed by 737 participants from numerous federal, state and local law enforcement agencies [and] serves as the central conduit for criminal intelligence sharing." The formation of the NYPD ISC can be traced back to federal grants from the High-Intensity Drug Trafficking Areas (HIDTA) program, one the main initiatives of the Office of National Drug Control Policy (ONDCP)—the formation of which, recalling the previous chapter, further consolidated the workfare-carceral state and today stands as a clear precursor to the DHS-recognized National Network of Fusion Centers. New York–New Jersey was one of the first five HITDAs designated in 1990, when ONDCP launched the program. The ISC opened soon after.[7] In the years since 9/11, the NYPD has massively expanded and reorganized their intelligence operations. As part of these reforms, the NYPD joined the Homeland Security Information Network (HSIN) platform, a data-sharing initiative for unclassified information that links DHS-recognized fusion centers. The NYPD used the HSIN to create "an unclassified community-of-interest Web portal . . . called the New York Situational Awareness Program." Forty-five police departments and other emergency responders participate in the endeavor. Even though New York City lacks a DHS-recognized fusion center, the NYPD has built the systems and relationships to facilitate what has been described as "network fusion."[8]

The experience of New York City shows that intelligence fusion is not a simple response to terrorism but a state strategy constitutive of the workfare-carceral state. New York City was a critical theater in this war to remake the United States. Indeed, in some ways, this struggle started with New York City's technical bankruptcy in 1975, which "amounted to a coup by the financial institutions against the democratically elected government of New York City." In the 1960s, deindustrialization and suburbanization led to the collapse of New York City's tax base. Meanwhile, a moral panic overtook the city, what commentators described as the nationwide "urban crisis," associated with militant social movements, rising crime, and generalized disorder. Until the 1970s, federal subsidies managed the crisis with an expanded public sector and social services. For a few years after the withdrawal of federal funds, big banks bridged the gap between tax revenue and public expenditure. In 1975, however, bankers refused to roll over the debt and New York City became a laboratory to test the austerity politics that still dominate global politics today. Like the "structural adjustments" that beset the developing countries of the world in the 1980s and 1990s or the more recent municipal bankruptcies in Camden or Detroit, finance capital staked the first claim on public revenue, leaving crumbs for the public.[9]

This financial coup led to an upward redistribution of the social surplus and inaugurated a new politics. David Harvey explains:

> Much of the social infrastructure of the city was diminished and the physical infrastructure (for example the subway system) deteriorated markedly. . . . [T]he New York investment bankers did not walk away from the city. They seized the opportunity to restructure it in ways that suited their agenda. The creation of a "good business climate" was a priority. This meant using public resources to build appropriate infrastructures for business (particularly in telecommunications) coupled with subsidies and tax incentives for capitalist enterprises. Corporate welfare substituted for people welfare. The city's elite institutions were mobilized to sell the image of the city as a cultural centre and tourist destination (inventing the famous logo "I Love New York"). The ruling elites moved, often fractiously, to support the opening up of the cultural field to all manner of diverse cosmopolitan currents. The narcissistic exploration of self, sexuality, and identity became the leitmotif of bourgeois urban culture. . . . New York became the epicentre of postmodern cultural and intellectual experimentation. Meanwhile the investment bankers reconstructed the city economy around financial activities, ancillary services such as legal services and the media (much revived by the financialization then occurring), and diversified consumerism (gentrification and neighbourhood "restoration" playing a prominent and profitable role). City government was more and more construed as an entrepreneurial rather than a social democratic or even managerial entity. Interurban competition for investment capital transformed government into urban governance through public-private partnerships. City business was increasingly conducted behind closed doors, and the democratic and representational content of local governance diminished.

The arrival of the new workfare order also immiserated the working class of the city. It was not just a matter of declining material wealth; rather, daily life—social reproduction—became a cruel war of one against all. In the early 1980s, crack cocaine created a new criminalized and clandestine economy, necessarily regulated by violence. While the drug economy created real economic opportunities for the now vilified poor, it "left many young people either dead, incarcerated, or homeless, only to be bludgeoned again by the AIDS epidemic that carried over into the 1990s."[10] In this context, the Giuliani administration came to power and set a new model of urban governance in the 1990s, a period when tax cuts, budget reform, and experiments in workfare sat alongside CompStat and broken-windows policing in a Manhattan Institute–authored policy portfolio.[11]

The formative experience of New York City further underscores the relational nature of the state-formation. Since the state is neither subject nor object but a social relation, it exists in a particular historical moment as a strategic field. No doubt, the state's institutional apparatus is a powerful mechanism, which does much to fabricate social order, but it is also riven with contradiction and conflict. The outcomes of social struggles within and apart from the state are iterative. They build upon themselves and inscribe certain biases into the state's institutional apparatus and the subjectivities of its cadres. In this way, the institutional apparatus is a "complex set of institutional mechanisms and political practices that serve to advance (or obstruct) particular fractional or class interests."[12] The battles fought and won in New York City advanced the interests of certain capital sectors: finance, real estate, and technology. Ideologically, it recast the postindustrial city, once seen as a squalid cesspool of disorder, as a center of creative innovation. Elites across the United States took note and sought to replicate the seeming triumph over economic decline and crime. Hence, intelligence fusion did not simply diffuse out from New York City. Instead, the social struggles fought in and around New York City were a key theater of struggle in the consolidation of the workfare-carceral state. As New York City became a seemingly self-evident success story of urban renewal, it eased the subsequent spread of certain strategies, including the policing practices now unified under the rubric of intelligence fusion and ILP.

Simply put, New York City's experience was formative. Proponents credit CompStat with New York City's dramatic crime drop. Between 1993 and 1999, murders decreased by 66 percent, assaults declined by 36 percent, robberies dropped by 58 percent, rapes fell by 40 percent, and motor vehicle thefts declined by 65 percent.[13] Although there is considerable debate about whether decreased crime could be attributed to CompStat, these doubts did not stop other cities from implementing the system.[14] By the early 2000s, many cities—including Baltimore, Houston, Newark, New Orleans, and Philadelphia—adopted CompStat, a process that often involved hiring NYPD administrators as police executives or consultants.[15] As part of a broader effort to modernize and encourage collaboration among law enforcement agencies throughout New York State, the Division of Criminal Justice Services (DCJS) created Operation IMPACT, a grant-driven interagency partnership between DCJS and the major law enforcement agencies (police departments, district attorney's offices, sheriffs, and parole) in the seventeen counties that, together, account for 80 percent of crime outside of New York City. As part of IMPACT, DCJS has promoted CompStat. "We saw the value of timely and accurate crime reporting that is paired with rapid reaction and relentless follow up," an administrator involved in the creation of IMPACT, told me. "We wanted to take what had been so effective in the city and apply the model to New York State."[16]

While New York City was an early leader in ILP and intelligence fusion, the rest of New York State and neighboring New Jersey soon followed. The counties closest to New York City were the first to build intelligence centers. The NY/NJ HIDTA provided the impetus and funding for Nassau and Suffolk Counties on Long Island and Westchester and Rockland Counties, just north of New York City, to set up their own intelligence centers, described as "satellites" of the NYPD's massive ISC.[17] In 2007, the DCJS followed suit and started setting up Crime Analysis Centers (CACs) in Upstate New York as part of IMPACT. By 2015, there were five of these CACs, located in Albany, Broome, Erie, Monroe, and Onondaga Counties. With the exception of the smaller Broome CAC, each CAC has a staff of between fifteen and twenty.[18]

The DHS-recognized fusion centers in New York and New Jersey, moreover, are some of the first and largest of their kind. The NYSIC was created in August 2003, approximately three years before DHS began to promote the concept of fusion centers.[19] At that time, the NYSP, working closely with the FBI field office in Albany, established the "first fusion center" to coordinate data sharing and intelligence analysis among state and local police, federal intelligence agencies, and private companies.[20] The New Jersey State Police (NJSP) founded The New Jersey Regional Operations (ROIC) in 2005. Today, the NYSIC and the ROIC rank among the largest fusion centers recognized by DHS. While most DHS-recognized fusion centers have around thirty staff, the NYSIC has ninety-four personnel deployed to the center, while the ROIC has "approximately 100."[21] In short, the New York region and, particularly, New York City is one of the crucibles of intelligence fusion. Not just an early adopter, it is a formative example that influenced the way these strategies were defined, understood, and implemented.

THE UNEVEN INSTITUTIONALIZATION OF INTELLIGENCE FUSION

While the experience of New York helped define intelligence fusion as a coherent state strategy, its institutionalization elsewhere is another matter. Rather than an involuntary causality produced by the power of example, the outcome is politically mediated through jurisdictional struggles within the state as a strategic field. These battles determine the particularities of intelligence fusion in each state. Points of conflict arise where jurisdictional rivalries cannot be overcome or battles stalemated. The victories produce pockets of information sharing, albeit ones with distinct centers of gravity. The result is not the seamless information-sharing environment envisioned after 9/11 but rather an uneven and conflictive system variously defined by clear conflicts between large agencies and regionalized pockets of enhanced collaboration. The very complexity and density of these arrangements underscores this point. The massive expansion of intelligence capacities of state and local governments is not a uniform process led by one agency or actor. Instead, it is a complex result of a series of overlapping and often conflicting programs. This finding confirms Poulantzas's prescient analysis of "authoritarian statism," what I reinterpret in the US context as the workfare-carceral state: "such statism does not designate a univocal strengthening of the State but constitutes the effect of a tendency to strengthening-weakening of the state, the poles of which develop in an uneven manner."[22]

The Institutionalization of Intelligence Fusion in New York State

The NYSIC exists in a crowded field of police agencies competing for resources, prestige, and mission space. In New York State, the three most powerful actors in law enforcement are the NYPD, the DCJS, and the NYSP, the lead agency at the NYSIC. "They're the three big dogs and they don't play nice," a retired police chief told me.[23] The founding of the NYSIC did little to mend these rivalries. The NYSP, working closely with the FBI, founded the NYSIC in August 2003, when DHS was not yet a year old. Interviewees gave conflicting information regarding the participation of the NYPD and DCJS in the founding of the NYSIC.[24] "When the state police set up the NYSIC, the FBI was their big partner. NYPD or DCJS may have played a bit role," one intelligence analyst explained. "I don't know for sure. I can tell you that they weren't visible at the start the way FBI was. It's petty, but I'm sure NYPD and DJCS saw this move as a power play. That's exactly what it was too. State police went to the feds to set up the first fusion center and ignored the other big players in the state."[25] Several interviewees, however, were able to confirm that the NYPD and NYSIC did have a formal information sharing agreement from 2003 to 2007.[26] "The relationship broke down," one intelligence analyst explained. "It was politics. I don't know the exact reason. It was above my pay grade, so to speak." Even before the breakdown, the relationship between NYPD and NYSIC was tense. "They didn't want to share information freely because they were afraid we would either steal cases or share information that should not be released."[27] As of June 2013, the NYSIC and NYPD did not have a signed "memoranda of understanding" with each other, meaning they did not officially share intelligence.[28]

The relationship between DCJS and the NYSIC is similarly strained. Through Operation IMPACT, DCJS competes with the NYSIC to meet the state's criminal intelligence needs. The mission of DCJS is to keep crime records and support law enforcement agencies by providing training, certifications, and specialized services (fingerprinting, forensics, information technology support). Operation IMPACT leveraged this role into great power and influence. For each funding cycle, DCJS identifies the most common Part I or index crimes in a given county.[29] On this basis, the county-level IMPACT partnerships bring together police departments, district attorney's offices, sheriffs, probation, parole, and corrections to propose "effective strategies" to reduce the specific "target crimes." Each year, DCJS disburses grants ranging from around $100,000 to over $1 million that can be spent on nearly anything: overtime for officers, salaries for crime analysts and field intelligence officers, and technological upgrades ranging from new software for records management or intelligence analysis to surveillance systems like closed-circuit television cameras, automated license plate readers, or GPS trackers. In ten years of operation, from the 2003–2004 funding cycle to the 2013–2014 funding cycle, IMPACT has dispersed over $118 million to the seventeen New York State counties that account for 80 percent of the crime outside of New York City.[30] In 2015, DCJS reformed Operation IMPACT and refocused the program on gun violence, renaming it the Gun Involved Violence Elimination (GIVE) initiative. Many viewed the shift as cynical rebranding. As one intelligence analyst who had worked in a number of IMPACT jurisdictions explained, "In the end, it will all be on paper and won't make a real noticeable difference in how the agencies spend the money. [Governor] Cuomo [D-NY 2011–present] just wanted something to stamp his name on. It would not be the first example of Cuomo using DCJS for a bit of political puffery."[31]

When DCJS starting using IMPACT to set up CACs in 2007, it exacerbated the rivalry between DCJS and NYSP and put the NYSIC on the defensive. "There's been some contention since the centers came up," one municipal police captain in an administrative role at a CAC explained. "We were asked to sit in on a NYSIC meeting and we were asked what our capabilities are. You know, what do we do? It felt like it wasn't done to help us work together. It was like they wanted to check us out to see if there was anything they needed to start doing."[32] The addition of CACs and their subsequent integration through a statewide information-sharing network called the Digital Information Gateway (DIG) also empowered the larger municipal police departments in relation to the state police. One police administrator used to assign a detective to the NYSIC, but, after the creation of the CAC in his jurisdiction, his reasoning changed: "I had somebody assigned there for a while. . . . I don't have anybody assigned there anymore. . . . Resources are at a premium. The cost/benefit just isn't there. We have our center now. We can access most of their data with DIG. I'm not going to take another detective out of our center to go work for the State Police."[33]

Internal institutional dynamics also shape the CACs. At the time of my fieldwork, the Onondaga Crime Analysis Center (OCAC), for example, was dominated by the Syracuse Police Department (SPD). Its DCJS-appointed director is a retired SPD officer, which exacerbates existing jurisdictional rivalries among the main players in the IMPACT partnership: the SPD, Onondaga County Sheriff's Office, and the Onondaga County District Attorney (DA). A series of disputes between the DA and the SPD has further aggravated this natural jurisdictional rivalry. In the most serious of these clashes, the DA wrote a letter to the mayor detailing the constitutional rights violations of the SPD, which ignored requests for lawyers, and refused the right to remain silent in interrogations.[34] As a result of this tension, the SPD exercised effective control over the OCAC. The county's once active chronic offender initiative, an IMPACT program reliant on both OCAC intelligence products and cooperation from the DA, became an empty formality.[35] Although the conflict in Onondaga County is the most acute, the collaboration fostered by IMPACT tilts in the direction of the largest agencies in the IMPACT partnership. These resultant pockets of information sharing are dominated by the largest agency, usually the police department in the county's population center.

Altogether, other agencies provide the NYSIC strong competition to meet the state's criminal intelligence needs. The NYPD and DCJS have hollowed out the mission of the NYSIC, which, under these conditions is left to fill the gaps left by the NYPD and NYSIC, mostly by providing statewide services: information brokerage and special services. According to a DCJS official, "The NYSIC fills the void for a lot of the other smaller agencies out there that don't get the benefit from [the CACs]. They don't have anyone to request information from. . . . [NYSP] has the statewide view of all these different counties. They also support a statewide agency of 4,400 people. I think the NYSIC and the Crime Analysis Centers are complementary."[36] Documents show that, in 2010, the NYSIC completed 9,300 requests and two years later the number fell to 7,720.[37] Since the CACs cover case support and criminal intelligence in the IMPACT jurisdictions, these numerous requests show that the NYSIC fills the gaps between New York's major urban areas.

The NYSIC's position as an information broker is clear in what is supposed to be the analytic core of the NYSIC: the Counterterrorism Center. In effect, this ultra-secret intelligence center within the fusion center simply vets and processes Suspicious Activity Reports—part of a nationwide program to promote intelligence reporting from law enforcement and the private sector—and directs information coming in through the NYSIC's Terrorism Tip Line to other agencies.[38] The hostility between NYPD and NYSP prevents the NYSIC from fulfilling its counterterrorism mission by effectively removing the largest jurisdiction and the most obvious target from its purview. "We're talking about a situation where 80 percent of the [terrorism] cases deal with New York City and we did not have access to those;" an intelligence analyst told me. "Our counterterrorism center was a referral service. We would answer the phone and refer the cases to the [FBI Joint Terrorism Task Force (JTTF)], or the NYPD. I understand that they publicly have to tout it as a huge success because that is where they are pouring all their money but, inside the NYSIC, most of the work that was done was actually criminal in nature, like most fusion centers across the US."[39] On the counterterrorism side, the NYSIC loses out to both the FBI and "Operation Sentry," the NYPD's expansive counterterrorism program.[40]

The reduction of the NYSIC Counterterrorism Center into a referral service is felt on the operational end. The five police chiefs I interviewed all identified the NYPD or the FBI as their most important partner for counterterrorism. One police administrator was particularly blunt on the issue:

> We have all these different venues and it gets so confusing that nobody knows who the hell is doing what. I know these are very important issues, but we are tripping over each other now. . . . I have been in this business for thirty-seven years . . . and I don't know who to go to. Say something comes up and I really have to get information, I go to my stand-by. I will call our guy on the JTTF and see what the FBI knows. You go to these other guys and they are out in the abyss somewhere. I'll be very frank with you: I don't even pay attention to them anymore. They just clog up the inbox with trash. I read two newspapers every morning. I don't need an email from the NYSIC to tell me there was a car bomb in Iraq. . . . I think what is going on is when the federal dollars came out for terrorism everyone rushed to get. Now they are trying to prove they are doing something with it, but everyone is doing the same crap and none of it is of any benefit to local PDs.[41]

Other police administrators were more measured, while making a similar point. One executive told me that the "NYSIC really doesn't give us too much useful information on counterterrorism. Our relationship with the NYPD through Operation Sentry is more important."[42] Another police administrator "get[s] [counterterrorism intelligence] through the JTTF and NYPD. We are members of Operation Sentry. We've got great relationships there and that's how I get my information. The NYSIC is pretty peripheral."[43]

The NYSIC has also tried to build on their statewide reach and set up a field intelligence officer program. This program, however, has been unable to supplant a rival field intelligence office program put in place by DCJS. In every IMPACT jurisdiction, even those without a CAC, DCJS provides funding for a field intelligence officer that collects intelligence for the CAC or the crime analysis team. In contrast, the NYSIC's field intelligence officer program is an unfunded effort to increase the flow of intelligence to the statewide fusion center. These field intelligence officers are asked to

> [b]e familiar with the functions of the NYSIC . . . [t]ake a proactive
> approach to observing suspicious activity . . . [r]eview previous shift
> arrests and incidents for information that may be of value to the
> NYSIC. . . [r]eceive and disseminate information and intelligence
> amongst members of your department" [and s]tay current on national
> and international terrorism events to maintain situational awareness.[44]

While the NYSIC command put forward the program as a great success in interviews, the NYSIC's own records reveal that it is struggling. About half of the program's 414 members are not active participants.[45] Many field intelligence officers "are unaware of their role and responsibilities." The program has no budget and no promotional items. A 2012 assessment concluded that "[e]xecutive level commanders are unaware of the program's fragile condition."[46] My interviews with municipal police and county sheriffs confirmed this conclusion. I interviewed twenty-four people who worked at municipal police departments or county sheriff's offices in New York State. Not a single person of this group—which included senior administrators of some of the largest police departments in the state—could name their department's NYSIC field intelligence officer. In short, the funded efforts of DCJS to create an intelligence network centered in IMPACT counties have marginalized the "first fusion center" recognized by DHS.

Although the NYSIC is largely redundant, it has used its statewide reach to provide niche products and services. For example, the NYSIC maintains two statewide databases related to gangs: Gang Reporting Intelligence Program (GRIP) and the Violent Gang and Terrorism Organization File

(VGTOF, pronounced "vig-tof").[47] GRIP is a database of dossiers on individual gang members. VGTOF is an alert system. It notifies police officers that a suspect is a gang member when their name is run against the National Crime Information Center, the electronic clearinghouse of crime data accessible to virtually every criminal justice agency in the nation. The NYSIC adapted VGTOF, a nationwide FBI system, to centralize referrals through NYSIC. Jurisdictions that participate in the program will report known gang members to the NYSIC, where a gang analyst will enter the information into the VGTOF database. When any police officer anywhere in the country runs a check on an individual entered into the database, the system will notify both the officer and analyst who entered the data. Since the VGTOF is centralized at the NYSIC, the system allows the NYSIC to gather more intelligence about the movements and whereabouts of alleged gang members. According to NYSP annual reports, between one thousand and two thousand individuals are added each year to GRIP and VGTOF. The system also registers approximately two thousand post-submission "hits" per year.[48]

Border intelligence is another niche the NYSIC fills. For some time, New York's institutional geography left the NYSIC in control over the border intelligence mission. New York's land border with Canada is far from any major urban center and, thus, far outside the reach of NYPD or, at the time of my research, any of the IMPACT-funded CACs. The NYSIC filled the gap with the Border Intelligence Unit (BIU), the only fusion center unit focusing on the US-Canada border. The work of the BIU covers three areas: (1) it builds databases on cross border criminal activity; (2) it encourages information sharing among relevant federal, state, local, and tribal law enforcement agencies; and (3) it directs multi-jurisdictional operations.[49] Although the NYSIC has established a presence on the Canadian border, competition is growing. New York Senator Chuck Schumer (D-NY 1999–present) successfully fought an increase for funding to allow the NY-NJ HIDTA to cover the counties on the Canadian border: Clinton, Franklin, and St. Lawrence Counties in 2010 and Niagara County in 2016.[50] In 2016, 2017, and 2018, moreover, DCJS opened four more CACs: the Niagara CAC in the northwesternmost county in New York State and the North Country Center in Franklin County, located in the Adirondacks region, the Mohawk Valley CAC in Utica; and the Hudson Valley CAC in Goshen.[51]

Altogether massive expansion in the intelligence capabilities of state and local law enforcement has not created an integrated information-sharing network across New York State. Instead, jurisdictional rivalries among the NYPD, NYSP, and DCJS created a conflictive system. The NYPD pulled many jurisdictions, particularly in Long Island and the Hudson River Valley, into its orbit. Meanwhile, DCJS, through Operation IMPACT, has created discontinuous pockets of intelligence sharing throughout New York State. Although information may be shared across the state through systems like DIG, information sharing and interagency collaboration, in practice, are circumscribed by institutional politics. There is simultaneous process decentralization and recentralization, where criminal justice agencies enter into information-sharing networks and collaborative programs that revolve around—and empower—larger jurisdictions. With NYPD and DCJS, the NYSP and the NYSIC, the state's official DHS-recognized fusion center, are sidelined and rendered largely superfluous.

The Institutionalization of Intelligence Fusion in New Jersey

The ROIC has little competition to meet the intelligence needs of New Jersey. On the federal level, the FBI has field offices and JJTFs in Newark and Philadelphia, just across the river from Camden. The NY/NJ HIDTA also funds the New Jersey Intelligence Center, which is co-located with the Newark office of the Drug Enforcement Administration (DEA). This intelligence center provides services to the six New Jersey counties closest to New York City.[52] The New Jersey Intelligence Center is much smaller than the ROIC. According to a ROIC analyst that formerly worked at the New Jersey Intelligence Center, the HIDTA-funded intelligence hub has only "five or six analysts. . . . We were encouraged to work more hand-in-hand with the Newark PD or Essex County Prosecutor's Office. A lot of it was case work, as opposed to here [at the ROIC], where a lot of our time is filled up with monitoring trends and data streams, rather than specific cases."[53] With its narrow focus on drugs, the New Jersey Intelligence Center does not compete much with the much larger ROIC, which has a more expansive "all-hazards" mission.

On the state and local level, the ROIC's biggest competitor comes from across state lines. The Philadelphia Police Department runs the Delaware Valley Intelligence Center (DVIC), which services the greater Philadelphia metro area, including four New Jersey counties. With a reported staff of 130, it is larger than either the ROIC or NYSIC.[54] The senior managers at the ROIC were peripherally involved in the planning of the Philadelphia metro fusion center, which they welcomed.[55] "We've been talking to the guys down at what will be the DVIC for a while. It will be good to have help in Camden. We have developed a lot of assets in North Jersey ... but Camden is in a crisis and it has been a little harder to get things started there;" a senior manager in the ROIC's intelligence division explained,

"The state took over the city, the entire governance, OK? Troopers have been down there for years. The DVIC will be a huge positive for the area."[56]

The centerpiece of the ROIC's efforts in North Jersey is a regional information sharing consortium for the municipalities along the urban corridor linking Newark and Paterson called CorStat, short for Corridor Statistics. Starting in September 2012, CorStat links together twenty-eight agencies, including federal agencies like the FBI or DEA, state agencies like the NJSP and New Jersey Parole Board, and municipal police departments. The partnership includes large cities—Newark and Paterson are, respectively, the largest and third-largest cities in the state—and a series of smaller municipalities. Representatives from each agency meet monthly to share intelligence and formulate responses to crime patterns and criminal networks. While the chief of detectives from the Essex County Prosecutor's Office CorStat chairs meetings, the ROIC also plays a major role. Each meeting begins with a presentation from ROIC personnel on regional crime trends and related matters of interest. In addition to supporting these physical meetings, the ROIC regularly produces specialized products for the CorStat region. It also set up a specialized web-based platform to facilitate information sharing between meetings and, importantly, avoid bombarding their other partners in the state with extraneous, regionally focused information.[57] In April, 2016, the ROIC partnered with the Newark Police Department, the Essex County Prosecutors Office, and the Rutgers University Police Institute to create a Real Time Crime Center (RTCC), for the CorStat region. Although located in Newark, the RTCC is a satellite of the ROIC. According to its founding documents, the RTCC is modeled after the ROIC and governed by its privacy policy. The RTCC commander also reports to the ROIC director.[58]

While the ROIC has little competition from other intelligence centers, there are internal interagency tensions at the fusion center. The ROIC was built around partnerships among NJSP, the New Jersey Office of Emergency Management (NJ OEM) and the New Jersey Office of Homeland Security and Preparedness (OHS&P).[59] Founded in 1980 as an independent office of the NJSP with its own director, NJ OEM has a well-defined mission area.[60] In 2007, the State Emergency Operations Center, the centerpiece of NJ OEM, merged with the ROIC. At this time, the ROIC expanded to its current staffing level, a moment long-tenured personnel described as the movement from "the pebble" to "the rock." Reflecting this relationship, the ROIC includes an emergency management function, a trait it shares with some other DHS-recognized fusion centers. While personnel from NJ OEM and the NJSP have a harmonious relationship, OHS&P's partnership with the ROIC is more conflicted. Founded in 2006, OHS&P competes with the NJSP for mission space. At the time of my research, half of the civilian analysts at the ROIC were OHS&P employees. They were deployed to the terrorism-focused threat unit inside the ROIC's Intelligence and Analysis Section. Some of the troopers that manage ROIC view the presence of OHS&P as a distraction. This conflict does much to animate the main professional struggle with the ROIC over the scope and nature of "intelligence."[61] With these interagency conflicts undermining work, OHS&P, in 2014, removed most of their analysts from the fusion center and refocused their staff on counterterrorism reporting.[62]

External pressures from the media and governor's office also shaped the ROIC. In March of 2006, Trenton, the state capital, witnessed seven shootings in a forty-eight-hour period. A stray bullet severely injured a seven-year-old girl, sparking a public controversy. Governor Corzine (D, 2006–2010), reeling from the bad press, allocated $750,000 for the NJSP, which immediately launched Project Watchtower.[63] The effort consisted of three programs that came to define the ROIC's routine operations. NJ Trace is a gun tracking system that runs ballistics data against records to track crime guns and map out illegal sales. Pins on Paper is a mapping program that charts shootings; identifies hotspots by region; provides temporal and spatial analysis; shows gang-involved shootings; and draws associations among weapons recovered, recidivist offenders, and shooting motivations across jurisdictional boundaries. And Targeting Activities of Gangs is an intelligence analysis effort to map out gang associations.[64] A senior manager described Project Watchtower as "opportunity [meeting] preparation. . . . We were a year old and had gotten ourselves to a position where we were capable of launching some programs. Along comes Governor Corzine and his crime strategy. It put us in motion."[65] The products have since changed but the focus of the ROIC's crime unit on guns and gangs continues.[66]

Altogether, the ROIC monopolizes intelligence analysis in its state but this position of dominance creates its own problems. "We are an all-hazards, all-threats, all-crimes fusion center but we can't be all things to everyone," the trooper heading the unit responsible for private sector outreach explained. "It's caused a strain on us as an entity and on the individual's working here."[67] The ROIC's most pressing demands are for criminal intelligence and case support. At the time of these interviews, three New Jersey cities ranked among the top twenty in crime rates: Camden topped the list, Newark at eight and Trenton at fifteen.[68] These demands increased in relation to the fiscal crunch of the "Great Recession." By 2010, the ROIC had been in operation for five years. It had established a reputation and built capabilities for crime mapping, predictive analytics, social network analysis, and telephone analysis. At the same time, public sector budgets contracted and municipal police cut staff. This confluence of forces conspired to transform the ROIC into the outsourced intelligence division for state's largest municipal police departments. As a result, the nature of work at the ROIC is frantic. A senior manager described it as "getting taskings, surging to address a tasking, and then going to the next fire to put that out."[69]

INTELLIGENCE FUSION AND THE INSTITUTIONAL UNEVENNESS OF THE WORKFARE-CARCERAL STATE

Intelligence fusion has been institutionalized in New Jersey and New York in a complex and often conflictive manner. In different ways, the ROIC, the NYSIC, and the IMPACT-funded CACs are defined by external lines of conflict and internal tensions. In New Jersey, the ROIC struggles to meet the intelligence needs of a densely populated state with high rates of violent crime. Externally, the ROIC has no major rivalries, but, internally, tension between the NJSP and OHS&P divided and, in many ways, defined the center from its establishment in 2005 until 2014, when the state homeland security office removed most their personnel from the fusion center. In New York, the environment is more complex. The NYPD is the largest police department in the world and exercises great power. Meanwhile, a series of county-level intelligence centers have crowded the NYSIC out of the crime analysis mission in the population centers outside of New York City. As a result, the NYSIC has the opposite problem of the ROIC. The NYSIC has to compete with other actors for its mission space and niche. The ROIC, in contrast, is so overextended that its management welcomed the addition of the Philadelphia-based DVIC to the state's intelligence landscape and created a satellite RTCC in Newark.

Altogether, these politics create an uneven and often conflictive intelligence system. This situation should be interpreted as failure. Instead, it reveals how fusion centers are a constitutive component of the larger workfare-carceral state. Intelligence fusion is animated by the same entrepreneurial ethos that defines workfare. The goal is cost-effectiveness and pragmatism, not the uniform application of policies. This approach is materially grounded in a system of competitive grant funding that fosters competition between government agencies and, in some ways, undermines construction of a seamless intelligence sharing system. This is an ongoing process of state-formation. The iterative reforms created a structural predisposition toward certain state strategies, easing the further institutionalization of intelligence fusion. In this way, the incorporated nature of this comparative study, explained in chapter 1, is especially appropriate. Comparing the institutionalization of intelligence fusion *through time* highlights the interactive nature of these two "cases" and the formative nature of struggles in New York City. Simultaneously comparing these instances *in time* illustrates the different ways a generalized state strategy—intelligence fusion—can be institutionalized, while still reflecting and advancing the larger formation of the workfare-carceral state.

The way police use their new intelligence capabilities and the ends to which they put them, however, are less clear. On paper, fusion centers have the potential to organize dramatic surveillance powers. In practice, however, what happens at fusion centers is circumscribed by the politics of law enforcement. The tremendous resources being invested in counterterrorism and the formation of interagency intelligence centers are complicated by organizational complexity and jurisdictional rivalries. These conflicts slow the pace of change but do not fundamentally alter the direction that policing is moving. The result is not a revolutionary shift in policing but the creation of uneven, conflictive, and often dysfunctional intelligence-sharing systems.[70] Paradoxically, this dysfunction provides a degree of autonomy for agents. It allows them to exploit ambiguity and, in certain cases, mobilize the state's capacities for pacification to address localized pockets of perceived social disorder. Most often, these resources are directed toward pacifying surplus populations. Today, this means policing decarceration.

4. Policing Decarceration

Mass Supervision, Manhunts, and the Continuing Advance of Workfare

In 2010, the US prison population had declined for three straight years. There year-to-year reductions were not dramatic, three tenths of percent in 2010, but it was trend.[1] In 2011, the prison population continued to fall, dropping by some fifteen thousand, a mere nine-tenths of a percent decrease.[2] The next year, the trend accelerated: 27,770 less people behind bars, nearly a 2 percent drop.[3] Significant reforms underpinned this reduction in the overall prison population. In 2008, Congress passed the Second Chance Act, which established grants for reentry initiatives. Two years later, the Fair Sentencing Act reduced the notorious sentencing disparity between crack and powder cocaine from a hundred to one to eighteen to one. Through executive orders and administrative actions, the Obama administration scaled back the use of solitary confinement, phased out private prisons in the Federal Bureau of Prisons, and reduced federal drug prosecutions. Obama also commuted the sentences of nearly one thousand incarcerated people, more than the previous three presidents combined. In the preceding years, some states foreshadowed this reform push with dramatic reductions in their prison populations, including New York and New Jersey.

Reformers and advocates celebrated decarceration—and called for more. The editorial board of the *New York Times* not only praised the Fair Sentencing Act and Second Chance Act but also identified their limits and called for further-reaching measures.[4] In 2010, Sasha Abramsky, author of four books on mass incarceration, told the readers of *The Nation* that "the [Obama] administration is laying the foundations for a new criminal justice system model that might, conceivably, end America's morally disastrous, fiscally ruinous, four-decade-long experimentation with mass incarceration."[5] More conservative and technocratic voices echoed this point. The next year, Joan Petersilia, director of Stanford University's Criminal Justice Center proclaimed, "These changes mean it is very likely that we are seeing the beginning of the end of America's long commitment to what some critics call 'mass incarceration.'"[6]

Subsequent developments moderated this optimism. In 2013, the total prison population increased by 4,300.[7] Although the decline continued again in 2014 and 2015 with prison population respectively dropping by 15,400 and 35,500, it focused attention on the limits of this apparent decarceration.[8] In 2013, the Sentencing Project, a research and advocacy organization dedicated to reducing imprisonment, calculated that, if annual reductions continued at the nearly 2 percent rate seen in 2012, it would take eighty-eight years—until the year 2101!—for the prison populations to return to 1980 levels.[9] A year later, Marie Gottschalk published a landmark study on the "prison state," its many manifestations, and its diverse and not necessarily overlapping consistencies. She contended that the current reforms were inadequate and superficial. Most people freed from prison were "non, non, nons"—non-serious, nonviolent, non-sexual offenders. Meaningful decarceration, she argued, will only happen if efforts extend beyond the most sympathetic offenders. Such changes also require a long-term, broad-based political movement: "Some of the most successful penal reform movements in the United States over the last century and a half raised penetrating questions about economic and social justice. These movements did not act in isolation but were buoyed by contemporaneous social and political movements."[10] Although many movements have been organizing against mass incarceration for decades, the fiscal crunch of the Great Recession, not grassroots mobilization, provided the main impetus for recent reform. "It now appears the Great Recession has put states in the position of having to rethink punishment," Elizabeth Brown writes in her review of correctional policy changes since 2008, "in some cases accelerating a process of corrections policy revision that began in the early 2000s."[11]

This chapter builds on the sobering conclusions of Gottschalk and others. Significant decarceration can occur without meaningfully changing the punitive character of the larger criminal legal system. In both New York and New Jersey, moreover, substantial decarceration occurred alongside expanding policing that targets the same criminalized populations being released from prison. In the past decade, four types of intelligence-led policing (ILP) operations have become routine in both states: warrant sweeps, compliance checks, chronic-offender initiatives, and saturation patrols. These programs are not part of nationwide policy initiatives. Following the previous chapter's focus on the conflictive and uneven institutionalization of intelligence fusion in each state, these ILP operations are organized in ways that reflect the particularities of New York and New Jersey. The different arrangements that surround these common practices raise an important point. These policing practices are part of a structural transformation. They have emerged organically from the same shifting social forces that are behind decarceration: chronic unemployment and deepening austerity that reduces incarceration and increases reliance on less labor-intensive forms of policing.

In this context, intelligence fusion is enabling a punitive form of decarceration that reduces prison populations without pushing penal policy toward rehabilitation and reintegration. These changes are not a narrow concern of the criminal legal system. They are part of a larger recalibration of the workfare-carceral state that is changing the dynamics of labor-formation. The explosive expansion of incarceration helped consolidate the workfare-carceral state, organizing labor-formation during the economic shift from an industrial to a postindustrial service-based economy. This transition is complete. Now in an era of austerity with incarceration in decline or at least retrenchment, mass supervision—the set of mechanisms developed to monitor and manage problem populations within their home communities—is becoming both more visible and more important. In New York and New Jersey, warrant sweeps, compliance checks, chronic-offender initiatives, and saturation patrols supplement contracting prison populations with a series of "intelligence-led manhunts," recasting police officers as prison guards for surplus populations that have become too costly to incarcerate and transforming entire communities into open-air prisons. These austerity politics are not just limited to the pragmatic reforms behind the modest decline in imprisonment. Just as decarceration has not brought a return to rehabilitation and reintegration, the Great Recession and its aftermath have failed to replace the workfarist arrangements that define the relations among the state, capital, and labor. Instead, the institutionalization of intelligence fusion and ILP has restructured police agencies and further extended market discipline into the public sector. The medium- and long-term consequences of these shifts are an open question, subject to ongoing developments, but the immediate implications are clear: punitive decarceration, the increasing prominence of a police-intensive strategy of mass supervision, and the continuing advance of workfare.

DECARCERATION AND MASS SUPERVISION

Both New York and New Jersey dramatically reduced their prison populations, long before any decrease was apparent in aggregated nationwide figures, as seen in table 1. Both states, moreover, closed major prisons. Since 2009, New York State shuttered sixteen adult prisons, ranging from small facilities that housed between one hundred fifty and three hundred people

TABLE 1. State Prison Populations in
New York and New Jersey, 2001–2016

Year	NY Prison Population	NJ Prison Population
2001	68,351	28,142
2002	67,658	27,891
2003	66,109	27,246
2004	64,905	26,757
2005	63,928	27,359
2006	64,410	27,371
2007	63,425	26,827
2008	60,933	25,953
2009	59,279	25,382
2010	57,229	25,007
2011	55,980	23,834
2012	54,865	23,225
2013	54,196	22,452
2014	53,157	21,590
2015	52,363	20,489
2016	51,406	19,453
Percent Change	*−24.79%*	*−30.87%*

SOURCE: New York State, Department of Corrections and
Community Supervision; State of New Jersey, Department
of Corrections.

to major prisons with a capacity of over one thousand.[12] While New Jersey
has not closed the same number of prisons as New York, in 2009, it did close
a large facility, the 800-bed Riverfront Prison located in Camden.[13] In 2017,
New Jersey reopened the 696-bed Mid-State Correctional Facility as a specialized drug treatment and detention center. The same year, the state also
announced plans to close the 250-person satellite unit of the Bayside State
Prison, located inside Ancora Psychiatric Hospital.[14]

While these reforms are releasing people from prison and diverting others into alternative programs, they are not challenging the processes of
criminalization that lead millions to a life of stigma and marginalization.
The 1.5 million caged in prisons must be considered in relation to the larger
criminalized population: the 4.6 million people on probation and parole, the
12 million more that spend some time in a county jail each year, and nearly

20 million people estimated to have a felony conviction. This criminalized mass of people is nine times larger than the prison population. Two-thirds of this group are poor and one-third is black. An even larger group, 100 million, have some kind of criminal record, which, as a result of electronic background checks and reporting requirements on applications, leads to systemic discrimination in housing, employment, and education. Altogether, one-third of adults in the United States are entangled in the criminal legal system in some way.[15] In recent years, scholars have used the term "mass supervision" to connote the systems put in place to manage millions of criminalized people outside of the prison. This scholarship focuses on post-incarceration strategies, such as probation and reentry programs, that "widen the net" of correctional control beyond the prison.[16]

When considered from the perspective of policing, however, mass supervision extends beyond the programs put in place to manage formerly incarcerated people. Many of the one hundred million people with some kind of criminal record have never been imprisoned or under community supervision, but all of them are entered into the law enforcement databases that provide much of the raw data for intelligence fusion. Moreover, since most incarcerated people are concentrated in relatively few communities, it means that anyone living in these areas are subjected to more aggressive policing and surveillance. This is not just an urban issue. Instead, the characteristics of hyper-ghettoization—dual segregation on the basis of race and class—can be found in rural areas, including poor white communities in places like Upstate New York.[17] The aggressive policing of hyper-ghettoized communities has only intensified in recent years as counterterrorism grants have led to the installation of surveillance systems such as security cameras, automated license plate readers, and "ShotSpotter" gunshot detectors in high-crime areas. These systems, moreover, often feed directly into police intelligence centers, whether fusion centers recognized by the Department of Homeland Security (DHS) or other intelligence hubs such as the crime analysis centers (CACs) set up throughout New York State or the real-time crime centers found in many cities. For this reason, I contend that intelligence fusion has become mass supervision's center of gravity in this moment of ambiguous decarceration. Intelligence fusion pulls policing, community supervision, and the courts together in a shared project to pacify criminalized surplus populations.

ILP OPERATIONS AND THE MANHUNT

The centrality of intelligence fusion to mass supervision is evident in the organic emergence of four ILP operations in New York and New Jersey during the period when both states dramatically reduced their prison populations. These programs target the same symbolically profaned surplus populations warehoused in prisons: the so-called criminal element that I found occupied the attention of New Jersey's Regional Operations Intelligence Center (ROIC) during my first visit to a fusion center. The first two programs—warrant sweeps and compliance checks—enforce the terms of administrative surveillance on formally criminalized individuals. Warrant sweeps are police raids to apprehend individuals with outstanding warrants. Where warrant sweeps target people already wanted for arrest, compliance checks partner probation or parole with police to continually enforce orders of supervision. Individuals on probation or parole forfeit freedom of movement and association in order to, respectively, avoid a prison sentence or be released from one. Often the terms will include specific requirements such as avoiding contact with certain people, remaining employed, staying sober, submitting to regular drug tests, abiding by a curfew, receiving substance-use treatment or psychological counseling, or performing community service. A violation can result in penalties, including incarceration. In compliance checks, probation or parole officers partner with police to conduct home visits, stripping community supervision of its social work mission.

While the formal criminalization entailed in the warrant process and codified in orders of community supervision provides the basis for warrant sweeps and compliance checks, chronic-offender programs and saturation patrols use intelligence analysis to preempt and pacify *potential* disorder. These programs show how mass supervision extends beyond the programs put in place to manage formally criminalized people to a broader effort that targets larger populations and communities. Chronic-offender programs begin with intelligence analysts, who use "specific and objective, data-led criteria to identify individuals who should be targeted."[18] These programs bring police agencies and district attorneys' (DA) offices together to identify and aggressively target individuals who are designated prolific offenders. The goal of this targeted policing is to keep "career criminals" off the streets at all costs, even if it means prosecuting minor offenses that result in short jail sentences. Saturation patrols are similar to chronic-offender initiatives in that they are driven primarily by intelligence analysis. Police executives plan data-driven deployments to target "hotspots." While these efforts are increasingly part of routine police administration, they are also used to respond to surges in crime, usually centered on gun violence, drug dealing, or property theft. In these instances, the DA often resorts to "enhanced prosecution," meaning no plea deals and harsh convictions that often derive from mandatory minimum sentences.

These operations exemplify one of the enduring practices of police power: the manhunt. Echoing Poulantzas's point about the role of state power in labor-formation, Neocleous notes that "police power was forged through the hunting of the idle poor, the beggar and the vagabond." He reinterprets the world-historic emergence of the proletariat through the lens of the police manhunt:

> [I]t is no exaggeration to say that capital's conquest . . . was founded on a vast manhunt that continued across the Continents for almost four centuries: the hunting of blacks in Africa, the hunting of "Indians" in the Americas and the East and West Indies, and the hunting of the poor across Europe . . . the hunt for pirates, the lynch-mob, the pogrom and the witch-hunt.

As an expression of the perpetual wars of pacification that produce and maintain capitalist social relations, these manhunts continue to the present, targeting the contemporary criminalized other: "the 'squeegee merchants', the 'feral youth', the 'delinquents.'"[19] Tyler Wall continues this analysis of the "foundational practice of police power where the 'reserve army of labour' is quite literally hunted and captured." He shows how police helicopters and drones "unman" the manhunt, extending "the police dream of pacification through air power—or a scopic verticality."[20] This chapter further elaborates this argument, showing how mass supervision extends "the police dream of pacification" through intelligence fusion—or a computerized legibility. These "intelligence-led manhunts," I contend, are a central aspect of the shifting dynamics of labor-formation in a conjuncture constituted by the Great Recession, decarceration, and austerity.

Warrant Sweeps

In both New York and New Jersey, intelligence fusion is the starting point for police manhunts for individuals with outstanding warrants. The records of probation and parole are essential. As a parole officer assigned full-time to the ROIC explained:

> Our system . . . Parole Board Information System has a lot of information and it's a very useful tool. We are able to filter by a lot of means: physical attributes, release data, criminal history. A lot of times, we are asked to run a profile and see what we can come up with or we're asked to look up a particular person. The way the database works, we still have information when the person is in the prison system or off on parole. The information is still in there and it's a tremendous resource. It may be someone that we can find because we used to have him. We can provide addresses, cell phones, girlfriends, family. Part of the deal

with parole is they have to give us all their information. Even prior to them being released, they need to provide a pre-parole address of where they want to live. The officers go out and conduct a pre-parole investigation and we learn about everyone who lives there. We learn about family members, girlfriends, everyone, children even. It's all documented and put into the system. We have more information than any other law enforcement agency, especially on the criminal population. Police can do a criminal background check and they'll just get their criminal history and the last address he gave. We have everything. . . . It really helps in an investigation. It will give you a half dozen or so addresses to check during a warrant sweep.[21]

A probation officer in New York State explained that they provide a similar quality of information to police: "We have great relationships with the police department. We have so much more information than they do. Their records are limited to basically just criminal histories, if they're lucky their intel or detective bureau will have a file on someone but that's hardly assured. We can give them a lot more: where they live, where their family members live, where they work."[22]

In New Jersey, warrant sweeps began in 2010 as a statewide effort organized by the Attorney General's Office. Parole and the ROIC provided the necessary intelligence. In July and August of 2010, interagency teams went hunting, arresting 1,298 individuals, including 385 parole violators.[23] These manhunts continued in Jersey City and Hudson County, where, again, the operation began at the ROIC with intelligence compiled by analysts and the two parole officers assigned there full-time. Renamed "Summer Shield," the warrant sweeps in Jersey City brought together the DEA, FBI, US Marshals Service, New Jersey State Police (NJSP), Parole, the Attorney General's Office, and other local law enforcement agencies in series of operations over the course of several months. In 2011, the manhunts led to 176 arrests.[24] In 2012, the sweeps resulted in 200 arrests and a raid on a barbershop that led to the seizure of over $25,000, and the confiscation of "several hundred of bags of heroin."[25] In 2013, the program was scaled back and renamed "Operation Safer Streets." The sweeps resulted in twenty-seven arrests in 2013 and twenty-four in 2014.[26] The ROIC also supports ad hoc warrants sweeps, such as the 2013 manhunt in Camden County that resulted in seventy-six arrests and the 2015 sweeps in Passaic and Essex Counties that led to fifty-five arrests.[27] "Almost every summer we work with the ROIC, the feds, some of the larger PDs to do warrant sweeps," the chief of detectives in a county prosecutor's office explained. "It's like going to the beach, it wouldn't be summer if we weren't kicking down some doors and getting these guys before they start causing real trouble."[28] In 2017, the Attorney General's Office, working with the ROIC and other agencies, relaunched statewide warrant sweeps, which led to a three-month "violent-offender fugitive sweep" and 150 arrests.[29]

In New York State, Operation IMPACT made warrant sweeps a fixture of policing. In 2006, the US Marshalls began a warrant sweep program dubbed "Operation Rolling Thunder," the same name used for the carpet bombing of Vietnam during the Johnson administration. By 2008, six IMPACT jurisdictions participated in the effort, including Oneida and Erie Counties, which, respectively, apprehended 106 and 140 people in two weeks of sweeps.[30] These manhunts focused on federal warrants. In 2009, the year after the Division of Criminal Justice Services (DCJS) set up its first crime analysis center, the Buffalo-based Erie Crime Analysis Center (ECAC), DCJS focused IMPACT jurisdictions on manhunting for state warrants. The Erie County IMPACT partnership piloted the "Violent Offender Interdiction Collaborative Effort," or Operation VOICE. The program started with ECAC analysts identifying a hotspot on Buffalo's East Side and compiling a list of outstanding warrants in the area. Armed with this intelligence, the Buffalo Police Department went hunting. It let loose the IMPACT-funded mobile response unit, "a proactive unit that consists of Buffalo police officers and New York State troopers who patrol areas of the city based on real-time crime information" from the ECAC. Over the course of a ninety-day period, 147 people "were systematically arrested and debriefed."[31] In the intervening years, warrants sweeps have become commonplace in most IMPACT jurisdictions. Erie County is still the most aggressive. During ten years of Operation IMPACT, the Buffalo police executed 39,734 warrants, including 4,855 in 2013 alone.[32]

Compliance Checks

Where warrant sweeps involve hunting people who are wanted by the state, compliance checks collapse community supervision into policing. In IMPACT jurisdictions, the county probation department and the statewide Department of Corrections and Community Supervision each designate one officer to act as field intelligence officers. These field intelligence officers partner with police officers and sheriff's deputies to conduct "authorized warrantless searches, warrant execution, curfew checks, alcohol tests, drug tests and computer/mobile device searches and have made efforts to ensure adherence to Orders of Protection."[33] As one probation officer explained, "We don't need a warrant to search our guys so, if a cop tells me one of my guys is dealing on this corner at this time, I can just show up and search him. For IMPACT details, we will partner up with the PD or Sheriff and do compliance checks on my higher risk cases."[34] In Monroe County, for example, the probation field intelligence officer conducted 185 of these home searches in 2013. In Erie County, the probation field intelligence officer performed 197 compliance checks, including 153 with the aid of the Buffalo Police Department's Canine Unit.[35] In New Jersey, probation and parole still conduct their compliance checks on their own and do not partner with law enforcement.

Chronic-Offender Initiatives

Chronic-offender initiatives are another type of police manhunt that is common in both New York and New Jersey. A point of doctrine ILP emphasizes is "disruption and prevention through both *strategic management* and effective enforcement strategies that target prolific and serious offenders."[36] This commitment to hunting "prolific and serious offenders" is manifest in the routine operations of the ROIC. When the ROIC is building up intelligence in anticipation of a larger police operation, such as "Operation Padlock" in Camden, which I discussed in the prologue of this book, analysts will assemble what they called "gator guides" or pocket-sized booklets with pictures, names, aliases, whereabouts, gang affiliations, and criminal histories of known offenders. "Gator guides are a good example of some of the small ways we add value to officers in the field," an analyst explained. "If you're on patrol and you see one of these known troublemakers, you now have the intelligence to attempt a field debriefing. If you round up a bunch of guys, you can use the Gator Guide to make sure they are who they say they are."[37] The dissemination of intelligence on chronic offenders is also part of the CorStat Program, the information sharing consortium among twenty-eight agencies in the urban corridor linking Newark and Paterson. At the monthly CorStat meetings, a parole officer presents information on recent parolees released to the area. Here, the idea is to alert law enforcement about the return of a potential offender to a community. The presentation includes information about an individual's criminal history, modus operandi, and previous areas of operation. The Newark-based Real Time Crime Center (RTCC), a satellite intelligence hub that operates under the ROIC and supports the CorStat region, has routinized this process. Opened in 2016, one of the RTCC's primary missions is to develop "in-depth 'persons of strategic interest' reports."[38]

In New York, hunting for chronic offenders takes a more structured form. In all IMPACT jurisdictions, DCJS encouraged the development of chronic-offender lists. The goal is to focus attention on "the most serious offenders by identifying and focusing on those who are known to commit a disproportionate percentage of the jurisdiction's violent crime. The work of crime analysts is critical to these initiatives, as they generally use very specific criteria to develop the list of chronic offenders."[39] Partnerships between the police agencies and DA's offices provide the foundation for these efforts. One of the most successful and publicized versions of these programs, the Chronic Offender Recognition and Enforcement (CORE) Program in Onondaga County, provides an illustrative example of how these programs work and why they are controversial. CORE used intelligence produced at the Onondaga County Crime Analysis Center (OCAC) to "target the estimated eight percent of criminals who commit about 80 percent of the crimes in the community."[40] The program was successful on its own terms. Police arrested all twenty-six "CORE offenders." Ten received state prison sentences ranging from one to seven years; eight were incarcerated for short sentences at the county jail. The US Attorney's Office sent another defendant to prison on federal charges.[41]

The program, however, became a victim of its own success. "The first CORE list we had was really successful," an assistant DA told me, "but the second CORE list, once you start getting the assholes off the street, the target-rich environment becomes less and less robust. Soon, you're questioning how 'chronic' these guys are. If your program is successful, it is going to end."[42] By the time of the third CORE list in 2010, interagency conflict had sunk the program. "CORE I and CORE II were extremely successful. CORE III started to take a turn and that's when the political stuff starting coming in," a police supervisor at the OCAC explained. "We started to see that we were arresting these guys and they weren't getting any different treatment than any normal person who would going through the system. Through a series of meetings, it was stated that we are not going to treat these guys any different than anyone else. So that didn't sit well with the law enforcement side of things."[43] From the perspective of the DA's office, police expected the prosecutors to bend the rules of criminal justice:

> You can't go into a court and tell a judge "This is a CORE offender. You need to treat him more harshly." That goes against every grain of American criminal justice system. Trying to explain that to the police is a different story. "We know he's a bad guy." Well, OK, that's great. We need proof. . . . Prosecutors have an ethical obligation, OK? All the stuff you've read in the IMPACT reports about the enforcement side of things needs to be tempered by claims of organizations like the Innocence Project, who say that all these people have been wrongfully convicted because of overzealous police or because of police or prosecutorial misconduct. . . . Our job is not to prosecute and convict people that the police arrest. Our job to evaluate a case and ensure that

(a) the person is the right person to prosecute and (b) that we have the right evidence to convict him and survive an appeal down the road.[44]

Similar tensions complicated other chronic-offender initiatives. As a result, the Office of Public Safety, the component of DCJS that oversees IMPACT, started to compile its Persistent Chronic Offender Lists in 2011. The statewide lists provide police agencies with the intelligence on chronic offenders, thus neutralizing tensions between police agencies and DA's offices and allowing the hunting of supposed chronic offenders to continue.[45]

Saturation Patrols

Other programs use intelligence fusion to define hunting grounds, where the police can freely target "the criminal element." These "saturation patrols" are premised on generalized suspicion, further underscoring the broad reach of mass supervision as a state strategy concerned not just with formerly incarcerated people but with the surplus populations quarantined in criminalized communities. In their simplest form, saturation patrols are a product of the managerial aspects of ILP: the use of crime analysis to direct police patrols. As one police administrator explained:

> The head analyst runs our weekly IMPACT meetings within the department. It's basically a gentler version of CompStat. We're not so big that I need to act like I'm running a Fortune 500 company and reduce everything to performance quotas and data analysis. I don't take officers to task like it's the NYPD, but I do use crime data to manage the department. It tells me where I need to focus the investigative division. It drives the patrol division. What they do is directly a result of the information and intelligence they develop.[46]

Saturation patrols can also involve intelligence collection. In the words of another police administrator:

> We do use crime analysis to manage resources. It really goes hand in hand with intelligence-led policing. We're looking to reduce the incidents of crime so we want to get on top of them and try to be proactive. Crime analysis allows you to recognize that you're having an increase in a certain type of crime. You have a hot spot. We don't always attack things with increased manpower either. Sometimes we decrease the manpower and we increase the undercovers. . . . Sometimes our saturation patrols don't take the typical form of lots of uniformed officers in the area. Sometimes they're surges of detectives and undercovers. If these surges of intelligence collectors work, they get to the root of the problem in a way that the normal saturation patrols don't. Scaring the bad guys away is fine enough, but identifying and disrupting a whole criminal network is better.[47]

As a police practice, saturation patrols can connote crime analysis to direct police deployments or they can be closer to the ideals of ILP, where police operations result in further intelligence collection.

In both New York and New Jersey, police agencies initiate more sustained saturation patrols linked to "enhanced prosecution." In New Jersey, for example, the ROIC and NJSP partnered with the Trenton Police Department, Mercer County Prosecutors Office, and the State Attorney General to address the ninety-four shootings that resulted in injuries to 120 people and nineteen deaths in Trenton in the first half of 2013.[48] The NJSP developed a saturation patrol component, Targeted Integrated Deployment Effort (TIDE), that began with intelligence produced at the ROIC. The "enhanced prosecution" element of the program, codenamed "the Targeted Anti-Gun Initiative" (TAG), makes use of New Jersey's 1981 Graves Act, which mandates a three-and-a-half-year minimum sentence for a series of gun crimes, including illegal possession.[49] In the seven months between August 2013 and April 2014, the TIDE-TAG manhunt led to the arrest of 3,223 people, and the seizure or recovery of 177 guns.[50]

In New York, saturation patrols are a hallmark of all IMPACT jurisdictions. Indeed, they are the basis of the program, which started with crime analysis directing "blue and gray patrols" or joint patrols of state police and municipal police officers and/or sheriffs' deputies.[51] Some IMPACT partnerships, however, target saturation patrols on a specific crime and connect them to enhanced prosecution. Operation Speeding Bullet in Albany County is a good example. It involves the Albany Crime Analysis Center, the Albany Police Department, the sheriffs' office, and the DA's office. Like other ILP initiatives, Operation Speeding Bullet begins with intelligence: crime analysts conducting a spatial and temporal breakdown of shots fired. With these crime maps, police patrol the area. The officers look to prevent future shootings, question known persons of interest connected to past shootings, and seize illegal guns. From 2008 to 2011, these hunts led to the recovery of between 90 and 120 guns per year.[52] An IMPACT-funded Gang and Gun Prosecutor in the DA's office—who operates on call twenty-four hours a day, seven days a week—handles all arrests and brings them to a grand jury instead of a preliminary hearing with a judge. These measures allow the prosecutor to set a higher bail. As a result of Operation Speeding Bullet, Albany County now moves a gun case from arrest to conviction in the average time of forty-five days. In the eleven-month period between July 2013 and June 2014, the DA's office "prosecuted almost 50 felony firearm cases with more then [sic] two dozen open cases during the grant year."[53]

Collectively, these now routinized ILP operations supercharge police manhunts with computerized legibility afforded by intelligence fusion. They extend police power deeper into criminalized communities, subsume probation and parole within policing, and place police power at the core of mass supervision. Warrant sweeps hunt subjects already monitored by the state. Compliance checks transform community supervision from a punitive form of social work into a continuous hunt for criminal behavior. Chronic-offender initiatives hunt the "criminal element." Saturation patrols use intelligence to define hunting grounds for open-ended police operations. Together, these four types of programs create a multilayered pacification project that supplements imprisonment. While these programs are widespread across New York and New Jersey and share a common convergence in intelligence fusion, they are institutionalized in different ways. In New York, the programs take a more standardized form as a result of Operation IMPACT. In New Jersey, in contrast, the programs are put in place on a more ad hoc basis. They revolve around the overextended ROIC, the DHS-recognized statewide fusion center. These different institutional origins suggest that these intelligence-led manhunts are an organic response to common conditions.

THE CONTINUING ADVANCE OF WORKFARE

Although different institutional mechanisms surround routinization of warrant sweeps, compliance checks, chronic-offender initiatives, and saturation patrols in New York and New Jersey, these ILP operations have become commonplace during the period defined by the Great Recession, which saw declines in police employment and rising police budgets. These trends, depicted in tables 2 and 3, below, further support Gottshalk's skeptical review of the declining prison population. Decarceration and the ILP operations now common in New York and New Jersey are changes, but they are not challenges to the dominant perspective informing social policy: workfare. Indeed, a deeper look into the nature of policing reveals that the *experience* of police labor has grown more punitive during this period. In this way, decarceration is not a break from the workfare-carceral state but, instead, represents its continuing development. This change is not only visible in the intelligence-led police manhunts at the center of mass supervision, it is also manifested in another development related to the institutionalization of intelligence fusion: the extension of the market of discipline over police labor.

The Great Recession and decarceration did not prompt a pendulum swing back to either welfare state–style policies or rehabilitation. Instead, most of the

TABLE 2. Unemployment, Police Employment, and Total Police Budgets in New York State, 2003–2017

Year	Unemployment Rate	Total Police Employment	Total Police Budgets
2003	10.2	no data	no data
2004	9.7	86,481	no data
2005	8.6	83,625	no data
2006	7.7	86,053	no data
2007	8.1	86,952	$7,642,649,000
2008	10	80,949	$8,152,669,000
2009	14.3	83,394	$8,360,054,000
2010	14.8	83,941	$8,707,895,000
2011	14.3	81,795	$9,005,989,000
2012	14.9	79,358	$9,272,858,000
2013	13.8	78,497	$9,332,470,000
2014	12.4	78,535	$9,401,996,000
2015	10.6	81,036	$9,597,553,000
2016	9.4	no data	no data
2017	8.6	83,642	no data

SOURCES: Federal Bureau of Investigation, Police Employment, 2004–2017; Bureau of Labor Statistics, Alternative Measures of Labor Underutilization for States (Archived Tables), 2017; Bureau of Justice Statistics, Justice Expenditure and Employment Extracts Series, 2009–2015.

approximately six hundred thousand people released from prison each year in the United States return to communities that are mired in violence, and lack employment opportunities.[54] Similarly, as social suffering ratchets up in an increasingly unequal and precarious economy, the only solutions offered remain workfarist ones, more attentive to the needs of capital than people. Hence, the signature domestic policy accomplishment of President Obama, the president many thought would be the second coming of Franklin Delano Roosevelt, was not a "Green New Deal" but "Obamacare," a tepid measure that used the state power to create new markets for insurance companies rather than de-commodifying health care as human right and universal social good.[55] With no significant investment in rehabilitation, or a comprehensive structural intervention at the level of political economy, formerly incarcerated and otherwise criminalized people of all races find themselves subjected to the aggressive policing that today forms the core of mass supervision.

TABLE 3. Unemployment, Police Employment, and
Total Police Budgets in New Jersey, 2003–2017

Year	Unemployment Rate	Total Police Employment	Total Police Budgets
2003	9	no data	no data
2004	7.7	40,195	no data
2005	7.7	40,810	no data
2006	7.8	36,456	no data
2007	7.4	41,672	$3,057,957,000
2008	9.5	42,022	$3,086,622,000
2009	15.2	39,996	$3,257,777,000
2010	15.7	41,609	$3,283,489,000
2011	16	36,854	$3,343,545,000
2012	15.7	37,881	$3,323,662,000
2013	14.7	31,931	$3,369,028,000
2014	12.4	38,778	$3,357,289,000
2015	10.4	39,376	$3,325,995,000
2016	9.7	no data	no data
2017	9.2	40,469	no data

SOURCES: Federal Bureau of Investigation, Police Employment, 2004–2017; Bureau of Labor Statistics, Alternative Measures of Labor Underutilization for States (Archived Tables), 2017; Bureau of Justice Statistics, Justice Expenditure and Employment Extracts Series, 2009–2015.

This continuing commitment to workfare is a key part of the ongoing regulation of surplus populations and pacification of social struggle. Workfare remains as a cynical way of managing people by engendering insecurity and transmuting class antagonisms into the individual struggle of one against all in a hyper-competitive labor market. The Great Recession caused a massive spike in unemployment, and, although job markets have ostensibly recovered to pre-crash levels, the more comprehensive measures of unemployment show that structural unemployment is a chronic problem. As explained in chapter 2, two economic crises punctuate the formation of DHS and the creation of the National Network of Fusion Centers: the "dot-com" crash and the Great Recession. The most complete measure of unemployment—which includes people unemployed for fifteen weeks or longer, people who have stopped looking for work altogether (so-called discouraged workers), underemployed workers, and others who eke by on the margins of the labor market—shows that New York and New Jersey emerged from the dot-com crash in 2003 with about one of every ten eligible workers unemployed (data on this more complete measure of unemployment are not available on a state-by-state basis before 2003). After the Great Recession hit, unemployment steadily rose, peaking at 16 percent in 2011 in New Jersey and 14.9 percent in 2012 in New York. Of course, unemployment does not affect everyone equally. According to 2016 data, the unemployment rates for African Americans and Latinos respectively were 56 percent and 35 percent higher than the white unemployment rate in New York and 49 percent and 12 percent higher in New Jersey.[56] In other words, structural unemployment is a chronic problem in both New York and New Jersey, and one—like incarceration and police-involved killings—that falls more heavily on racial minorities. In a context of decarceration, the work of managing these surplus workers increasingly falls to the police, hence the routinization of intelligence-led manhunts in both states.

However, the mass supervision is not just a product of chronic unemployment and punitive decarceration, predicated on empowered, high-technology policing. The extension of the workfare regime to the core of state—the police agencies that, in part, comprise the state's physical monopoly on violence—also clarifies another, important dimension of mass supervision: labor control. As general unemployment rose, full-time employment in police agencies contracted in both states. In 2004, the first year where data is available, police agencies in New York and New Jersey respectively employed 86,481 and 40,195 full time employees. In New York, this number dropped by just over 9 percent to 78,535 in 2014 before rebounding to 83,642 in 2017. In New Jersey, the dynamic was similar. Full time employment at police agencies saw an even sharper decrease, falling by over 20 percent to 31,931 in 2013 before sharply increasing the next year. In all, full-time police employment decreased by nearly 4 percent in New York and almost 3 percent in New Jersey in the decade following the Great Recession. Despite the arrival of austerity, however, there is no indication that the total public investment in policing declined. Total budgets for police agencies in New York and New Jersey actually increased in the years immediately following the Great Recession. From 2007 to 2012, total police budgets in New York State shot up by 25 percent from $7.6 billion to $9.5 billion. In New Jersey, the total jump was less dramatic but still notable, an increase of 8.7 percent from $3 billion to $3.3 billion during those same years. Taken together, the state put police *labor* on the chopping block during lean years after the Great Recession. This austerity, however, did not affect the police *institution*, which grew, due, in part, to the continual investment in counterterrorism and homeland security.

These contradictory trends—declining police employment and rising investment in policing—suggest that decarceration is not a meaningful departure but a new stage in the ongoing formation of the workfare-carceral state. Starting in the early 1970s, four decades of class warfare from above created a situation Bernard Harcourt called "neoliberal penalty," a set of arrangements where "the penal sanction is marked off from the dominant logic of classical economics as the only space where order is legitimately enforced by the State."[57] Decarceration and the contemporaneous rise of intelligence fusion and ILP, however, challenge this notion. Since the "Great Recession," the fiscal crisis of the state put immense pressure on the public sector, prompting decarceration and austerity. In this context, fusion centers and ILP appear as a mechanism that is further reorganizing policing around the discipline of the market. There are three processes informing the extension of workfare on police agencies: the ongoing recentralization of police agencies around fusion centers; the managerial aspects of CompStat and ILP; and the funding mechanisms underpinning the spread of intelligence fusion.

As chapter 3 demonstrates, the institutionalization of intelligence fusion has created simultaneous processes of decentralization and recentralization, where criminal justice agencies enter into information-sharing networks and collaborative programs that revolve around—and empower—larger agencies that manage fusion centers or CACs. The public sector austerity associated with the Great Recession added further momentum to this process. "The recession is actually pushing people towards us," one senior supervisor at the ROIC explained.

> It would be great if people said "that's a really great idea and let me dig into this and find out" . . . [but] it doesn't happen until people either have to do it—[are] commanded to do it—or [are] forced by circumstance like having a quarter of your officers laid off.[58]

Here, he is referring to the example of Paterson. Like many formerly industrial cities in the United States, Paterson is in decline and locked into a seemingly permanent fiscal crisis. In 2011, the city laid off 125 officers, about one-fourth of the force.[59] As the third-largest city in the state, Paterson already had a close relationship with the ROIC, but budget cuts increased the city's reliance on the fusion center. A detective with the Paterson Police described the ROIC as "one-stop shopping," an outsourced intelligence division. It provides routine case support: in minutes, analysts can assemble comprehensive criminal histories drawn from local, state, and federal databases, work that used to take the detective "several phone calls and the better part of a day, if not days." The fusion center also provides higher-level intelligence products. "I don't do any mapping here anymore, especially with the manpower restrictions," the detective explained. "If I want to map a certain area or look at hotspots or do some predictive analyses, if we have a string of shootings, I'll just pick up the phone and call the ROIC."[60]

This dynamic is not limited to Paterson. Between 2008 and 2013, the number of full-time employees at police agencies declined in New Jersey's largest cities: Newark (down 431), Trenton (down 121), Jersey City (down 116), and Elizabeth (down 51). More aggressive proposals to restructure police agencies accompanied these reductions. Recalling the example that introduced this book, the State of New Jersey, in 2011, withdrew financial support from Camden, prompting the police department to lay off 168 of 368 officers and causing violent crime to spike. This austerity and the crescendo of violence were a prelude to the imposition of workfare on the police department. The reformed and no longer unionized Camden County Police cut pensions and health care benefits by 65 percent, reducing the average costs per officer from $182,168 to $99,605.[61] Governor Chris Christie (R-NJ 2010–2018), moreover, unsuccessfully advocated for other jurisdictions to follow the Camden model.[62] The general reduction of police employment and the restructuring of Camden's police force underscores the class politics at work in these changes. The institutionalization of intelligence fusion and ILP further advances the workfare regime to the core organs of the state's coercive power—the armed men (and they are mostly men) that *embody* the monopoly on force—are now subjected to the discipline of the market.

The extension of market discipline over police agencies is also facilitated by the managerial aspects of CompStat and ILP. In general, these increasingly common strategies enhance the supervision of police labor. As an officer in an IMPACT-funded intelligence center on Long Island explained:

> We're becoming more surgical. This is the twenty-first-century model of targeted enforcement. We're lean and effective. The previous model was to saturate public space with police. This was ineffective because the criminals would learn when police were going to be in certain places. It was inefficient and expensive as well because it required so much manpower. Now, we use intel to dial down on the recidivist 20 percent that accounts for 80 percent of crime. This is how we do more with less. Some patrol officers and precinct commanders may not like CompStat and ILP because it means more supervision and control from above but it works and it's the future. There's no fighting it.

This officer went on to criticize the more centralized model of DHS-recognized fusion centers in terms consonant with the workfarist emphasis on flexibility and competitiveness:

> The fusion center idea is fantastic if everyone has equal investment, but that doesn't happen. Petty empires are gobbling up fusion centers, driving everyone away and ruining the partnerships. It is getting so one agency lords over and runs everyone else out. We don't make demands on the people that want to use us. "You need to send us two officers full time to be part of this." That kind of demand hurts collaboration. We have a business model and we try to excel at customer service so the customer will come back. It is like a McDonalds or Bennigans. Good service builds trust and trust creates real relationships.[63]

Although these sentiments are not universally shared and there is significant rank-and-file resistance to this new regime of labor discipline in police agencies, CompStat and ILP are the core of new relations between labor and management in police agencies.[64]

In New York State, moreover, the emphasis on measurability, results-based initiatives, and accountability associated with the CompStat and ILP are central to the way DCJS manages Operation IMPACT and its successor program, Gun-Involved Violence Elimination. These programs revolve around two kinds of meetings: monthly meetings among all the partners in a county, and irregular crime-trend meetings between the partnership and DCJS officials. The purpose of both meetings is to tighten the managerial control over police labor, statistically manage police resources, and hold executives accountable for their decisions. At the crime-trend meetings in Albany, all the partner agencies "get questioned." As the DJCS deputy commissioner explained, "They do a formal presentation and we will ask how probation is working with the police to address the following issue. We'll identify crimes that are up and ask them what they are doing to address it and how it's working. . . . These meetings are an opportunity to share ideas as well as hold everyone accountable."[65] For those on the other side of the table, the meetings are "a magnifying glass. . . . It's definitely a level of accountability that you don't necessarily have with other grant programs," a lieutenant deployed to a CAC told me. "For the analysts, sergeant and myself, it's very stressful. You're on pins and needles, especially if you're up in a crime type."[66] As CompStat and ILP become increasingly common, then, managerial oversight of police agencies intensifies. Internally, police executives use data and intelligence to determine deployments and hold middle management accountable, while, externally, grant-giving bodies can use the same techniques to encourage departments to adopt particular policies.

The broader politics of grants are the third means through which the institutionalization of intelligence fusion extends the logic of workfare to police agencies. Recalling chapters 2 and 3, the various grant programs that have facilitated the spread of fusion centers build on the example of the High-Intensity Drug Trafficking Area (HIDTA) program, which the a HIDTA administrator described as "an investment fund." Launched in 1990, HIDTA was an important point in ratcheting up the consolidation of the workfare-carceral state. Its grant-funded structure fostered competition between government agencies, and the policies it promoted advanced the drug war. Regarding workfare, HIDTA is less concerned with central regulation and the uniform application of programs than it is with cost effectiveness. "The idea is to build on existing efforts and relationships," the same HIDTA administrator. "We are building a decentralized network, not a central hub. . . . You also need some way to hold everyone accountable. That what's great about HIDTA. If a program is not producing results or using their money wisely, we're not going to fund it next year."[67]

Some of the funding mechanisms set up by DHS also replicate the HIDTA model. Of these, Urban Area Security Initiative (UASI) is the most important to fusion centers. The program designates thirty-nine urban areas and allocates funds to a program manager who disperses them on a competitive basis to different initiatives to "enhance . . . [the] capacity to prevent, protect against, mitigate, respond to, and recover from acts of terrorism." This program distributes substantial resources. In fiscal year 2014, for example, the total budget of UASI was $587 million, which included $178 million for the New York City Area UASI and a $22 million budget for the Newark/Jersey City Area UASI.[68] The federal official familiar with the Newark/Jersey City UASI described the initiative "as HIDTA for counterterrorism and urban security. I don't really know if it was designed with HIDTA in mind but, without a doubt, UASI brings the HIDTA approach to a different set of issues."[69] In an even more direct way, HIDTA informs Operation IMPACT. Key personnel from the NY/NJ HIDTA were also involved in the launch of Operation IMPACT. "We took a lot from HIDTA when we were designing Operation IMPACT. . . . It wouldn't be incorrect to call IMPACT a descendent of HIDTA."[70]

While these grant programs generally reorganize policing along the competitive and flexible lines of workfare, they also encourage and perhaps even coerce agencies to allocate budgets toward particular ends when the grants dry up or are withdrawn. This dynamic is clearly at work with National Network of Fusion Centers recognized by DHS. The federal government provided seed money to help set up the centers but does not provide "sustainment funding."[71] As table 4 shows, overall investment in the National Network of Fusion Centers has increased even as direct federal investments in fusion centers have declined.

In the aftermath of the Great Recession, this dynamic caused worries among fusion center directors. "Nationally, there is some concern about fusion centers closing their door, primarily in those USASI cities that don't receive USASI funding anymore," a senior NYSIC administrator explained. "Here in New York, we're not going away. We've leveraged from grant funding for specific homeland security programs, but I would venture that we'd support it with our state police budget if we needed to sustain those programs."[72] This situation can engender resentment among municipal police. As a police officer in a North Jersey city told me, "We're in the midst of fiscal crisis, OK? I mean we're laying off police officers in a city where a dozen, two dozen people are murdered each goddamn year. Does Christie— that stupid fat fuck—does he help us out? No, look what he's doing to Camden! I'm sure he wants to do it here too." Soon after, the lieutenant compared his department to the ROIC. "I don't think the State Police and their fancy fusion center are on the chopping block. I was there a few weeks ago. That fucking compound must cost millions and millions. They had dozens of people working there with brand new equipment and fancy fucking software. Over here, where people are killing each other, we can't even keep our guys employed."[73]

These deepening workfare arrangements reveal the shallowness of decarceration. This effort to reduce the prison population is not part of broader effort to address the sharp inequalities that define American society. Prison populations are dropping, but the break with mass incarceration is only in form, not in spirit. Decarceration is occurring as mass supervision is becoming a more prominent and visible strategy. In New York and New Jersey, the reduced prison populations are complemented by a series of intelligence-led manhunts: warrant sweeps, compliance checks, chronic-offender initiatives, and saturation patrols. These reforms in the criminal legal system, moreover, are not part of a broader shift in social policy. Indeed, the same changes enabling these aggressive ILP operations are also restructuring police agencies along market models. The extension of the logic of workfare over *the* core organ of the state, the physical monopoly on force, demonstrates the durability of the workfare-carceral state. Workfare continues its advance, and the punitive spirit of the carceral state remains, even if its edifice of imprisonment continues to crumble.

In the near term, these trends are clear. The increased prominence of mass supervision is systemic. The structural nature of this change is visible in the organic institutionalization of four types of intelligence-led manhunts in New York and New Jersey—despite the different institutional arrangements that enable intelligence fusion in both states and, as this chapter shows, the

TABLE 4. Total Funding for National Network of Fusion Centers, 2011–2016

Year	Federal Grants Expended	Direct Federal Expenditures	State	Local	Tribal	Territorial	Private Sector	Total
2011	$52,258,930	$97,456,195	$83,338,580	$34,144,222	no data	no data	no data	$267,197,927
2012	$71,219,656	$76,888,662	$90,980,473	$63,778,109	$0	$57,000	$1,293,000	$304,216,900
2013	$65,231,769	$69,653,432	$102,150,253	$70,304,104	$100,256	$153,658	$642,770	$308,236,242
2014	$73,499,366	$68,216,940	$113,297,136	$71,519,890	$0	$860,307	$892,685	$328,286,324
2015	$63,707,217	$68,502,223	$108,401,575	$79,519,890	$0	$937,064	$724,830	$321,432,687
2016	$72,225,816	$50,081,782	$111,581,875	$80,949,377	$0	$3,751,072	$698,330	$322,147,399
Percent Change	38.46%	−48.45%	33.73%	135.29%	NA	6480.83%	−46.99%	20.57%

SOURCE: Department of Homeland Security, *National Network of Fusion Centers: Final Report*, 2012, 2013, 2014, 2015, 2016.

unique histories behind each iteration of each program. Absent dramatic political push from below—the broad movement pressure identified by Gottschalk as a requisite for systemic change—this moment may well mark the stabilization of incarceration rates and the dramatic expansion of mass supervision around the logic of ILP and intelligence fusion. This outcome, however, is far from assured. Whether or not these arrangements are a glimpse of the future or a passing monster of a morbid moment will, of course, be determined by ongoing social struggles. An important factor to consider in this unfolding drama is the very state strategies used to regulate the social surplus and pacify class struggle. Indeed, policing and the wider administrative apparatus of the state do not simply enforce order. They also fabricate it. In this way, the state strategies deployed in this current moment of capitalist crisis and increasingly sharp political contention will do much to determine what arrangements emerge from this chaotic interregnum. For this reason, the final section of this book considers the ways fusion centers and ILP fabricate social order.

5. Beyond COINTELPRO

*Intelligence Fusion and Patchwork
Political Policing*

From 1956 through 1971, the FBI engaged in a counterintelligence campaign
to pacify social movements. Known as COINTELPRO, the program started to
"increase factionalism, cause disruption and win defections" within the
Communist Party USA. It soon targeted the newly formed Southern
Christian Leadership Conference, the civil rights organization led by Martin
Luther King Jr.[1] By the time the Citizen's Commission to Investigate the FBI
broke into an FBI field office, stole documents, and exposed the program, the
FBI was targeting every major left group in the United States.[2] No mere
surveillance program, COINTELPRO sought to "'expose, disrupt, misdirect,
discredit, or otherwise Neutralize'" its targets.[3] It used a strategy of escalation: first, infiltration (informants to gather information *and* to sow mistrust
and discord); second, psychological (planted stories, false communications
and pamphlets, and other efforts to discredit and divide); third, harassment
through the legal system (discriminatory enforcement of the tax code, grand
jury subpoenas, and other attempts to intimidate and waylay activists); and
finally, illegal force (break-ins, assault, and even assassination).[4]

   The full scope of the program is unclear. Officially, the FBI admitted to
2,218 separate COINTELPRO actions, many involving illegal activity, such
as warrantless phone taps, and break-ins.[5] These records, however, are a
partial account. Former FBI officials told Congress that the "most heinous
and embarrassing actions" were not put into writing.[6] Subsequent research
revealed that the FBI covered up its role in the assassination of Black
Panther Party (BPP) leaders and hid its extensive operations against the
Puerto Rican independence and Chicano movements from Congress.[7]
COINTELPRO was an incredibly successful pacification program. It is
implicated in the breakup of major organizations and coalitions. It fostered
tensions within the leadership of the BPP and Liberation News Service. It

eased the splits between the BPP and Student Nonviolent Coordinating Committee, and the Socialist Workers Party and various antiwar coalitions. It encouraged the open hostilities between the BPP and the US Organization, and stoked tensions between the Students for a Democratic Society and Women's Liberation Movement.[8] While other factors contributed to the decline of the movements of "the sixties," COINTELPRO undoubtedly played a significant role.

This impact is not lost on contemporary observers. Indeed, "the specter of COINTELPRO"—to quote the subtitle of one report on fusion centers—still haunts the politics of the United States.[9] On the left, many activists and commentators see fusion centers as "the most expansive surveillance network targeting radicals in the United States since the tumultuous days of the Federal Bureau of Investigation's (FBI's) COunter INTELligence PROgram" and the starting point for "neo-COINTELPRO operations."[10] On the right, radio personality Alex Jones claims that fusion centers are part of a larger "globalist" conspiracy. During the Obama administration, these concerns led a group of libertarian activists to create the now-defunct Liberty Restoration Project, and launch Operation Defuse, a nationwide tour of fusion centers and related political education events.[11] In the aftermath of the crackdown on Occupy Wall Street, some commentators even alleged that the president, Congress, DHS, and powerful corporate interests used the National Network of Fusion Centers to coordinate the crackdown on Occupy.[12]

While fusion centers are implicated in political policing, they are not federally directed like COINTELPRO, nor are they part of some all-encompassing conspiracy. These conclusions attribute too much coherence to the state and too much unity to elites. The state is not an instrument of repression that politicians and other elites can controlled in a direct and simple way. Instead, political struggles continually shape and reshape the character of state power. The nature of political policing in the United States today is the outcome of struggles. It is shaped by important conflicts within the state, like the intelligence reforms in the late 1970s, their post-9/11 rollback, and contemporary controversies over the designation of far-right groups as domestic terrorists. It also shifts in relation to struggles outside of the state, namely the rise and fall of left movements and the reactionary forces that challenge them.

In other words, the transformation of the *herrenvolk*-welfare state into the workfare-carceral state also transformed the dynamics of political policing. After the exposure of COINTELPRO and related scandals, Congress reformed the security apparatus to curtail abuses, while leaving space for a seemingly limited human rights compliant political policing. These reforms reaffirmed the legitimacy of the security apparatus, while legalizing many existing practices. Over time, human rights complaint political policing interacted with the increasing emphasis on "terrorism," and the wider workfarist reformation of the state apparatus to produce new patterns of political policing. Today, political policing operates through overlapping interagency intelligence networks, including the National Network of Fusion Centers. This decentralized model is more permeable to local political pressures. Indeed, private interests—not politicians or government officials—appear to be the leading actors in some of the most notorious recent examples of political policing, like the crackdown on Occupy and the showdown over the Dakota Access Pipeline. In many other cases, secrecy and organizational complexity complicate a clear parsing of events and actors. This decentralized system produces diverse outcomes, a patchwork of political policing. It is also harder to expose and redress than the highly centralized COINTELPRO program and, as a suppler system, may be a more effective means to pacify class struggle.

"HUMAN RIGHTS COMPLIANT" POLITICAL POLICING OF "TERROR IDENTITIES"

The COINTELPRO exposé was part of a larger day of reckoning for the security apparatus. By 1975, the scandals leading to Nixon's resignation compelled the Ford administration and Congress to act. Vice President Nelson Rockefeller led a special presidential commission to investigate the CIA. Congress created the Church Committee in the Senate and the Pike Committee in the House to launch the first sustained investigations into intelligence activities. The inquiries revealed much of what we know of the sordid dealings of the Cold War: coups and covert action, secret psychological research that produced the torture techniques now politely called "enhanced interrogation," and the varied military and intelligence efforts to surveil Americans and subvert political activities. After the investigations, Congress made the intelligence committees permanent. In 1978, legislators passed the Foreign Intelligence Service Act (FISA), creating a specialized surveillance court and erecting a "wall" that blocked information sharing between the law enforcement agencies, including most of the FBI, and the intelligence community.[13]

These changes only went so far. The investigations paradoxically relegitimized security agencies by demonstrating their apparent accountability, while simultaneously allowing controversial practices to continue by covering them with a patina of legality. The result was a seemingly limited version of human rights compliant political policing, a strategy that endeavors to protect political rights and facilitate peaceful protest while still combating "extremism."[14] As Kathryn Olmsted contends in her critical history of the investigations, the reforms "strengthen[ed] the agencies and the laws protect[ed] their secrecy." The response to domestic spying, for example, "was to make that spying legal."[15] Indeed, from 1979 to 2012, the FISA court rejected just 11 of approximately 33,900 warrant applications.[16] A similar process played out at the state and local level. During COINTELPRO, the FBI regularly worked with the intelligence units of local police. As discussed in chapter 2, these "red squads" had their origins in the pacification of labor struggles in the late nineteenth and early the twentieth centuries. They became less prominent in the conservative period after World War II. The recrudescence of radicalism in 1960s and 1970s, however, also brought a renaissance of red squads.[17]

Like the larger COINTELPRO program, the renewed red squads were partially self-defeating. Movements fought back. Kristian Williams explains:

So what kills a red squad? In Washington, D.C., it was a combination of lawsuits and pressure from city council. In Birmingham, it was the success of civil rights efforts, and the shift of power that accompanied it. Official investigations and a change in local statutes did in the Baltimore unit. A series of court rulings, a change in political climate, the election of a liberal mayor, attacks in the media, and a sudden loss of allies conspired against the red squad in Detroit. A series of scandals finally cost the Los Angeles unit the last of its credibility, leading to its break-up. In Philadelphia, it was the combination of a Federal Civil Rights Commission investigation, lawsuits, judicial rulings, and a loss of public support stemming from widespread corruption. In Seattle, a city ordinance outlawed the red squad's activities. In Memphis and Chicago, lawsuits produced consent decrees limiting political investigations. A change in political climate brought New York City a liberal mayor and police commissioner; combined with lawsuits, court rulings, and an overall loss of credibility, the change of administration spelled doom for the red squad.[18]

As with the investigations of the FBI and CIA, the death of red squads did not end political policing on the state and local levels. In New York City, for example, a 1971 class action suit against the NYPD led to the creation of the "Handschu guidelines," which created a three-person oversight committee to authorize investigations into political activity if the police could provide evidence of criminal activity.[19]

Overtime, the ambit of acceptable investigations gradually increased. This expansion happened through the construction of "terror identities," capacious categories that link together loosely affiliated or ideologically aligned individuals, movements, and events into a general category, which, in turn, justifies further intelligence gathering.[20] Terror identities are the antagonists within the prose of pacification. They are the "Invisible Power" that Neocleous, drawing on Hobbes's foundational writings on the state, sees as "permeat[ing] the whole problematic of security," creating a "category of the Enemy open to endless modification." In this paranoid domain of cultural production, the "function and status of that perennial propagator of banalities, the 'security expert', is thereby reinforced. . . . The emptiness also allows those same people to name and rename the Enemy." Hence, the very existence of intelligence analysts, police officers, academic security specialists, and others is predicated on the proliferation of terror identities, the subjects of an institutionalized body of expert knowledge that organizes the provisioning of "security." In a broader sense, "the abstract ghostly emptiness of the Enemy would also . . . demand[s] the permanent ghostly presence of the police power, that all-pervasive power that lies at the heart of the state."[21] For at least that last three decades, "terrorism" has been the "Enemy" in narratives that define the limits of legitimate politics and justify continuous pacification.

Starting the 1980s, the increasing emphasis on "terrorism" and the proliferation of other, more specific terror identities redefined political policing. The FBI's first Joint Terrorism Task Force (JTTF), an interagency group chaired by the FBI and charged with investigating "terrorism," was an important shift. Formed in New York City, the Taskforce partnered FBI agents with NYPD detectives. Their first targets included the Revolutionary Armed Taskforce, an urban guerilla force of former Weather Underground cadres operating under the leadership of the Black Liberation Army. After a robbery of a Brinks truck that resulted in the deaths of a guard and two police officers, the JTTF began an investigation that conflated dissent with terrorism. The taskforce searched for links between the urban guerillas and other organizations like the May 19th Communist Organization, another splinter of the Weather Underground. In this expanding investigation, the FBI described nonviolent actions like attending antiwar demonstrations and participating in sit-ins at South African Airways to protest apartheid as "terrorism."[22] This investigation into the militant fragments of the mass of movements of the "sixties" gave way to broader efforts against the new movements. Again, under the guise of the investigating terrorism, the FBI monitored groups criticizing government policy, including the Committee in Solidarity with the People of El Salvador, Witness for Peace, and AIDs Coalition to Unleash Power. They also investigated Jesse Jackson and the Plowshares movement for links to Libya and the Soviet Union.[23]

Starting in the late 1980s, JTTF investigations produced a new terror identity: "eco-terrorism," which—foreshadowing later "post-9/11" developments—provided the pretext for specialized legislation. The FBI focused on the radical environmental movement, first the Animal Liberation Front (ALF) and later Earth Liberation Front (ELF). Their efforts to sabotage, vandalize, and damage agribusinesses, construction projects, and similar sites prompted JTTF investigations, often entailing informers, infiltration, and entrapment. These investigations further refined "counterterrorism" as a state strategy. Almost a decade before the "war on terror," Congress passed the 1992 Animal Enterprise Protection Act, which created the crime "animal enterprise terrorism" and provided harsh sentencing guidelines, including life in prison. The arrests, convictions, and grand jury indictments piled up. Critics called it "the Green Scare."[24]

After 9/11, lawmakers further expanded the meaning of "terrorism," increased the state's "counterterrorism" capacities, and dismantled many post-COINTELPRO reforms. The 2001 Patriot Act created another terror identity: "domestic terrorism," defined as acts "dangerous to human life" that violate of the criminal law and are intended to intimidate or coerce civilians and influence government policy through intimidation, coercion, mass destruction, assassination, or kidnapping.[25] The Patriot Act dismantled "the FISA wall," allowing the FBI to collect information without evidence of criminal activity. It weakened the 1974 Privacy Act, limiting citizens' right to know what information agencies collected about them and freeing information to circulate among the FBI, Department of Homeland Security (DHS), state and local police, and fusion centers.[26] A similar rollback occurred at the state and local level. The New York Police Department (NYPD) went to court over the Handschu guidelines and won the power to initiate investigations for a year at a time and authorize undercover operations for four months without any evidence of criminal activity. The three-person advisory board lost its power to prevent NYPD investigations. Now, it could only investigate NYPD practices.[27] As this rollback occurred, "counterterrorism" capacities expanded. The FBI increased the number of JTTFs from 35 in 2001 to 56 in 2002 to 104 today.[28] Of course, Congress formed DHS, which set up the National Network of Fusion Centers.

The stage now seemed to be set for a new COINTELPRO: an expanded security apparatus animated by heightened fears of terrorism. This expectation, however, overlooks important changes. As a new element of the security apparatus and one constitutive of the workfare-carceral state, JTTFs decentralized state power and emphasized cost effectiveness. In contrast to the centrally directed COINTELPRO program, JTTFs "respond to terrorism leads" that other law enforcement agencies refer to them.[29] As taskforces, JTTFs bring together state, local, and federal agencies under the chairmanship of the FBI. This arrangement, which also characterizes fusion centers, allows the JTTF to "policy shop" or pick "from overlapping sets of laws" and avoid "privacy laws, open-records acts, and civil liability."[30] Specifically, state and local authorities assigned to JTTFs "are ostensibly acting as federal agents" freeing them from "the supervision of local authorities" and protecting their work within the envelope of FBI secrecy. "The FBI meanwhile can rely on other agencies to do the heavy lifting, thus avoiding the unseemly impression of excessive federal involvement."[31] A similar dynamic defines DHS-recognized fusion centers, which fall under the Code of Federal Regulations, Part 23. This statute prevents law enforcement from collecting or storing information in absence of "reasonable suspicion" of criminal activity.[32] Not all fusion center partners, however, operate under these restrictions, opening loopholes such as passing the investigation over to an FBI agent assigned to the fusion center. This decentralization and coordination, moreover, is not just a measure to get around post-COINTELPRO regulations. It is also a cost-saving mechanism. For example, JTTFs are "a cost-efficient structure of cooperation" that allows the FBI to leverage the resources of other agencies.[33]

Taken together, JTTFs and the National Network of Fusion Centers form a permeable system that different actors can operate through and mobilize toward different ends. The JTTFs direct attention upward, taking "terrorism leads" and, in cases like Operation Backfire targeting the ALF and ELF in 2005 and 2006, developing them into multistate investigations.[34] The National Network of Fusion Centers is a more horizontal network that empowers state and local police with advanced analytic capabilities. An important contrast to the more secretive and secure JTTFs, the fusion centers produce intelligence products for a wider scope of users, including the private sector. This arrangement opens them up to more pressures, further muddling the causality behind any episode of political policing. The taskforce organization—a reflection of the emphasis on structural competitiveness central to the workfare-carceral state—intensifies the scope and intensity of political struggles within the state, creates more opportunities for plausible deniability, muddles command hierarchies, and increases the likelihood of both dysfunction and abuse. The result is not a simple return to past patterns. Instead, there is real change: a decentralized patchwork of human rights compliant political policing.

FUSION CENTERS AND THE PATCHWORK
OF POLITICAL POLICING

Journalists began uncovering fusion centers' role in monitoring political activities almost as soon as soon as state and local governments began to form the interagency intelligence hubs. The targets of surveillance included a patchwork of political positions: anarchists and the anti-globalization movement, anti-death-penalty campaigners, antiwar groups, Black Lives Matter, environmentalists, immigrant rights advocates, indigenous activists, LGBTQ advocates, libertarians, militias, Occupy Wall Street, pro-life and pro-choice activists, and third-party supporters, among others.[35] The majority of these incidents simply involved gathering information and entering it into various databases. In other cases, often related to specific protest actions, authorities actively subverted political activity. All these examples fit the model of human rights compliant political policing, where law enforcement monitors political activities for "situational awareness" and, under the rubric of different terror identities, investigates ostensibly only to prevent violence.

The "Maryland Spy Scandal" and the known instances of monitoring Black Lives Matter are good examples of surveillance without disruption. A 2008 investigation by the Maryland attorney general revealed that the Maryland State Police, in 2005 and 2006, labeled fifty-three people associated with a variety of progressive causes as "terrorists" or "security threats." Police entered their information into the databases of two intelligence hubs, including Maryland's fusion center. The eventual investigation required the data to be deleted. Despite fears of being included in "terror watch lists" that would restrict their movements, none of the fifty-three activists reported any difficulties traveling.[36] All documented examples of fusion centers' surveillance of Black Lives Matter also fit this pattern of monitoring, often at a distance and through social media.[37] When infiltrators have been involved, they have not been connected to fusion centers, nor is there evidence that they were agent provocateurs intent on sowing mistrust among activists or pushing people into incriminating action. Strict informants, their involvement has been limited to intelligence collection.[38]

A few of these incidents, however, included attempted subversion of political activity. Consider the preemptive arrests before the 2008 Republic National Convention (RNC) in St. Paul, Minnesota. In anticipation of the convention, the Minnesota Joint Analysis Center (MNJAC), the statewide fusion center, "carried out 'over 1,000 hours of support to intelligence operations' and 'disseminated approximately 17 RNC situation reports to over 1,300 law enforcement recipients.'" During the lead-up to the RNC, detectives with the Ramsey County Sheriff's Department viewed a satirical

YouTube video posted by the RNC Welcoming Committee, a small anarchist group. The video featured what one journalist called "juvenile satire of popular anarchist imagery" such as using a dummy Molotov cocktail to light a charcoal grill. This seemingly innocuous video prompted "a $300,000 investigation." An undercover officer and two informants infiltrated the group.[39] Two days before the RNC, the Sheriff's Department raided three houses and arrested five activists with the RNC Welcoming Committee. Deputies arrested one more activist later in the day and two others the day of the convention. The group, dubbed the "RNC 8," was charged with "conspiracy to riot in furtherance of terrorism."[40] One member of the group accepted a plea deal that landed a ninety-one-day sentence. The other seven went to trial. They accepted a gross misdemeanor charge that carried no jail time after the judge dismissed all felony charges.[41]

While MNJAC clearly was involved in wholesale surveillance of activists leading up to the RNC, the role of the fusion center in the infiltration of the RNC Welcoming Committee is unclear, as is the sequence of events that culminated with the preemptive arrest of the RNC 8. The incident was part of a larger effort to pacify the protest. Authorities arrested eight hundred protesters during the RNC (only seventeen received criminal convictions).[42] Prior to the convention, DHS designated the RNC as a National Security Special Event, requiring the Secret Service and a local agency, the St. Paul Police Department, to coordinate security. They established a Multi-Agency Communication Center (MACC), a temporary intelligence center staffed by representatives from fifty-five different government agencies and private sector organizations. The resultant "Civil Disturbance Management Plan" named the MACC as "the primary communication center" and "not a command center." As with other security taskforces, agency representatives "must be able to continually liaison between MACC and their home agency" and "will maintain their respective command and control."[43] In this context and absent evidence to the contrary, the infiltration of the RNC Welcoming Committee may be what journalists presented it as: an independent operation of the Sheriff's Department.

The policing of the 2008 RNC parallels another lower-profile incident involving the Connecticut Intelligence Center (CTIC):

> On January 3, 2007, [Kenneth] Krayeske was taking photographs of
> Connecticut Governor M. Jodi Rell at her inaugural parade. He was not
> engaged in protest at the time. While serving as the manager of the
> Green Party's gubernatorial candidate, he had publicly challenged
> Governor Rell over the issue of why she would not debate his candidate.
> At the parade, police promptly arrested Krayeske (after he took 23
> photographs) and later charged him with "Breach of Peace" and

"Interfering with Police." [The CTIC] had conducted a threat assessment for the event and had circulated photographs of Krayeske and others to police in advance. . . . The person who read Krayeske his Miranda rights and attempted to interview him in custody was Andrew Weaver, a sergeant for the City of Hartford Police Department who *also* works in the CTIC fusion center.[44]

It is not clear in whether Weaver was acting as a member of the Hartford Police Department or a CTIC representative when he questioned Krayeske. When he arrested Krayeske, was he acting on his own accord or following orders? During the preliminary stages of my research, I interviewed a CTIC official, who denied any involvement in what she called "the Krayeske matter."[45] In response to an open-records request for the inaugural parade threat assessment, the CTIC's parent agency released a reply to an earlier request from Krayeske that stated that there were no responsive documents.[46]

While both incidents involved fusion centers, the pattern is not unique to them. They reflect the changing dynamics of protest policing that developed to pacify the anti-globalization movement. This new approach was clarified to the world during the demonstrations against the 2004 meeting of the Free Trade Area of the Americas in Miami, Florida. This "Miami model" took the "hard" approach to protest, escalated force, and synthesized it with the "soft" negotiated management model. The "hard" measures evident in the arrest of the RNC 8—infiltration, police raids, preemptive and mass arrests—are supplemented by "soft" mechanisms such as the permit negotiations that constrain protest, public relations campaigns to smear protesters as disorderly or otherwise burdensome, and the intimidating presence of massive deployments police in riot gear.[47] In this new paradigm, escalated force and negotiated management are not separate models so much as distinct poles in a continuum.

The Miami model was a response to changing movement strategy. In his study of protest policing, Luis Fernandez argues that "modes of repression always follow innovations in resistance." As anarchist tendencies influenced the anti-globalization movement, protesters rejected the permit process. Police agencies responded by adopting disciplinary quarantines: containing protests far from the center of activity in rural areas and, in urban areas, tracking protests with mobile police teams and "kettling" or corralling demonstrations with mobile police squads.[48] When discussing the parallelism between protesters and police, however, Fernandez focuses on mobilization of activists and the physical deployment of police forces. He does not consider organizations. If the current era of social movements are "leaderless" and horizontally organized, do fusion centers represent the emergence of an equally decentralized political policing? The response to Occupy Wall Street, the claims made about it, and documents subsequently released to civil liberties organizations provide the necessary perspective on this question.

A VARIEGATED CRACKDOWN

Occupy was a surprise success. The initial, audacious encampment in Manhattan's financial district inspired nearly a thousand allied actions in eighty-two different countries in just two months.[49] By February 2012, however, police forces had forcibly removed most occupations. Despite some attempts to "reoccupy" parks, police had completely driven Occupy out of public spaces by June 2012. In the process and related protest actions, authorities arrested 7,775 people.[50] In November 2011, following the eviction of occupations in Denver, Portland, Salt Lake City, Oakland, and Manhattan, all within a ten-day span, many wondered whether the federal government coordinated the crackdown. Writing in *The Guardian*, Naomi Wolf alleged that DHS, under direct orders from members of Congress and President Obama, organized the evictions.[51] The article resonated and generated debate: a million people viewed it in three days, a thousand commented on *The Guardian*'s webpage, nearly a quarter of a million shared it on social media.[52] Following the release of documents to the Partnership for Civil Justice Fund (PCJF), a civil liberties organization, Wolf implicated fusion centers in her conspiracy.[53] Drawing on the same documents, Dave Lindorff concluded that the National Operations Center, a national fusion center connected to the White House Situation Room, organized the crackdown.[54] Both Wolf and Lindorff pointed to reports of two conference calls involving mayors and police executives as evidence of DHS coordination. In subsequent months, DHS, FBI and the National Park Service released over four thousand pages of documents to PCJF.

These records do not support the allegations of a federally directed attack on Occupy. No documents implicate President Obama or any member of Congress in the response to Occupy. Most of the records are emails addressing media inquiries about DHS's attitude toward Occupy. Lindorff's argument hinges on an email message from an employee of the DHS Office of Internal Affairs:

> Since these protests are lawfully protected First Amendment activities, we are treating all "Occupy" demonstrations as peaceful. We are working with [General Services Administration] and each city government to ensure that all parties concerned are safe and secure.

When a protest area on federal property is deemed unsanitary or unsafe by GSA or a city, we work with those officials to develop a plan to evacuate the participants in a safe manner.

We have held standard coordination calls and face-to-face meetings with our partners to ensure that the proper resources are available for operations such as street closures, etc. The only eviction [Federal Protection Services] has been involved with was assisting the Portland Police Bureau at the federally-owned Terry Schrunk Plaza where FPS arrested two people.[55]

Lindorff interprets this message as an oblique admission of a coordinated crackdown. At the time, it was easy to jump to this conclusion. The near-simultaneous eviction of multiple Occupy encampments provided an impression of a highly coordinated and repressive state. The PCJF documents, moreover, do provide ample evidence of the surveillance of Occupy, including military and private sector participation in the monitoring.[56] In the heady days of Occupy's charismatic moment, it was tempting to take these documents, make a few leaps, and resuscitate J. Edgar Hoover in the guise of then-DHS Secretary Janet Napolitano.

Such allegations, however, attribute too much coherence to the state, erase the dysfunction and conflict internal to the state apparatus, and downplay the fundamental indeterminacy of politics. Many of the documents show confusion within DHS: a group of government bureaucrats struggling to address what was obviously not part of the routine. On the federal level, the DHS took a limited role, and, repeating the mantras of human rights–compliant political policing, redirected requests for information to fusion centers. As one DHS official explained

We have received a number of questions and requests for information regarding Occupy Wall Street from a number of component partners and intelligence officers. Recognizing that this is a first amendment protected activity, we have recommended (on an ad hoc basis when we received requests) that our Intelligence Officers refer inquiries to Fusion Centers and avoid the topic altogether.[57]

When these requests arrived at fusion centers, some explained that they deliberately chose not to monitor Occupy. An officer at Delaware's fusion center, for example, responded to an inquiry from another fusion center by explaining that "[o]ur fusion center has distanced itself from the movement because of 1st Amendment rights and because we have not seen any criminal activity to date."[58]

My research sites New Jersey Regional Operations Intelligence Center (ROIC) and the New York State Intelligence Center (NYSIC) showed the same dynamics in play. Senior personnel at both sites claimed to respect the constitutional rights and reported on Occupy only for "officer safety" and "situational awareness." Officials at the ROIC acknowledged monitoring the "Occupy Highway" march from New York City to Washington, D.C., in November 2011. As one ROIC administrator explained:

> We were monitoring the traffic to make sure [Department of Transit] and our constituents that operate the highway know that there will be significant delays. We made sure to add the caveat that they had their first amendment rights to do this. So as long as they weren't endangering anyone, there was nothing law enforcement could do but direct traffic and tell people to expect delays. It was all in the wording. We don't infiltrate them. That's the biggest thing. We're not even monitoring them to figure out what they are doing.[59]

The only reports from the ROIC in the PCJF collection corroborate these claims.[60]

While also speaking in terms of human rights compliant political policing, comments from NYSIC command suggest that they *may* have taken a more active role in relation to Occupy. As one NYSIC administrator explained:

> We are aware of them from an officer safety perspective and that is the only reason we ever look at any type of demonstrations but we, as the fusion center, are not necessarily monitoring the Occupy events. When criminal activity starts to happen, that's a different story. When people start getting arrested for disorderly conduct and trespassing and so forth, we start to monitor it a bit more. . . . Our effort, when it came to Occupy, was very minimal, situational awareness only. We want to be aware. It could be Occupy. It could be a different group. We are interested in letting law enforcement know if there is going to be demonstrations and what they will look like: How many people? Whether it's permitted or unpermitted. What's their intent? Do they have a history of violence? Do they have a criminal history? Are there known persons of interests who will be at this demonstration?[61]

Another officer in a management position at the NYSIC reiterated this point:

> They have a right say whatever they want. They have a right to be assholes. We are not going to look at them until it becomes criminal or until they cross the line and act like extremists. That's when we are going to be interested. People have the right to protest about whatever moves them. Those are their beliefs. Those are the ideologies that they carry. They want to tell the world about it. Have at it, but we're going to

be focused in to determine whether they are going to commit crimes in furtherance of that stuff. That's where we become interested.[62]

While these comments suggest that the NYSIC was more inclined to monitor Occupy than the ROIC, there are no publicly available documents that confirm this possibility.

Across the country, responses to Occupy varied. Occupy Providence negotiated their departure from Burnside Park, leaving when the city opened a day shelter for the homeless.[63] Occupy Albany, while it was eventually evicted, lasted until late December 2011, largely because the district attorney defied the governor and refused to prosecute any arrests for nonviolent civil disobedience.[64] On the other end of the spectrum, Arizona's fusion center, the Arizona Counter Terrorism Information Center (ACTIC), became the center of an aggressive effort to monitor, infiltrate, and disrupt Occupy Phoenix. Importantly, however, the ACTIC became a vessel for private interests: the American Legislative Exchange Council (ALEC), a nonprofit organization that brings together state legislators and representatives of corporations like Exon Mobile, Koch Industries, and Pfizer, among many others, to collaborate on draft legislation for state legislatures.

In Arizona, ALEC became controversial for its role in the drafting of Support Our Law Enforcement and Safe Neighborhoods Act. Also known as Arizona Senate Bill (SB) 1070, the legislation mandated that all resident aliens carry proof of legal residence or face a misdemeanor charge. It also required law enforcement officers to attempt to determine immigration status during a stop, detention, or arrest. Critics viewed it as legalized racial profiling. Moreover, the two largest private prison corporations—GeoGroup and the Corrections Corporation of America (known as CoreCivic since October 2016)—were ALEC members when SB 1070 became law. Since Immigration and Customs Enforcement mostly contracts out the work of immigration detention, these firms directly profited from the bill. Reflecting the broader movement's desire to limit corporate power, Occupy Phoenix identified SB 1070 and ALEC's role in state politics as a major issue. In this context, ACTIC, the state's fusion center, assigned an officer to monitor Occupy Phoenix and liaise with ALEC. The ACTIC provided ALEC with intelligence reports on the movement, including a "face sheet" of persons of interests who planned direct actions to disrupt an ALEC conference in Scottsdale, Arizona. To pacify the protest, ALEC contracted off-duty Phoenix Police Department officers, who violated department policy by providing uniformed security at the events. Armed with ACTIC reports, the moonlighting officers preemptively arrested "persons of interest" for trespassing.[65]

These divergent responses to Occupy protests illustrate the historical transformation of the security apparatus, one consonant with the larger change from the *herrenvolk*-welfare state to the workfare-carceral state. J. Edgar Hoover personally directed COINTELRPO and reviewed every operation. On several occasions, FBI special officers in charge (SACs) wanted to discontinue a program area because specific movement categories, such as New Left or Black Power, did not exist in their jurisdiction. Hoover never approved any such requests. This intransience compelled SACs "to avoid censure by identifying 'worthy' targets in the absence of political protest through the construction of deviance narratives that connect[ed] subversion to visible personal characteristics." With no organized New Left activity to subvert, for example, FBI agents focused on "homosexuality and Jewishness" to explain "the 'spoiled' and 'non-conformist' tendencies of various affluent college students" who sympathized with New Left causes and adopted the aesthetic of the counterculture but were not actively organized.[66] This centralization was COINTELPRO's undoing. When activists exposed COINTELPRO, the paper trail clearly implicated Hoover.

In contrast, a decentralized, variegated crackdown pacified Occupy Wall Street (OWS). At each site, the participating agencies and pressures from more external forces such as local politicians and corporations produced different dynamics. In some instances, for example, Providence or Albany, local politics constrained police in ways that gave Occupy more leeway. In others, as in Phoenix, corporate power operated through and mobilized the fusion center to crush the movement. These arrangements also produced the seemingly coordinated crackdown on several encampments in November 2011. The conference calls highlighted by Wolf and Lindorff as evidence of federal direction were not organized DHS or the FBI. Instead *private* associations—the National Conference of Mayors and the Police Executive Research Forum—took the lead.[67]

The fact that these nominally private organizations are made up of public officials further underscores the particular context of the workfare-carceral state. In this institutional order, national agencies lose some power to local agencies and "stakeholders" from business and civil society, including organizations such as those that orchestrated the infamous conference calls. Yet the national state has not disappeared. Instead, it directs and facilitates "governance" across and between administrative levels.[68] Hence, the DHS secretary does not have the ability to control fusion centers or even select their directors. Instead, DHS helped define the policy framework within which fusion centers operate, while also facilitating the flow of information through the National Network of Fusion Centers. As the newest federal department and one established in the era of the workfare-carceral state, DHS is—*by its very design*—incapable of centrally planning the Occupy crackdown. Unlike SACs in Hoover's FBI, fusion center directors are not federal employees, nor are they managed by the DHS secretary. Instead, they are officers of the state or local police department that DHS recognizes as the lead agency at a given fusion center. Operationally independent from DHS, fusion center directors work within the loose framework of "recommendations" and "baseline capabilities."[69]

The reorganization of the state's institutional apparatus through competitive mechanisms means that different agencies are compelled to fight for their own financial and organizational well-being.[70] These dynamics increase the scope, intensity, and stakes of the struggles within the state. They make political processes more indeterminate and expand the range of potential outcomes immanent in this historical moment. A product of the era of monopoly capitalism largely contained within state boundaries, the centralized *herrenvolk*-welfare state, narrowed the state's response to political challenges as seen in the uniform aggressiveness of COINTELPRO. In contrast, the contemporary workfare-carceral state, a reflection of increasingly globalized capital and the related extension of commodification and competition to all aspects of life, has reorganized the work of political policing on a market models. In this environment, fusion centers tailor their services in response to the unique needs of their local partners. For political policing, this arrangement creates a range of potential outcomes, where some political struggles, such as Occupy Providence, are resolved with the velvet glove of negotiated management and others, such as Occupy Phoenix, feel the iron hand of escalated force. This situation is fundamentally ambiguous and indeterminate. Are incidents of political policing examples of overzealous officers empowered to act independently? Is there direction by elites in government or the private sector? When COINTELRPO was exposed, the answers to these questions were clear. The Occupy files do not contain similar revelations.

ESCALATED POLITICAL POLICING AND SEEMING STATE CAPTURE

In the years since the rise and fall of Occupy and the first mobilizations to chant the refrain "Black Lives Matter," there have been two important developments: one, the confrontations among police, protesters, and counterprotesters have intensified; and two, Donald Trump's presidency marks a new political conjuncture that, at least in the short term, is more conducive to political policing. This political shift, however, cannot be reduced to Trump's surprising victory. While it may appear that the fossil fuel sector and white supremacists have "captured" the security apparatus, these seeming shifts began during the Obama administration. These ongoing struggles, both within and outside the state, underscore an important point, even if the immediacy of events and the secrecy that surrounds them prevents a full accounting. The state is not a "thing" to be seized by particular interested and mobilized to particular ends. It is an ever-shifting condensation of power relations. The decentralized and competitive nature of the workfare-carceral state has produced a patchwork of political policing, which creates new opportunities for local political forces to escalate or constrain political policing. The general intensification of class struggle since the Great Recession and the renewal of protest do not just produce more aggressive political policing. They also intensify struggles within the state apparatus.

The pacification of the mobilization against the Dakota Access Pipeline (DAPL) is a clear escalation of previous patterns. In the spring of 2016, the Standing Rock Sioux began to organize against the DAPL, which would cut through their lands and endanger water supplies. The effort eventually drew thousands to the area, including representatives from at least three hundred indigenous nations, making it the largest gathering of Native American peoples in more than a century. The "water protectors," as the protesters became known, assembled in three encampments and launched direct actions to stop construction. As with the 2008 RNC and other mass protest actions, numerous government entities came together to form a temporary taskforce to pacify the protests. In this case, the FBI, Bureau of Indian Affairs, US Marshals, and the US Attorney's Office for North Dakota, and state and local police, including North Dakota's fusion center, North Dakota State and Local Intelligence Center (NDSLIC) created an "Intelligence Group" to provide real-time monitoring and a coordinated response. Importantly, TigerSwan—a security contractor hired by Energy Transfer Partners, the firm building the pipeline, to provide security on the construction site—also joined the taskforce.

Best known for its work in US-occupied Iraq and Afghanistan, TigerSwan quickly became a dominant and aggressive force in the Intelligence Group. As documents obtained by journalists Alleen Brown, Will Parrish, and Alice Speri show, TigerSwan led the effort to pacify protest.[71] With echoes of COINTELPRO-style countersubversion, the security contractor went beyond monitoring and sought to exploit "ongoing native versus non-native rifts, and tribal rifts between peaceful and violent elements" in order to "delegitimize the anti-DAPL movement."[72] TigerSwan complemented these efforts with psychological warfare, euphemistically called a "social engagement plan," to "protect the reputation of DAPL."[73] No mere public relations push, this work also included arresting journalists and imposing a no-fly zone over the protest encampments.[74] As the demonstration continued, repression ratcheted up. In September, private security sicced dogs on protesters obstructing the bulldozing of a sacred site. In October, riot police used tasers, pepper spray, beanbag rounds, and sound cannons to disperse a blockade that had stopped traffic for days. In the process, they arrested 127 demonstrators. In November, they sprayed protesters with fire hoses in below-freezing weather and shot tear gas and rubber bullets to clear protesters who were blocking a bridge. Over 300 people received treatment for hypothermia, and 26 were hospitalized.[75]

These escalating confrontations punctuated the daily intelligence gathering. The camps were subject to aerial surveillance and penetrated by infiltrators and informants. In addition, NDSLIC analysts trolled social media and mined databases to create reports that the Intelligence Group reviewed in daily meetings at the emergency operations center in Bismarck, the state capitol. One of these analyses was a network analysis that included Red Fawn Fallis, a water protector who was singled out by police and arrested in an October confrontation. During the arrest, officers wrestled Fallis to the ground, where they claim she fired three shots from a revolver. Parrish later reported that the owner of the gun, Heath Harmon, was a paid FBI informant that infiltrated the protest encampment and entered a romantic relationship with Fallis.[76] By the time security forces cleared the encampment in February 2017, police arrested nearly five hundred protestors, six of whom, including Fallis, faced felony charges.[77]

The pacification of the anti-DAPL protest is an intensification of the most aggressive measures used to disrupt Occupy. Akin to the response to Occupy Phoenix, the confrontations between security forces and water protectors show how private interests operate through and mobilize fusion center networks. In an apparent escalation from the Occupy crackdown, fossil fuel interests continued to work through fusion centers after the disruption of the anti-DAPL demonstrations. Indeed, TigerSwan's efforts to pacify the Standing Rock encampments grew into what Brown, Parrish, and Speri described as a "multistate dragnet." The security contractor monitored another protest camp in Iowa, and tracked two activists who sabotaged the pipeline in North Dakota and Iowa.[78] After security forces dispersed the protests in North Dakota, TigerSwan targeted what they called the "Anti-DAPL diaspora," monitoring other protests against pipeline construction and demonstrations opposing the then-incoming Trump administration in Illinois, Iowa, Minnesota, Oklahoma, Oregon, Pennsylvania, South Dakota, and Texas.[79] These efforts were not frictionless. One document noted tensions between TigerSwan and law enforcement in Iowa, where, "Calhoun, Boone and Webster county law enforcement are not supportive of DAPL Security's mission" because they were reluctant "to arrest or cite trespassing individuals."[80] TigerSwan's leading role and the tensions between the security contractor and some police agencies mark the episode as a discreet instance of pacification, another piece in the patchwork of contemporary political policing.

As the policing of Occupy and the DAPL illustrate, fusion centers are not *the* center of political policing. They are a channel through which particular interests can flow. Fusion centers advance specific class interests by providing conduits for terror identities and the prose of pacification to circulate. After the showdown at Standing Rock, for example, fusion center analysts produced intelligence products that accepted TigerSwan's analysis of movements opposing the construction of fossil fuel infrastructure. For example, the DHS Office of Intelligence and Analysis (I&A) jointly produced an intelligence report with fusion centers in Iowa, Illinois, North Dakota, Montana, South Dakota, and Washington that detailed the "targeting, tactics, and procedures" used to pacify "suspected environmental rights extremists."[81] The NDSLIC collaborated with another DHS-recognized fusion center, the Central Florida Information Exchange, to draft an assessment on impact the anti-DAPL movement was having on the Sabal Trail Pipeline, a natural gas conduit constructed in Alabama, Georgia, and Florida during 2016 and 2017.[82] Fusion centers in Oklahoma, Arkansas, and Tennessee also partnered with DHS I&A to report on the threat of "environmental rights extremists" to the Diamond Pipeline, project constructed in those three states in 2016 and 2017.[83]

Fusion centers are an institutional network within a larger security apparatus that spans the seeming divides of public-private and foreign-domestic. This is further underscored by the "militarized" institutional culture that suffuses security agencies, regardless of their jurisdiction. TigerSwan products used the language of "find, fix, and eliminate"—a clear allusion to the terminology of "find, fix, finish" used "abroad" by drone operators and Special Forces. This is not the first time this language has been used to organize a pacification project within the United States. As a fusion center intelligence analyst with a background in military intelligence told me years before the showdown at Standing Rock, "In the military, it is find, fix, finish. That's what we do. We can try and blend some of the mind-set but here we are talking find, fix, turn. Can we develop informants?"[84] These rhetorical affinities reveal the way that the prose of pacification both animates this institutional apparatus of the state and resides within it.

As political struggles wax and wane, the practices and knowledges that organize administration, the prose of pacification, can be either discredited—and, potentially, purged from institutional memory—or freed to circulate unhindered. The reforms that followed the 1975 investigations sullied the security apparatus, but they failed to displace the prose of pacification as the logic animating administration. Instead, they retrenched the prose of pacification in modified form, what this chapter has described in the "domestic" context as human rights compliant political policing. The Reagan administration's attacks on its political enemies, the FBI's campaigns against radical environmentalists, the post-9/11 period were all moments where the prose of pacification metastasized, increasing the currency of terror identities and expanding state capacity to pacify class struggle and administer poverty. The current conjuncture appears to be a similar moment.

Undoubtedly, Trump's election created a more permissive climate for political policing. In the lead up to the inauguration, police in Washington, D.C., infiltrated DisruptJ20, an umbrella coalition that planned a series of direct actions to disrupt the inauguration and related events. The DC Superior Court later indicted 214 protesters on felony riot charges.[85] In the weeks immediately following the inauguration, moreover, officers connected to a JTTF interviewed three anti-DAPL protesters.[86] While it is unclear whether the interviews were part of a broader investigation, this incident joined a cascade of similar reports detailing intensifying political policing. On August 9, 2017, the FBI released an intelligence assessment predicting an "increase in premeditated, retaliatory lethal violence against law enforcement" by "Black Identity Extremists."[87] This new terror identity appears in fusion center products. In an undated "Domestic Extremism Threat Update" produced between April and August 2017, the Northern California Regional Intelligence Center named five groups as "Black Identity Extremists."[88]

This new terror identity becomes even more suggestive when placed in its broader context. The FBI released the report nine days before the "Unite the Right" rally in Charlottesville, Virginia, which brought together white supremacist and fascist organizations in a torch-lit march where participants chanted "white lives matter," "Jews will not replace us," and the Nazi slogan "blood and soil." The two-day demonstration climaxed with street fighting between the protestors and counter-protestors that resulted in thirty-eight injuries and one death, caused by a white supremacist who rammed his car into a crowd. After the deadly confrontations, many criticized the tepid police response. Although approximately one thousand officers were present at the protest, they stood aside and let the clashes work themselves out. In the lead up to the demonstration, moreover, Solidarity Cville, a grassroots media collaborative, presented evidence to city officials that rally organizers were planning violent action, an intention openly broadcast on social media. The Virginia Fusion Center did not report on these public threats. Instead, they worked with DHS I&A to issue an assessment three days before the rally that predicted likely "domestic terrorist violence" but focused mostly on a different terror identity: "anarchist extremists."[89] Charlottesville is not an isolated incident. Journalists uncovered similar episodes in California, where "police investigating a violent white nationalist event worked with white supremacists in an effort to identify counter-protesters and sought the prosecution of activists with 'anti-racist' beliefs."[90]

At first glance, the pacification of anti-DAPL protests and clashes in Charlottesville suggest that fossil fuel interests and white supremacists have "captured" key pieces of the security apparatus. In a certain sense, this may well describe what is happening under the Trump administration. However, this conclusion fails to consider the specificity of the workfare-carceral state. As explained in this chapter and previous ones, the decentralized and competitive nature of this state-form increases the scope and intensity of struggles within the state, making particular pieces of the state apparatus more susceptible to local political inclinations. In this context, what happened at Standing Rock or Charlottesville cannot be generalized without further investigation. Indeed, the over two thousand pages of documents concerning FBI, DHS, and fusion center reporting on contemporary movements obtained by journalists contains countless intelligence reports that define white supremacists as threats. On May 10, 2017, for example, DHS and FBI released a Joint Intelligence Bulletin titled "White Supremacist Extremism Poses Persistent Threat of Lethal Violence." The report, based on an assessment of sixteen years of white supremacist violence, concludes that white supremacists remain a threat, and are most likely to target racial minorities with "lone wolf" attacks.[91] An assessment produced by DHS and Nevada's two fusion centers on sovereign citizen and militia extremists as the most likely domestic terrorism threat to Nevada.[92] Other reports document the far-right organization's recruitment efforts, symbols, and violent clashes at demonstrations. In short, many in fusion centers and the wider security apparatus clearly see white supremacists and other far-right movements as "domestic terrorists." What do these reports mean in relation to other instances where police have ignored or even collaborated with far-right groups?

STRUGGLES WITHIN THE SECURITY APPARATUS

The seeming hesitancy of the security apparatus to target the far-right more aggressively can be traced two sources: the constraints of human rights compliant political policing, and the internal struggle within state around the far-right and their efforts to infiltrate the security apparatus. Human rights compliant political policing treats all political activity the same, regardless of its content. White supremacists advocating genocide and an ethnostate have the same rights to freedom of speech and assembly as leftist calling for a borderless world and a transition to socialism. This ethos is entrenched in police agencies. It was even put forward as official policy, when I observed a January 2013 Fusion Liaison Officer training conducted by one of the senior managers at the ROIC.[93] The section of the training on civil liberties demonstrated a high degree of self-awareness. The officer explained many of the concerns with fusion centers, citing the 2007 ACLU report on the subject.[94] He then discussed how the ROIC dealt with large protest actions. He referenced their monitoring of Occupy to show how limited reporting for situational awareness and officer safety was appropriate but anything more would have violated constitutional rights and ROIC's privacy policy. He also brought up a 2011 Neo-Nazi rally in Trenton as an example. While the trooper presented Occupy in a neutral tone, he described Neo-Nazis as "scum" and "the worst people you can possibly imagine." However, he noted that their protest was permitted and, even though the rally was advocating odious positions, the fusion center could only take the same limited measures they took toward Occupy. With both examples, the intended point was that investigation required a "nexus" to crime or terrorism.

During my interviews and observations at the ROIC, several interviewees explained how these policies limited intelligence analysis. For example, law enforcement across the country are concerned with sovereign citizens, a far-right movement that believes citizens are subject only to "natural law." Sovereign citizens have attacked officers, sometimes in situations that escalated from routine encounters. "It's an officer safety issue;" one officer explained, "These guys make their own licenses and think the law doesn't apply to them. They'll snap and shoot at officers."[95] Of the 163 ROIC products I obtained, 31 report on "sovereign citizen." These references, however, are limited to brief mentions of contacts such "Identified male claimed to be a sovereign citizen, fought with the police, and was arrested in Linden, New Jersey" or "An identified male responded to a request for payment by the [New Jersey Transit Authority] and refused to pay the tolls using Sovereign Citizen rhetoric in Lincoln Park, NJ."[96] Analysts complained that they could not compile a comprehensive report on sovereign citizens. "We could put together a nice product to give background on sovereign citizens. Cops should be familiar with their rhetoric and common behaviors but management doesn't want to go anywhere near anything in-depth like that. It's too controversial."[97]

Similar dynamics were also evident with fusion center reporting on left movements. One ROIC analyst objected to the heavy edits to their report on anarchists:

> Over last year, there was a lot of panic about Occupy. Are anarchists violent? I did an analysis that said basically, "Calm down, there is no indication that anarchists in New Jersey are violent or are planning any violent actions. They are few in number and basically irrelevant." That sort of negative reporting is valuable. Every time you hear about a protest at a local university don't activate the SWAT team and be concerned.[98]

The officer supervising the analysts saw value in the product but also found reasons to be concerned:

> The tricky part of the project was, unless they were doing something criminal and it was documented, you couldn't really report on them. . . . If you're reporting that they are assembling, it presumes that the assembling is illegal. . . . We went back and forth on it a lot on that product. . . . I'm not trying to get us in the front page of the *Star-Ledger*. This is America. These people have the right to believe whatever they want."[99]

Taken together, the police managing fusion centers respond to radicals on the right and left in the same way: they fear bad press and hew close to the law. This dynamic provides perspective on Charlottesville. When left counter-protesters disrupt a white supremacist rally, this registers as an attack on white supremacists' right of assembly. After all, the title of the controversial intelligence report on "anarchist extremists" released days before the Unite the Right Rally was "Domestic Terrorist Violence at *Lawfully Permitted* White Supremacists Rallies Likely to Continue."[100]

Human rights compliant political policing, however, does not fully explain the hesitancy displayed at Charlottesville. Indeed, some participants in the Unite the Right Rally broadcast their intent to fight leftist counter-protestors on social media. Here, the political struggle around white supremacists and their efforts to infiltrate the security apparatus provides some perspective. During the Obama administration, the status of far-right movements as domestic terrorists was point of bitter controversy. In April 2009, DHS I&A predicted an increase in far-right violence and identified four causes: prolonged economic downturn, the election of a Black president, renewed debates over gun control and the return of military veterans to civilian life.[101] The report was leaked to the press. Conservative commentators sensationalized it. Pat Roberson, the television evangelist, encouraged his viewers to call DHS and complain. The American Legion objected to the depiction of veterans. To quell the controversy, DHS Secretary Napolitano apologized to the national commander of the conservative veterans group.[102]

Eventually, Napolitano shut down the unit that produced the report, leaving DHS I&A with no analysts focusing on the far-right. In 2011, Daryl Johnson, the primary author of the contested report, resigned and, moved by several deadly attacks perpetuated by far-right militants, took his story to the media.[103] Johnson's whistleblowing did not change policy. For years, DHS ignored violence from the far-right, leaving the matter to the FBI and fusion centers. Indeed, subsequent DHS I&A assessments on far-right movements, like the 2015 report on Sovereign Citizens, were produced in collaboration with the FBI.[104] In September 2015, DHS Secretary Jeh Johnson created the Office of Community Partnerships to fund community-based counter-radicalization programs. Unsatisfied with these efforts and dismayed by continuing far-right violence, fifteen Democratic members of Congress unsuccessfully petitioned President Obama to order DHS to update the controversial assessment on far-right violence and reopen the office that produced it.[105] Shortly after the inauguration, the Trump Administration rolled back the outgoing administration's late and half-hearted attempt to counter domestic extremism, reviewing all grants from Office of Community Partnerships and rescinding two that focused on the far-right.[106]

These conflicts around the meaning of "domestic terrorism" are occurring alongside counterintelligence efforts to combat the infiltration of the security apparatus by the far-right. In 2006, the FBI produced an internal intelligence assessment document concerning the far-right's attempts to infiltrate police agencies and influence officers. While highly redacted, the declassified portions of the report state that "white supremacist groups have historically engaged in strategic efforts to infiltrate and recruit from law enforcement communities."[107] While almost nothing is known about the FBI's efforts to address this issue, it is apparently a cause of some concern. The FBI recently released a 2015 Counterterrorism Policy Guide. The document states that "domestic terrorism investigations focused on militia extremists, white supremacist extremists, and sovereign citizen extremists often have identified active links to law enforcement officers."[108]Although there are no public records detailing the scope or number of FBI investigations into far-right infiltration of law enforcement, the Policy Guide explains that the FBI can identify officers as suspected terrorists and enter them in the Known or Suspected Terrorist File as "silent hit," which limits the access to the record. For journalist Alice Speri, this procedure implies "that extremist infiltration is enough of a concern that the FBI has built-in protocols to prevent domestic terrorism investigations from being obstructed by members of law enforcement."[109]

The limitations of human rights compliant political policing and efforts of the far-right to infiltrate law enforcement cast an ominous shadow over the violence in Charlottesville and similar clashes. Although there is no evidence that white supremacists infiltrated the Charlottesville Police or the Virginia State Police, the lead agency at the Virginia Fusion Center, an independent review of the response to the Unite the Right Rally by a former federal attorney shows that police downplayed the white supremacist threat. The report documents several intelligence analyses received by the Charlottesville Police that predicted violence from far-right militants. It also provides some anecdotes of individual law enforcement officers downplaying the threat from the far-right and positioning left counter-protestors as more problematic. For example, a Charlottesville police detective contacted the FBI for information about the Traditionalist Workers Party, a white nationalist group with documented history of violence. The FBI agent responded that they were "not likely to cause problems" but that "the counter-protesters might." The report also details an overture from a New York Police Department detective who shared intelligence with Charlottesville Police about Black Lives Matter activists that were planning on attending the rally. While the report concludes that poor training, insufficient coordination, and conflict between police and city council explained the violence, it gives hints of other dynamics at work.[110]

A SUPPLE SECURITY SYSTEM OR AN OVERWROUGHT ORGANIZATIONAL LEVIATHAN?

Altogether, fusion centers and the wider institutionalization of intelligence fusion has transformed political policing in the United States. Contemporary instances of police repression do not reproduce the highly centralized COINTELPRO model. Instead, the exposure of the FBI's infamous countersubversion operations led to a seemingly limited human rights compliant mode of political policing. This attempt to legally constrain police repression paradoxically retrenched abusive practices. It also produced pressures to criminalize dissent in order to expand the ambit of investigation. These

dynamics help explain the increasing emphasis on "terrorism" and its frag-
mentation into increasingly specific "terror identities." Human rights compliant political policing and counterterrorism are now the dominant state
strategies organizing political policing. These struggles to redefine and rel-
egitimate the security apparatus interacted with wider processes of state-
formation. Indeed, political policing now operates through the overlapping
intelligence networks, JTTFs and DHS-recognized fusion centers, which,
themselves, are mutually constituting parts of the larger whole, the workfare-carceral state. Reflecting the decentralized and competitive nature of
this state-form, these intelligence networks are subject to varied political
pressures, such as the external forces that shaped the divergent responses to
different Occupy encampments or the internal struggles within the state
that complicate the relations between the security apparatus and far-right
movements.

This patchwork of political policing is a complex and convoluted arrangement. It is both a supple security system and an overwrought organizational
leviathan. Enhanced coordination creates organic opportunities for plausible
deniability. It is hard to discern the leading actors and exact sequence of
events. It muddles command hierarchies. Are officers and analysts acting
without oversight or approval? Are private interests undermining the relative autonomy of the security apparatus, effectively transforming police
departments and intelligence centers into crude instruments of particular
class interests? Currently, these questions cannot be answered definitively.
This lack of clarity is only partially caused by secrecy and the proximity of
events. Increased political indeterminacy is also built into the very structure
of workfare-carceral state. This means the current patchwork of political
policing is much harder to expose and redress than COINTELPRO. If it is
difficult to discern exact dynamics behind a given instance of political policing, it makes it hard to name the problem and build consensus about a solution. If these arrangements can withstand their own internal contradictions,
they may be a more effective means to pacify class struggle.

Of course, "political policing" only targets the self-conscious mobilization of a class-for-itself, the efforts of organized movements. Intelligence
fusion—and police power in general—also attends to less explicit manifestations of class struggle: the ill-understood and often illegible survival
strategies of disarticulated segments of the working class. These practices
are often dismissed and overlooked as the anarchic turbulence of the "criminal element." The varied genres of the prose of pacification code it as
"crime" or "the street economy." Sometimes, it explodes as a "riot." These
activities do not target "politics" as such but focus instead on the ragged

edges of capitalism. Here, we find the surplus populations who are not (fully) incorporated within capitalist social relations, the structurally excluded people whose needs and desires cannot be (fully) satisfied within the constraints of capitalist social relations. This social space is a privileged domain of police power, where the state's role in producing and maintaining the most basic social relations that define capitalism are laid bare.

6. Pacifying Poverty

Police Power and Moral Economies of Poverty

While activists worry about a new COINTELPRO, reformers bemoan waste and mission failures, and watchdogs fret about civil liberties, intelligence fusion subjects entire populations to constant surveillance and aggressive intelligence-led policing (ILP) operations. These activities continue with little controversy because they target a group with almost no formal political power: the surplus populations warehoused in hyperghettoized communities doubly segregated by race and class. As I learned during my first visit to a fusion center and explained in the prologue, this "criminal element" is the main object of intelligence fusion. This situation reflects the basic mandate of police power: to regulate poverty and fabricate capitalist forms of order. This conclusion becomes clear in light of other ILP operations enabled by intelligence fusion. In addition to the "intelligence-led manhunts" that complement and enable decarceration, police also engage in a series of ILP operations that share a common convergence in the criminalization of "moral economies of poverty," the ill-understood survival strategies of those struggling at the bottom of the crushing inequalities that define capitalist societies.

These police projects attempt to reorganize social reproduction on terms that do not challenge the state or capital. Much of this work centers on the drug economy. Today, intelligence fusion helps police launch multiagency investigations into drug trafficking networks. These operations are attempts to regulate and, through asset forfeiture laws, tax the criminalized labor at the core of moral economies of poverty. They often push the drug economy off the street and indoors. Here, landlord training, trespass affidavit, and narcotics eviction programs enlist non-state actors in the work of pacification, compelling landlords to police the survival strategies and quotidian behaviors of surplus populations. Finally, secondhand dealer laws provide police new tools to not only monitor and manage the trade in stolen goods but also (re)produce the market and reaffirm the power of capital. In targeting these clandestine and criminalized exchanges, police operations pacify poverty and fabricate capitalist forms of order.

These examples, like those in the previous chapter on political policing, show that intelligence fusion, ILP, and the work of "security" in general are not simple responses to "disorder." Instead, security is the political work of managing poverty and pacifying class struggle. Structurally, policing is always and already an attempt to fabricate order around the logic of accumulation. Of course, the exact organization continually changes as a social formation develops through time. In the contemporary United States, intelligence fusion does not just supercharge the hunt for surplus populations with computerized legibility and police radical politics through a patchwork of interagency intelligence networks. It also works to disrupt moral economies of poverty. These efforts continually (re)produce capitalist social relations by subsuming threatening forms of labor within the criminal legal system, enforcing legal subjectivities, and constructing administratively legible market relations.

THE DIALECTIC OF POLICE POWER AND
MORAL ECONOMIES OF POVERTY

In the sixteenth century, the idea of "police" emerged during the transition from feudalism to capitalism. It developed, first, to provide coherence to the destruction of pre-capitalist social relations and, later, to organize capital's perpetual war against labor. Capitalism destroyed an old way of life and created of a new one. In famous passages of *Capital*, Marx analyzed these processes of expropriation and criminalization, wherein "the agricultural folk [were] first forcibly expropriated from the soil, driven from their homes, turned into vagabonds, and then whipped, branded and tortured by grotesquely terroristic laws into accepting the discipline necessary for the system of wage-labour."[1] The conversion of common and church lands into private property, the dispossession of the peasantry, and their transformation into proletarians—what Marx denounced as "grotesquely terroristic laws" and "bloody legislation—was, at the time, known as "police science."

The philosophers, proto-political economists, and administrators who first used the term "police" held that "the main interest of police was the development of commerce and the production of wealth." As Neocleous explains, the "police" idea was always "concern[ed] with subsistence in general, the state of work and, most crucially, the condition of poverty." He elaborates:

Behind the police of the state of prosperity as the basis of order was a
more specific concern over the place of the poor and the potential threat
posed by the new "class" of poverty to the emerging structures of
private property. "Order" is hardly threatened unless there is a force
which appears to possess the potential of undermining it, and as
bourgeois social relations began to stamp themselves across the face of
society, the major threat appeared to be the labouring poor. Thus, the
need to shape the workforce played an increasingly significant part
in policing. . . . [O]ne finds that the poor had a presence in texts on
police, either as beggars and vagrants (or at least, potential beggars
and vagrants) or as a general category subject to police. . . . This is
because the administration of poverty was and is the heart of the
police project.

The class content of policing was evident from the beginning. The London
Metropolitan Police, considered by most to be first "modern" police force,
"criminalize[d] traditional activities which were either recreational or
rooted in an alternative economic mode of life and which centred on the
street—the 'proletarian public sphere.'" Again Neocleous:

In particular, the police necessarily became involved in removing the
possibility of obtaining non-wage subsistence. Traditional activities
which labour used to eke out an existence—casual labour for payment
in kind, grazing cattle on public byways, pilfering wood, picking fruit
and vegetables for either consumption or sale, poaching, fishing from
rivers without licence, hawking, peddling and street selling—all became
targets for police action. . . . [O]ne should see the street powers granted
to the police as an expression of the state's contribution to class
formation as well as class domination. The new forms of police
operation coming into existence were fundamental to the imposition of
the money wage as a means of making the working class, and thus need
to be seen in the broader context of the role of police in the fabrication
of a new, bourgeois, order.[2]

These dynamics also characterized other antecedents of the police forces we
would recognize today. In the 1790s, Patrick Colquhoun, a Scottish merchant
and magistrate, created the Thames River Police, a private force funded by
London merchants. They imposed strict surveillance on "lumpers"—that is,
"longshoremen"—to end pre-capitalist compensation practices. Within capitalism, "taking the fruits of what one has worked on with one's hands had
to be eliminated as a practice."[3] Across the Atlantic, in 1785, the Guard and
Watch in Charleston, South Carolina, assumed broad powers to regulate
slaves who had been "hired out" to work in the city. While the personal
control of slave owners and slave patrols reigned in rural areas, Charleston

created arguably the first "modern" police force in the world to manage bonded black workers in urban industries.[4]

This critical reinterpretation of the "police" idea highlights the power of the state to administer civil society and, thus, fabricate social order. As explained in chapter 1, this theorization recuperates the productive theory of micropowers associated with poststructuralism into a humanist and historical Marxism, a holistic approach that attends to both the specificity of social structures and the dynamics of class struggle. From the sixteenth century through the mid-nineteenth century, "police science" connoted what would now be recognized as "social policy." It was a broad science of social order that included what became public law, administrative science, political economy, public health, and urban planning. Over time the meaning of "police" gradually narrowed, downgrading "'police science' from a master discipline aimed at the preservation and extension of the means of the state to a technical subdiscipline of instrumental criminology."[5] Despite the narrowing of "police," its origins left indelible marks on policing and the various categories of social policy that grew out of the old "master discipline" of police science. These policy discourses are thus distinct genres of the prose of pacification. Their abiding concern is the protection of private property, the creation of markets, the regulation of poverty, and the separation of the worthy or deserving poor from the undeserving and inscrutable "criminal element." Hence, Frances Fox Piven and Richard Cloward, in *Regulating the Poor*, their seminal study of social assistance, note that "most of the features of modern welfare—from criteria to discriminate the worthy poor from the unworthy to strict procedures for surveillance of recipients and measures for their rehabilitation—were present in" the first experiments in "poor aid" in sixteenth century Europe.[6] In this regard, the history of the idea of policing recasts "social policy" as "social police" and highlights how the productive powers of administration form the working class and fabricate capitalist forms of order.[7]

This conception of police and social policy refocuses politics around class struggle. Reflecting the humanist and historical Marxism that underpins this analysis, *class struggle* connotes both the formal politics of a mobilized class-for-itself and the substantive—but not always self-consciously articulated—political content manifest in the activities and social reproduction strategies of a class-in-itself. The notion of a "moral economy" clarifies this expansive understanding of class struggle and connects this historical reinterpretation of policing with contemporary ILP operations. The social historian E. P. Thompson coined the term *moral economy* to analyze "food riots" in eighteenth-century England. Rather than dismissing such eruptions as irrational violence, he reinterpreted them as political acts grounded upon a consistent traditional view of social norms and obligations, of the proper economic functions of several parties within the community, which, taken together, can be said to constitute the moral economy of poverty. An outrage to these moral assumptions, quite as much as actual deprivation, was the usual occasion for direct action.[8]

The moral economy, in other words, is the shared values that organize the social reproduction practices of the working class, the commonly held values that animate the work households and constitute what communities do to sustain themselves from day to day and generation to generation. In this way, the moral economy is point of contrast to and—potentially—grounds for resistance against the capitalist economy. Capital demands that the market govern all human conduct, while actually existing communities often insist on other arrangements.

Recently, ethnographers George Karandinos, Laurie Hart, Fernando Castrillo, and Philippe Bourgois have reinterpreted the seemingly antisocial violence associated with "the inner city" on these terms. Drawing on observations of a hyperghettoized Philadelphia neighborhood, they identify a "moral economy of violence" defined by "a destructive solidarity" that "amplifies the prevailing sense of physical insecurity and further elevates the symbolic and practical importance of commanding violent resources." Violence becomes "a valuable but fragile resource: unstable cultural and social capital that meshes ethically with gender and kin-based roles and is cast not as choice but as obligation to both individuals and the local community." This conclusion is consonant with other ethnographies that analyze the symbolic code and institutions that create bottom-up forms of social order and solidarity in hyperghettoized areas. Although these studies use terms like "the code of the street," "alternative governance," and "the art of running" over the "moral economy," they show that the violence of the hyperghetto cannot be reduced to a pathological "criminal element."[9] Instead, it is structural, based in *both* the neglect and divestment connected to deindustrialization and the imposition of workfare *and* the agency of criminalized surplus populations.[10]

The emphasis on agency is important. Moral economies of poverty are contested and should not be romanticized. They are "moral" in the sense of commonly accepted understanding of conduct, not in the sense of "good" ethics. As Elijah Anderson notes in his ethnography of hyperghettoized Philadelphia neighborhoods, there are often tense relations between "decent" and "street" people:

The fact that decent people, as a rule civilly disposed, socially conscious, and self-reliant men and women, share the neighborhood streets and other public places with those associated with the street, the inconsiderate, the ignorant, and the desperate, places the "good" people at special risk. In order to live and function in the community, they must adapt to a street reality that is often dominated by people who are at best suffering severely in some way and who are apt to quickly resort to violence to settle disputes. This process of adapting means learning and observing the code of street.

This learning process means even "decent" people participate in moral econ-omies. It explains why entire communities, including "decent" people, have fraught relations with police. For example, Anderson contends that drug dealing is "recognized as work," albeit "an occupation that overwhelming numbers of residents surely despise." Still, "many people are afraid to report obvious drug dealing or other crimes to the police. . . . [T]hey believe that the police are unlikely to come or, if they do come, they may even harass the very people who called them."[11] The complex and varied stances toward "crime" and police power produce a bottom-up form of social solidarity, creating a coherent "moral economy," but not one free of contradiction. Police seek to exploit those tensions but they cannot resolve them, as they are structural features of the workfare-carceral state.

In addition to explaining the production of social solidarity in a situation of privation, the notion of a "moral economy" also connotes a broader rela-tion to historical capitalism. Just as Thompson's moral economy exists in relation to the world-economy, "moral economies of violence" are con-nected to "capitalist economies of pacification." Indeed, elites and more privileged segments of the population interpret the violence of hyperghet-toized communities in ways that advance security politics:

> The violence that is irregularly but spectacularly reported on local
> television news stations pathologizes the poor as dangerous "others,"
> legitimizing zero tolerance carceral repression in the name of public
> safety and moral retribution and fueling more rounds of institutional
> and structural violence (disinvestment by the private sector and
> decreases in public funds for welfare, health, education, and housing).
> Perhaps most importantly, the de-facto apartheid boundaries of the US
> inner city are normalized by the fact that most people in the United
> States fear they will be ripped limb from limb if they set foot in the
> ghetto.[12]

The moral economy of violence is dialectically related to police power. The existence of a moral economy of violence legitimates policing and naturalizes the structural inequalities—"the de-facto apartheid boundaries of the US inner city"—produced through the long history of capital accumulation and class struggle. It engenders a politics of racial fear and class resentment, easy fodder for security.

This dialectic is self-perpetuating. As Rigakos contends, security is "materially and ideologically, the blast furnace of global capitalism, fueling both the conditions for the system's perpetuation while feeding relentlessly on the surpluses it has exacted."[13] The relationship between moral economies of poverty and police power, like the larger dialectic of labor and capital, is an intrinsic contradiction of historical capitalism. Its perpetual churn produces a bewildering variety of situations, but the essential antagonism cannot be resolved without a fundamental change of social relations, a systemic transformation. Today, intelligence fusion and ILP operate to pacify poverty and disrupt moral economies of poverty. Not only do these operations target the survival strategies and social reproduction practices that sustain hyperghettoized communities in the face of extreme hardship. They also attempt to pacify these inchoate expressions of class struggle through the administrative subsumption of threatening forms of labor, the enforcement of legal subjectivities, and the construction of administratively legible market relations. In this way, policing fabricates social order around the logic of accumulation.

POLICING THE DRUG ECONOMY AND TAXING CRIMINALIZED LABOR

The structural mandate of policing to pacify moral economies of poverty is evident in the way intelligence fusion and related ILP operations administratively subsume criminalized labor within the security apparatus. After decades of market reform and punitive social policy, the drug trade has become a tremendous source of wealth for deindustrialized, disinvested, and hyperghettoized communities. The United Nations Office on Drugs and Crime releases annual drug reports but has not estimated the total value of the global drug trade since 2005, when they set it at $320 billion per year. A 2017 study by a nonprofit that studies illicit economies appraised the size of the global drug trade to between $426 and $652 billion. Both projections put this criminalized commerce at about 1 percent of global GDP. Reflecting demand in the United States, North America accounts for nearly half of the global drug market.[14]

The Northeast, as a major population center, is one the main hubs of this activity. In 2009, the New York/New Jersey High Intensity Drug Trafficking

Area (HIDTA) estimated that financial institutions in the New York metropolitan region launder $4 to $8 billion in drug money each year.[15] In 2013, the NY-NJ HIDTA funded programs that seized $111.3 million in drugs, and $257.6 million in cash and other assets. That same year, the Philadelphia/Camden HIDTA confiscated $20.7 million in drugs, and $1.7 million in cash, while the New England HIDTA seized $75.2 million in drugs, and $34.3 million in cash and property.[16] For the surplus populations warehoused in hyperghettoized communities, this criminalized commerce is labor. As mentioned in the prologue, $250 million in drugs reportedly moves through Camden each year, and, according to one state trooper, an individual "drug set" can make $20,000 in one day.[17]

The sheer size of the drug trade makes it central to moral economies of poverty. Susan Phillips, in her ethnography of the drug war in Los Angeles, explains:

> [U]nderstanding the tie between the drug trade and very real economic need is critical to comprehending how people grow toward a tacit or explicit acceptance of drug-based or other illegal monies. . . . Youth in particular sometimes choose drug dealing to give their family economic stability. Unlike legitimate forms of employment, drug dealing is rooted in neighborhoods where people already live, requires little education and can withstand the interruption of prison time and community reentry.

By providing a livelihood that can resist the disruptions of policing and incarceration, the drug economy creates a social cohesion in a context of privation. As Phillips notes, "the game"—"the colloquial term for the drug trade"—ties together "growers, manufacturers, suppliers, dealers, servers, addicts, cops, agents, snitches, wires, GPS units, computers and confidential sources." It creates "new possibilities for social integration and disintegration." No one "wins" the game. Instead, it continually (re)produces the criminalized labor and social reproduction practices that constitute moral economies of poverty. "[T]he war on drugs," she explains, "is a legal construct that paradoxically reinforces unconventional or illegal forms of cooperation." The interconnections among "the people and systems" that constitute the drug war form "social life as whole. . . . Both violence and the lack of violence are indexes of social order. Whether people experience violence as victim or perpetrator, it bonds them in life-changing ways and becomes a counterforce to the state's own violent actions."[18]

The drug economy both organizes the moral economies of poverty *and* animates the work of the security apparatus. Police and drug traffickers play "the game" in a distinct social space, an "invisible interstice" that

Alfred McCoy, the venerable historian of US intelligence, calls the "covert netherworld." He explains:

> The study of police and scandal takes us beneath the visible surface of politics into a murky realm between the formal and informal, licit and illicit that we call, for want of better words, the "covert netherworld.". . .[T]this covert netherworld is an invisible interstice, within both individual nations and the international system, inhabited by criminal and clandestine actors with both the means and the needs to operate outside of conventional channels. . . . [P]olice are not simply guardians of an impregnable social frontier that keeps moral outcasts at a safe remove from polite society but serve instead as informal gatekeepers between the state and its social margins, patrolling the boundaries of parallel social systems, civil society and its criminal netherworld. This hidden sector of social commercial vice—gambling, prostitution and addictive drugs—is . . . the meeting ground of high and low, a leveling marketplace were the privileged and underprivileged exchange goods and services otherwise prohibited by moral and legal sanctions. Through methods, legal and extralegal, police regulate this informal marketplace.[19]

Indeed, as McCoy's scholarship on the involvement of the Central Intelligence Agency in global heroin trade shows, states often operate through the "covert netherworld" to advance their interests.[20] Similar dynamics occur throughout the security apparatus. For the police agencies running fusion centers, the drug trade not only orients and legitimates their work, it also provides resources.

Perversely, police agencies tax the drug trade and regulate criminalized labor. Through asset forfeiture laws, money and property seized in criminal investigations can be expropriated by police agencies. In both New York and New Jersey, police can seize money that is derived from criminal activities or properties associated with it. While there is no centralized data on asset forfeiture in New Jersey, police in New York State, from 1990 to 2010, seized nearly $244 million in cash alone and distributed over $88 million to police agencies.[21] In some jurisdictions, the conflict of interest generated by this for-profit policing is blatant. In New York's Nassau County, their IMPACT-funded intelligence center, the Lead Development Center (LDC), sits under the Asset Forfeiture *and* Intelligence Unit. The LDC operates at no budgetary cost for the department. It is funded exclusively through asset seizures and grants.[22] While the LDC is an extreme example, it underscores the role drug operations play in regulating a criminalized market that cannot be suppressed.

These efforts to police the drug economy amount to a tax on criminalized labor that imposes legal subjectivities on surplus populations that are weakly connected to labor markets. Recalling the discussion from chapter 2, the recognition of organized labor pacified the working class by incorporating them within capitalist states. This administrative subsumption of labor is one the primary ways state administration continually (re)produces capitalist social relations. Neocleous explains:

> In order to fashion a fully-fledged capitalist market the state had to form the legal subjectivity of the parties to its essential feature—the contract. This constitution is a dual process, involving the constitution of both individual and collective legal subjects. In the case of individual legal subjects this meant the fashioning of labour power through the consolidation of wage-labour as the means of subsistence of the working class. In the case of collective subjects . . . trade unions were given quasi-corporate form as the legal subjectivity of the working class, through which the state recognized the social power of collective labour. By specifying the nature and form that this power could take the state shaped working-class collective action into a series of organs which, while able to formally express the social power of labour, also limit it in accordance with state policy.[23]

Policing accomplishes this same process for the criminalized workers of the drug economy. Instead of subsuming legal labor within the confines of "labor law," it envelopes criminalized labor within the "drug war." Police surveillance and intelligence gathering track the drug trade and identify its key players. Arrest and prosecution imposes legal subjectivities on both individual and collective actors: people involved in the drug economy and the "criminal conspiracies" they create. The prohibition of drugs creates a caste of criminalized labor that policing regulates and taxes. Cumulatively, these efforts pacify class struggle by dividing the working class into a profaned "criminal element" and "decent" people.

Intelligence fusion intensifies these processes. Since fusion centers are interagency organizations, they can expand investigations into larger operations. In New York State, for example, the New York State Intelligence Center (NYSIC) developed a Border Intelligence Unit (BIU) that leads a taskforce of law enforcement agencies on both sides of the border to intercept drugs. In 2009, for example, the BIU supported eight operations that led to forty-four arrests and the seizure of 129 pounds of marijuana and $283,639 in cash.[24] Each IMPACT county also mounts their own ILP operations targeting the drug trade. In Rensselaer County, for example, the Troy Police Department regularly conducts undercover buys on the basis of intelligence from their IMPACT-funded crime analysis team. "Crimes are linked to drug activity," the analyst told me, "The mapping I do helps the chief decide where to send undercovers."[25] This basic procedure can sometimes develop into a large operation. An officer with the department explains:

> We see a lot of larcenies. We see a lot of burglaries and it's all—I think—it's all because of this drug issue. They're burglarizing and ripping people off to buy drugs. . . . A few years ago, maybe four or five, it was out of control. We reached out to the Sherriff and then the State Police, the [The Drug Enforcement Administration (DEA)] over in Albany, and some others. It became a multiagency thing. It was big deal.

The officer is referring to a 2008 initiative, where the multiagency county IMPACT partnership collaborated with the DEA and other federal agencies to combat crime associated with the drug economy. He elaborated:

> We did joint patrols. We'd make arrests and gather intel. Our analyst worked with their guys: run the plates, check the databases, and work up bios. We did lots of surveillance. We had our [confidential informants]. The feds had theirs. We kept at it for months. It was a cycle: patrols, arrests, surveillance, intel work, more arrests.[26]

During the course of these "proactive operations," multiagency "teams made approximately 800 arrests"—accounting for fifth of all arrests in Troy in 2008—and seized, three-quarters of a pound of crack cocaine, sixty-five pounds of marijuana, three vehicles, ten firearms, and $52,000.[27]

In New Jersey, similar operations revolve around the DHS-recognized fusion center. The Regional Operations Intelligence Center (ROIC) participates in the Violent Enterprise Source Targeting (VEST) program, which brings together federal, state, and local law enforcement to work high-level drug cases in Jersey City, Newark, Perth Amboy, and Trenton. The goal of VEST, in the words of one officer, is "to go after higher-end narcotics dealers and cut off the head of the snake." This requires resources beyond the scope of municipal police department:

> At the municipality level, you have to rely on the prosecutor's office for anything that was outside of the realm . . . but, a lot of times, we had targets that were above us and above the County Prosecutor's level. VEST lets us work with the FBI, DEA and organizations that are bigger than even the county. That allowed us to enhance our capability to target and go after bigger targets. It broadened our horizons and gave us contacts where we didn't have contacts before. It was really beneficial for us because it allowed us to go after people that were out of reach for a long time.[28]

Another officer in the same department explained how these increased resources, available through VEST, allowed them to expand the scope of an investigation:

So we focused on a group and, with resources from federal agencies, we were able to track someone who was buying large amounts of heroin and cocaine. . . . It reached all way to the Bronx. The person in the Bronx had the connection to Colombia. We would have never been able to reach this point on our own because we are normally so focused on our town. This led us to make buys and reach a higher level in the distribution network. That is where VEST has been successful. Here at the ROIC, they have an analytic product that profiles persons of interest. They can do a background check and see if there are warrants and maybe get some good information that came from a field intelligence officer. They know their patterns in town, but they can't see their [Internal Revenue Service] information or see if they've been leaving on flights. All of that [Immigration and Customs Enforcement] can do, FBI can do. So with that, they were able to connect the dots. We were able to knock out the whole group and get the bigger fish. We would never be able to that before because we could only use about $2,000 on any given job. Usually we make three buys, get a no-knock warrant, lock 'em up and that's where it stays . . . but to reach all the way to Colombia [and] shut down a whole network is something entirely different.[29]

The coordination that enables programs like VEST is important not just because they increase the reach of local jurisdictions by partnering them with state and federal agencies. They also enable police agencies to offset the costs of austerity and do more with less resources.

In an era defined by austerity, punitive decarceration, and the increasing prominence of mass supervision, these types of ILP take on greater importance as sources of revenue for struggling municipalities. Recalling the discussion of the continuing advance of workfare in chapter 4, public sector austerity compelled municipal police to work more closely with fusion centers. For example, Paterson turned to the NJ ROIC for help to address a surge in violence following the 2011 layoffs of one quarter of the force.[30] With shootings occurring at twice the rate of the previous year, the Paterson Police, the State Police, the County Prosecutor, and the Sherriff began to work on what would become "Operation Fourth Down." As a first step, the ROIC created combined density maps of shootings, narcotics arrests, and gun recoveries to identify the center of the problem. They identified a hotspot in Paterson's fourth ward. The analysts zeroed in on two blocks, .07 percent of the city's total area that accounted for 22 percent of the narcotics arrests, 14 percent of the shootings, and 11 percent of the robberies. The Paterson Police knew this area as the home of the Fruit Town Brims, a Bloods gang set. They began gathering intelligence. When there would be a shooting in the area, the analysts at the ROIC would work with the Paterson

Police to link various types of data—criminal histories, social network analyses, ballistic information—to produce intelligence to help them apprehend persons of interest and gather more intelligence about the incident. After eleven months of planning, Operation Fourth Down went live. During early morning sweeps, a multiagency group executed nine search warrants and twenty-four arrest warrants. They arrested 170 people, and seized twelve guns, and four thousand bags of heroin, crack, marijuana, and other drugs.[31]

For the ROIC, Operation Fourth Down was just another successful drug operation. Supporting this work is routine. In May 2012, they provided intelligence support for "Operation Billboard," a multiagency investigation into a Camden-based Latin King set that culminated in twenty-five arrests, and the seizure of three-quarters of a kilo of heroin, approximately $52,000 in cash, $20,000 in counterfeit currency, one handgun, and seventeen vehicles.[32] In November 2012, the Paterson Police, New Jersey State Police (NJSP), and ROIC again partnered with a collection of other agencies to launch Operation Dismayed. After six months of investigation, multiagency teams raided ten residences, arrested fifteen people, seized four kilos of heroin, and $255,000 in cash.[33] In November 2013, the ROIC; NJSP; Camden County Police; and other state, local, and federal agencies carried Operation North Pole, which climaxed with forty-seven arrests, and seizures of $200,000, six guns, more than five ounces of cocaine, ten cars, and one "party bus."[34] In May 2013, Operation Blok Buster brought together Atlantic City Police, NJSP and other agencies in early morning raids on eighteen properties that led to twenty-eight arrests, and the confiscation of four guns and "significant quantities of heroin and cocaine."[35] In January 2014, NJSP, the ROIC, the New Brunswick Police Department and other state, local, and federal agencies collaborated on Operation Smokescreen, which resulted in ten arrests and the seizure of thirty-six weapons, $10,000 in cash and $130,000 in drugs.[36] These operations are only a sample of the routine drug investigations that the ROIC supports. These operations join countless others across the country to form a larger structure of police power: an administrative project to disrupt moral economies of poverty, subsume criminalized labor within the criminal legal system, and perversely tax the drug economy through asset seizures.

EXTENDING THE REACH OF POLICE POWER

These efforts often drive the drug trade off the streets and into homes. To extend the reach of police power into "private" spaces, police agencies seek to enlist civilians in their program. They pressure some to become complicit in the operation of police power. They create specialized a system of penalties and fines to govern the conduct of households, individuals, and third-party service providers, administratively subsuming social reproduction practices. A good example of this process is the landlord training, trespass affidavit, and narcotics eviction initiative in New York's Albany County. Here, the District Attorney's (DA) office, working with Albany Police Department (APD) and Albany Crime Analysis Center (ACAC) developed two interconnected programs to bring the drug war inside homes. The initiative compels landlords and tenants to become agents of police power. Under threat of fines and investigation, police pressure landlords to monitor "problem tenants" and threaten them with eviction. These programs discourage both landlords and tenants from either tacitly or explicitly accommodating the drug economy, thus disrupting moral economies of poverty and encouraging residents of hyperghettoized communities to accept "honest work" in the formal economy.

Albany County's landlord training, trespass affidavit, and narcotics eviction initiative revolves around two connected programs: Safe Homes–Safe Streets, a community outreach program run by the DA's office and, Operation Reclamation, an ILP effort of the APD. For Safe Homes–Safe Streets, the DA's office assigned a dedicated assistant district attorney (ADA) to train property owners to screen tenants in order to "identify criminal behaviors." The ADA also provides examples of "Zero tolerance leases with clauses for criminal behavior" and encourages landlords to rely on the DA for support in evicting "problem tenants."[37] The "zero tolerance lease" permits landlords to evict tenants for several reasons: "Any criminal, violent or drug-related activity *on or off* the leased premises that the Landlord determines may interfere with or threatens the health, safety, or right to peaceful enjoyment of the premises by other tenants;" the use of "a controlled substance, or abuse of alcohol that the Landlord determines . . . may interfere with the health, safety, or right to peaceful enjoyment of the premises by other tenants, or persons residing in the immediate vicinity of the premises or persons legally on the premises"; and the "display, use or possess[ion] of any firearm (operable or inoperable) or other offensive weapon that is illegal or is used . . . [il]legally."[38] The program not only encourages landlords to evict tenants, it penalizes them if they do not. "In cases where the landlord fails to act in a timely manner, the DA's Office will step in and execute the eviction. When the DA's Office takes this step, it will also name the landlord as a respondent to the action subjecting the landlord to possible fines of up to $5,000 plus legal fees."[39]

The ADA also organizes the trespass affidavit component of the program. The ADA recruits landlords to provide lists of all tenants, post a "No

Trespassing" sign, and encourages tenants to report trespassers.[40] Participating landlords also grant "full permission and authority to the Albany County Police Departments, its employees and agents to enter upon the above described premises and the stoop/stairs attached thereto at any and all hours of the day for the purpose of arresting those persons found thereon who are not tenants, their family members or invited guests."[41] The trespass affidavit program also allows police to search properties "for illegally stashed weapons and drugs."[42] The Safe Homes–Safe Streets transforms rental properties into quasi-correctional spaces. The program creates serious risks for landlords who collect rents from tenants involved in the drug trade. Through the threat of fine, the program compels landlords to actively support law enforcement in policing tenants' behavior. Tenants, meanwhile, lose their privacy to the police, who are free to question and search anyone on the property.

The involvement of police in the landlord training, trespass affidavit, and narcotics eviction initiative also includes ILP operations. In 2010, the APD launched a pilot program called "Operation Reclamation," which centered on the identification of "Code Red" properties. First, ACAC analysts identified a seventy-seven-block area that accounted for more than half of the crime in the county.[43] Analysts then used the department's records management system to create "premise histories" for 165 properties in the area. They scored each property based on calls for service and identified eleven "Code Red" properties. The APD and DA then contacted the landlords and compelled them to join the trespass affidavit program. By the end of 2010, the eleven houses were no longer designated "Code Red." This experience motivated the APD to create a "Code Red Team," a multiagency response team to execute search warrants on drug houses. Before the execution of a warrant, ACAC analysts will generate a report on the property "that will include information pertaining to each agency so that those agencies may respond with the appropriate remedies." The APD "believes that such a response will permanently shut down the drug location by disrupting business on multiple levels . . . utilizing such things as inspection or home visits." The success of the initial pilot program convinced the Albany County impact partnership to expand the use of "Code Red" assessments: "In the near future, we hope that all properties within the County of Albany will be scored in such a manner."[44]

The scope of the program is impressive. From 2009 to 2014, the Albany IMPACT partnership shut down nineteen "drug houses," executed 100 evictions, trained over 770 landlords, and registered over 1000 properties.[45] The Albany IMPACT partnership did not produce these results with persuasion alone. Landlords who do not voluntarily join Safe Homes–Safe Streets become targets. In addition to "civil court proceedings to recover costs of investigations and prosecution associated with their properties," the DA's office focused on "repeat offender landlords." To this end, ACAC analysts created "property owner trees" to map out landlords' other properties in an attempt "to reveal a pattern and/or history of criminal activity," and identify "property owners that are working directly with those committing offenses." At the same time, APD's Code Red Team targeted the properties of uncooperative landlords, canvassing the area to gather intelligence through informal interviews with residents willing to speak to officers. These teams also aggressively issued citations and conducted arrests for offenses observed on or around the properties of uncooperative landlords. To this end, the Code Red Team often relied on their partners in probation, parole, and the school district to enforce orders of protection and conduct home visits.[46]

Through these combined efforts, the landlord training, trespass affidavit, and narcotics eviction initiative extends the reach of police power into "private" spaces. While this program is unlike any other in New York State and perhaps the entire United States, it shares some features with the broader strategy of mass supervision. Ruben Miller and Forrest Stuart find mass supervision empowers third-party service providers, such as landlords, "to manage, correct, sanction and care for" criminalized surplus populations. They also note that mass supervision entails "new laws, sanctions and regulatory penalties, numbering in the tens of thousands" that shape "the social, civic and economic participation of people with criminal records."[47] Clearly, this program reproduces these patterns. However, the landlord training, trespass affidavit, and narcotics eviction initiative also underscores the centrality of police power to mass supervision. It disrupts moral economies of poverty by coercing landlords and tenants to act as agents of administrative surveillance, driving a wedge within hyperghettoized communities and encouraging residents to avoid any accommodation with the drug economy. Importantly, the initiative also shares the concern with poverty and promotion of wealth associated with the original police idea. A police administrator discussed the program in these terms. "We're trying to get at the root problems that have been plaguing certain neighborhoods for years," he told me, "You can't just arrest your way out of it but, if you can educate landlords and tenants and drive out problems, maybe you can turn the neighborhood around? This is policing at its best, its most ambitious. We're trying to create opportunity. It could open the way for revitalization and investment in neighborhoods that really need it."[48]

POLICING AND PRODUCING THE MARKET

While the drug war organizes much of the present police project to pacify poverty, other operations target criminalized commerce in general. Here, secondhand dealer laws are particularly important because they reveal the way policing produces market relations even in "mature" capitalist societies like the United States. In recent years, there has been a push to update regulations to require *electronic* reporting of transactions at pawnshops, scrap yards, and other secondhand dealers. These revised regulations create new databases that enable to police to target underground markets in stolen goods. In New York, several municipalities and counties have already passed such laws, including Canandaigua, New York City, and Rochester, and Erie, Broome, Cortland, Oneida, Onondaga, Ontario, and Steuben Counties.[49] In Onondaga County, the law became controversial. The rise, fall, and reinstitution of the law not only shows how secondhand dealer laws provide police new tools to disrupt the moral economies of the poor. It also reveals how these efforts (re)produce market relations and reinforce the power the capital.

Police agencies use secondhand dealer laws to investigate theft. In Onondaga County, electronic reporting of every transaction allows police investigators and intelligence analysts to, in the words of the police captain managing the Onondaga County Crime Analysis Center (OCAC),

> do bulk quer[ies] on all stolen property. . . . They will get hits on stuff like GPS units, televisions, anything with a serial number. We also check the pawn logs in reverse. The analysts know who are the problem burglars so they will look them up in the [database] to see if they've been pawning anything and then try to match that back to what is stolen.[50]

In 2009, for example, an elderly woman suspected that one of her home health aides stole a ring. An OCAC analyst ran the names against electronically reported records of pawn transactions and found a match, leading to the recovery of the ring and the arrest of the aide.[51] The database also allows OCAC analysts to refine investigative leads out of pawn records and create cases in the absence of any reported theft. In 2009, for example, the OCAC generated nineteen leads in this manner.[52]

Secondhand dealer laws also allow police to check shopkeeper's compliance. The same police captain explains:

> We also will do compliance checks. We send an informant into a store with stolen Red Bull or some other secondhand merchandise that you need a license to sell. The corner stores will take in stolen property, put

it right on the shelf, and sell it. So we will do that a couple times to establish a pattern and then cite them. We mark the merchandise with [an ultraviolet marker] and then we will go back in and buy the same product that we know they got through the informant and then we will arrest them for violating the secondhand dealer law. We also will take stolen goods—DVDs still in the case—and take them to registered pawnshops and have the informant come in and say "I just boosted this stuff. I don't have ID. Will you take it?" And if they take it without the ID, we will come in and see if it makes the log and we will cite them.[53]

In 2013, the Syracuse Police Department (SPD) mounted a six-month investigation using these methods, which culminated in raids on seven stores that resulted in forty-nine charges against nine individuals. At the press conference announcing the arrest, representatives from corporate retailers—Tops, Walgreens, and Wegmans—flanked the police chief and mayor. The operation actually began at the behest of private security working for the corporate retailers who began sharing intelligence on "boosters" who steal baby formula, razor blades, energy drinks, cigarettes, electronics, and other retail goods to resell to corner stores.[54] These corner stories are not just centers of criminalized commerce. They also offer other services that meet the needs of the most marginalized, making them organizational hubs of moral economies of poverty. Unlike corporate retailers, corner stores often allow their "regulars" to buy on credit in order to manage insufficient and unsteady incomes. They organize illegal gambling, and provide outlets for other "illegal products" including weapons, and home-made alcohol.[55] In this context, the police use secondhand dealer laws not just to suppress the market in stolen goods but also to disrupt wider moral economies of the poverty.

These class politics are manifest in the geography of Syracuse depicted in figure 1. The nine individuals charged were all non-white proprietors of small, independent businesses that were located in high-poverty census tracts. The corporate retailers, in contrast, are all located in the high-income neighborhoods on the edges of the city's borders. The map reflects the wider finding of a 2015 analysis of census data, which shows that extreme poverty has spread out from the city's core to the Near South, Near Southwest and North Sides. In 2000, nine census tracks in Syracuse were "extreme poverty" neighborhoods, meaning more than 40 percent of residents live in poverty. By 2013, the number of such census tracks increased to thirty. Textbook hyperghettos, these impoverished neighborhoods are mostly black and brown, leaving Syracuse with the highest rate of black and Hispanic poverty out the 100 largest cities in the United States.

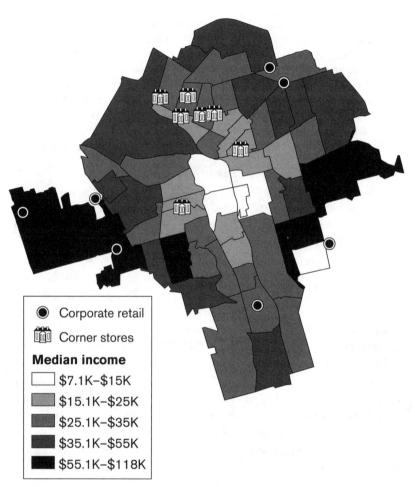

FIGURE 1.   Median income, corporate retail, and corner stores in Syracuse, New York. Source: 2010 American Community Survey. Production credit: Cassie Follet.

Syracuse also is also home to white hyperghettos. The city has the fifth-highest rate of poverty among non-Hispanic whites.[56]

The class character of secondhand dealer laws is also evident in the controversy that surrounded it in Onondaga County. In August 2010, a county judge struck down both the city and county's secondhand dealer laws. In a case regarding the search of a Syracuse resident's home, which was used as an unlicensed pawnshop, the judge concluded the police used "administrative search" provisions of the local laws as a "ruse employed by the detectives to effect a warrantless entry and search of [the defendant's] premises in order to uncover additional evidence of criminal activity."[57] The decision echoes concerns about secondhand dealer laws in New York City, where similar provisions have been denounced as "electronic stop and frisk" that allows police "to perform warrantless dragnets and exploratory searches of pawnbrokers' records" and "reverse engineer investigations of criminal activity."[58]

When city council and county legislators reintroduced the laws, protests erupted. The controversy, however, had no connection to the judge's concerns. In both the city and county, the revised legislation required all secondhand dealers, not just pawnshops to report data, which led to protests from the owners and customers of antique stores and used music stores. Eventually, the Syracuse City Council granted an exception for a used music store. The county executive vetoed the revised regulations before signing a law that exempted antique shops and trade shows.[59] The political negotiation of the secondhand dealer laws shows how police power operates on lines of class power to construct capitalist markets and disrupt moral economies of poverty. The protests around the bill were not concerned with the expansion of police power but instead focused on ensuring the viability of "respectable" businesses. In the rise, fall, and reinstitution of the law, new powers for surveillance were politically negotiated in such a way as to both construct administratively legible market relations and generate local consent for the political attack on the surplus populations quarantined in Syracuse's hyperghettoized neighborhoods.

As intelligence fusion becomes more entrenched, police agencies are advocating for revisions to secondhand dealer laws. In New Jersey, for example, state legislators have been debating mandated statewide electronic reporting for pawnshops since at least 2013.[60] While these bills have not passed, the NJSP's Legislation and Research Unit and the New Jersey State Police Benevolent Association lobbied for the bills. At a meeting of CorStat, the regional information-sharing consortium for the urban corridor linking Newark and Paterson, a state trooper assigned to the ROIC gave a presentation about a 2013 proposal, even before legislators formally introduced the bill. He encouraged municipal police departments to lobby for the legislation. The ROIC was ahead of the legislators in other ways. In 2012, before the matter was debated in the state assembly, detectives "expressed frustration regarding current inadequate reporting requirements for secondhand businesses" at CorStat meetings. In response, the ROIC's Fusion Liaison and Intelligence Training (FLIT) Unit "commenced the Pawn Shop initiative." The FLIT Unit collaborated with the State Office of Weights and Measure, and NJSP's Legislation and Research Unit "to draft the necessary verbiage to amend the current legislation" and "make reporting requirements . . . mandatory and to implement statewide usage of technology such the Regional Automated Property Information Database (RAPID) to capture these transactions at the point-of-sale"[61] In 2014, Atlantic City, Egg Harbor Township, and Ocean County adopted the FLIT Unit's model legislation and mandated that all pawnshops record all transactions into the RAPID.[62] By 2016, Bayonne, Belleville, East Rutherford, and Jersey City followed.[63] That same year, the first pawnshop owners were prosecuted in an investigation involving the RAPID.[64]

PACIFYING POVERTY AND PRODUCING THE ORDER OF CAPITAL

Taken together, these ILP initiatives—multiagency drug war operations; landlord training, trespass affidavit, and narcotics eviction programs; and secondhand dealer laws—show how policing fabricates capitalist social relations. In different ways, these programs disrupt moral economies of poverty, the ill-understood survival strategies of the working class. In the contemporary United States, these practices revolve around regulating the surplus populations laboring in the drug trade and other criminalized forms of commerce. Multiagency drug operations are the centerpiece of this effort. These police offenses administratively subsume criminalized labor within the criminal legal system. Specifically, through intelligence analysis, arrest, and prosecution the drug war imposes legal forms of subjectivity on individuals and organizations that reproduce themselves outside of the formal economy. This process both regulates a criminalized market that cannot be suppressed and continually (re)forms the security apparatus. The prohibition of drugs and the violence that surrounds it orients the work of police agencies, stimulates their development, and provides them with a source of revenue through asset seizures. Landlord training, trespass affidavit, and narcotics eviction initiatives extend the reach of police power into "private" spaces. Under the threat of fines, legal action, and eviction, these programs coerce landlords and tenants into collaborating with police. They transform rental properties into quasi-correctional spaces. They disrupt moral economies of poverty by discouraging both landlords and tenants from either tacitly or explicitly accommodating the drug economy. Finally, the ILP operations enabled by secondhand dealer laws allow police to attack the broader market in stolen and otherwise criminalized goods. Through these efforts, police disrupt moral economies of poverty, (re)produce administratively legible market relations, and reaffirm the power of capital.

Most importantly, these operations focus our attention on the essential contradiction of security: the dialectic between moral economies of poverty and police power. The contemporary institutionalization of intelligence fusion and related ILP operations are products of the endless churn of this dialectic. Structurally, policing pacifies poverty. In earlier epochs of historical capitalism, police power destroyed the last vestiges of pre-capitalist, communal economies. It proletarianized people and forced them to sell their labor. In the contemporary United States, decades of deindustrialization and disinvestment, a consequence of the imposition of workfare, has produced a different outcome: growing numbers of surplus populations structurally excluded from or weakly connected to the formal economy. This situation, coupled with the rise of mass incarceration, helped create moral economies of poverty that largely revolve around the drug trade. Today, policing monitors, manages, and administratively subsumes this criminalized labor regime and related social reproduction practices. Moral economies of poverty are sites of class struggle and potential bases of resistance to capital and state. While their substantive political content is rarely expressed in self-conscious terms, it is no less threatening than other forms of "politics." If the aggressive police response is a useful yardstick, moral economies of poverty may be more threatening to the existing social orders than the organized political movements existing today. In any case, these activities—not "terrorism" or even political radicalism—are the most common targets of intelligence fusion and ILP. Poverty is the fulcrum of police power, pacification, and mass supervision.

Conclusion: The Camden Model and the Chicago Challenge

Police Reform and Abolition

In 2015, President Obama traveled to Camden to highlight the success of the new county police force. After the budget crisis, layoffs, and crime surge in 2011 and 2012, the Camden County Police committed to community policing. By the end of 2014, the number of violent crimes fell by over 20 percent and the number homicides was cut in half. Obama praised the city as "a symbol of promise for the nation." He noted its community policing practices: officers "walk[ing] the beat" and "actually getting to know the residents—to set up basketball games, to volunteer in schools, to participate in reading programs, to get to know the small businesses in the area." The feel-good story provided the backdrop to announce the President's Task Force on Twenty-First Century Policing, a commission created in December 2014 to recommend reforms that would "strengthen community policing and trust among law enforcement officers and the communities they serve—especially in light of recent events around the country." Five months later, at the annual meeting of the International Association of Chiefs of Police (IACP), Obama cited Camden, "where they used to have complete mistrust between the department and local residents, and where the crime rate was sky high. And they're now using community policing and data to drive down crime."[1]

The president was trying to sell a "smarter" version of community policing to address the post-Ferguson crisis of police legitimacy, the Camden model. The Task Force recommend reforms in five areas: a cultural shift to "embrace a guardian—rather than a warrior—mindset;" "clear and comprehensive policies" for use of force, mass demonstrations, and consent for searches; expanded use of technology; community policing; more training; and increased emphasis on officer safety and "wellness."[2] The language of "guardians" may very well be derived from Camden. Since the May 2013 relaunch as the Camden County Police, Chief Scott Thomson has explained the department's community policing approach in these terms. "The most important roles for the police are as guardian figures and community builders," he told a reporter in December 2014, five months before the release of the Task Force's report; "Police must strive to employ the greatest force multiplier—the people—to coalesce around the common objective of safety and well being."[3] Police reformers and media outlets also praised Camden's de-escalation training, the "Guardian Culture Program." From July 2015 to October 2016, Camden police responded to over twenty-four hundred calls for armed persons, made 370 arrests and had only one "officer-involved shooting."[4] The reformed force was also using cutting-edge technology. In addition to the surveillance systems detailed in the prologue, the reformed department also opened a Real Time Tactical Operational Intelligence Center (RT-TOIC), a fusion center "that pulls together data from an array of cameras, gunshot location devices and automated license plate readers." The RT-TOIC runs predicted analytics software, "CrimeScape," produced by CivicScape, a technology firm founded by a former Chicago cop. It uses the software to "to determine what blocks warrant heightened police presence or even which people are most likely to be involved."[5] Of course, these efforts provide the details that frame the dramatic lead: "Crime Numbers Plummet in Camden."[6]

When I traveled to Camden in October 2016, community activists told me a different story, one that resonated with my broader conclusion that intelligence fusion and intelligence-led policing (ILP) are reconfiguring state administration around a strategy of mass supervision. "When they started, they were out in force, very aggressive," one activist working on youth leadership development told me, "Cops were everywhere doing foot patrols, squad cars on the corners with their lights on all night, writing tickets for everything, talking to everybody."[7] In practice, the much touted "community policing" efforts blurred with the aggressive enforcement of misdemeanors, what has been variously called broken window, public order, or quality-of-life policing. The municipal court struggled to process the nearly 125,000 cases on its docket from July 2013 and 2014, a 97,000-case increase from the previous year. Many of these were petty offenses. From July through October 2014, for example, the Camden County Police wrote ninety-nine tickets for riding a bicycle without a bell. They issued one in the previous year.[8] "Community policing is just how they're selling broken windows," an activist with the Camden chapter of the National Association for Advancement of Colored People (NAACP) told me. "They're increased contacts with the community by citing people for anything and everything."[9] This method of "actually getting to know the residents" came at a cost. In 2014, excessive force complaints reached sixty-five, nearly twice the number of the previous year and more than the combined total for Newark and Jersey City, the two largest cities in the state.[10]

An ILP offensive lurked behind the media-friendly optics of community engagement and the daily grind of broken-windows policing. All "contacts" between police and residents also double as moments of intelligence collection. In October 2016, I accompanied a Camden police officer on a "directed patrol" in a "guardian zone." It was a rebranding of "saturation patrols" in a "hot spot." The officer explained:

> The guardian zones are basically a way for us to proactively address crime conditions. . . . In this area, we're supposed address assault incidents, and possible drug-related conditions. . . . We're expected to be proactive, so we make lots of pedestrian stops, not necessarily in a negative way but we get out and talk to residents. . . . If we see a moving violation, we'll stop somebody and that gives us an opportunity to talk and get some information. . . . Occasionally, you'll stop somebody, you'll talk to somebody who will share information about a crime that they witnessed or maybe something they've heard. We'll do what's called a Community Intelligence Report to record the information. Even if they don't want their identity shared with law enforcement, we'll fill out the report and leave out their information. We'll also write up Field Contact Cards for any interaction we have, even if it's something that's not a citation or any obvious intelligence information. All these cards get reviewed by the Strategic Analysis Unit and they use that intelligence to analyze the crime conditions. They use the information we get from citizens.

During the ride along, the officer stopped to speak to a homeless man whom she knew by name. She also stopped a middle-aged man to warn him for jaywalking. "Normally, I would've written up a field contact for that," she explained. Later, we drove past a man rolling a marijuana cigarette in public. "He's walkin' down the street rolling a blunt! I should write him up and lock him up and I will. Now, I'm officially pissed off." She circled back, but the man had disappeared from sight. "If I was by myself, I'd find him and put him in the back of this car." When I asked if she would consider confiscating the marijuana and giving a warning, she repeated the mantra of broken-windows policing: "It's against the law and they know it's against the law. Why I should I give you discretion when you're blatantly disrespecting the law? It doesn't make any sense! If I did, they'd think it was OK and then it goes from walking down the street smoking a blunt to selling on this block. It just escalates. We don't want that."[11] Shortly after this incident, the ride along ended. An announcement from the RT-TOIC came across the radio that all reports needed to be in by 12:30.

Camden's much-hyped community policing was a little thin. No doubt, I saw only a tiny sliver of the city's community policing programs. The officer I interviewed also did outreach in schools and held neighborhood "pop-up barbeques." She did not, however, organize beat meetings to institute the "collaborative problem solving" that supposedly defines community policing.[12] Instead, Camden activists explained that "community outreach" had only produced personal relationships with officers. "Somebody was driving on one of the football fields at night and tore it up," an organizer who focused on youth programming told me. "I now know an officer I can call and they'll actually be out there the next night. That's new." Even these connections between police and key community figures, moreover, have an intelligence component. Criminologists writing about "community intelligence-led policing" have identified "'neighbourhood sentinels'... mothers with children, postal delivery workers, people who are engaged in local groups" as important sources of information. "There's officers who know me. They talk to me;" the same activist elaborated, "We both tryin' to get something out of it. They're tryin' to learn a little about the community from me and I just want them to stop bothering every young person walkin' down sidewalk. I want them to do something that actually helps."[13]

Camden's much-celebrated crime reduction was also more complicated than presented. From 2010 to 2013, Camden logged between 1,900 and 2,100 violent crimes each year. After the budget crisis and the layoffs, murders rose by 80 percent from thirty-seven in 2010 to sixty-seven in 2012. The reformed police began with an aggressive campaign of intelligence collection and misdemeanor enforcement. The total number of violent crimes dropped down to 1,550 in 2014 and in the 1,500 range until 2017, when it fell to 1,467. Homicides fell to thirty-three and thirty-four in 2014 and 2015 but increased to forty-four in 2016. In 2017, there were only twenty-two homicides, the lowest number since 1980.[14] "Our crime rate is too high," the NAACP activist told me, "It's better than a few years ago, but that's nothing to brag about." He also raised some doubts about the accuracy of the numbers. "I think there's some smoke and mirrors stuff going on. Right now, we're concerned they're underreporting. We think they might be putting assault in as simple assault to the numbers look better."[15] While officials denied the allegations, year-end data for 2016 showed that simple assaults increased over a fifth to reach a total of 3,026.[16]

Others doubted that police or the larger government would do much to improve Camden's fate. "There used to be drug sets on every corner in North Camden," a community activist and small business owner told me, "they cleared them out here, but they can't stop it everywhere and they

can't do anything to change *the reasons* why there's so much drugs here."
He went on to discuss the surge in shootings in 2016, identifying the
underlying dynamics that I analyze as the dialectic relation between police
power and moral economies of poverty:

> A lot of what have going on with the spike in murders is drug dealers
> working it out after the police came through the way they did. . . .
> You've got to understand what made Camden so major was
> manufacturing. That went away and the drug trade ushered in. It kinda
> subsidized the city. . . . Whether you want to admit or not, that's what
> happened. That's what kept this city alive. . . . But now you've cut down
> the drug trade and you haven't replaced it or the manufacturing jobs. So
> what do you think is going to happen? They're robbin,' they're stealin,'
> they're fightin' for what's left of the drug trade. That's why you had all
> those killings. People from other parts of the town that never had to
> interact with each other now trying to sell on the same turf. . . . You
> have guys saying, "OK, let's get together" but then there's no trust. So,
> it's like, you know, "I don't know this guy. I'll get in with 'em for a
> while and then rob his ass." So you have this spike. . . . Everybody who
> lives here knows what's going on. It's no mystery. It's a spike and it'll
> settle when the turf wars settle and they're settling now. . . . The cops all
> know this. They won't say it, but they're not stupid. They know what's
> going on. They're just about keeping a lid on it.

He also was skeptical about the states broader strategy to redevelop
Camden:

> It's a sad thing. There's twelve hundred unemployed people here. Just
> the other day, I heard that the [Economic Development Authority]
> proposed $130-some million tax rebate for a hotel on the waterfront.
> It's going to guarantee fifty-five jobs for $130-some million. I'm like,
> "Really? Fifty-five jobs for millions and millions? . . . I'm not just so
> sure about the geniuses planning this stuff. They've brought the Sixers
> and Holtec to Camden. I mean I'm not against that, but let's be real for
> a minute. At the end of the day, it's not gonna make a dent in those
> twelve hundred unemployed.[17]

Here, he was citing the $139 million tax incentive given to CHP Land LLC to
open a Hilton Hotel in Camden that was eventually approved in June 2017.
He also referenced two earlier tax abatements: $260 million to entice Holtec
International, Inc. to manufactures nuclear reactor parts in Camden and $82
million for the Philadelphia Seventy-Sixers to open a practice facility.[18] By
the end of 2016, these abatements seemed to deliver. Camden's job market
grew by 3.7 percent, tied for highest in the nation.[19] In interviews, however,
Camden community leaders were quick to point out that many of these jobs

are out of reach for many residents. "We're talking about a city where there's a lot of third-generation drug dealers, where the public schools have been underfunded for generations," the activist focusing on youth leadership development told me. "So, sure, you can bring jobs here but there's a lot people that are already out of the running for them. A lot of those jobs are going to go people who will commute from the suburbs or Philly."[20]

While these corporate handouts are unlikely to reverse Camden's long-term economic decline, they do underscore the broader context of the much-hyped police pacification project. The response to Camden's crisis is corporate tax abatements and police pacification. Along with the cost-cutting restructuring of Camden's police, previously discussed in the prologue, these measures show that the logic of workfare remains the guiding principle for policy makers. Additionally, the fact that this drama is playing out in New Jersey, one the early leaders in the now nationwide reduction in prison populations, also further supports the analysis in earlier chapters. Decarceration does not challenge the punitive approach of mass incarceration. Instead, it realigns the criminal legal system around mass supervision, an administrative strategy that emphasizes policing and surveillance over imprisonment to manage class struggle and continually (re)produce capitalist social relations. During a time of crisis and change, Camden is the site of a dramatic pacification project. It exhibits certain relations in exaggerated fashion and provides a clear expression of the tendency for intelligence fusion and related police operations to create quasi-correctional environments, open air prisons. However, there are pockets of Camden in most communities, hyper-policed neighborhoods that house the criminalized sections of the working class, and, as previous chapters have shown, many of the practices on display in Camden are evident elsewhere.

Although Camden is not a political center, local leaders are voicing many of the same criticisms as larger movements. Black radicals often use the term "Black Freedom Movement," to connote the long struggle of black peoples, not simply to distribute the ill-gotten gains of historical capitalism, but to defeat racism, restore our sullied humanity, and expand the domain of freedom.[21] The Black Lives Matter (BLM) movement is the latest expression of this struggle. Camden did not have any organizations explicitly adopting the BLM banner, but the movement's influence was evident. A month before I traveled to Camden, a high school football team made news by taking a knee to join the protest against police violence sweeping across the National Football League. "We don't want to disrespect the people that fought for our freedom," one student told a reporter "but, at the same time, the way we live, we're not free all the way."[22] When I asked the small business owner and community activist about the football team taking a knee, he spoke in terms consonant with claims of BLM. "The police here are an occupying army. It's changed a little but not enough even to make me think about disagreeing with those kids for second."[23]

The Black Freedom Movement, moreover, has long been a feminist movement, something that BLM has made especially clear.[24] This means more than female leadership. It means, in Saidiya Hartman's words, a politics that centers the labor of care and social reproduction as "the antidote to violence" and an alternative basis for social order.[25] The small business owner and community activist also advocated for investment into the grassroots efforts that sustain social life in environments of privation and trauma. "There needs to be more investment in the grassroots organizations that are here. I feel that they're the real heroes." He then listed off dozens of people involved in various projects, including a local dance school, a mutual-aid association, "the chess club ... the football leagues ... the comedy shows ... the people fighting hard for our schools, and, I mean, the people that really hold this city together. The people that give and give and give." He reasoned that "if they left the day after tomorrow, this would really be a warzone. . . . I don't care about what police force you put in or how many cameras you put up, this city would a warzone. It would be another riot and this city would be burned to the ground."[26]

These sentiments reflect the specificities of this historical moment and, like the increasingly prominent strategy of mass supervision, they extend beyond Camden. When President Obama spoke at the IACP meeting to promote his agenda for police reform, the police association happened to be meeting in Chicago, home to vibrant examples of the Black Freedom Struggle, like Black Youth Project (BYP) 100 and We Charge Genocide (WCG). Activists obstructed the entrance to conference for hours. Chicago Police eventually cleared the blockades, arresting sixty-six people. The day after Obama's closing speech, BYP 100, WCG, and other organizations released a collaborative grassroots report on Chicago's long-running community policing program. *The Counter-CAPS Report: The Community Engagement Arm of the Police State* denounced community policing and called for "divestment from [the Chicago Police Department] and reinvestment in social services like education and public health that will meet real community needs."[27] This was the clash of two historical forces. The Camden model of police reform met the Chicago challenge of abolition. With the Camden model, Obama was trying to create a liberal coalition for police reform. At the IACP, he was trying to build consensus among law enforcement. He had already won the support of moderates within BLM. In

August 2015, Britney Packett, Deray McKesson, and other visible BLM activists launched Campaign Zero, a police reform campaign largely drawn from the recommendations from Obama's task force.[28] The IACP shutdown, in contrast, was organized by a black-led, multiracial coalition of mostly youth activists. It was another upswelling of the same social forces behind national movements like Occupy, BLM, the Fight for $15, and the reinvigorated Democratic Socialists of America (DSA).

Indeed, the protests at the IACP meeting was one many actions and political education events in larger campaign against police violence. We Charge Genocide formed to document the harm of the system, while centering and uplifting the experiences of young people of color most targeted by police violence. Evoking the 1951 report that the Civil Rights Congress, an important civil rights organization in the late 1940s and early 1950s, presented to the United Nations (UN), We Charge Genocide organized collaborative grassroots research and compiled an independent assessment on police violence in Chicago. They later sent a delegation of black youth to present the report to the UN Committee against Torture.[29] Meanwhile, BYP 100 built a national organization, participated in countless protest actions, and compiled two comprehensive reports that called for structural reforms. *The Agenda to Keep Us Safe* advocated for community control over police, an end to the drug war, and other measures to reduce the scope police power.[30] *The Agenda to Build Black Futures* demanded reparations, a worker's bill of rights, universal health care, and other mechanisms to redistribute wealth and address enduring racialized inequalities.[31] In March 2015, WCG, BYP 100, and other organizations, won a major victory. After months of organizing, the Chicago City Council passed a repatriations bill to compensate the 110 black men tortured by the "midnight crew" of John Burge, an infamous Chicago Police commander active in the 1970s and 1980s. The bill provided $5.5 million in damages, counseling, and other services. It also mandated that Chicago Public Schools include the city's history of police torture in the curriculum.[32] Seven months later, these organizations helped disrupt the IACP meeting, released a report challenging the Camden model, and demanded reinvestment in social services.

These campaigns are explicitly abolitionist. In other words, they seek to dismantle the security apparatus—police, prisons, the military, and intelligence community. They call for structural reforms: reinvestment universal public goods, and specialized programs to redress historical injustices. Hence, abolitionists fight "for non-reformist reforms" what Dan Berger, Mariame Kaba, and David Stein define as "measures that reduce the power of an oppressive system while illuminating the system's inability to solve the crises it creates." This abolitionism "engage[s] these contradictions by pursuing reforms that shrink the state's capacity for violence." In this way, the abolitionist project tries to avoid the trap of traditional reformist politics. Citing fraught reforms like the shift from indeterminate sentencing into mandatory minimums and the recent creation of "gender-responsive" prison, Berger, Kaba, and Stein contend that "reform . . . often grow[s] the state's capacity to punish."[33] This position resonates with my earlier critique of surveillance scholars and civil libertarians. By trying to limit surveillance with privacy, they paradoxically legalize, codify, and entrench the very abuses they wish to curtail. In this way, even seemingly "critical" scholars or oppositional stances get drawn into the prose of pacification, the discourses and practices that animate administration, organize the state apparatus, and encourage its growth.

In the years since BLM emerged, abolitionist perspectives have become more prominent. In August 2016, a coalition of fifty organizations released *A Vision for Black Lives: Policy Demands for Black Power, Freedom and Justice*, an expanded version of the earlier policy platforms from BYP 100. The agenda is clearly abolitionist. Its proposals for criminal justice reform, couched as "end[ing] the war on black people," are rolled into a larger set of demands for economic justice and political empowerment, including a divest-reinvest strategy to redirect resources for policing, prisons, war, and fossil fuel development toward universal public goods.[34] The next year, the DSA, a once-marginal organization that now counts tens of thousands of members, endorsed the abolitionist agenda of *Vision for Black Lives*: the abolition of police and prisons through a divest-reinvest strategy. Simultaneously, local movement coalitions began organizing campaigns for a series of non-reformist reforms. Across the country, organizers are creating community bail funds to limit pretrial detention. In 2018, Philadelphia elected Larry Krasner, "the most radical district attorney in the country," who immediately worked to reduce incarceration and bring greater accountability to police. Other campaigns to elect "progressive district attorneys" followed. In Chicago, many of the same individuals and organizations that won the reparation bills and shutdown the IACP meeting are working to block a $95 million proposal to build a police training complex and redirect the resources to public education. Carlos Ramirez-Rosa, an alderman and DSA member, is the campaign's lone supporter on the City Council. In the summer and fall of 2018, the Trump administration's hard-line immigration policies had made the demand to abolish Immigration Customs Enforcement *both* a rallying cry for protest (including some militant direct actions) *and* a talking point for some Democratic politicians.

At this juncture, the medium-term outlook is far from clear. Is mass incarceration really unraveling? Are we witnessing the beginning of the end or the end of the beginning? With the world-economy mired in low growth and low profitably, is neoliberal globalization finally over? Is the workfare-carceral state collapsing or transforming? The answers to these questions are impossible to determine, as they depend on the outcomes of ongoing political struggles, both those outside and within the state. The lines of struggle are sharpening, and American politics are polarizing. The white supremacist and neo-fascist movements are rising alongside the ascendant American left. Perhaps the left will provide the bottom-up pressure necessary for comprehensive institutional change. Perhaps the law and order emphasis of the Trump administration will close the door on this moment of reform. As it stands, street fighting among rival partisans and terrorism from the far right are threatening to tear the fabric of civil society apart. Will the security apparatus hold the center together, as liberals hope? Will the state stand aside and let the fighting continue? Will it, as many leftists fear, intervene on behalf of the reactionaries and counterrevolutionaries and move the United States toward a more naked form of authoritarianism?

I researched and wrote *Pacifying the Homeland* while struggling with these questions and supporting these movements. This book explains the genesis of police power in the United States and details the forms it takes today. It shows how policing—and the state's broader pacification projects—administer poverty, create the working class, shape the state apparatus, and continually (re)form the larger social formation we call the United States. The story of intelligence fusion has deeper roots than 9/11, DHS, and the war on terror. It begins with the crisis of the *herrenvolk*-welfare state and the consolidation of the workfare-carceral state, the transition from a formally segregated, industrial society to a "colorblind," postindustrial one. When the prison population exploded in the 1980s and 1990s, intelligence fusion was an unacknowledged future of mass supervision, the underappreciated corollary to mass incarceration. In the last two decades of economic crisis and war, intelligence fusion has become more prominent. Due to the particular structure of the workfare-carceral state, intelligence fusion has been institutionalized in an uneven and conflictive pattern, as the comparison between New York and New Jersey shows. Despite this complexity, however, the general state strategy is clear. Intelligence fusion has become the center of gravity of mass supervision. It draws together police, courts, and the wider security apparatus in a shared practice to monitor dissent and, most importantly, manage poverty. If these arrangements can manage their contradictions, namely organizational dysfunction, they may allow a reconfigured workfare-carceral state to weather the current crisis.

In this way, *Pacifying the Homeland* encourages us to think more systemically about police power, and its centrality to the state. The state is not a "thing" to be seized or smashed. It is the institutional condensation of social relations in the form of political power. This materiality of the state—the fundamental contribution of Poulantzas—means the state is inescapable, both politically and analytically. The state is present in the formation of class powers. Through police power, it administers poverty and continually shapes the working class. The bloody legislations against vagabonds and today's intelligence-led manhunts in the postindustrial city are historically specific manifestations of capital's endless hunt for workers. There is a continuum between the enclosure of commons at the dawn of the capitalist epoch and today's efforts to pacify the moral economies of poverty rooted in the drug trade. The central importance of police power to the modern state reveals one of the fundamental contradictions of capitalist society: the dialectic relation between police power and moral economies of poverty. Like the antagonism between labor and capital, this contradiction can only be resolved by systemic transformation. In the absence of a dramatic social change, police power manages these contradictions and continually (re)produces capitalist social relations: private property, market relations, wage labor, and the commodity form.

This analysis raises challenging questions, for example about the divest-reinvest approach to abolition. Undoubtedly, the proponents of this project do not want to divest from police *departments* in order to invest in other social policy responses that also bear the marks of *police power*. Mass supervision by the kinder gentler "social police" would not be the radical break that these movements demand. Instead, the substantive concern must be how to exorcise *police power* and the prose of pacification from social life. In this regard, non-reformist reforms need to extend beyond defensive "measures that reduce the power of an oppressive system while illuminating the system's inability to solve the crises it creates." Can we think of non-reformist reforms as measures to shift power relations to the advantage of the working class and institutionalize different ways of living? Rather than simply rolling back oppression, can non-reformist reforms build power, transform institutions, and help produce a new way of living outside of the dictatorship of the bourgeoisie? Thinking of police power in a more structural way, I contend, helps advance this task. For example, it reminds us that divestment from police will not advance abolition unless there is reinvestment in something that challenges the specificity of capitalist social relations. Not just investment in "social services" but the re-creation of the commons through de-commodifying public goods such as housing, health care, education, and other necessities of social reproduction understood as inalienable rights. These questions, I contend, are the type that can open up wider political horizons. This book was written to advance them.

Research and the World of Official Secrets

A Methodological Note

On the morning of May 14, 2013, I was driving to the New York State Intelligence Center (NYSIC) for my first site visit. I was about halfway there when the NYSIC security/privacy officer emailed me. The message had no salutation or explanation: "We do a site security check for those we allow onto the premises. What is your date of birth? That way we can get it done before you arrive." I pulled over at the next gas station, sent a quick reply on my BlackBerry—"Lt. Veepings, My date of birth is May 12, 1985. See you soon, Brendan"—and got back on the highway.[1] I spent the last forty minutes of the drive worrying that they were going to turn me away when I arrived. At 9:45, I pulled up to a nondescript intersection in the suburban sprawl surrounding Albany. I had fifteen minutes to find the place and review my notes one last time. I passed a Hilton, a Ford dealership, a Rite-Aid, a sparse strip mall anchored by a Mr. Sub and a Dollar General but no fusion center.

I circled back and found the right address: two large, windowless steel buildings so close that they first appeared as one L-shaped structure. A blue and white sign read "World Class Gymnastics Academy." On the far side of the other building, I noticed a door. There was no sign but there was a security camera and, on the far end of the building, perimeter fencing that secured the parking lot. When investigative journalists Dana Priest and William Arkin looked into what they called "top secret America"—the interwoven and rapidly expanding world of federal intelligence agencies and security contractors—they found intelligence outposts in otherwise unremarkable office parks all over the Washington, D.C., metro area: National Geospatial-Intelligence Agency office in the shadow of a Michaels craft store and a Books-A-Million, an annex of the National Security Agency near an airport parking garage, an "alternative geography" of official secrets hidden in plain sight.[2] There it was, New York's fusion center hidden behind "one of the Northeast's premier gymnastic training facilities."

I walked to the door and went inside: a small foyer, another door, and a middle-aged secretary, sitting behind a window, "Can I help you?"

"My name is Brendan McQuade. I'm here to see Lieutenant Veepings."

"I'll call him for you." She handed me a clipboard. "Please sign in." She picked up the phone and spoke quietly into the receiver. "Sit down. He will be with you shortly."

"Thank you." I sat down on the bench and exhaled loudly, too loudly.

"Are you nervous? Don't be!" she chirped from behind the glass. I waited for another fifteen minutes. Eventually, the lieutenant came through the second door. We exchanged empty pleasantries, and he showed me to their conference room. Everyone was there: the NYSIC director, an FBI special agent from the Albany field office, a representative from DHS, the assistant director of the New York State Office of Counter Terrorism within the New York State Division of Homeland Security and Emergency Service, the open-records officer working on my long-delayed Freedom of Information Law request to the New York State Police, the NYSIC chief analyst, and three more state troopers in management positions. I tried to cut the tension a bit. "Well, this is a little intimidating," I said.

A state trooper looked at me, made eye contact and said, "That is exactly how we want this to be, Brendan." Everyone laughed. I didn't think it was very funny. After a PowerPoint presentation, they opened the floor to my questions. I planned for one-on-one interviews but adjusted well enough to stretch the group interview for two and a quarter hours. By the end of the interview, some were visibly annoyed. There was fidgeting. I talked to the director for another twenty minutes and the privacy officer for fifteen minutes. I spent another half hour with director and open-records officer negotiating what records they would release. After the meeting, they said I could come back and interview analysts. I scheduled the interviews, twice. They were canceled, twice, both times without reason. Eventually, the NYSIC command sent me 392 terse and uninformative words that responded to a nine-question interview template, three of which they refused to answer. At the end of the group interview, the NYSIC director also gave me his office number and encouraged me call him with any follow-up questions. I made dozens of calls and left as many messages. They were never answered or returned. I had broken down the doors of the castle, only to confront a well-disciplined and unified palace guard. I had hit a wall.

The "wall" I confronted was the invisible but very real boundaries of a vast and indistinct social space: the world of official secrets. Today, over five million Americans hold security clearances. In contrast, just 1.8 million work in the non-classified parts of the federal government. Of those millions with security clearances, 1.5 million have access to "top secret" information.[3] This world of official secrets represents accumulated knowledge, by some estimates yearly outnumbering publicly produced knowledge by five times.[4] Could I break into this world? From the outside, fusion centers looked unapproachable. But how did I appear from the point of view of fusion centers managers? Undoubtedly, I was an outsider. I had no family or friends who worked in the field. The sociology department at Binghamton University, where I was enrolled as a PhD student at the time, did not have any faculty members who could broker my access. I had to find my own way in.

I sent formal interview requests to seven nearby fusion centers. This was a practical matter. Having failed to secure a research grant, I funded my own research and these fusion centers were within driving distance. I made follow-up phone calls. Lots of them. Starting in June 2012, when I sent out my initial letters, I would begin every week with what became my Monday-morning ritual: cold calling fusion centers and, soon, their "law enforcement partners" like municipal police departments, district attorney's offices, and other government agencies or offices. Sometimes, you have to hit your head against the wall until you make the cracks yourself. By August, I had a contact at New Jersey's fusion center, the Regional Operations Intelligence Center (ROIC). We played phone tag for weeks, while trying to do a preliminary interview. He was a busy man and hard to pin down.

Despite innumerable phone calls and brief conversations on his morning commute, I never formally interviewed him for my study. Eventually, he invited me to observe an interagency intelligence meeting in North Jersey in September. He introduced me to the senior staff of the ROIC and asked a trooper to help schedule a few research visits. As soon as I was making headway, I had a setback. My first trip to the ROIC to conduct interviews was delayed by Hurricane Sandy, which hit New Jersey hard in late October. The ROIC doubled as the state's emergency operations center. My visit was delayed until late January 2013. All the while, my Monday-morning ritual of cold calling fusion centers continued. The Connecticut Intelligence Center and the Pennsylvania Criminal Intelligence Center gave me preliminary interviews but declined to participate in my study. The Boston Regional Intelligence and the Commonwealth Fusion Center eventually acknowledged requests but they too declined. The best I got from the Rhode Island State Fusion Center was an empty promise that the director would return my call.

I later realized that the ROIC granted me access because they had a uniquely public profile for a fusion center. This position grew from the recent history the New Jersey State Police (NJSP), the ROIC's parent agency. We owe the term "racial profiling" to the NJSP's pattern of discriminatory enforcement in the 1980s and 1990s. The department was notorious for "ghost stops," unreported stops where troopers searched cars and let drivers go if they did not find anything illegal. Joe Collum, the journalist who coined the term "racial profiling," found that 76 percent of New Jersey Turnpike arrests in 1988 and 1989 were African Americans for possession of drugs and weapons. Collum also interviewed people who had been stopped and searched, but not charged, and concluded that blacks and dark-skinned Hispanics made up 90 percent of those pulled over.[5]

The issued exploded into national news in 1998, when troopers opened fire on van with four black men during a traffic stop. As a result, the NJSP signed a consent decree, agreeing to federal oversight. The decree was not lifted until 2009. Under the consent decree, the NJSP installed dashboard cameras to videotape traffic stops, changed training, and implemented new policies to record road stops. The experience transformed the NJSP. It adopted a "smarter" image. Under the tenure of Colonel Rick Fuentes, NJSP police superintendent from 2003 to 2017, the tighter management systems and more detailed reporting imposed under the consent decree gave way to a broader reform movement centered on intelligence-led policing (ILP). In 2005, the NJSP reorganized their investigations branch around their intelligence functions of police work in order to facilitate the proactive disruption of crime envisioned as "intelligence-led policing."[6] The next year, the NJSP and the Manhattan Institute, a neoliberal think tank that had previously worked with the administration of New York City mayor Rudolph Giuliani to advance controversial policing practices, released *The New Jersey State Police Practical Guide to Intelligence-Led Policing.*[7]

As part of this public embrace of ILP, the NJSP have made the ROIC part of their public image. The fusion center appears in press releases extolling successful police operations. It features in government newsletters, and trade publications. The leadership at the ROIC also welcomed other researchers and facilitated two other dissertations.[8] One of the ROIC's senior managers was a visible police reformer, who had written on the subjects for *Police Chief*, the official publication of the International Association of Chiefs of Police. The director and assistant director of the ROIC held master's degrees in homeland security and defense from the Naval Postgraduate School. While I was doing my field work, the Naval Postgraduate School accepted another trooper at the ROIC for their master's degree program. My research was following a precedent. All told, I interviewed thirty-three state troopers, intelligence analysts, and others that worked in intelligence in New Jersey. I also observed nine meetings: internal meetings of the ROIC's intelligence and analysis unit, regional information-sharing meetings in North Jersey, a training session for the Fusion Center Liaison Officer program, and an operationally focused interagency task force on narcotics.

The connections I made at the ROIC also helped me access the NYSIC. Again, my work was made possible by law enforcement professionals who had sympathies with my position as a young scholar. My broker was a retired municipal police officer who held a federal position that required him to travel to fusion centers across the Northeast. Many years previously, he had started a PhD program but did not continue after obtaining his master's degree. "I always was intrigued by the academic lifestyle," he told me. The eventual expansion of my research into New York was a tremendous advance for my study. Although I was never achieved the same of access to NYSIC that I had to the ROIC, there is always a back door. For much of the spring and summer of 2013, I worked around the obstinacy of the NYSIC command to find entrance or at least a window to peer through. I tracked down former NYSIC analysts who moved on to other positions in government or academia. I also expanded my study to include Operation IMPACT and its county Crime Analysis Centers. Altogether, I interviewed forty-two state troopers, intelligence analysts, municipal police officers, assistant district attorneys and others working in intelligence in New York State.

The specific vector of my research also shaped the type of data I gathered and my methods. I entered into the world of official secrets by trading on scholarly credentials. I found sympathetic officials who granted me access to the ROIC, where my access was largely unobstructed, and later to the NYSIC, where my admission was tightly controlled. From here, New York State's crowded institutional environment and competing intelligence programs presented two avenues for further research: an indirect approach to get at the NYSIC by contacting former employees and partner agencies, and an expansion of the study to consider the same practice, intelligence fusion, as it is instituted through a different mechanism, Operation IMPACT. These dynamics also shaped my methods. Concretely, I started where the practical nature of my research demands I begin, the ethnographic present or the observed reality of intelligence fusion and ILP. I approached research as a generative exercise that develops through successive cycles of data collection, analysis, and reflection. Taking a particularly historical approach to the practice of "grounded theory," I simultaneously undertook data collection and analysis, constructing analytic codes and categories from data, not from preconceived logically deduced hypotheses.[9] Instead of beginning with ideal typical categories that are said to align with empirical data, a movement of thought from concept to indicator, I "mov[ed] out by successive determinations, bringing in successive parts—themselves abstract processes—in constant juxtaposition."[10] In this way, recalling the discussion of "incorporated comparisons" in chapter 1, I built a conceptual whole out of empirical research, rather than assuming a whole that can be filled with empirical content. My "research sample" developed organically in the form of a "snowball" sample.[11] My analytic attention was not geared toward "representativeness" but theory construction.[12]

Altogether, I completed over a year of fieldwork where I observed nine meetings and interviewed seventy-five people who work in intelligence in New York and New Jersey. While I conducted most of these interviews in 2013, I did a smaller set of interviews in 2014. When I reconceptualized the dissertation as a book, I traveled to Camden, New Jersey, and conducted five more interviews in October 2016. At this time, I did a ride-along with a Camden County police officer and public affairs official. The county public affairs office had arranged for me to interview the police chief and the head of Camden's real-time crime center, but both were suddenly unavailable the day of our scheduled interview. I rescheduled a phone interview with the chief nearly a dozen times, only to find that he was too busy to speak every time I called. I also reached out to community leaders, who were far more receptive than the police department. In Camden, I interviewed three community activists and observed a meeting of a grassroots mutual aid association. I also interviewed two more activists over the phone. With these additions, I formally interviewed eighty-two people over the course of three years. These were semi-structured interviews that ranged from a half hour to over two hours. In addition to these interviews, I gathered publicly available primary sources: government reports and documents, whether leaked or released under open-government laws. As a historical sociologist, I approached these materials in a qualitative and constructivist mode. I used historical analysis to trace the processes behind the emergence of these police intelligence systems and the pressures shaping their operation. I mapped out the constitutive relationships that shape intelligence gathering and structure its analysis, dissemination, and operational use.

This project was only successful because I remained flexible and persistent. My initial research questions concerned public-private partnerships and the degree of business influence on fusion centers. When I first got access to the ROIC, I shifted my focus to criminal intelligence because that was their obvious priority. As documents concerning the policing of Occupy and subsequent movements became public, I considered fusion centers' involvement in political policing. When I confronted the wall of official secrets at the NYSIC, I labored to find a way around it. The eventual expansion of the study to cover Operation IMPACT was especially fruitful. It broke the tendency to abstract "fusion centers" out of their constitutive historical and social context and focused my attention on the broader concept of the institutionalization of intelligence fusion. At this point, my historical approach to grounded theory felt especially appropriate. The mass of data collected started to take shape into a coherent project. The resultant 2015 dissertation, however, was rough around the edges. I put too much in the pot and not all of it was fully cooked. Subsequently, I published four essays derived from this research. Two of these analyzed the fine professional struggles within "the bureaucratic field" and "spaces of intelligence fusion."[13] Having separated these aspects of the argument from the larger historical and structural analysis, the other two essays gave the opportunity to further refine my thinking. Although it is not fully evident in these pieces, writing them convinced me to abandon the dissertation's attempt at theoretical synthesis and to reconceptualize the project in terms of Nicos Poulantzas's work and the critique of security.[14] The final product, this book, represents my best efforts and the culmination of these years of research and writing.

Notes

PROLOGUE: POLICING CAMDEN'S CRISIS

1. US Senate, Permanent Subcommittee on Investigations, *Federal Support for and Involvement in State and Local Fusion Centers* (Washington, DC, October 3, 2012), 11–13, https://www.hsgac.senate.gov/imo/media/doc/10-3-2012%20 PSI%20STAFF%20REPORT%20re%20FUSION%20CENTERS.2.pdf.

2. Jon Whittin, "New Jersey is 7th Worst State for Income Inequality," New Jersey Policy Perspective, December 15, 2016, https://www.njpp.org/budget/new -jersey-is-7th-worst-state-for-income-inequality (accessed January 17, 2017).

3. New Jersey Building Authority, *New Jersey Building Authority Annual Report* (Trenton: New Jersey Building Authority, 2008), 14, https://dspace .njstatelib.org/xmlui/handle/10929/15935 (accessed January 30, 2013).

4. The phrase appears throughout the literature on fusion centers and in my interview sample. Proponents and critics of fusion centers both use the expression to, respectively, assert that fusion centers meet the unique needs of their jurisdictions or bemoan the lack of standardization. See: Justin Lewis Abold, Ray Guidetti, and Douglas Keyer, "Strengthening the Value of the National Network of Fusion Centers by Leveraging Specialization: Defining 'Centers of Analytical Excellence,'" *Homeland Security Affairs* 8, no. 1 (2012); Hilary Hylton, "Fusion Centers: Giving Cops Too Much Information?" *Time*, March 9, 2009, https://content.time .com/time/nation/article/0,8599,1883101,00.html (accessed March 13, 2012).

5. Brendan McQuade, "The Puzzle of Intelligence Expertise: Spaces of Intelligence Analysis and the Production of 'Political' Knowledge," *Qualitative Sociology* 39, no. 3 (2016); Brendan McQuade, "Police and the Post-9/11 Surveillance Surge: 'Technological Dramas' in 'the Bureaucratic Field.'" *Surveillance & Society* 14, no. 1 (2016).

6. Mike Davis, "The Urbanization of Empire: Megacities and the Laws of Chaos," *Social Text* 22, no. 4 (2004); Saskia Sassen, *Expulsions: Brutality and Complexity in the Global Economy* (Cambridge, MA: Harvard University Press, 2014).

7. Ruth Gilmore, *Golden Gulag: Prisons, Surplus, Crisis, and Opposition in Globalizing California* (Berkeley: University of California Press, 2006); Christian Parenti, *Lockdown America: Police and Prisons in the Age of Crisis* (New York: Verso, 2000); Jordan T. Camp, *Incarcerating the Crisis: Freedom Struggles and the Rise of the Neoliberal State* (Berkeley: University of California Press, 2016).

8. Reuben Jonathan Miller and Amanda Alexander, "The Price of Carceral Citizenship: Punishment, Surveillance, and Social Welfare Policy in an Age of Carceral Expansion," *Michigan Journal of Race & Law* 21 (2015): 294; Reuben Jonathan Miller, and Forrest Stuart, "Carceral Citizenship: Race, Rights and Responsibility in the Age of Mass Supervision," *Theoretical Criminology* 21, no. 4 (2017); Fergus McNeill and Kristel Beyens, eds., *Offender Supervision in Europe* (New York: Palgrave Macmillan, 2013).

9. David Garland, *The Culture of Control: Crime and Social order in Contemporary Society* (Chicago: University of Chicago Press, 2012), 27–52.

10. For general reviews, see: Marie Gottschalk, *Caught: The Prison State and the Lockdown of American Politics* (Princeton: Princeton University Press, 2016), 165–94; Matthew Epperson and Carrie Pettus-Davis, eds. *Smart Decarceration: Achieving Criminal Justice Transformation in the 21st Century* (New York: Oxford University Press, 2017); for analysis of community supervision and prison reentry, see: Carl Takei, "From Mass Incarceration to Mass Control, and Back Again: How Bipartisan Criminal Justice Reform May Lead to a For-Profit Nightmare," *University of Pennsylvania Journal of Law and Social Change* 20, no. 2 (2017); Joshua M. Price, "Serving Two Masters? Reentry Task Forces and Justice Disinvestment," in *After Prisons? Freedom, Decarceration, and Justice Disinvestment*, ed. William G. Martin and Joshua M. Price (Lanham, MD: Lexington Books, 2016), 77–98; Reuben Jonathan Miller, "Devolving the Carceral State: Race, Prisoner Reentry, and the Micro-Politics of Urban Poverty Management," *Punishment & Society* 16, no. 3 (2014); for more on deferred prosecution and specialized courts, see: Mary D. Fan, "Street Diversion and Decarceration," *American Criminal Law Review* 50 (2013); Mary D. Fan, "Street Diversion and Decarceration," *American Criminal Law Review* 50 (2013); Allegra M. McLeod, "Decarceration Courts: Possibilities and Perils of a Shifting Criminal Law," *Georgetown Law Journal* 100 (2011); for analysis of jail expansion see: Andrew Pragacz, "Is This What Decarceration Looks Like? Rising Jail Incarceration in Upstate New York," in Martin and Price, *After Prisons?*, 99–214; Joan Petersilia, "California Prison Downsizing and its Impact on Local Criminal Justice Systems," *Harvard Law & Policy Review* 8 (2014).

11. William Martin, "Decarceration and Justice Disinvestment: Evidence from New York State," *Punishment & Society* 18, no. 4 (2016), 493; Michelle S. Phelps, "Mass Probation: Toward a More Robust Theory of State Variation in Punishment," *Punishment & Society* 19, no. 1 (2017).

12. Systems Administrator, ROIC, Interview by author, West Trenton, NJ. January 29, 2013.

13. Matt Taibbi, "Apocalypse, New Jersey: A Dispatch from America's Most Desperate Town," *Rolling Stone*, December 11, 2013, http://www.rollingstone .com/culture/news/apocalypse-new-jersey-a-dispatch-from-americas-most -desperate-town-20131211 (accessed June 1, 2014).

14. Howard Gillette, *Camden after the Fall: Decline and Renewal in a Post-Industrial City* (Philadelphia: University of Pennsylvania Press, 2005), 42.

15. Blake Ellis, "Counting the Homeless in America's Poorest City," *CNNMoney*, February 13, 2014, http://money.cnn.com/2014/02/12/pf/home less-count/index.html (accessed June 1, 2014); US Census Bureau, *Selected Economic Characteristics from the 2006–2010 American Community Survey 5-Year Estimates for Camden City* (Washington, DC: US Census Bureau, 2010), https://factfinder.census.gov/faces/tableservices/jsf/pages/productview .xhtml?src=bkmk (accessed June 1, 2014); Shoshana Guy, America's 'Invincible' City Brought to Its Knees by Poverty, Violence," *NBC News*, March 7, 2013, http://www.nbcnews.com/feature/in-plain-sight/americas-invincible-city -brought-its-knees-poverty-violence-v17225824.

16. Taibbi, "Apocalypse, New Jersey."

17. James Osborne, "Nearly 40 People Arrested in North Camden Drug Sweep," *Philadelphia Inquirer*, August 19, 2012, http://articles.philly.com/2012 -08-19/news/33262050_1_open-air-drug-markets-drug-trade-police-sweep (accessed June 1, 2014).

18. "Police administrator, Municipal Police Department, Recorded phone interview, June 28, 2013.

19. Taibbi, "Apocalypse, New Jersey"; State Trooper, Intelligence & Analysis Unit, Crime Zone-South, ROIC.

20. Federal Bureau of Investigation, "Crime in the United States 2012, Table 8, New Jersey, Offenses Known to Law Enforcement," 2012, https://ucr.fbi.gov /crime-in-the-u.s/2012/crime-in-the-u.s.-2012/tables/8tabledatadecpdf/table -8-state-cuts/table_8_offenses_known_to_law_enforcement_by_new_jersey _by_city_2012.xls (accessed June 1, 2014).

21. Gillette, *Camden after the Fall*, 201–10.

22. Matt Katz, "Camden's Waterfront—and Its Woes," *Philadelphia Inquirer*, November 9, 2009, http://articles.philly.com/2009-11-09/news /24987966_1_municipal-rehabilitation-poorest-city-aquarium (accessed June 1, 2014).

23. Claudia Vargas, "Camden Tax Collection Inches Up," *Philadelphia Inquirer*, July 10, 2013, http://articles.philly.com/2013-07-10/news/40471880_1 _county-force-collection-rate-city-money (accessed June 1, 2014).

24. Matt Katz, "Camden Recovery Aids Some," *Philadelphia Inquirer*, November 10, 2009, http://www.philly.com/philly/news/special_packages /inquirer/20091110_Recovery_aids_some_areas.html (accessed June 1, 2014).

25. Gillette, *Camden after the Fall*, 25.

26. Taibbi, "Apocalypse, New Jersey"; John Rudolf, "Chris Christie Pushes Camden Police Force to Disband, Despite Questions over New Plan's Finances," *Huffington Post*, November 19, 2012, http://www.huffingtonpost.com/2012

/11/19/chris-christie-camden-police_n_2025372.html (accessed June 1 2014); Jason Laday, "Camden County Towns to Study Possible Merger of Police Departments," *South Jersey Times*, July 23, 2013, http://www.nj.com/camden /index.ssf/2013/07/camden_county_municipalities_to_study_merger_at _police_departments.html#incart_river (accessed February 14, 2018); Jenna Portnoy, "Christie: Trenton Should Copy Camden's Regional Police Force," *Star-Ledger*, August 21, 2013, http://www.nj.com/politics/index.ssf/2013/08/christie _in_camden_education.html (accessed June 10, 2104).

27. Darran Simon, "Christie Sends Troopers into Camden amid Crime Surge," *Philadelphia Inquirer*, December 12, 2011. http://articles.philly.com/2011-12-12 /news/30507131_1_state-troopers-police-force-law-enforcement.

28. Systems administrator, NJ ROIC, Recorded personal interview by author, January 29, 2013.

29. Taibbi, "Apocalypse, New Jersey"; Brendan McQuade, "Demilitarization Ruse," *Jacobin*, May 24, 2015. https://www.jacobinmag.com/2015/05/camden -obama-police-brutality-black-lives-matter/ (accessed May 24, 2015).

30. McQuade, "Demilitarization Ruse"; Matt Skoufalos, "3 from Collingswood Collared in Camden Drug Bust," *Collingswood Patch*, September 12, 2012, http:// collingswood.patch.com/groups/police-and-fire/p/3-from-collingswood-collared -in-camden-drug-bust (accessed June 1 2014); Lucas Murray, "535 Arrested in Camden Drug Sweeps," *Courier-Post*, November 7, 2012, http://archive.courier postonline.com/article/20121008/CRIME/310070036/535-arrested-Camden -drug-sweeps (accessed June 1, 2014).

31. Original Emphasis. Mark Neocleous, "Security as Pacification," in *Anti-Security*, ed. Mark Neocleous and George Rigakos (Ottawa: Red Quill Books, 2011) 24.

32. Ellis, "Counting the Homeless"; Kevin Shelley, "Survey: Nearly 15 percent of Camden Properties Abandoned," *Courier-Post*, August 14, 2014, http:// www.courierpostonline.com/story/news/local/south-jersey/2014/08/14 /survey-nearly-percent-camden-properties-abandoned/14059361/ (accessed July 14, 2017).

33. George Rigakos, *Security/Capital: A General Theory of Pacification* (Edinburgh: Edinburgh University Press, 2016), 96–102; Karl Marx, "On the Jewish Question," *Marxist.org*, September 2009. https://www.marxists.org /archive/marx/works/1844/jewish-question/ (accessed August 1, 2017); see also: Mark Neocleous, *Critique of Security* (Edinburgh: Edinburgh University Press, 2008), 30–32.

34. Neocleous, *Critique of Security*, 5–7, 30; see also Mark Neocleous, "Security, Liberty and the Myth of Balance: Towards a Critique of Security Politics," *Contemporary Political Theory* 6, no. 2 (2007).

35. Taibbi, "Apocalypse, New Jersey."

36. Neocleous, "Security as Pacification," 36–42.

37. George S Rigakos, John L. McMullan, Joshua Johnson, and Gulden Özcan, *A General Police System: Political Economy and Security in the Age of Enlightenment* (Ottawa: Red Quill Books, 2009).

38. Brendan McQuade, "The Prose of Police Power: Pacification, Critical Theory and Socialist Strategy," *Social Justice*, forthcoming (Brooklyn, NY: Verso, forthcoming 2020).

39. Subsequent critiques of security developed these ideas to analyze colonialism and counterinsurgency, economic development, policing, and immigration, among other topics; see: Alissa R. Ackerman, Meghan Sacks, and Rich Furman, "The New Penology Revisited: The Criminalization of Immigration as a Pacification Strategy," *Justice Policy Journal* 11, no. 1 (2014): 1–20; Will Jackson, Helen Monk, and Joanna Gilmore, "Pacifying Disruptive Subjects: Police Violence and Anti-fracking Protests," *Contention* 3, no. 2 (2015); Travis Linnemann, *Meth Wars: Police, Media, Power* (New York: New York University Press, 2016); Christopher McMichael, "Urban Pacification and "Blitzes" in Contemporary Johannesburg," *Antipode* 47, no. 5 (2015); Brendan McQuade, "A Critical View of Counterinsurgency: World Relational State (De)formation," *Yonsei Journal of International Studies* 4 no. 1 (2012); Mark Neocleous, "'A Brighter and Nicer New Life': Security as Pacification," *Social & Legal Studies* 20, no. 2 (2011); Stuart Schrader, "To Secure the Global Great Society: Participation in Pacification," *Humanity: An International Journal of Human Rights, Humanitarianism, and Development* 7, no. 2 (2016); Maíra Siman and Victória Santos, "Interrogating the Security–Development Nexus in Brazil's Domestic and Foreign Pacification Engagements," *Conflict, Security & Development* 18, no. 1 (2018); Tyler Wall, Parastou Saberi, and Will Jackson, eds., *Destroy, Build, Secure: Readings on Pacification* (Ottawa: Red Quill Books, 2017).

40. Jerry Ratcliffe, *Intelligence-Led Policing* (Cullompton, UK: Willan Publishing, 2008).

41. Jerry Ratcliffe and Ray Guidetti, "State Police Investigative Structure and the Adoption of Intelligence-Led Policing," *Policing: An International Journal of Police Strategies & Management* 31, no. 1 (2008).

42. Jerry H., Ratcliffe, Evan T. Sorg, and James W. Rose, "Intelligence-Led policing in Honduras: Applying Sleipnir and Social Psychology to Understand Gang Proliferation," *Journal of Police and Criminal Psychology* 30, no. 2 (2015), 113–14; Adam Isacson and Sarah Kinosian, "Which Central American Military and Police Units Get the Most U.S. Aid?" *WOLA: Advocacy for Human Rights in the Americas*, April 16, 2016, https://www.wola.org/analysis/which-central -american-military-and-police-units-get-the-most-u-s-aid/ (accessed December 7, 2016).

43. Ranajit Guha, "The Prose of Counterinsurgency," in *Culture/Power/ History: A Reader in Contemporary Social Theory*, ed. Nicholas Dirks, Geoff Eley, and Sherry Ortner (Princeton, NJ: Princeton University Press), 336–37.

44. Camp, *Incarcerating the Crisis*, 17.

45. Jason Laday, "Camden Police Security at July 2012 Concert Cost $77K in Overtime: Documents," *South Jersey Times*, January 14, 2016. http://www .nj.com/camden/index.ssf/2014/01/camden_police_security_at_july_2012 _concert_cost_77k_in_overtime_documents.html (accessed October 24, 2016).

46. Gulden Özcan and George Rigakos, "Pacification," in *The Wiley-Blackwell Encyclopedia of Globalization*, ed. George Ritzer (Hoboken, NJ: Wiley-Blackwell, 2014), 3. https://onlinelibrary.wiley.com/doi/10.1002/9780470670590.wbeog621

CHAPTER 1. CONNECTING THE DOTS BEYOND
COUNTERTERRORISM AND SEEING PAST
ORGANIZATIONAL FAILURE

1. National Commission on Terrorist Attacks upon the United States, *The 9/11 Commission Report: Final Report of the National Commission on Terrorist Attacks upon the United States* (New York: WW Norton & Company, 2004), 253.

2. Jerry Ratcliffe, *Intelligence-Led Policing* (Cullompton, UK: Willan Publishing, 2008), 104–12.

3. Ratcliffe, *Intelligence-Led Policing*, 54–58; John E., Eck, and Ronald V. Clarke, *Intelligence Analysis for Problem Solvers* (Washington, DC: Office of Community Oriented Policing Services, Department of Justice, September 2013), 13, https://popcenter.asu.edu/sites/default/files/library/reading/PDFs/Intell-Analysis-for-ProbSolvers.pdf (accessed June 14, 2014); The U.S. Department of Justice's Global Justice Information Sharing Initiative, *Common Competencies for State, Local, and Tribal Intelligence Analysts* (Washington, DC: The Department of Justice and Department of Homeland Security, June 2010), 5–8 https://it.ojp.gov/documents/d/common%20competencies%20state%20local%20and%20Tribal%20intelligence%20analysts.pdf (accessed March 12, 2012).

4. US Senate, Permanent Subcommittee on Investigations, *Federal Support for and Involvement in State and Local Fusion Centers* (Washington, DC, October 3, 2012), 2, https://www.hsgac.senate.gov/imo/media/doc/10-3-2012%20PSI%20STAFF%20REPORT%20re%20FUSION%20CENTERS.2.pdf (accessed October 3, 2012).

5. Robert O'Harrow, "DHS 'Fusion Centers' Portrayed as Pools of Ineptitude and Civil Liberties Intrusion," *Washington Post*, October 2, 2012, https://www.washingtonpost.com/investigations/dhs-fusion-centers-portrayed-as-pools-of-ineptitude-and-civil-liberties-intrusions/2012/10/02/10014440-0cb1-11e2-bd1a-b868e65d57eb_story.html (accessed October 2, 2012).

6. James Risen, "Inquiry Cites Flaws in Counterterrorism Offices," *New York Times*, October 2, 2012, http://www.nytimes.com/2012/10/03/us/inquiry-cites-flaws-in-regional-counterterrorism-offices.html (accessed October 2, 2012).

7. Federal official, Telephone interview by author, March 14, 2013.

8. Michael Isikoff, "Unaware of Tsarnaev Warnings, Boston Counterterror Unit Tracked Protesters" *NBC News*, May 9, 2013, http://investigations.nbcnews.com/_news/2013/05/09/18152849-unaware-of-tsarnaev-warnings-boston-counterterror-unit-tracked-protesters.

9. For review of the first five years of reporting on fusion center, see: Torin Monahan and Neal A. Palmer, "The Emerging Politics of DHS Fusion Centers," *Security Dialogue* 40, no. 6 (2009).

10. In 2008, The DHS Office of the Inspector General identified a series of problems: a vague mission, a lack of federal DHS personnel at fusion centers, poor coordination, and a reliance on informal networks rather than formal liaison relationships. Working simultaneously and independently, researchers with the Congressional Research Service found several issues that undermined information sharing: incompatible information systems, over-classification, an ill-defined mission that undermined oversight, and, "the culture of ownership," DHS Office of Inspector General, "DHS' Role in State and Local Fusion Centers Is Evolving," OIG-9-2012 (Washington, DC, 2008), http://www.oig.dhs.gov/assets/Mgmt /OIG_09-12_Dec08.pdf (accessed March 12, 2012); Todd Masse, Siobhan O'Neil, and John Rollins, *Fusion Centers: Issues and Options for Congress*, (Washington, DC: Congressional Research Services, 2007), http://epic.org/privacy/fusion/crs _fusionrpt.pdf (accessed March 12, 2012); John Rollins, *Fusion Centers: Issues and Options for Congress* (Washington, DC: Congressional Research Services, 2008), 29–32, http://www.dtic.mil/cgi-bin/GetTRDoc?AD=ADA482006 (accessed March 12, 2012).

11. Mike German and Jay Stanley, *What's Wrong with Fusion Centers* (Washington, DC: ACLU, December 2007), http://www.aclu.org/files/pdfs/pri vacy/fusioncenter_20071212.pdf (accessed January 3, 2012); Michael Price, "National Security and Local Police," The Brennan Center for Justice, December 10, 2013: https://www.brennancenter.org/publication/national-security-local-police (accessed December 15, 2013); Matt Mayer, "Consolidate Domestic Intelligence Entities under the FBI" (Washington, DC: American Enterprise Institute, March 2016), https://www.aei.org/wp-content/uploads/2016/03/Fusion-Center.pdf (accessed March 27, 2016).

12. Bart Johnson and Shelagh Dorn, "Fusion Centers: New York State Strategy Unifies Law Enforcement," *The Police Chief* 75, no. 2 (2007), www.policechiefmag-azine.org/magazine/index.cfm?fuseaction=display_arch&article_id=1419&issue _id=22008 (accessed January 4, 2012); Raymond Guidetti, "Rethinking the Purpose of Fusion Centers," *The Police Chief*, 77, no. 2 (2010), http://www .policechiefmagazine.org/magazine/index.cfm?fuseaction=display_arch&article _id=2017&issue_id=220100 (accessed, August 4, 2012); Raymond Guidetti, "Local Policing: Expanding Reach with Limited Resources through Fusion Centers," *The Police Chief*, 74, no. 2 (2012), http://www.policechiefmagazine.org/local-policing -expanding-reach-with-limited-resources/ (accessed August 4, 2012); Joseph Pfeifer, "Network Fusion: Information and Intelligence Sharing for a Networked World," *Homeland Security Affairs* 8 (2012); US House of Representatives, Committee on Homeland Security, *Majority Staff Report on the National Network of Fusion Centers* (Washington, DC, July 2013), https://www.archives .gov/files/isoo/oversight-groups/sltps-pac/staff-report-on-fusion-networks -2013.pdf (accessed July 27, 2013).

13. Beau Hodai, *Dissent or Terror: How the Nation's Counter Terrorism Apparatus, in Partnership with Corporate America, Turned on Occupy Wall Street* (Madison, WI: Center for Media and Democracy & BDA Press, May 2013), http://www.prwatch.org/files/Dissent%20or%20Terror%20FINAL.pdf

(accessed May 20, 2013); ACLU-Massachusetts and National Lawyers Guild-Massachusetts, *Policing Dissent: Police Surveillance of Lawful Political Activity in Boston* (Boston: ACLU–Massachusetts and National Lawyers Guild–Massachusetts, 2012), http://www.aclum.org/sites/all/files/policing_dissent _101812.pdf (accessed October 15, 2012).

14. Brian Peteritas, "Fusion Centers Struggle to Find Their Place in the Post-9/11 World," *Governing*, June 2013, http://www.governing.com/topics /public-justice-safety/gov-fusion-centers-post-911-world.html (accessed July 7, 2013).

15. US Senate, *Federal Support for . . . Fusion Centers*, 4.

16. These include FBI Field Intelligence Groups and the Bureau-chaired Joint Terrorism Task Forces, the Department of Justice's Regional Information Sharing Systems, the Office of National Drug Control Policy's High Intensity Drug Trafficking Area Investigative Support Centers, and state and major metro area fusion centers recognized by the Department of Homeland Security. The total count of 268 does not include county crime analysis centers, municipal real-time crime centers, and a variety of interagency intelligence-sharing taskforces, which may not have a physical location but do the work of a fusion center. Government Accountability Office, *Information Sharing: Agencies Could Better Coordinate to Reduce Overlap in Field-Based Activities*, Government Accountability Office, April 4, 2013, http://www.gao.gov/products/GAO-13-471 (accessed April 14, 2013).

17. There are several reasons for this shift. In the absence of terrorism, fusion center employees "have to use their time and skills constructively" and find ways "to be valuable to their states." To meet these practical demands, fusion centers developed to needs of the police agencies managing them. In this context, fusion center investigators "found" that many acts of terrorism have a "nexus" with crime, which, in theory, makes the former a window into the latter. Similarly, fusion centers' information-sharing mission led many to contend that intelligence fusion illuminated criminal patterns across jurisdictions. Finally, some of the grants available to fusion centers were also linked to emergency preparedness, encouraging expansion to an "all hazards" approach. Priscilla Regan and Torin Monahan, "Beyond Counterterrorism: Data Sharing, Privacy and Organizational Histories of DHS Fusion Centers," *International Journal of E-Politics* 4, no. 3 (2013): 10; David L. Carter and Jeremy G. Carter, "The Intelligence Fusion Process for State, Local, and Tribal Law Enforcement," *Criminal Justice and Behavior* 36, no. 12 (2009): 1327.

18. Richard Jackson, *Writing the War on Terrorism: Language, Politics and Counter-terrorism* (Manchester, UK: Manchester University Press, 2005); Lee Jarvis, *Times of Terror: Discourse, Temporality and the War on Terror* (New York: Springer, 2009).

19. Lisa Stampnitzky, *Disciplining Terror: How Experts Invented "Terrorism"* (New York: Cambridge University Press, 2013) 13, 187–89.

20. Quoted in Jonathan Powell, *Terrorists at the Table: Why Negotiating Is the Only Way to Peace* (New York: St. Martin's Press, 2015), 15.

21. Watson Institute for International Affairs, "Costs of War," Brown University, undated, http://watson.brown.edu/costsofwar/papers/summary (accessed May 4, 2018); National Priorities Project, "U.S. Security Spending Since 9/11," May 26, 2011, https://www.nationalpriorities.org/analysis/2011/us-security-spending-since-911/ (accessed May 4, 2018).

22. Joseph Stiglitz and Linda J. Bilmes, "The True Cost of the Iraq War: $3 Trillion and Beyond," *Washington Post*, September 5, 2010, http://www.washingtonpost.com/wp-dyn/content/article/2010/09/03/AR2010090302200.html (accessed June 24, 2018).

23. Jackson, *Writing the War on Terrorism*, 2.

24. Jarvis cites Foucault as his theoretical and methodological influence. Jackson does indirectly. His approach is "critical discourse analysis," an interdisciplinary approach derived, in part, from Foucault. Stampnitzky's work is not an example of critical terrorism studies. Instead, she takes the field theory of Pierre Bourdieu to analyze the struggles over terrorism expertise. The general thrust of my critique, however, also applies to this approach. Field theory can explain why terrorism studies is a dysfunctional field, but it cannot explain why the demand for terrorism expertise exists in the first place. Answering this question requires an approach that is more attuned to how both wealth and power accumulate. Foucault's has no "economic" theory, and his political theory is lacking. Field theory can offer insight into many political questions but cannot explain how "economic capital" is created and distributed. See Jarvis, *Times of Terror*, 12–22; Jackson, *Writing the War on Terrorism*, 24–27. Stampnitzky, *Disciplining Terror*, 8–13; for this criticism of Bourdieu and field theory, see: Göran Bolin, "The Forms of Value: Problems of Convertibility in Field Theory," *tripleC* 10, no. 1 (2012).

25. Michel Foucault, *Discipline and Punish: The Birth of the Prison* (New York: Vintage, 1995); Michel Foucault, *Madness and Civilization: A History of Insanity in the Age of Reason* (New York: Vintage, 1988); Michel Foucault, *The Birth of the Clinic: The Archeology of Medical Perception* (New York: Routledge, 2012).

26. Michel Foucault, "Confessions of the Flesh," in *Power/Knowledge: Selected Interviews and Other Writings, 1972–1977*, ed. Colin Gordon (New York: Pantheon 1980), 194.

27. Nicos Poulantzas, *State, Power, Socialism* (New York: Verso, 1978), 44, 69, 149. Despite Poulantzas's direct engagement with Foucault, Foucault never directly responded. However, many scholars argue that "late Foucault" moved closer to Poulantzas and Marxism. Hence, Étienne Balibar argues that Foucault moved from clear critique to an unambiguous appropriation, where

> the first invovl[ed] a global critique of Marxism as a "theory" and the second a partial usage of Marxist tenets or affirmations compatible with Marxism. . . . Thus, in contradictory fashion, the opposition to Marxist "theory" grows deeper and deeper whilst the convergence of the analyses and concepts taken from Marx becomes more and more significant.

On the question of the state and the materiality of power, Jessop's meticulous essay on Poulantzas and Foucault notes that Foucault obliquely responded to Poulantzas's critique of his "metaphysical and mystical" conception of power:

> on state power, whilst still arguing for the dispersion of powers, insisting that the state, for all its omnipotence, does not occupy the whole field of power relations, and claiming that the state can only operate on the basis of other, already existing power relations, Foucault also conceded that the State invests and colonizes these other power relations in a conditioning-conditioned relationship to generate a kind of "meta-power" that renders its own functioning possible.

Indeed, according to Foucault, "power relations have been progressively governmentalized, that is to say, elaborated, rationalized, and centralized in the form of, or under the auspices of, state institutions." Regardless of these gestures, Foucault's theory of power still lacks a clear grounding in material relations. One is left with the impression of separate systems of power relations that may overlap yet still have no "other basis than itself." Hence, in a 1977 interview, Foucault clarified that "relations of power are interwoven with other kinds of relations (production, kinship, family, sexuality) for which they play at once a conditioning and a conditioned role." Due to this ambiguity, I conclude that Poulantzas's criticisms still hold, despite Foucault's continuing evolution. For this reason, I frame this study in relation to the humanist and historical strand of Marxism and ground my understanding of power in relation to material processes of social reproduction (see chapter 2). Étienne Balibar "Foucault and Marx: the Question of Nominalism," in *Foucault, Philosopher: Essays Translated from French and German*, ed. Timothy J. Armstrong (New York: Routledge, 1992), 53; Bob Jessop, "Pouvoir et stratégies chez Poulantzas et Foucault," *Actuel Marx* 36 (2007): 89–107; English translation online available at https://www.researchgate.net/publication/312506809 _Poulantzas_and_Foucault_on_Power_and_Strategy_Pouvoir_et_strategies _chez_Poulantzas_et_Foucault (accessed January 4, 2018); Michel Foucault, "Power and Strategies," in *Power/Knowledge: Selected Interviews and Other Writings, 1972–1977*, ed. Colin Gordon (New York: Pantheon 1980), 142.

28. Original emphasis, Mark Neocleous, *Administering Civil Society* (New York: Palgrave Macmillan Ltd, 1996), 57, 66–67, 70, 72; see also: Andreas Kalyvas, "Stateless Theory: Poulantzas's Challenge to Postmodernism," in *Paradigm Lost: State Theory Reconsidered*, ed. Stanley Aronowitz and Peter Bratsis, 105–42 (Minneapolis: University of Minnesota Press, 2002), 105–42. Akin to the substitution of "bodies" for legal subjects, a similar ahistorical denial of the specifics of "power" is seen in Foucault's analysis of sexuality, which, as Federici shows, ignores social reproduction, collapses "female and male histories into an undifferentiated whole," and is "so disinterested in the 'disciplining' of women that it never mentions one of the most monstrous attacks on the body perpetrated in the modern era: the witch-hunt." Silvia Federici, *Caliban and the Witch: Women, the Body, and Primitive Accumulation* (Brooklyn, NY: Autonomedia, 2004), 8.

29. Urs T. Linder, "State, Domination, and Politics: On the Relationship Between Poulantzas and Foucault," in *Reading Poulantzas*, ed. Alexander Gallas, Lars Bretthauer, John Kannankulam, and Ingo Stützle (Pontypool, UK: Merlin Press, 2011), 138.

30. Jessop, "Pouvoir et stratégies chez Poulantzas et Foucault," 8–13.

31. Poulantzas, *State, Power, Socialism*, 45, 69, 73.

32. Nicos Poulantzas, *Political Power and Social Classes* (London: New Left Books, 1973), 99–119. Although some criticize *Political Power and Social Classes* for class reductionism, it also can be read in a more open way when considered in relation to *State, Power, Socialism* and the humanist and historical conception of class formation presented in chapter 2. Theda Skocpol, "Political Response to Capitalist Crisis: Neo-Marxist Theories of the State and the Case of the New Deal," *Politics & Society* 10, no. 2 (1980).

33. Michel Foucault, *The Birth of Biopolitics: Lectures at the Collège de France, 1978–1979* (New York: Macmillan, 2010), 77. Recently translated work from Foucault shows that this dominant interpretation of Foucault as vulgarly "poststructuralist," dogmatically opposed to the analysis of centralized forms of political power, is a misreading. While Foucault avoided using the term *the state*, his work offers a genealogy of the modern state formation (see also note 27). This reading of Foucault, however, runs counter to his reception in the Anglophone academe, where a distinct strand of scholarship "selectively appl[ies Foucault's] initial insights on governmentality to new areas." These so-called "Foucaultians" have created a "distinctive academic field: governmentality studies," which draws

> on *Discipline and Punish* and the lecture on government from his 1977–78 course at the Collège de France, which appeared, out of context, in English in 1979. . . . The coherence of this field rests on its narrow understanding of governmentality and resulting neglect of its place in Foucault's intellectual and political reflections—including its import for the logic of capital and forms of political domination.

Bob Jessop, "Constituting Another Foucault Effect: Foucault on States and Statecraft," in *Governmentality: Current Issues and Future Challenges*, ed. Ulrich Bröckling, Susanne Krasmann, and Thomas Lemke (New York: Routledge, 2010), 58; see also: Bob Jessop, *State Power: A Strategic-Relational Approach* (Cambridge: Polity, 2008), 140–56.

34. For extended critiques of surveillance studies and securitization theory, see: Brendan McQuade, "*Windows into the Soul* or the Clouded Glass of Surveillance Studies," *Critical Sociology* 44, nos. 4–5 (2018): 815–24. Mark Neocleous, "From Social to National Security: On the Fabrication of Economic Order," *Security Dialogue* 37, no. 3 (2006); Mark Neocleous, *Critique of Security* (Edinburgh: Edinburgh University Press, 2008), 79.

35. Poulantzas, *State, Power, Socialism*, 32.

36. Ingo Stützle, "The Order of Knowledge: The State as a Knowledge Apparatus," in *Reading Poulantzas*, ed. Alexander Gallas, Lars Bretthauer, John

Kannankulam, and Ingo Stützle, 170–85 (Pontypool, UK: Merlin Press, 2011), 175–76.

37. National Consortium for the Study of Terrorism and Responses to Terrorism, Global Terrorism Database, University of Maryland, 2017, https://www.start.umd.edu/gtd (accessed March 28, 2017).

38. Terry Miller, Kenneth Kolosh, Kevin Fearn, and Kathleen Porretta, *Injury Facts, 2015 Edition* (Washington, DC: National Safety Council, 2015), http://www.nsc.org/Membership%20Site%20Document%20Library/2015%20Injury%20Facts/NSC_InjuryFacts2015Ed.pdf (accessed March 27, 2017).

39. Institute for Economics and Peace, "Global Peace Index, 2016," in *Quantifying Peace and Its Benefits* (Sydney: IEP, 2016), 8, http://economic-sandpeace.org/wp-content/uploads/2016/06/GPI-2016-Report_2.pdf (accessed March 27, 2016).

40. Mattea Kramer and Chris Hellman, "'Homeland Security': The Trillion-Dollar Concept That No One Can Define," *TomDispatch.com*, February 28, 2013. http://www.tomdispatch.com/post/175655/ (accessed March 1, 2013); US Senate, *Federal Support for . . . Fusion Centers*, 61.

41. Michael Elliott, "The Shoe Bomber's World," *Time*, February 16, 2002, http://content.time.com/time/world/article/0,8599,203478,00.html; Corey Kilgannon and Michael S. Schmidt, "Vendors Who Alerted Police Called Heroes," *New York Times*, May 2, 2010, http://www.nytimes.com/2010/05/03/nyregion/03vendor.html; Anahad O'Connor and Eric Schmitt, "Terror Attempt Seen as Man Tries to Ignite Device on Jet," *New York Times*, December 26, 2009, sec. US. http://www.nytimes.com/2009/12/26/us/26plane.html.

42. US Senate, *Federal Support for. . . Fusion Centers*, 83.

43. Trevor Aaronson, *The Terror Factory: Inside the FBI's Manufactured War on Terrorism* (Brooklyn, NY: Ig Publishing, 2013): 15; Trevor Aaronson and Margot Williams, "Trial and Terror," *The Intercept*, August 30, 2018 (last update), https://trial-and-terror.theintercept.com/ (accessed October 2, 2018).

44. US Senate, *Federal Support for . . . Fusion Centers*, 31.

45. Emphasis added, New York State Intelligence Center, "Threat Assessment: Major Terror Attacks against Hotels, 2002–2011, March 29, 2012," *Public Intelligence*, February 1, 2013, http://publicintelligence.net/nysic-hotel-attacks/ (accessed February 26, 2013).

46. New Jersey Regional Operations Intelligence Center, "Situational Awareness Report: Attack on Afghan Resort Demonstrates Vulnerability of Hotels, June 26, 2012," *Public Intelligence*, July 10, 2012, http://publicintelligence.net/njroic-kabul-hotel-bombing/ (accessed August 14, 2012).

47. New Jersey Regional Operations Intelligence Center, Intelligence Analysis Threat Unit, "ROIC Intelligence and Analysis Threat Unit Daily Overview, New Jersey Regional Operations Intelligence Center, March 14, 2014.

48. New Jersey Regional Operations Intelligence Center, Intelligence Analysis Threat Unit, "ROIC Intelligence and Analysis Threat Unit Daily Overview," The New Jersey Regional Operations Intelligence Center, July 25, 2014.

49. For extended discussion of these issues, see: Brendan McQuade, "The Puzzle of Intelligence Expertise: Spaces of Intelligence Analysis and the Production of 'Political' Knowledge," *Qualitative Sociology* 39, no. 3 (2016).

50. Police administrator, NYSIC, Recorded personal interview by author, May 14, 2013b.

51. Police administrator, NJ, ROIC, Recorded personal interview by author, January 2, 2013.

52. "'If You See Something, Say Something™' Campaign," Department of Homeland Security, http://www.dhs.gov/if-you-see-something-say-something %E2%84%A2-campaign (accessed August 1, 2014).

53. Joshua Reeves, "If You See Something, Say Something: Lateral Surveillance and the Uses of Responsibility," *Surveillance & Society* 10, nos. 3–4 (2012).

54. Police administrator, NJ ROIC, Recorded personal interview by author, January 28, 2013a.

55. Analyst, Recorded personal interview by author, May 14, 2013.

56. Ibid.

57. Police officer, NYSIC, Recorded personal interview by author, May 14, 2013a.

58. Police administrator, NYSIC, Recorded personal interview by author, May 14, 2013c.

59. The meeting's budget was $46,321. New York State Police, "SIS Budget 2012," New York State Police, 2012.

60. Police administrator, NYSIC, Recorded personal interview by author, May 14, 2013d.

61. Intelligence Analyst, Personal interview by author, August 2, 2013.

62. Christos Boukalas, *Homeland Security, Its Law and Its State: A Design of Power for the 21st Century* (New York: Routledge, 2014), 76, 220, original emphasis.

63. Foucault, *Discipline and Punish*, 234.

64. Mikaela Cooney, Jeff Rojek, and Robert J. Kaminski, "An Assessment of the Utility of a State Fusion Center by Law Enforcement Executives and Personnel," *Journal of Intelligence Analysis* 20, no. 1 (2011); Raymond Guidetti and James Morentz, "Geospatial Statistical Modeling for Intelligence-Led Policing," *The Police Chief* 77, no. 8 (2010), http://www.policechiefmagazine .org/magazine/index.cfm?fuseaction=display_arch&article_id=2152&issue_ id=82010 (accessed August 4, 2012); Raymond Guidetti and Thomas Martinelli, "Intelligence-Led Policing—A Strategic Framework," *The Police Chief* 76, no. 10 (2012), http://www.policechiefmagazine.org/magazine/index.cfm? fuseaction=display&article_id=1918&issue_id=102009 (accessed, August 4, 2012); Bart Johnson and Shelagh Dorn, "Fusion Centers: New York State Strategy Unifies Law Enforcement," *The Police Chief* 75, no. 2 (2007), http:// www.policechiefmagazine.org/magazine/index.cfm?fuseaction=display_arch &article_id=1419&issue_id=22008 (accessed January 4, 2012); Jerry Ratcliffe and Kyle Walden, "State Police and the Intelligence Center: A Study of

Intelligence Flow to and From the Street," *Journal of Intelligence and Analysis* 19, no. 1 (2010).

65. Nina Cope, "Intelligence Led Policing or Policing Led Intelligence: Integrating Crime Analysis into Policing," *British Journal of Criminology* 44, no. 2 (2004); David Dannels and Heather Smith, "Implementation Challenges of Intelligence Led Policing in a Quasi-Rural County," *Journal of Crime and Justice* 24, no. 2 (2001); Arrick Jackson and Michael Brown, "Ensuring Efficiency, Interagency Cooperation, and Protection of Civil Liberties: Shifting from a Traditional Model of Policing to an Intelligence-Led Policing (ILP) Paradigm," *Criminal Justice Studies* 20, no. 2 (2007); Renee Graphia-Joyal, "Are Fusion Centers Achieving Their Intended Purposes? Findings from a Qualitative Study on the Internal Efficacy of State Fusion Centers," *Journal of Intelligence Analysis* 19, no. 1 (2010).

66. US Department of Justice's Global Justice Information Sharing Initiative, *Fusion Center Guidelines Developing and Sharing Information and Intelligence in a New Era* (Washington, DC: The Department of Justice and Department of Homeland Security, August 2006), https://www.fema.gov/pdf/government/grant/2010/fy10_hsgp_fusion.pdf (accessed March 12, 2012); US Department of Justice's Global Justice Information Sharing Initiative, *Baseline Capabilities for State and Major Urban Area Fusion Centers* (Washington, DC: The Department of Justice and Department of Homeland Security, September 2008), https://www.fema.gov/pdf/government/grant/2010/fy10_hsgp_fusion.pdf (accessed March 12, 2012); US Department of Justice's Global Justice Information Sharing Initiative, *Common Competencies for State, Local, and Tribal Intelligence Analyst* (Washington, DC: The Department of Justice and Department of Homeland Security, June 2010), https://it.ojp.gov/documents/d/common%20competencies%20state%20local%20and%20Tribal%20intelligence%20analysts.pdf (accessed March 12, 2012).

67. Police administrator, NYSIC, Recorded personal interview by author, May 14, 2013b.

68. Priscilla Regan and Torin Monahan, "Beyond Counterterrorism: Data Sharing, Privacy and Organizational Histories of DHS Fusion Centers," *International Journal of E-Politics* 4, no. 3 (2013); Priscilla Regan and Torin Monahan, "Fusion Center Accountability and Intergovernmental Information Sharing," *Publius: The Journal of Federalism* (2014): doi: 10.1093/publius/pju016; Priscilla Regan, Torin Monahan, and Krista Craven, "Constructing the Suspicious: Data Production, Circulation, and Interpretation by DHS Fusion Centers," *Administration and Society* (2013), doi: 0095399713513141.

69. Torin Monahan and Priscilla Regan, "Zones of Opacity: Data Fusion in Post-9/11 Security Organizations," *Canadian Journal of Law and Society* 27, no. 3 (2013): 302.

70. Krista Craven, Torin Monahan, and Priscilla Regan, "Compromised Trust: DHS Fusion Centers' Policing of the Occupy Wall Street Movement," *Sociological Research Online* 20, no. 3 (2015).

71. German and Stanley, "What's Wrong with Fusion Centers," 22–23.

72. Regan and Monahan, "Beyond Counterterrorism"; Regan and Monahan, "Fusion Center Accountability."

73. Aaron Henry, "The Perpetual Object of Regulation: Privacy as Pacification," *Socialist Studies/Études Socialistes* 9, no. 2 (2013): 99, 106; see also: Mark Neocleous, "Privacy, Secrecy, Idiocy," *Social Research* 69, no. 1 (2002).

74. US House of Representatives, Committee on Homeland Security, *Majority Staff Report on the National Network of Fusion Centers* (Washington, DC, July 2013), 5–6.

75. US Department of Justice's Global Justice Information Sharing Initiative, *Baseline Capabilities for State and Major Urban Area Fusion Centers*, 2; see also: Justin Lewis Abold, Ray Guidetti, and Douglas Keyer, "Strengthening the Value of the National Network of Fusion Centers by Leveraging Specialization: Defining 'Centers of Analytical Excellence,'" *Homeland Security Affairs* 8, no. 1 (2012).

76. Renee Graphia-Joyal, "How Far Have We Come? Information Sharing, Interagency Collaboration, and Trust within the Law Enforcement Community," *Criminal Justice Studies* 25, no. 4 (2012).

77. Philip McMichael, "Incorporating Comparison within a World-Historical Perspective: An Alternative Comparative Method," *American Sociological Review* (1990); Terrence Hopkins, "World-Systems Analysis: Methodological Issues," in *World-Systems Analysis: Theory and Methodology*, ed. Terrence Hopkins and Immanuel Wallerstein (Thousand Oaks, CA: Sage, 1982), 134–58.

78. C. Wright Mills, *The Sociological Imagination* (New York: Oxford University Press, 2000), 50–52.

CHAPTER 2. THE RISE AND PRESENT DEMISE OF THE WORKFARE-CARCERAL STATE

1. Jonathan Simon, *Governing through Crime: How the War on Crime Transformed American Democracy and Created a Culture of Fear* (New York: Oxford University Press, 2007), 11.

2. The six multistate centers are the Middle Atlantic Great Lakes Organized Crime Enforcement Network, the Mid-States Organized Crime Information Center, the New England State Police Information Network, the Rocky Mountain Information Network, Regional Organized Crime Information Center (for the Southeastern states) and the Western States Information Network. Donna Rogers, "Missing Link: A New Link Chart Capability Adds Functionality to RISSNet Criminal Intelligence Reports," *Law Enforcement Technology* 31, no. 7 (2004); Office of Inspector General, *Review of the Drug Enforcement Administration's El Paso Intelligence Center*, (Department of Justice, June 2010), i, http://www.justice.gov/oig/reports/DEA/a1005.pdf (accessed May 25, 2013). For more on modernization and computerization of policing during this period see also: Tony Platt, Jon Frappier, Ray Gerda, Richard Schauffler, Larry Trujillo, Lynn Cooper, Elliot Currie, and Sidney Harring, *The Iron Fist and the Velvet Glove: An Analysis of the US Police* (San Francisco:

Synthesis Publications, 1982) and Elizabeth Hinton, *From the War on Poverty to the War on Crime: The Making of Mass Incarceration in America* (Cambridge, MA: Harvard University Press, 2016).

3. James Kilgore, *Understanding Mass Incarceration: A People's Guide to the Key Civil Rights Struggle of Our Time* (New York: The New Press, 2015), 1.

4. For an account of the variation across workfare states in North America and Europe, see: Joel F. Handler, *Social Citizenship and Workfare in the United States and Western Europe: The Paradox of Inclusion* (New York: Cambridge University Press, 2004); Jamie Peck, *Workfare States* (New York: Guilford Press); Barbara Vis, "States of Welfare or States of Workfare? Welfare State Restructuring in 16 Capitalist Democracies, 1985–2002," *Policy & Politics* 35, no. 1 (2007).

5. Kilgore, *Understanding Mass Incarceration*, 1

6. Danielle Kaeble and Mary Cowhig, "Correctional Populations in the United States, 2016," US Department of Justice, Bureau of Justice Statistics, April 2018, https://www.bjs.gov/content/pub/pdf/cpus16.pdf (accessed May 17, 2018).

7. These data on incarceration rates by race are derived from the 2010 census. More current data on race are only available for "imprisonment rates" in state and federal prisons, which excludes jail populations. According to 2015 data compiled by the Bureau of Justice Statistics (BJS), the "imprisonment rate" is 820 per 100,000 Hispanics, 1,745 per 100,000 blacks and 317 per 100,000 whites. Leah Sakala, "Breaking Down Mass Incarceration in the 2010 Census: State-by-State Incarceration Rates by Race/Ethnicity," Prison Policy Initiative, May 24, 2014. http://www.prisonpolicy.org/reports/rates.html (accessed July 10, 2014); Danielle Kaeble and Lauren Glaze, "Correctional Populations in the United States, 2015," US Department of Justice, Bureau of Justice Statistics, December 2016, https://www.bjs.gov/content/pub/pdf/cpus15.pdf (accessed March 22, 2016).

8. Jamie Peck, "Workfare: A Geopolitical Etymology," *Environment and Planning D: Society and Space* 16, no. 2 (1998): 156, original emphasis. This study draws mostly on the work of Bob Jessop and his analysis of the distinct state-form he calls the "Schumpeterian Post-national Workfare Regime." For reasons of style and clarity, I use the simpler language employed by scholars like Jamie Peck: *workfare states*. Bob Jessop, *The Future of the Capitalist State* (Malden, MA: Polity, 2002); Peck, *Workfare States*.

9. Giovanni Arrighi, *Adam Smith in Beijing: Lineages of the 21st Century* (New York: Verso, 2009); David Harvey, *A Brief History of Neoliberalism* (New York: Oxford University Press, 2005); Bob Jessop and Ngai-Ling Sum, *Beyond the Regulation Approach: Putting Capitalist Economies in Their Place* (Northampton, UK: Edward Elgar Publishing, 2006); Roberto Patricio Korzeniewicz and Timothy Patrick Moran, *Unveiling Inequality: A World-Historical Perspective* (New York: Russell Sage Foundation, 2009).

10. Associated Press, "U.S. Has Highest Rate of Imprisonment in World," *New York Times*, January 7, 1991, http://www.nytimes.com/1991/01/07/us/us-has-highest-rate-of-imprisonment-in-world.html (accessed May 12, 2017).

11. The following studies comprise the key intellectual contributions that developed out of these conversations: Michelle Alexander, *The New Jim Crow: Mass Incarceration in the Age of Colorblindness* (New York: The New Press, 2012); Ruth Gilmore, *Golden Gulag: Prisons, Surplus, Crisis, and Opposition in Globalizing California* (Berkeley: University of California Press, 2006); Marie Gottschalk, *The Prison and the Gallows: The Politics of Mass Incarceration in America* (New York: Cambridge University Press, 2006); Jeff Manza, and Christopher Uggen, *Locked Out: Felon Disenfranchisement and American Democracy* (New York: Oxford University Press, 2006); Marc Mauer, *Race to Incarcerate* (New York: The New Press, 2006); Christian Parenti, *Lockdown America: Police and Prisons in the Age of Crisis* (New York: Verso, 2000); Simon, *Governing through Crime*; Loïc Wacquant, *Deadly Symbiosis: Race and the Rise of the Penal State* (Malden, MA: Polity, 2009); Loïc Wacquant, *Punishing the Poor: The Neoliberal Government of Social Insecurity* (Durham, NC: Duke University Press Books, 2009); Bruce Western, *Punishment and Inequality in America* (New York: Russell Sage Foundation, 2006).

12. Jessop, *The Future of the Capitalist State*, 3.

13. Alexander, *The New Jim Crow*; Wacquant, *Deadly Symbiosis*.

14. Naomi Murakawa, *The First Civil Right: How Liberals Built Prison America* (New York: Oxford University Press, 2014); Hinton, *From the War on Poverty to the War on Crime*.

15. Mauer, *Race to Incarcerate*; Western, *Punishment and Inequality*.

16. While Bureau of Justice Statistics (BJS) documents "arrest-related deaths," jurisdictions are not required to record or report the data and many—including the entire state of Florida—do not. Since BJS does "not attempt to estimate for partial or non-responding jurisdictions," their findings are "more representative of the nature of arrest-related deaths than the volume at which they occur." In response to the Black Lives Matter movement and increased awareness of "police-involved killings," the *Washington Post* and the *Guardian* began maintaining their own independent counts of people killed by police. In 2015, the *Guardian* documented 1,146 individuals killed by police, while the *Washington Post* recorded 991. For 2016, the *Guardian* tallied 1,093 deaths and the *Washington Post* counted 963. For 2017, the *Guardian* stopped compiling data and the *Washington Post* recorded 987 "police-involved killings." While these data show that racial minorities are killed by police at higher rates than whites, these independent counts reveal that whites make up a larger percentage of those killed by police than what the BJS data indicate. The *Guardian*'s data set shows that 51 percent and 52 percent of those killed by police in 2015 and 2016 were white. Using *Washington Post* data, these percentages change to 50 percent and 48 percent (and 46 in 2017). Andrea Burch, "Arrest-Related Deaths, 2003–2009—Statistical Tables," US Department of Justice, Bureau of Justice Statistics, November 2011, 1, https://www.bjs.gov/content/pub/pdf/ard0309st.pdf (accessed March 25, 2014); *Guardian*, "The Counted: People Killed by Police in the US, *Guardian*, June 1, 2015, https://www.theguardian.com/us-news/ng-interactive/2015/jun/01/about-the-counted (accessed May 5,

2017); *Washington Post,* "Fatal Force: More Than 250 People Have Been Fatally Shot by Police Officers in the First Three Months of 2016," *Washington Post,* undated, https://www.washingtonpost.com/policeshootings/?utm_term =.148246b81e5c (accessed June 25, 2018).

17. James Forman Jr., "Racial Critiques of Mass Incarceration: Beyond the New Jim Crow," *New York University Law Review* 87 (2012); James Kilgore, "Mass incarceration: Examining and Moving Beyond the New Jim Crow," *Critical Sociology* 41, no. 2 (2015); Marie Gottschalk, *Caught: The Prison State and the Lockdown of American Politics* (Princeton, NJ: Princeton University Press, 2016), 119–38.

18. The literature on workfare state is not alone in ignoring race, as Jung and Kwon point out, "the classic works of state theory" have "essentially ignored the causes and effects of state enforced race discrimination." See: Moon-Kie Jung and Yaejoon Kwon, "Theorizing the US Racial State: Sociology since Racial Formation," *Sociology Compass* 7, no. 11 (2013): 927.

19. William Martin, "From Mass Imprisonment to Decarceration and Justice Disinvestment," in *After Prisons? Freedom, Decarceration, and Justice Disinvestment,* ed. William Martin and Joshua Price (Lanham, MD: Lexington Books, 2016), 1.

20. Western, *Punishment and Inequality in America,* 198.

21. Judith Greene and Marc Mauer, *Downscaling Prisons: Lessons from Four States* (Washington DC: The Sentencing Project, 2010), https://www .sentencingproject.org/wp-content/uploads/2016/01/Downscaling-Prisons -Lessons-from-Four-States.pdf (accessed July 30, 2014).

22. Here, I mean the strands of Marxism that emphasize autonomy and self-determination of historically specific working classes and particularities of the actually existing modern capitalist world-system over and above the neat theoretical systems constructed by more "scientific" Marxists. This perspective is analogous to Dyer-Witheford's "red thread" within Marxism that focuses on not just "the dominative power of capital, but on people's capacity to contest that power." This red thread ties together "the young Marx"; the humanism of Luxemburg and Gramsci; the insistence of socialist feminists and black radicals that we must look past the wage relation to fully understand capital accumulation; the refusal of world-systems analysts to separate the study of historical capitalism from theories of capitalist development; and the willingness of autonomist Marxists, Nicos Poulantzas, and anti-security scholars to question old orthodoxies, address the limitations of Marxism, and renew the tradition through a consideration of the pressing questions of our times. Nick Dyer-Witheford, *Cyber-Marx: Cycles and Circuits of Struggle in High Technology Capitalism* (Urbana: University of Illinois Press, 1999), 62–65.

23. Jordan T. Camp, *Incarcerating the Crisis: Freedom Struggles and the Rise of the Neoliberal State* (Berkeley: University of California Press, 2016); Gilmore, *Golden Gulag;* Stuart Hall, Chas Critcher, Tony Jefferson, John Clarke, and Brian Roberts, *Policing the Crisis: Mugging, the State and Law and Order* (New York: Palgrave Macmillan, 2013); Nicos Poulantzas, *State Power Socialism* (New York: Verso, 1978), 203–4.

24. Karl Marx, *Capital, Vol. 1: A Critique of Political Economy* (New York: Penguin).

25. My understanding of social surplus is a synthesis of Marx's original formulation and Alessandro De Girogi's work. For Marx, social surplus connoted excess product that settled, "civilized" societies produced beyond subsistence. Hence, Ernest Mandel writes that "Marx's theory of historical materialism does indeed include comparative economic analysis—for example an examination of the evolution of human labour, human labour productivity, *social surplus* product and economic growth, from slave society through feudalism to capitalism" (emphasis added). These different societies produced different social surpluses. Slave or feudal societies produced wealth: a collection of things. These ruling classes consumed the social surplus as personal luxury, distributed the surplus to their retinue, and/or acquired more land or slaves. By reinvesting wealth in the process of production itself, capitalist societies accumulate capital. This process causes the constant transformation of social relations to produce an ever-expanding mass of wealth (i.e., capital) that exploits labor with increasing efficiency. De Girogi, in his analyses of post-Fordist punishment, introduced a different notion of social surplus as "the complex of subjectivities that are *beyond the reach of disciplinary technologies*" (original emphasis). He identifies these "subjectivities" as the contemporary manifestations of surplus populations: "the underclass, the permanently unemployed, working poor, informal workers, etc." Di Girogi uses this notion of "social surplus" to contrast post-Fordist punishment as a system predicated on the management of surplus, in contrast to Fordism punishment, which managed scarcity. For De Girogi, social surplus, in the Fordist period,

> was on the side of capital, whose requirement had to be imposed to the labour force: a surplus of organization, discipline, scientific management and productivity . . . the labour force was inadequate, unprepared and thus in need of discipline in order to reach the level of cooperation and economic efficiency required by capital.

In this period of productive expansion, labor was scarce and "it was reasonable to consider unemployment and social exclusion as consequences of an individual deficit." In contrast, during the post-Fordist period of financial expansion, the surplus is on the side of labor, which requires regulation not to be disciplined into productive workers but to be pacified as a restive surplus population. While this argument has some merits, it, like the wider cognitive capitalism hypothesis upon which it draws, tends to erase colonial difference and overvalue the stability of labor markets during Fordism. From a world-historical perspective, proletarianization is always partial. Fordism is the exception and "precarity" is the norm. The fundamental precarity of proletarianized labor, however, further demonstrates the usefulness of Di Girogi's notion of "social surplus." Historically and today, capital needs to manage potential disruptions of the social surplus: the excess capital, labor, and subjectivities that result from accumulation. For this reason, I fold Di Girogi's notion of social surplus back into Marx's notion of social surplus *product*. Ernest Mandel, Introduction to *Capital, Vol. 1: A Critique of Political Economy*, by Karl Marx (New York: Penguin, 1992), 13; Alessandro De Giorgi, *Re-thinking the Political Economy of Punishment: Perspectives on Post-Fordism and Penal Politics* (Burlington, VT: Ashgate, 2006), 53, 74–75; Brendan McQuade, "Cognitive Capitalism and Contemporary Politics: A World Historical Perspective" *Science and Society* 79, no. 3 (2015).

26. Starting with Rosa Luxemburg in the early twentieth century, Marxist intellectuals and, especially, socialist feminists theorized social reproduction to disabuse us of the tendency to view capital accumulation as an enclosed, self-correcting system. On a world scale, the broader reproduction of historical capitalism, understood as a world-system that extends beyond the bounds of any individual nation state, would also include the various ways capital accumulation relies upon "unproductive" forms of labor like "housework" and subsumes seemingly non-capitalist, non-waged systems of production (petty commodity production in the household, debt peonage, or slavery). While this expanded notion of social reproduction is strongly associated with socialist feminism, black radicals have consistently emphasized the ways non-waged forms of labor share a common convergence in world-scale processes of capital accumulation. Rosa Luxemburg, *The Accumulation of Capital* (New York: Routledge, 2003); Maria Mies, *Patriarchy and Accumulation on a World Scale: Women in the International Division of Labour* (New York: Palgrave Macmillan, 1998); Cedric J. Robinson, *Black Marxism: The Making of the Black Radical Tradition* (Chapel Hill: University of North Carolina Press, 1983).

27. Antonio Gramsci, *Selections from the Prison Notebooks*, edited by Quintin Hoare and Geoffrey Nowell Smith (New York: International Publishers Co, 1971), 140.

28. James Scott, *Weapons of the Weak: Everyday Forms of Peasant Resistance* (New Haven, CT: Yale University Press, 1987); James Scott, *Domination and the Arts of Resistance: Hidden Transcripts* (New Haven, CT: Yale University Press, 1992).

29. Marx, *Capital, Vol. 1*. 798.

30. David Greenberg, *Crime and Capitalism: Readings in Marxist Criminology* (Philadelphia: Temple University Press, 2010) 39, 41; Mark Neocleous, *The Fabrication of Social Order: Critical Theory of Police Power* (London: Pluto Press, 2000), 1–9.

31. Marx also identified three other subcategories of surplus populations. See: Marx, *Capital, Vol. 1*, 794–98.

32. Frances Fox Piven and Richard Cloward, *Regulating the Poor: The Functions of Public Welfare* (New York: Vintage, 2012); Neocleous, *The Fabrication of Social Order*.

33. Mark Neocleous, *Administering Civil Society* (New York: Palgrave Macmillan Ltd, 1996), 140.

34. Poulantzas, *State, Power, Socialism*, 218–19.

35. Bob Jessop, *State Power: A Strategic-Relational Approach* (Cambridge: Polity, 2008), 7–8, 79.

36. Giovanni Arrighi, Terence K. Hopkins, and Immanuel Wallerstein, *Anti-Systemic Movements* (New York: Verso, 1989), 99–101.

37. Indeed, subsequent revolutionaries would view other social classes as the revolutionary agent. Mao Zedong privileged the peasantry, while Huey Newton later looked to the lumpenproletarian. These "revisionist" tendencies are responses to the uneven development of capitalism. Different social formations were incorporated into the world-market at different "stages" of development, creating a complex world-system where a bewildering diversity of class structures and social property relations shared a common convergence in world-scale accumulation processes. For an example of these processes, see the extended discussion of the "two different, though intersecting, histories" of black working class in the UK in: Hall et al., *Policing the Crisis*, 374–89.

38. George Rigakos and Aysegul Ergul, "Policing the Industrial Reserve Army: An International Study," *Crime, Law and Social Change* 56, no. 4 (2011); George Rigakos and Aysegul Ergul, "The Pacification of the American Working Class: A Time Series Analysis," *Socialist Studies/Études Socialistes* 9, no. 2 (2013).

39. Karl Marx and Friedrich Engels, "The Manifesto of the Communist Party," in *The Marx-Engels Reader, Second Edition*, edited by Robert Tucker (New York: WW Norton, 1978), 469–500.

40. Aníbal Quijano, "Coloniality of Power and Eurocentrism in Latin America," *Nepantla: Views from South* 1, no. 3 (2000): 534.

41. Oliver Cromwell Cox, *Caste, Class, and Race: A Study in Social Dynamics* (New York: Monthly Review Press, 1948), 300–345.

42. Aníbal Quijano and Immanuel Wallerstein, "Americanity as a Concept; or, The Americas in the Modern World," *International Social Science Journal* 44, no. 4 (1992): 551; see also: Kelvin Santiago-Valles, "The Fin de Siècles of Great Britain and the United States: Comparing Two Declining Phases of Global Capitalist Hegemony," in *Endless Empire: Spain's Retreat, Europe's Eclipse, America's Decline*, ed. Alfred W. McCoy, Josep M. Fradera, and Stephen Jacobson (Madison: University of Wisconsin Press, 2012), 182–90.

43. Hall et al., *Policing the Crisis*, 386–87.

44. Roderick Bush, *The End of White World Supremacy: Black Internationalism and the Problem of the Color Line* (Philadelphia: Temple University Press, 2009).

45. Theodore Allen, *The Invention of the White Race, Vol. 2: The Origin of Racial Oppression in Anglo-America* (New York: Verso, 1997).

46. Poulantzas, *State, Power, Socialism*, 129, 148 (emphasis in the original). See also: Jessop, *State Power*.

47. Kelvin Santiago-Valles, "'Race,' Labor, 'Women's Proper Place,' and the Birth of Nations: Notes on Historicizing the Coloniality of Power," *CR: The New Centennial Review* 3, no. 3 (2003): 53.

48. *Herrenvolk* is a German term meaning "master folk" that was used to justify European colonialism. The term *Herrenvolk democracy* was first

introduced by Kenneth Vickery to explain the compatibility of professed demo-cratic equality and overt racial oppression. It was introduced to a wider audience by the work of David Roediger; Kenneth P. Vickery, "'Herrenvolk' Democracy and Egalitarianism in South Africa and the US South," *Comparative Studies in Society and History* 16, no. 3 (1974); David Roediger, *The Wages of Whiteness: Race and the Making of the American Working Class* (New York: Verso, 2007).

49. Joel Olson, *The Abolition of White Democracy* (Minneapolis: University of Minnesota Press, 2004), 42.

50. Ben Brucato, "Fabricating the Color Line in a White Democracy: From Slave Catchers to Petty Sovereigns," *Theoria* 61, no. 141 (2014): 31, 36.

51. W. E. B. Du Bois, *Black Reconstruction in America, 1860–1880* (New York: Free Press, 1999), 700–701; see also: Roediger, *The Wages of Whiteness*.

52. Brucato, "Fabricating the Color Line in a White Democracy," 38–41; Noel Ignatiev, *How the Irish Became White* (New York: Routledge, 2009), 170–204; Rashad Shabazz, *Spatializing Blackness: Architectures of Confinement and Black Masculinity in Chicago* (Urbana: University of Illinois Press, 2015), 11–30.

53. Nikhil Pal Singh, *Race and America's Long War* (Berkeley: University of California Press, 2017), 48–53.

54. Frank J. Donner, *Protectors of Privilege: Red Squads and Police Repression in Urban America* (Berkeley: University of California Press, 1990); Sidney Harring, *Policing Class Society: The Experience of American Cities, 1865–1915* (New Brunswick, NJ: Rutgers University Press, 1983), 148; Alfred W. McCoy, *Policing America's Empire: The United States, the Philippines, and the Rise of the Surveillance State* (Madison: University of Wisconsin Press, 2009), 314–15.

55. Khalil Gibran Muhammad, *The Condemnation of Blackness: Race, Crime and the Making of Modern Urban America* (Cambridge, MA: Harvard University Press, 2010), 20, 272–73.

56. Bruce Nelson, *Divided We Stand: American Workers and the Struggle for Black Equality.* (Princeton, NJ: Princeton University Press, 2002).

57. James Boggs, "Uprooting Racism and Racists in the United States," *The Black Scholar* 2, no 2 (1970): 6.

58. Labor law did not cover domestic household labor or agriculture, the sectors where most black people worked. While the GI Bill was not written in a discriminatory fashion, it was administered locally, which meant thousands of black veterans were denied housing and business loans and job-training pro-grams in emerging fields. Ira Katznelson, *When Affirmative Action Was White: An Untold History of Racial Inequality in Twentieth-Century America* (New York: WW Norton and Company, 2005).

59. This emphasis on the racially differentiated modes of punishment sepa-rates my analysis of the *Herrenvolk*-welfare state from De Giorgi's argument of Fordist punishment. De Giorgi, *Re-thinking the Political Economy of Punishment.* See also note 24 in this chapter.

60. David Rothman, "Perfecting the Prison: The United States, 1789–1865," in *The Oxford History of the Prison: The Practice of Punishment in Western Society*, ed. Norval Morris and David J. Rothman (New York: Oxford University Press, 1995), 100–116.

61. Du Bois, *Black Reconstruction*, 699; Santiago-Valles, "'Race,' Labor, 'A Woman's Proper Place' and the Birth of Nations," 52.

62. Boggs, "Uprooting Racists," 7, 8.

63. Arrighi, Hopkins, and Wallerstein, *Anti-Systemic Movements*, 97–116.

64. Sidney M. Milkis and Jerome M. Mileur, *The Great Society and the High Tide of Liberalism* (Amherst: University of Massachusetts Press, 2005).

65. From Marx and Engels, "The Manifesto of the Communist Party":

> The bourgeoisie, by the rapid improvement of all instruments of production, by the immensely facilitated means of communication, draws all, even the most barbarian, nations into civilisation. The cheap prices of commodities are the heavy artillery with which it batters down all Chinese walls, with which it forces the barbarians' intensely obstinate hatred of foreigners to capitulate. It compels all nations, on pain of extinction, to adopt the bourgeois mode of production; it compels them to introduce what it calls civilisation into their midst, i.e., to become bourgeois themselves. In one word, it creates a world after its own image.

Also available at: https://www.marxists.org/archive/marx/works/1848/communist-manifesto/ch01.htm.

66. Giovanni Arrighi, *The Long 20th Century: Money, Power, and the Origins of Our Times* (New York: Verso, 1994), 309–35; Harvey, *A Brief History of Neoliberalism*, 9–19.

67. Jessop, *The Future of the Capitalist State*, 95–103, 119–32, 141–71, 250–54.

68. Although it's not meaningfully considered in this study, the many wars of pacification that defined the Cold War—counterinsurgency, security assistance, and development aid—also informed these shifts in "domestic" policy. Indeed, one of the main contributions of the critique of security has been to link war power with police power. See: Markus Kienscherf, "Beyond Militarization and Repression: Liberal Social Control as Pacification," *Critical Sociology* 42, nos. 7–8 (2016); Mark Neocleous, *War Power, Police Power* (Edinburgh: Edinburgh University Press, 2014); Ananya Roy, Stuart Schrader, and Emma Shaw Crane, "'The Anti-Poverty Hoax': Development, Pacification, and the Making of Community in the Global 1960s," *Cities* 44 (2015); Stuart Schrader, "To Secure the Global Great Society: Participation in Pacification," *Humanity: An International Journal of Human Rights, Humanitarianism, and Development* 7, no. 2 (2016); Micol Seigel, "Objects of Police History," *Journal of American History* 102, no. 1 (2015).

69. Hinton, *From the War on Poverty to the War on Crime*, 2.

70. Julilly Kohler-Hausmann, "Guns and Butter: The Welfare State, the Carceral State, and the Politics of Exclusion in the Postwar United States," *Journal of American History* 102, no. 1 (2015); Murakawa, *The First Civil Right*.

71. Hinton, *From the War on Poverty to the War on Crime*, 3.

72. Alexander, *The New Jim Crow*, 236–45; Eduardo Bonilla-Silva, "Color-Blind Racism," in *Race, Class, and Gender in the United States: An Integrated Study*, ed. Paula Rothenberg (New York: Worth Publishers, 2007); Brucato, "Fabricating the Color Line," 41–48.

73. Keeanga-Yamahtta Taylor, *From #Blacklivesmatter to Black Liberation* (New York: Haymarket Books, 2016), 75–106.

74. Camp, *Incarcerating the Crisis*, 80–82.

75. Julilly Kohler-Hausmann, "'The Attila the Hun Law': New York's Rockefeller Drug Laws and the Making of a Punitive State," *Journal of Social History* 44, no. 1 (2010): 74.

76. Kilgore, *Understanding Mass Incarceration*, 40.

77. Parenti, *Lockdown America*, 9–18.

78. Hinton, *From the War on Poverty to the War on Crime*, 181–216; Parenti, *Lockdown America*, 12.

79. Tony Platt et al., *The Iron Fist and the Velvet Glove*, 50–54, 84.

80. Joseph A. McCartin, *Collision Course: Ronald Reagan, the Air Traffic Controllers, and the Strike That Changed America* (New York: Oxford University Press, 2011).

81. Parenti, *Lockdown America*, 39, 4043.

82. Gilmore, *Golden Gulag*.

83. Hinton, *From the War on Poverty to the War on Crime*, 310–14, 317; Kilgore, *Understanding Mass Incarceration*, 61–65; Murakawa, *The First Civil Right*, 68–71, 99–100; Parenti, *Lockdown America*, 49–58.

84. Hinton, *From the War on Poverty to the War on Crime*, 318.

85. The act also added further anti-drug provisions: mandatory minimums for possession of five grams of crack cocaine, mandatory drug testing for all federal employees, prohibiting drug users from receiving federal grants or assistance, including public housing. See: Hinton, *From the War on Poverty to the War on Crime*, 319–20; Murakawa, *The First Civil Right*, 121–22.

86. Office of National Drug Control Policy, *High Intensity Drug Trafficking Areas (HIDTA) Program*, The White House, undated, https://www.whitehouse.gov/ondcp/high-intensity-drug-trafficking-areas-program (accessed August 17, 2014).

87. Federal official/former state administrator, Personal interview, September 27, 2013.

88. Government Accountability Office, *Information Sharing: Agencies Could Better Coordinate to Reduce Overlap in Field-Based Activities* (Washington, DC, April 4, 2013), 11, http://www.gao.gov/products/GAO-13-471 (accessed April 14, 2013).

89. Kilgore, *Understanding Mass Incarceration*, 31–32.

90. Wacquant, *Punishing the Poor*, 78, 108, original emphasis.

91. While Wacquant's argument holds much merit, scholars have criticized it on multiple grounds. Jessop notes that while Wacquant gestures at political economy, he does not meaningfully consider capital accumulation or class

struggle. Instead—as Camp and others contend—the horizons of Wacquant's political imaginary are limited to politics within the state. This account of the workfare-carceral state separates itself from Wacquant's analysis of the "neoliberal state" in that it grounds analysis in four interconnected processes: labor-formation, racial-formation, pacification, and state-formation. At the same time, it is important to recognize that Wacquant, particularly in *Deadly Symbiosis*, takes race much more seriously than scholars of the workfare state. For this reason, I recuperate aspects of his argument into an expanded analytic that is attentive to capital accumulation and class struggle. See: Camp, *Incarcerating the Crisis*, 6–7; Bob Jessop, "Putting Neoliberalism in Its Time and Place: A Response to the Debate," *Social Anthropology* 21, no. 1 (2013); Wacquant, *Deadly Symbiosis*.

92. Arrighi, *Adam Smith in Beijing*, 112–20; 189–203.

93. Jelle Visser, "Union Membership Statistics in 24 Countries," *Monthly Labor Review* 129, no. 1 (2006): 38–49; Thomas Piketty, *Capital in the Twenty-First Century* (Cambridge: Belknap, 2014), 23–25.

94. Kilgore, *Understanding Mass Incarceration*, 11–12.

95. Giovanni Arrighi and Beverly Silver, "The End of the Long Twentieth Century," in *Business as Usual: The Roots of the Global Financial Meltdown*, ed. Craig Calhoun and Georgi Derluguian (New York: New York University Press, 2011), 53, 63.

96. Christos Boukalas, *Homeland Security, Its Law and Its State: A Design of Power for the 21st Century* (New York: Routledge, 2014), 42.

97. National Priorities Project, "U.S. Security Spending Since 9/11," May 26, 2011, https://www.nationalpriorities.org/analysis/2011/us-security-spending-since-911/ (accessed May 4, 2017).

98. Boukalas, *Homeland Security*, 130–31.

99. David Harvey, *The Enigma of Capital and the Crises of Capitalism* (London: Profile Books, 2011), 5–6, 118.

100. Michael Roberts, *The Long Depression: How It Happened, Why It Happened, and What Happens Next.* (Chicago: Haymarket Books, 2016).

101. Boukalas, *Homeland Security*, 217.

102. Saskia Sassen. *Expulsions: Brutality and Complexity in the Global Economy* (Cambridge, MA: Harvard University Press, 2014), 14–15, 21–35, 83–116, 121–46.

103. Saskia Sassen, "A Savage Sorting of Winners and Losers: Contemporary Versions of Primitive Accumulation," *Globalizations* 7, nos. 1–2 (2010): 46.

104. US Department of Homeland Security, *Budget in Brief, Fiscal Year 2009* (Washington DC, undated), https://www.dhs.gov/sites/default/files/publications/budget_bib-fy2009.pdf (accessed May 1, 2017); US Department of Homeland Security. *Budget in Brief, Fiscal Year 2017.* (Washington, DC, undated), https://www.dhs.gov/sites/default/files/publications/FY2017_BIB-MASTER.pdf (accessed May 1, 2017).

105. Boukalas, *Homeland Security*, 212.

CHAPTER 3. THE INSTITUTIONALIZATION OF INTELLIGENCE FUSION

1. US Senate, Permanent Subcommittee on Investigations, *Federal Support for and Involvement in State and Local Fusion Centers* (Washington, DC, October 3, 2012),1, https://www.hsgac.senate.gov/imo/media/doc/10-3 -2012%20PSI%20STAFF%20REPORT%20re%20FUSION%20CENTERS .2.pdf (accessed October 3, 2012).

2. William F. Walsh, "Compstat: An Analysis of an Emerging Police Managerial Paradigm," *Policing: An International Journal of Police Strategies & Management* 24, no. 3 (2001).

3. Bernard Harcourt, *Illusion of Order: The False Promise of Broken Windows Policing* (Cambridge, MA: Harvard University Press, 2009): 47–51.

4. Alex Vitale, *City of Disorder: How the Quality of Life Campaign Transformed New York Politics* (New York: New York University Press, 2008), 1–2.

5. William F. Walsh and Gennaro F. Vito, "The Meaning of Compstat Analysis and Response," *Journal of Contemporary Criminal Justice* 20, no. 1 (2004): 51–69.

6. ILP has varied origins. While New York City's experience with CompStat are important precursors, they are not the only ones. For more, see: Jerry Ratcliffe, *Intelligence-Led Policing* (Cullompton, UK: Willan, 2008), 6, 15–40, 83–87.

7. The NYPD ISC was originally referred as the Regional Intelligence Center (RIC) and was renamed the ISC in 2012, when the term became the standardized name for all HIDTA-funded intelligence centers. The exact date for the founding of the NYPD ISC is unclear. The oldest HIDTA report I found is from 2001. At the time, the RIC/ISC was operational. The staff size of 737 is from the 2011 report. Since the ONDCP is exempt from the Freedom of Information Act and since my other efforts to obtain older reports were unsuccessful, I was unable to determine the date that the RIC/ISC was founded. See: Office of National Drug Control Policy, *National Drug Control Strategy: High Intensity Drug Trafficking Areas (HIDTA) Program, 2001 Annual Report* (Washington, DC: Office of National Drug Control Policy, 2001), 78–83, https://www.ncjrs.gov/ondcppubs/publications/enforce/hidta2001/hidta2001 .pdf (accessed August 17, 2014); Executive Office of the President, *High Intensity Drug Trafficking Areas Program Report to Congress* (Washington, DC: Office of the National Drug Control Policy, June 2011), 101, https:// obamawhitehouse.archives.gov/sites/default/files/ondcp/policy-and-research /hidta_2011.pdf (accessed August 25, 2013); NY/NJ HIDTA Director/Former DCJS Director, Personal interview, New York, NY, September 27, 2013.

8. Joseph Pfeifer, "Network Fusion: Information and Intelligence Sharing for a Networked World," *Homeland Security Affairs* 8 (2012), 4.

9. David Harvey, *A Brief History of Neoliberalism* (New York: Oxford University Press, 2005), 44.

10. Ibid., 47–48.

11. For more on the Giuliani administration and the role of the Manhattan Institute, a neoliberal think tank, in shaping its policy platform, see: Jamie Peck, *Constructions of Neoliberal Reason* (New York: Oxford University Press, 2010), 134–51.

12. Jessop discusses this structural bias in terms of the "strategic selectivity" of the state or the "selective filtering of information; systemic lack of action of certain issues; definition of mutually contradictory priorities and counter-priorities; the uneven implementation of measures originating elsewhere in the state system; the pursuit of *ad hoc* and uncoordinated policies concerned with specific conjectural problems affecting particular branches of the state system." Bob Jessop, State *Power: A Strategic-Relational Approach* (Cambridge: Polity, 2008) 125–29.

13. Vincent E. Henry, *The Compstat Paradigm: Management Accountability in Policing, Business and the Public Sector* (New York: Looseleaf Law Publications, 2002), 1–3.

14. In general, it is difficult to link changes in crime with specific policies. The crime drop was a nationwide trend that has been attributed to many factors, including increasing numbers of police, the rising prison population, the waning of the crack boom, the normalization of drug markets, the social isolation caused by racial segregation, and the disruptive effects of mass incarceration. Such nuances, however, did not dissuade American policy makers from embracing the illusory clarity offered by reducing complex social problems to measurable units and performance metrics. As Sampson and Raudenbush observed, "Tough police tactics may thus be a politically popular but perhaps analytically weak strategy to reduce crime." Robert J. Sampson and Stephen W. Raudenbush, "Systematic Social Observation of Public Spaces: A New Look at Disorder in Urban Neighborhoods," *American Journal of Sociology* 105, no. 3 (1999): 638; Ben Bowling, "The Rise and Fall of New York Murder: Zero Tolerance or Crack's Decline?," *British Journal of Criminology* 39, no. 4 (September 1, 1999); Steven D Levitt, "Understanding Why Crime Fell in the 1990s: Four Factors That Explain the Decline and Six That Do Not," *Journal of Economic Perspectives* 18, no. 1 (2004); Bruce Johnson et al., "The Rise and Decline of Hard Drugs, Drug Markets, and Violence in Inner-City New York," in *The Crime Drop in America*, ed. Joel Wallman and Alfred Blumstein (New York: Cambridge University Press, 2000); Edward S. Shihadeh and Nicole Flynn, "Segregation and Crime: The Effect of Black Social Isolation on the Rates of Black Urban Violence," *Social Forces* 74, no. 4 (1996); Todd R. Clear, *Imprisoning Communities: How Mass Incarceration Makes Disadvantaged Neighborhoods Worse* (New York: Oxford University Press, 2009); Richard Rosenfeld et al., "Did Ceasefire, Compstat, and Exile Reduce Homicide?," *Criminology & Public Policy* 4, no. 3 (2005).

15. Henry, *The Compstat Paradigm*, 304–9.

16. Federal official/former state administrator, Personal interview, September 27, 2013.

17. BOTEC Analysis Corporation, *Assessment of the HIDTA Program: High Intensity Drug Trafficking Areas* (Washington, DC: National Criminal

Justice Reference System, April 2002), 106, https://www.ncjrs.gov/pdffiles1 /nij/grants/194118.pdf (accessed August 17, 2014).

18. State administrator, Email Message to Author, June 30, 2014.

19. US Senate, *Federal Support for . . . Fusion Centers*, 10.

20. The NYSIC was originally called the Upstate New York Regional Intelligence Center (UNYRIC) and, through a partnership with the FBI field office in Albany, covered Vermont in addition to Upstate New York (the FBI field office in Albany covers Vermont). The UNYRIC became the NYSIC in March 2008, when it became formally designated by the governor and DHS as New York State's primary fusion center. I have been unable to find documentary evidence that names the NYSIC as "the first fusion center." Many interviewees referred to the NYSIC as "the first fusion center" and documents released to me confirm the August 2003 founding of the center; see: Bart Johnson, Memorandum to William DeBlock, February 14, 2007, "Information Sharing Environment Implementation Plan—Request for Correspondence from the Governor Designating the Upstate New York Regional Intelligence Center as New York State's Primary Center"; Bart Johnson, Memorandum to Preston Felton, March 26, 2007, "Upstate New York Regional Intelligence Center"; Preston Felton, Memorandum to All Personnel, March 12, 2008, "New York State Intelligence Center (NYSIC) Designation as State Fusion Center."

21. Monahan and Regan found that "[t]he size of fusion centers also varied quite widely with one having as few as 4 staff, most having around 30 staff, and a few with 80 staff." In an email communication, the privacy/security officer at the NYSIC provided the exact staffing for the NYSIC: 16 federal agency personnel assigned to NYSIC, seven sworn, nine civilian; 75 state agency personnel assigned to NYSIC, 49 sworn, 26 civilian; three local state agency personnel assigned to NYSIC, three sworn, zero civilian. During my interviews with ROIC personnel, no one could give an exact number for the size of the staff. The figure of "approximately 100" comes from a 2012 article written by the then-assistant director of the ROIC. Regan and Monahan, "Beyond Counterterrorism" 5; State administrator, Email message to author, June 30, 2014; Raymond Guidetti, "Local Policing: Expanding Reach with Limited Resources through Fusion Centers," *The Police Chief* 74, no. 2 (2012): http://www.policechiefmagazine.org/magazine /index.cfm?fuseaction=display&article_id=2599&issue_id=22012 (accessed August 4, 2012).

22. Nicos Poulantzas, *State, Power, Socialism* (New York: Verso, 1978), 205.

23. Retired police administrator, Recorded interview by author, August 8, 2013.

24. The documents I collected do not clarify the matter. Documents related to the founding of the NYSIC were denied in the response to my request. A 2005 document, when the NYSIC was still officially known as the Upstate New York Regional Intelligence Centers, show that the NYSIC's field intelligence officer program was set up with the assistance of the NY/NJ HIDTA. At that time, a HITDA administrator involved in the creation of IMPACT told me that he "was invited to help set up the NYSIC, but I didn't do too much. I helped

them identify initial funding sources. The money didn't come from HIDTA or DCJS. I think asset forfeiture funds or from somewhere else in the state." Federal official/former state administrator, Personal interview, September 27, 2013; Upstate New York Regional Intelligence Center, "Field Intelligence Officers (FIO) Establishment Plan," New York State Police, 2005.

25. Intelligence Analyst, Telephone interview by author, July 27, 2013.

26. Intelligence analyst, Recorded telephone interview by author, August 8, 2014; Intelligence analyst, Recorded phone interview, July 1, 2013; Intelligence analyst, Personal interview by author, August 2, 2013; Retired police administrator, Recorded personal interview by author, August 8, 2013.

27. Intelligence Analyst, Telephone interview by author, July 27, 2013.

28. In response to my open-records request, the NYSP released all their MOUs in June 2013. At that time the NYSIC (or its parent agency, the NYSP) had formal information-sharing arrangements with the following third parties: Neustar (telecom and security company that operates a massive cell phone registry); CSX Transportation (a freight rail operator); the New York National Guard; the Social Security Administration; the Department of Motor Vehicles; US Attorney's Office; the New York City Fire Department; the New York City Department of Environmental Protection Police; the Drug Enforcement Administration; Interpol; the Sûreté du Quebec; the DHS Domestic Nuclear Detection Office; the Bureau of Alcohol, Tobacco, and Firearms and Explosives; US Border Patrol; Immigration and Customs Enforcement.

29. Part I crimes are reported to DCJS by all New York State law enforcement agencies as part of the federal Uniform Crime Reporting (UCR) program. They are violent crimes of murder, rape, robbery, and aggravated assault as well as the property crimes of burglary, larceny, and motor vehicle theft.

30. The 2009 annual report included budget figures from fiscal year (FY) 2003/2004 through FY 2008/2009. The rest were taken from the year reports. The total year IMPACT budget was added to get the full IMPACT budget. Division of Criminal Justice Services, *Operation IMPACT—Annual Report 2009* (Albany, NY: Division of Criminal Justice Services, 2009), 11; Division of Criminal Justice Services, *Operation IMPACT—Annual Report 2010* (Albany, NY: Division of Criminal Justice Services, 2010), 5; Division of Criminal Justice Services, *Operation IMPACT—Annual Report 2011* (Albany, NY: Division of Criminal Justice Service, 2011), 4; Division of Criminal Justice Services, *Operation IMPACT—Annual Report 2012* (Albany, NY: Division of Criminal Justice Services, 2012); Division of Criminal Justice Services, *Operation IMPACT—Annual Report 2013* (Albany, NY: Division of Criminal Justice Services, 2013), 4.

31. Intelligence Analyst, Telephone interview by author, March 10, 2014.

32. Police officer, Municipal Police Department Recorded personal interview by author, August 6, 2013.

33. Police administrator, Municipal Police Department, Recorded personal interview by author, August 2, 2013.

34. John O'Brien and Jim O'Hara, "Onondaga County DA: Syracuse Police Violations of Suspects' Rights 'Shocking,'" *Syracuse Post-Standard*, January 11,

2013, http://www.syracuse.com/news/index.ssf/2013/01/onondaga_county_da
_syracuse_po.html (accessed June 20, 2013).

35. State official, District Attorney's Office, Recorded telephone interview, June 26, 2013; Police officer, Municipal Police Department, Recorded personal interview by author, August 6, 2013.

36. State administrator, New York Department of Criminal Justice Services, Office of Public Safety, Recorded personal interview by author, June 13, 2013.

37. New York State Police, "NYSP Office of Counter Terrorism-Prevention: The New York State Intelligence Center," (Albany: New York State Police, 2012); New York State Police, "New York State Intelligence Center-2011," (Albany: New York State Police, 2013).

38. The Counterterrorism Center and the Sensitive Compartmented Information Facility (SCIF) are separate from the main floor of the NYSIC. "The Terrorism Tips Line is a 24/7 operation manned by personnel at the New York State Intelligence Center." Leads that are not terrorism related are "referred to the appropriate law enforcement agency for investigation." Leads related to New York City "will be forwarded to NYPD for investigation." All other leads are forwarded "to the appropriate FBI Joint Terrorism Task Force . . . [which] has the right of first refusal." Declined leads will be forward to the NYSP's Trooper Counter Terrorism Intelligence Unit. Daniel Cooney, Memorandum to Bart Johnson, October 24, 2004, "New York State Terrorism Tips Line."

39. Intelligence Analyst, Recorded telephone interview by author, July 1, 2013.

40. There are over 100 Joint Terrorism Taskforces (JTTFs) in the United States (see chapter 5 for an extended discussion of JTFFs), three of which are located in New York State: Albany, Buffalo, and New York City. For more on Operation Sentry, see: Raymond Kelly, "10 Years after 9/11: Lessons Learned by the New York City Police Department," *The Police Chief* 78, no. 9 (2010) http://www.policechiefmagazine.org/magazine/index.cfm?fuseaction=display
_arch&article_id=2473&issue_id=92011 (accessed July 20, 2013).

41. Police administrator, Municipal Police Department, Recorded telephone interview by author, June 28, 2013.

42. Police administrator, Municipal Police Department, Recorded personal interview by author, July 19, 2013.

43. Police administrator, Municipal Police Department, Recorded personal interview by author, August 2, 2013.

44. New York State Intelligence Center, "NYSIC Field Intelligence Officer," New York State Police (Undated).

45. New York State Police, "NYSP Office of Counter Terrorism-Prevention: The New York State Intelligence Center," New York State Police (2012); New York State Intelligence Center, "Current Assessment, 11/27/2012," in *Field Intelligence Office Guide Book* (Albany: New York State Police, 2012), 8.

46. New York State Intelligence Center, "Current Assessment, 11/27/2012," 7–8.

47. In 2009, the FBI renamed the database the Known or Suspected Terrorist File. Despite the change, the law enforcement officers interviewed referred to the

system as VGTOF, hence my use of the outdated name. Civil Liberties and National Security Clinic, Yale Law School, *Trapped in Black Box: Growing Terrorism Watchlisting in Everyday Policing* (Washington, DC: The American Civil Liberties Union, April 2016), 16, https://law.yale.edu/system/files/area/clinic/wirac_9-11 _clinic_trapped_in_a_black_box.pdf (accessed February 20, 2017).

48. New York State Police, *Annual Report, 2007* (Albany: New York State Police, 2007), 87; New York State Police, *Annual Report, 2008* (Albany: New York State Police, 2008), 115; New York State Police, *Annual Report, 2009* (Albany: New York State Police, 2009), 111; New York State Police. *Annual Report, 2010* (Albany: New York State Police, 2010), 107.

49. Police administrator, Recorded personal interview by author, May 14, 2013; New York State Police, *Annual Report, 2009*, 109.

50. Federal official/Former state administrator, Personal interview, September 27, 2013; Office of Senator Charles Schumer, Press Room, "Schumer Announces, after His Push, New Crime Fighting Resources Coming to Niagara County with Designation of County as 'High Intensity Drug Trafficking Area,'" Office of Senator Charles Schumer, Press Release, October 13, 2016, https:// www.schumer.senate.gov/newsroom/press-releases/schumer-announces-after -his-push-new-crime-fighting-resources-coming-to-niagara-county-with-desi gnation-of-county-as-high-intensity-drug-trafficking-area_designation-will -now-mean-additional-resources-to-fight-scourge-and-help-disrupt-trafficking (accessed June 1, 2017).

51. Office of Governor Andrew Cuomo, Press Room, "Newest of Seven Centers Supported by $5.5 Million from New York State to Help Police and Prosecutors More Effectively Solve, Reduce and Prevent Crime," Office of Governor Andrew Cuomo, Press Release, October 12, 2016, https://www .governor.ny.gov/news/governor-cuomo-announces-new-north-country -crime-analysis-center (accessed June 1, 2017); Office of Governor Andrew Cuomo, "Governor Cuomo Announces New Crime Analysis Center in Niagara County, Newest of Seven Supported by New York State," Office of Governor Andrew Cuomo, Press Release, February 29, 2016, https://www.governor .ny.gov/news/governor-cuomo-announces-new-crime-analysis-center -niagara-county-newest-seven-supported-new (accessed June 1, 2017); Office of Governor Andrew Cuomo, Press Room, "Governor Cuomo Announces Expansion of New York's Crime Analysis Center Network to the Hudson Valley Region," Office of Governor Andrew Cuomo, Press Release, June 13, 2018, http://www.criminaljustice.ny.gov/pio/press_releases/2018-6-13_press release.html (accessed June 26, 2018).

52. NY/NJ HIDTA covers Bergen, Essex, Hudson, Middlesex, Passaic, and Union counties. See: Executive Office of the President, *High Intensity Drug Trafficking Areas Program Report to Congress*, 99, 103.

53. Intelligence Analyst, Recorded personal interview by author, January 29, 2013.

54. The DVIC covers Burlington, Camden, Cumberland, Gloucester, and Salem counties in New Jersey; see: Joseph Myers, "Intelligence Center Eyes

Safety," *South Philly Review,* June 3, 2013, http://www.southphillyreview.com /news/cover-story/Intelligence-Center-eyes-safety-214136631.html (accessed June 15, 2014).

55. The DVIC director received his MA from the Naval Postgraduate Schools Center for Homeland Defense and Security, where some of the ROIC's senior managers also received their degrees. The DVIC director wrote his MA thesis before the DVIC opened. The thesis reviews the best practices at "four proficient fusion centers." The ROIC is included as one of these cases. Walter Smith, "Developing a Model Fusion Center to Enhance Information Sharing" (MA thesis, Naval Post Graduate School, 2011).

56. Police administrator, ROIC, Recorded personal interview by author, January 29, 2013.

57. State administrator, County Prosecutor's Office in North Jersey, Recorded telephone interview by author, June 9, 2013; Police officer, ROIC Liaison, Municipal Police Department, Recorded personal interview by author, February 27, 2013; Police officer, Municipal Police Department, Recorded telephone interview by author, June 11, 2013; Police administrator, ROIC, Recorded personal interview by author, February 27, 2013a.

58. Joseph Fuentes, "MOU Concerning the Establishment of the Real Time Crime Center," memorandum to A. Ponenti, April 21, 2016.

59. Christian A. Schultz, "The Homeland Security Ecosystem: An Analysis of Hierarchical and Ecosystem Models and Their Influence on Decision Makers" (MA thesis, Naval Postgraduate School, 2012), 30.

60. "Emergency Management in New Jersey—A Historical Perspective," NJ Office of Emergency Management, n.d., http://ready.nj.gov/about-us/history .shtml (accessed June 28, 2014).

61. Brendan McQuade, "The Puzzle of Intelligence Expertise: Spaces of Intelligence Analysis and the Production of 'Political' Knowledge," *Qualitative Sociology* 39, no. 3 (2016).

62. Rosemary Martorana, Dean Baratta, and Kimberly Brown, "Intelligence Reform at the State Level: Lessons Learned," State of New Jersey Office of Homeland Security and Preparedness, https://www.njhomelandsecurity.gov /media/webinar-intelligence-reform-at-the-state-level-lessons-learned (accessed June 1, 2017).

63. Judith Miller, "Intelligent Policing Comes to New Jersey," *City Journal* 18, no. 3 (2008), http://www.city-journal.org/2008/18_3_snd-new_jersey _policing.html (accessed October 24, 2012).

64. Anne Milgram, "Attorney General Law Enforcement Directive No. 2008-1: Submission and Analysis of Information Relating to Seized and Recovered Firearms," State of New Jersey, Office of Attorney General, Department of Law and Public Safety, March 17, 2008, http://www.nj.gov/oag /newsreleases08/dir20080318.pdf (accessed January 20, 2012); Raymond Guidetti, and James Morentz, "Geospatial Statistical Modeling for Intelligence -Led Policing," *The Police Chief* 77, no. 8, (2010), http://www.policechiefmaga zine.org/magazine/index.cfm?fuseaction=display_arch&article_id=2152 &issue_id=82010 (accessed August 4, 2012).

65. Police administrator, ROIC, Recorded personal interview by author, January 29, 2013.

66. At the time of my fieldwork, NJ TRACE remained a core component of the ROIC's services. The Pins on Paper program had changed formats: "We started producing the POP report, which is Pins on Paper and that developed into a monthly product. It was a good product, but it was very time consuming to produce so we took that from a monthly product and broke it up into a North, Central, and South Jersey product and assigned a few staff members to each region of the report so that made life a little easier. We weren't putting so much time into that report but we were doing a more customer-oriented, three-sectional report that was distributed by region. That's currently the basic format we use. We don't produce biweekly reports anymore. We do North and South report; the state is broken in half now. The central area was combined into the North and South. The Central region really only included Trenton and New Brunswick, and there wasn't a ton of incidents taking place. The initial concept went from an idea to a platform to capture the information to a report to a little more intelligence-based, useful tactical report that we're putting out."

Targeting Activities of Gangs never really got off the ground. The analysts and managers at the ROIC found the extensive gun mapping and link analysis organized under the POP program meet the same need: "You can't promise everything to everyone so TAG dropped away. What area of study? What measurable can take us into all of these other worlds? Shootings. Alright, we can track shootings. Where they happened? Who was involved? What weapon? You add it all up and it can tell you a lot. We found out, through our tracking of violent crime and our emphasis on problem people and problem places, that we really didn't need an independent focus on gangs. We focused on violent crime because that's where people get hurt. We picked our area or subject matter of expertise and we made those decisions."

Intelligence Analyst, Personal interview by author, January 28, 2013; Intelligence analyst, Recorded personal interview by author, January 29, 2013; Police administrator, ROIC, Recorded personal interview by author, February 27, 2013a.

67. Police administrator. NJ ROIC, Recorded personal interview by author, January 28, 2013a.

68. Scott Morgan, Kathleen O'Leary-Morgan, and Rachel Boba Santos, *City Crime Rankings 2014* (Thousand Oaks, CA: CQ Press, 2014), xxvi.

69. Police administrator, NJ ROIC, Recorded personal interview by author, January 29, 2013.

70. Brendan McQuade, "Police and the Post-9/11 Surveillance Surge: 'Technological Dramas' in 'the Bureaucratic Field.'" *Surveillance & Society* 14, no. 1 (2016).

CHAPTER 4. POLICING DECARCERATION

1. Paul Guerino, Paige M. Harrison, and William J. Sabol, "Prisoners in 2010," Bureau of Justice Statistics, February 9, 2012, https://www.bjs.gov/content/pub/pdf/p10.pdf (accessed June 23, 2017).

2. E. Ann Carson and Daniela Golinell, "Prisoners in 2011," US Department of Justice, Bureau of Justice Statistics, December 2012, https://www.bjs.gov /content/pub/pdf/p11.pdf (accessed April 10, 2014).

3. E. Ann Carson and Daniela Golinell, "Prisoners in 2012," US Department of Justice, Bureau of Justice Statistics, July 2013, https://www.bjs.gov/content /pub/pdf/p12ac.pdf (accessed April 10, 2014).

4. Editorial Board, "Shrinking the Prison Population," *New York Times*, May 10, 2009, http://www.nytimes.com/2009/05/11/opinion/11mon2.html (accessed June 23, 2017); Editorial Board, "Reducing Unjust Cocaine Sentences," *New York Times*, June 29, 2011, http://www.nytimes.com/2011/06/30 /opinion/30thu3.html (accessed June 23, 2017).

5. Sasha Abramsky, "Is This the End of the War on Crime?" *The Nation*, July 5, 2010, https://www.thenation.com/article/end-war-crime/ (accessed June 23, 2017).

6. Joan Petersilia, "Beyond the Prison Bubble," *Wilson Quarterly* 35, no. 1 (2011): 50.

7. E. Ann Carson, "Prisoners in 2013," Department of Justice, Bureau of Justice Statistics, September 30, 2014, https://www.bjs.gov/content/pub/pdf /p13.pdf (accessed June 23, 2017).

8. E. Ann Carson, "Prisoners in 2014," Department of Justice, Bureau of Justice Statistics, September, 2015, https://www.bjs.gov/content/pub/pdf/p14. pdf (accessed June 23, 2017); E. Ann Carson, and Elizabeth Anderson, "Prisoners in 2015," Department of Justice, Bureau of Justice Statistics, December 2016. https://www.bjs.gov/content/pub/pdf/p15.pdf (accessed June 23, 2017).

9. Marc Mauer, "Can We Wait 88 Years to End Mass Incarceration?" *Huffington Post*, February 19, 2014, http://www.huffingtonpost.com/marc -mauer/88-years-mass-incarceration_b_4474132.html (accessed June 23, 2017).

10. Marie Gottschalk, *Caught: The Prison State and the Lockdown of American Politics* (Princeton, NJ: Princeton University Press, 2016), 271.

11. Elizabeth K. Brown, "Foreclosing on Incarceration? State Correctional Policy Enactments and the Great Recession," *Criminal Justice Policy Review* 24, no. 3 (2012): 318.

12. William Martin, "Decarceration and Justice Disinvestment: Evidence from New York State," *Punishment & Society* 18, no. 4 (2016): 484; for an extended treatment of decarceration in New York State, see: William Martin and Joshua Price, eds., *After Prisons? Freedom, Decarceration and Justice Disinvestment* (Lanham, MD: Lexington Books, 2016).

13. MaryAnn Spoto, "Plan to Close Riverfront State Prison in Camden Draws Controversy," *NJ Advance Media for NJ.com*, March 9, 2009, http:// www.nj.com/news/index.ssf/2009/03/plans_to_close_riverfront_stat.html (accessed June 23, 2017).

14. Daniel Cruz, "Christie Marks Re-Opening of Mid-State Correctional Facility as Treatment Center," NJ TV News, April 10, 2017, http://www.njtvonline .org/news/video/christie-marks-re-opening-mid-state-correctional-facility-treat ment-center/ (accessed June 23, 2017); S.P. Sullivan, "Christie Will Shut Down

250-Inmate N.J. Prison Unit," *NJ Advance Media for NJ.com*, February 28, 2017, http://www.nj.com/politics/index.ssf/2017/02/christie_will_shut_down_250 -inmate_nj_prison_unit.html (accessed June 23, 2017).

15. Danielle Kaeble and Mary Cowhig, "Correctional Populations in the United States, 2016," US Department of Justice, Bureau of Justice Statistics, April 2018, https://www.bjs.gov/content/pub/pdf/cpus16.pdf (accessed May 17, 2018); Reuben Jonathan Miller and Forrest Stuart, "Carceral Citizenship: Race, Rights and Responsibility in the Age of Mass Supervision," *Theoretical Criminology* 21, no. 4 (2017): 534.

16. Reuben Jonathan Miller and Amanda Alexander, "The Price of Carceral Citizenship: Punishment, Surveillance, and Social Welfare Policy in an Age of Carceral Expansion," *Michigan Journal of Race & Law* 21 (2015): 293–94; Michelle S. Phelps, "Mass Probation: Toward a More Robust Theory of State Variation in Punishment," *Punishment & Society* 19, no. 1 (2017); Fergus McNeill and Kristel Beyens, eds., *Offender Supervision in Europe* (New York: Palgrave Macmillan, 2013).

17. Loïc Wacquant, *Deadly Symbiosis: Race and the Rise of the Penal State* (Malden, MA: Polity, 2009); Robert J. Sampson and Charles Loeffler, "Punishment's Place: The Local Concentration of Mass Incarceration," *Daedalus* 139, no. 3 (2010); John M. Eason, "Extending the Hyperghetto: Toward a Theory of Punishment, Race, and Rural Disadvantage," *Journal of Poverty* 16, no. 3 (2012); John M Eason, *Big House on the Prairie: Rise of the Rural Ghetto and Prison Proliferation* (Chicago: University of Chicago Press, 2017): 40–65.

18. Division of Criminal Justice Services, *Operation IMPACT—Annual Report 2008* (Albany, NY: Division of Criminal Justice Services, 2008), 11.

19. Mark Neocleous, "The Dream of Pacification: Accumulation, Class War, and the Hunt," *Socialist Studies/Études Socialistes* 9, no. 2 (2013): 14–17.

20. Tyler Wall, "Unmanning the Police Manhunt: Vertical Security as Pacification," *Socialist Studies/Études Socialistes* 9, no. 2 (2013): 34, 42.

21. Parole officer, Recorded personal interview by author, April 24, 2013a.

22. Probation officer, County Probation Department, Recorded personal interview by author, May 13, 2014.

23. New Jersey Regional Operations Intelligence Center, "New Jersey SWEEP Report: Summer Warrant Effective Enforcement Program, 7/1/2010 –9/1/2010," September 15, 2010, http://www.nj.gov/oag/newsreleases10 /pr20100914a-Sweep-Stats.pdf (accessed April 20, 2013).

24. Michaelangelo Conte, "Jersey City Cops, Other Law Enforcement Arrest 176 through Operation Summer Shield," *Jersey Journal*, June 4, 2011, http:// www.nj.com/jjournal-news/index.ssf/2011/06/jersey_city_cops_other_law_ enf.html (accessed April 20, 2013).

25. Stan Eason, "Summer Shield Closes with 200 Arrests: Feds, States and Locals Join to End Drug Trade in City," City of Jersey City, Press Release, September 21, 2012, http://www.cityofjerseycity.com/uploadedFiles/Public _Notices/Press_Releases/majorOPreleasefinal1%5B1%5D.pdf (accessed April 20, 2013).

26. Michaelangelo Conte, "Hudson County Sheriff's Officers Nab 27 'Fugitives' in Sweep," *Jersey Journal*, May 30, 2013, http://www.nj.com/hudson/index.ssf/2013/05/hudson_county_sheriffs_officer_6.html (accessed August 1, 2014); Michaelangelo Conte, "24 Netted by Hudson Sheriff's Office in Jersey City Warrant Sweep," *Jersey Journal*, July 25, 2014, http://www.nj.com/hudson/index.ssf/2014/07/post_573.html (accessed August 1, 2014); Parole officer, Recorded personal interview by author, April 24, 2013a; Parole officer, Recorded personal interview by author, April 24, 2013b.

27. Greg Adomaitis, "Camden County Warrant Sweep Nets 76 Arrests, Authorities Say," *South Jersey Times*, December 21, 2013, http://www.nj.com/camden/index.ssf/2013/12/camden_county_warrant_sweep_nets_76_arrests_authorities_say.html (accessed April 20, 2014); Office of Public Affairs, "Multi-Agency Fugitive Sweeps Put 55 Wanted Persons in Jail," New Jersey State Police, Press Release, June 24, 2015. http://www.nj.gov/lps/njsp/news/2015/20150624.shtml (accessed July 14, 2017).

28. Administrator, County Prosecutor's Office, Recorded telephone interview, July 2, 2013.

29. Office of Attorney General, The State of New Jersey, "Violent Crime Initiative Captures over 150 Fugitives throughout the State," Office of Attorney General, Press Release, January 25, 2017, http://www.nj.gov/oag/newsreleases17/pr20170125c.html (accessed June 10, 2018).

30. Division of Criminal Justice Services, *Operation IMPACT—Annual Report 2008*, 10; Janine Kava, "Crime Fighting Efforts in Western New York Get a Boost," Division of Criminal Justice Services, Press Release, July 7, 2008, http://www.criminaljustice.ny.gov/pio/press_releases/2008-07-07a_press release.html (accessed April 3, 2013).

31. Division of Criminal Justice Services, *Operation IMPACT—Annual Report 2009* (Albany, NY: Division of Criminal Justice Services, 2009), 24, 40, http://www.criminaljustice.ny.gov/crimnet/ojsa/impact/2009annualreport.pdf (accessed April 3, 2013).

32. Division of Criminal Justice Services, *Operation IMPACT—Annual Report 2013* (Albany, NY: Division of Criminal Justice Services, 2013), 13 http://www.criminaljustice.ny.gov/crimnet/ojsa/impact/2010annualreport.pdf (accessed April 3, 2013).

33. Division of Criminal Justice Services, *Operation IMPACT—Annual Report 2013*, 19.

34. Probation officer, Recorded personal interview by author, City in New York's Mohawk Valley May 13, 2014.

35. Division of Criminal Justice Services, *Operation IMPACT—Annual Report 2013*, 14, 16, 19.

36. Jerry Ratcliffe, *Intelligence-Led Policing* (Cullompton, UK: Willan Publishing, 2008), 182.

37. Intelligence analyst, Recorded personal interview by author, West Trenton, New Jersey, February 27, 2013d.

38. Joseph Fuentes, "MOU Concerning the Establishment of the Real Time Crime Center," Memorandum to A. Ponenti, April 21, 2016, 6.

39. Division of Criminal Justice Services, *Operation IMPACT—Annual Report 2013*, 6.

40. Jim O'Hara, "New Program Targets Chronic Criminals," *Syracuse Post-Standard*, May 6, 2008, http://www.syracuse.com/news/index.ssf/2008/05/new_program_targets_chronic_cr.html (accessed August 3, 2013).

41. Division of Criminal Justice Services, *Operation IMPACT—Annual Report 2009*, 11.

42. State official, District Attorney's Office, Recorded personal interview by author, June 26, 2013.

43. Police officer, Municipal Police Department, Recorded personal interview by author, August 6, 2013.

44. State official, District Attorney's Office, Recorded telephone interview by author, June 26, 2013.

45. Police officer, Municipal Police Department, Recorded personal interview by author, August 6, 2013; State administrator, New York Department of Criminal Justice Services, Office of Public Safety, Recorded personal interview by author, June 13, 2013; Police administrator, Crime Analysis Center, Recorded personal interview by author, July 15, 2013.

46. Police administrator, Municipal Police Department, Recorded personal interview by author, August 22, 2013.

47. Police administrator, Municipal Police Department, Recorded personal interview by author, August 2, 2013.

48. Alex Zdan, "Trenton Sees 19 Homicides, Sharp Increase in Shootings in First 6 Months of the Year," *Times of Trenton*, July 7, 2013, http://www.nj.com/mercer/index.ssf/2013/07/trenton_sees_spikes_in_homicides_shootings_in_first_six_months_of_2013.html (accessed August 4, 2014).

49. Paul Horvitz and *Inquirer* Trenton Bureau, "N.J. Gun Law: A Question of Fairness," *Philadelphia Inquirer*, July 25, 1986, http://articles.philly.com/1986-07-25/news/26099338_1_sentencing-judge-gun-law-excessive-sentences (accessed August 4, 2014); Paul Lorique, Peter Aseltine, and Brian Polite, "Attorney General Announces Two-Pronged Strategy to Combat Rising Gun Violence in Trenton," Office of Attorney General and New Jersey State Police. Press Release, August 15, 2013, http://nj.gov/oag/newsreleases13/pr20130815b.html (accessed August 4, 2014).

50. Penny Ray, "AG Announces Greater Police Presence on Trenton Streets," *Trentonian*, May 14, 2014, http://www.trentonian.com/general-news/2014 0514/ag-announces-greater-police-presence-on-trenton-streets (accessed August 4, 2014).

51. State administrator, New York Department of Criminal Justice Services, Office of Public Safety, Recorded personal interview by author, June 13, 2013.

52. Albany Police Department, "Response IX (part B): Strategy for Addressing Firearm Related Crimes," Albany Police Department, 2012; Police administrator, Crime Analysis Center, Recorded personal interview by author, July 15, 2013.

53. Albany Police Department, "Operation IMPACT X: Agency Budget Narrative for the Period July 1, 2013 through June 30, 2014," Albany Police Department, 2014.

54. James Kilgore, *Understanding Mass Incarceration: A People's Guide to the Key Civil Rights Struggle of Our Time* (New York: The New Press, 2015), 91, 102–3.

55. Howard Waitzkin and Ida Hellander, "Obamacare: The Neoliberal Model Comes Home to Roost in the United States—If We Let It," *Monthly Review* 68, no. 1 (2016), https://monthlyreview.org/2016/05/01/obamacare/ (accessed July 4, 2017).

56. Due to the sample-size limitations, the Bureau of Labor Statistics does not provide state-by-state analyses of unemployment by race, gender, or age, using the more complete measure of unemployment rate (the u-6 measure). For this reason, I calculated the relative difference between African American and Latino unemployment, on the one hand, and white unemployment, on the other, to show underlying phenomena. Bureau of Labor Statistics, "Preliminary 2016 Data on Employment Status by State and Demographic Group," January 27, 2017, https://www.bls.gov/lau/ptable14full2016.pdf (accessed July 7, 2017).

57. Bernard E. Harcourt, "Neoliberal Penality: A Brief Genealogy," *Theoretical Criminology* 14, no. 1 (2010): 77.

58. Police administrator, NJ ROIC, Recorded personal interview by author, January 29, 2013.

59. Zach Patburg, "Paterson Layoff of 125 Police Officers Draws Protests," *The Record*, April 18, 2011, http://www.northjersey.com/news/041811 _Paterson_layoff_of_125_police_officers_draws_protests.html (accessed January 20, 2012).

60. Police officer, Municipal Police Department, Recorded personal interview by author, January 30, 2013.

61. Matt Taibbi, "Apocalypse, New Jersey: A Dispatch from America's Most Desperate Town," *Rolling Stone*, December 11, 2013, http://www.rollingstone .com/culture/news/apocalypse-new-jersey-a-dispatch-from-americas-most -des perate-town-20131211 (accessed June 1 2014); John Rudolf, "Chris Christie Pushes Camden Police Force to Disband, Despite Questions over New Plan's Finances," *Huffington Post*, November 19, 2012, http://www.huffingtonpost .com/2012/11/19/chris-christie-camden-police_n_2025372.html (accessed June 1, 2014).

62. Jenna Portnoy, "Christie: Trenton Should Copy Camden's Regional Police Force," *Star-Ledger*, August 21, 2013. http://www.nj.com/politics/index .ssf/2013/08/christie_in_camden_education.html (accessed June 10, 2104).

63. Police officer, County Police Department, Personal interview, August 13, 2013.

64. Brendan McQuade, "Police and the Post-9/11 Surveillance Surge: 'Technological Dramas' in 'the Bureaucratic Field,'" *Surveillance & Society* 14, no. 1 (2016).

65. State administrator, New York Department of Criminal Justice Services, Office of Public Safety, Recorded personal interview by author, June 13, 2013.

66. Police officer, Municipal Police Department, Recorded personal interview by author, August 6, 2013.

67. Federal official/former state administrator, Personal interview, New York, NY, September 27, 2013.

68. US Department of Homeland Security, *Funding Opportunity Announcement (FOA) FY 2014 Homeland Security Grant Program* (Washington, DC: Department of Homeland Security, 2014), 4, 27, http://www.fema.gov /media-library-data/1395161200285-5b07ed0456056217175fbdee28d2b06e /FY_2014_HSGP_FOA_Final.pdf (accessed July 3, 2014).

69. Federal official, Recorded personal interview by author, August 8, 2013.

70. Federal official/former state administrator, Personal interview, September 27, 2013.

71. Priscilla Regan and Torin Monahan, "Fusion Center Accountability and Intergovernmental Information Sharing," *Publius: The Journal of Federalism* (2014), doi: 10.1093/publius/pju01

72. Police administrator, NYSIC, Recorded personal interview by author, May 14, 2013b.

73. Unfortunately, the state's level of support for the ROIC is not clear. The New Jersey State Police, New Jersey Attorney General's Office, and New Jersey Office of Management and Budget all denied repeated open-records requests for the budget of ROIC. The response was always the same: such records do not exist. Police officer, Municipal Police Department, Personal interview, January 30, 2013.

CHAPTER 5. BEYOND COINTELPRO

1. Tim Weiner, *Enemies: A History of the FBI* (New York: Random House, 2013), 195, 200.

2. Betty Medsger, *The Burglary: The Discovery of J. Edgar Hoover's Secret FBI* (New York: Knopf, 2014).

3. Weiner, *Enemies*, 271.

4. Brian Glick, *The War at Home: Covert Action against U.S. Activists and What We Can Do About It* (Boston: South End Press, 1989), 39–65.

5. Ward Churchill and Jim Vander Wall, *The COINTELPRO Papers: Documents from the FBI's Secret Wars against Dissent in the United States* (Boston: South End Press, 1990), 303.

6. Glick, *The War at Home*, 8.

7. Hans Bennett, "The Black Panthers and the Assassination of Fred Hampton," *Journal of Pan African Studies* 3, no. 6 (2010); Churchill and Vander Wall, *The COINTPRO Papers*, 303.

8. Churchill and Vander Wall, *The COINTPRO Papers*, xi, 18, 56–60, 126–34, 193–98, 228–30, 256–60.

9. Electronic Privacy Information Center, "Spotlight on Surveillance: 'National Network' of Fusion Centers Raises Specter of COINTELPRO," EPIC, June 2007, https://www.epic.org/privacy/surveillance/spotlight/0607/default .html (accessed March 4, 2014).

10. Brendan Maslauskas Dunn, "New Evidence Shows U.S. Government Spied on Wobblies, Activists" *Industrial Worker*, April 2014, https://libcom.org/library/new-evidence-shows-us-government-spied-wobblies-activists (accessed June 5, 2014); Kevin Gosztola, "The Risks Homeland Security Fusion Centers Pose to Americans' Civil Liberties," *Shadow Proof*, October 5, 2012. https://shadowproof.com/2012/10/05/the-risks-homeland-security-fusion-centers-pose-to-americans-civil-liberties/ (accessed March 4, 2014).

11. Catherine Bleisch, "Path to Freedom," YouTube video, 48:18, Posted by "TheLRP," November 30, 2012, https://www.youtube.com/watch?v=vedfu-ulmbA (accessed July 5, 2014); Alexander Zaitchik, "Meet Alex Jones," *Rolling Stone*, March 2, 2011, http://www.rollingstone.com/politics/news/talk-radios-alex-jones-the-most-paranoid-man-in-america-20110302?print=true (accessed July 12, 2014).

12. Dave Lindorff, "Did the White House Direct the Police Crackdown on Occupy?" *Counterpunch*, May 14, 2012, http://www.counterpunch.org/2012/05/14/did-the-white-house-direct-the-police-crackdown-on-occupy/ (accessed May 20, 2012); Dave Lindorff, "Evidence Homeland Security Coordinated Occupy Crackdown," *Counterpunch*, March 23, 2012, http://www.counterpunch.org/2012/03/23/evidence-homeland-security-coordinated-occupy-crackdown/ (accessed March 30, 2012); Naomi Wolf, "The Shocking Truth about the Crackdown on Occupy," *Guardian*, November 25, 2011, http://www.theguardian.com/com mentisfree/cifamerica/2011/nov/25/shocking-truth-about-crackdown-occupy (accessed November 25, 2011); Naomi Wolf, "The Crackdown on Occupy Controversy: A Rebuttal," *The Guardian*, December 2, 2011, http://www.the guardian.com/commentisfree/cifamerica/2011/dec/02/crackdown-occupy-contro versy-rebuttal-naomi-wolf?commentpage (accessed December 2, 2012); Naomi Wolf, "Revealed: How the FBI Coordinated the Crackdown on Occupy," *The Guardian*, December 29, 2012, http://www.theguardian.com/commentisfree/2012/dec/29/fbi-coordinated-crackdown-occupy (accessed December 28, 2012).

13. L.K. Johnson, *A Season of Inquiry Revisited: The Church Committee Confronts America's Spy Agencies* (Lawrence: University Press of Kansas, 2015).

14. Will Jackson, Joanna Gilmore, and Helen Monk, "Policing Unacceptable Protest in England and Wales: A Case Study of the Policing of Anti-fracking Protests," *Critical Social Policy* 39, no. 4 (2018), doi: 10.1177/0261018317753087

15. Kathryn S. Olmsted, *Challenging the Secret Government: The Post-Watergate Investigations of the CIA and FBI* (Chapel Hill: University of North Carolina Press, 2000).

16. Evan Perez, "Secret Court's Oversight Gets Scrutiny," *Wall Street Journal*, June 9, 2013.

17. Frank J. Donner, *Protectors of Privilege: Red Squads and Police Repression in Urban America* (Berkeley: University of California Press, 1990), 65–90.

18. Kristian Williams, *Our Enemies in Blue: Police and Power in America* (Cambridge, MA: South End Press, 2007), 164–65.

19. Matt Apuzzo and Adam Goldman, *Enemies Within: Inside the NYPD's Secret Spying Unit and Bin Laden's Final Plot against America* (New York: Simon and Schuster, 2013), 47–50.

20. Jeffrey Monaghan and Kevin Walby, "Making Up 'Terror Identities': Security Intelligence, Canada's Integrated Threat Assessment Centre and Social Movement Suppression," *Policing and Society* 22, no. 2 (2012).

21. Mark Neocleous, *The Universal Adversary: Security, Capital and "the Enemies of All Mankind'* (New York: "Routledge, 2016) 2, 4–5.

22. Churchill and Vander Wall, *The COINTPRO Papers*, 309–15.

23. Ivan Greenberg, *The Dangers of Dissent: The FBI and Civil Liberties since 1965* (Lanham, MD: Lexington Books, 2010), 142.

24. Will Potter, *Green Is the New Red: An Insider's Account of a Social Movement Under Siege* (San Francisco: City Lights Publishers, 2011), 122.

25. American Civil Liberties Union, "USA Patriot Act: Further Analysis," https://www.aclu.org/other/usa-patriot-act-further-analysis (accessed March 4, 2018).

26. Dana Priest and William Arkin. *Top Secret America: The Rise of the New American Security State* (New York: Little, Brown & Co. 2011), 134–35.

27. Apuzzo and Goldman, *Enemies Within*, 50–52.

28. Williams, *Our Enemies in Blue*, 280, footnote 137; Federal Bureau of Investigation, "Joint Terrorism Task Forces," Federal Bureau of Investigation, undated, https://www.fbi.gov/investigate/terrorism/joint-terrorism-task -forces (accessed March 4, 2018).

29. US Department of Justice, Office of the Inspector General, Evaluation and Inspections Division, *The Department of Justice's Terrorism Task Forces* (Washington, DC: US Department of Justice, June 2005), 16, https://oig.justice .gov/reports/plus/e0507/final.pdf (accessed March 4, 2018).

30. Mike German and Jay Stanley, *What's Wrong with Fusion Centers* (Washington, DC: American Civil Liberties Union, December 2007), 10, http:// www.aclu.org/files/pdfs/privacy/fusioncenter_20071212.pdf (accessed January 3, 2012); Susan N. Herman, "Collapsing Spheres: Joint Terrorism Task Forces, Federalism, and the War on Terror," *Willamette Law Review* 41 (2005).

31. Williams, *Our Enemies in Blue*, 167.

32. German and Stanley, *What's Wrong with Fusion Centers*, 11.

33. Mathieu Deflem, "Joint Terrorism Task Forces," in *Counterterrorism: From the Cold War to the War on Terror, Volume 1*, ed. Frank G. Shanty (Santa Barbara, CA: Praeger/ABC-CLIO, 2012), 425.

34. Potter, *Green Is the New Red*, 182–90.

35. For a review of incidents of political policing involving fusion centers from 2005 to 2011, see: Torin Monahan, "The Future of Security? Surveillance Operations at Homeland Security Fusion Centers," *Social Justice* 37, nos. 2–3 (2010/2011): 88–92. This chapter covers more recent examples.

36. Anthony Newkirk, "The Rise of the Fusion-Intelligence Complex: A Critique of Political Surveillance after 9/11," *Surveillance & Society* 8, no. 1 (2010).

37. George Joseph, "Exclusive: Feds Regularly Monitored Black Lives Matter, *The Intercept,* July 24, 2015, https://theintercept.com/2015/07/24/documents -show-department-homeland-security-monitoring-black-lives-matter-since -ferguson/ (accessed July 24, 2015); Darwin Bond-Graham, "Counter-Terrorism Officials Helped Track Black Lives Matter Protesters," *East Bay Express,* April 15, 2015, https://www.eastbayexpress.com/oakland/counter-terrorism-officials -helped-track-black-lives-matter-protesters/Content?oid=4247605 (accessed April 15, 2015); George Joseph, "NYPD Officers Accessed Black Lives Matter Activists' Texts, Documents Show," *The Guardian,* April 4, 2017, https://www .theguardian.com/us-news/2017/apr/04/nypd-police-black-lives-matter -surveillance-undercover (accessed April 4, 2017); Bill Dries, "Tennessee Fusion Center Monitored July Protests In Memphis, Emails Reveal," *Memphis Daily News,* March 14, 2017, https://www.memphisdailynews.com/news/2017/mar/14 /tennessee-fusion-center-monitored-july-protests-in-memphis-emails-reveal/ (accessed March 14, 2017).

38. George Joseph, "Undercover Police Have Regularly Spied on Black Lives Matter Activists in New York," *The Intercept,* August 18, 2015, https://theinter- cept.com/2015/08/18/undercover-police-spied-on-ny-black-lives-matter / (accessed August 18, 2015); George Joseph and Murtaza Hussain, "FBI Tracked an Activist Involved with Black Lives Matter as They Travelled Across the U.S., Documents Show," *The Intercept,* March 19, 2018. https://theintercept. com/2018/03/19/black-lives-matter-fbi-surveillance/ (accessed March 19, 2018).

39. G.W. Schulz, "Assessing RNC Police Tactics: Missteps, Poor Judgments and Inappropriate Detentions," *MinnPost,* September 1, 2009, http://www.min npost.com/politics-policy/2009/09/assessing-rnc-police-tactics-missteps-poor -judgments-and-inappropriate-deten (accessed March 2, 2012); Sam Stoker, "Framing the 'RNC 8," *In These Times,* October 8, 2008, http://inthesetimes .com/article/3962/framing_the_rnc_8 (accessed March 2, 2012).

40. Emily Gurnon, "Last 'RNC 8' Protesters Admit Guilt—but Remain Defiant," *St. Paul Pioneer Press,* October 20, 2010, http://www.twincities.com /news/ci_16382084 (accessed March 2, 2012).

41. Madeleine Baran, "Man Sentenced to 91 Days in RNC Protest Case," Minnesota Public Radio, August 27, 2010, http://www.mprnews.org/story/2010 /08/27/rnc-plea (accessed March 3, 2012); Madeleine Baran, "Charges Dismissed against Three of RNC 8 Suspects," Minnesota Public Radio, September 16, 2010, http://www.mprnews.org/story/2010/09/16/rnc-charges -dismissed (accessed March 3, 2012).

42. Paul Demko, "Lawsuits Field Alleging Police Misconduct around RNC," *The Minnesota Independent,* February 27, 2009, http://minnesotaindependent .com/27788/lawsuits-filed-alleging-police-misconduct-around-rnc (accessed March 2, 2012).

43. RNC Civil Disturbance Subcommittee, "Civil Disturbance Management Plan," August 14, 2008, 4, https://www.stpaul.gov/DocumentCenter /View2/7395.pdf (accessed March 3, 2012); Terri Smith, "Special Event Planning 2008 Republican National Convention," Homeland Security and

Emergency Management, 2008, 16, http://downloads.wikileaks-press.org/file /rnc-2008-homeland-security-planning.pdf (accessed July 3, 2014).

44. Monahan, "The Future of Security?" 90.

45. State official, Connecticut Intelligence Center, Recorded personal interview by author, August 22, 2012.

46. Brenda Bergeron to Kenneth Krayeske, "RE: FOI Request 11-517," November 25, 2011.

47. Luis Fernandez, *Policing Dissent: Social Control and the Anti-Globalization Movement* (New Brunswick, NJ: Rutgers University Press, 2008), 68–91; Alex Vitale, "The Command and Control and Miami Models at the 2004 Republican National Convention: New Forms of Policing Protests," *Mobilization: An International Quarterly* 12, no. 4 (2007).

48. Fernandez, *Policing Dissent*, 165.

49. Simon Rogers, "Occupy Protests around the World: Full List Visualised," *The Guardian*, November 14, 2011, http://www.theguardian.com/news/data blog/2011/oct/17/occupy-protests-world-list-map (accessed July 7, 2014).

50. Occupy Arrests, June 24, 2014, http://occupyarrests.moonfruit.com/ (accessed July 7, 2014).

51. Wolf, "The Shocking Truth about the Crackdown on Occupy."

52. Matt Seaton, "Naomi Wolf: Reception, Responses, Critics," *The Guardian*, November 28, 2011, http://www.theguardian.com/commentisfree/cifamerica /2011/nov/28/naomi-wolf-reception-responses-critics (accessed November 30, 2011); Wolf, "The Crackdown on Occupy Controversy: A Rebuttal."

53. Wolf, "Revealed: How the FBI Coordinated the Crackdown on Occupy."

54. Lindorff, "Did the White House Direct the Police Crackdown on Occupy?"

55. Robert Davis to Matthew Chandler. "RE: CBS News Media Request," November 16, 2011, http://www.justiceonline.org/docs/dhs-occupy-documents -1-398.pdf (accessed December 31, 2012).

56. The private sector was involved through the Domestic Security Alliance Council, a partnership between the FBI and the 200 largest US corporations. "DSAC Liaison Information Report," Domestic Security Alliance Council, December 9, 2011, http://www.justiceonline.org/docs/fbi-occupy-documents-1 .pdf (accessed December 31 2012).

57. Shala Byers to [redacted], "Guidance Requested: Occupy Wall Street," October 17, 2011, http://www.justiceonline.org/docs/dhs-occupy-documents -4-pt1.pdf (accessed December 31, 2012).

58. Todd Karpel to Mark Wiessman, "RE: Occupy Movements," November 26, 2011, http://s3.documentcloud.org/documents/1151739/surveillance-of-occupy -groups.pdf (accessed May 22, 2014).

59. Police administrator, NJ ROIC, Recorded personal interview by author, January 28, 2013.

60. New Jersey Regional Operations Intelligence Center, "Advisory: Occupy Wall Street March to Washington D.C.: Potential Impacts in New Jersey," November 9, 2011, http://www.documentcloud.org/documents/1094053-occupy -docs-set-4.html (accessed May 30, 2014); New Jersey Regional Operations

Intelligence Center Analysis Element to Anthony Tisdale, "Occupy Wall Street March to Washington D.C.: Potential Impacts in New Jersey," November 9, 2011, http://www.documentcloud.org/documents/1094053-occupy-docs-set-4.html (accessed May 30, 2014).

61. Police administrator, NYSIC, Recorded personal interview by author, May 14. 2013d.

62. Police administrator, NYSIC, Recorded personal interview by author, May 14, 2013b.

63. Jeff Nickerson, "Occupy Providence to Vacate Burnside Park after Reaching Agreement with the City," *Greater City Providence*, http://www.gcpvd.org/2012/01/24/occupy-providence-to-vacate-burnside-park-after-reaching-agreement-with-the-city/ (accessed July 14, 2014).

64. Bryan Fitzgerald, "Has Occupy Albany Movement Marched into History?," *Times Union*, http://www.timesunion.com/local/article/Has-Occupy-Albany-movement-marched-into-history-3965918.php#src=fb (accessed July 14, 2014).

65. Beau Hodai, *Dissent or Terror: How the Nation's Counter Terrorism Apparatus, in Partnership with Corporate America, Turned on Occupy Wall Street* (Madison, WI: Center for Media and Democracy & BDA Press, May 2013), 46–73, http://www.prwatch.org/files/Dissent%20or%20Terror%20FINAL.pdf (accessed May 20, 2013).

66. David Cunningham and Barb Browning, "The Emergence of Worthy Targets: Official Frames and Deviance Narratives within the FBI," *Sociological Forum* 19, no. 3 (2004): 351–52, 360–63.

67. Associated Press, "Mayors, Police Chiefs Talk Strategy on Protests," *Las Vegas Sun*, November 15, 2011, http://www.lasvegassun.com/news/2011/nov/15/us-occupy-cooperation/ (accessed December 28, 2011); Andy Kroll, "Mayors and Cops Traded Strategies for Dealing with Occupy Protesters," *Mother Jones*, November 16, 2011, http://www.motherjones.com/mojo/2011/11/occupy-protest-coordinate-crackdown-wall-street (accessed November 16, 2011); Hodai, *Dissent or Terror*, 41–45.

68. Bob Jessop, *The Future of the Capitalist State* (Malden, MA: Polity, 2002), 172–215, 250–54.

69. US Department of Justice's Global Justice Information Sharing Initiative, *Baseline Capabilities for State and Major Urban Area Fusion Centers* (Washington, DC: Department of Justice and Department of Homeland Security, September 2008), 2, https://www.fema.gov/pdf/government/grant/2010/fy10_hsgp_fusion.pdf (accessed March 12, 2012).

70. Stuart Schrader makes a similar analysis of the policing of Occupy:

> Unable to turn to tax revenue to cover the costs . . . many agencies turned to philanthropy, foundations, and private donations to make ends meet, even (or especially) in large, relatively fiscally sound cities. The foundation that received JPMorgan's donation, for example, has paid for expensive hardware, including body armor and computers . . . the instrumentalist accusation understands transactions like the

JPMorgan donation as not only symbolizing, but actually constituting, the relationship of capital and the state, and it proclaims that the police are enrolled in the management of that relationship. . . . It does not, however, look at the conditions that give rise to such transactions. . . . [T]he theory I am using—the state as a social relation, the subject-object of changing relations of forces—suggests that austerity itself has taken on a modified purpose since 2008.

Stuart Schrader, "Policing Political Protest: Paradoxes of the Age of Austerity," *Periscope: Social Text Collective,* December 9, 2012, http://what-democracy-looks-like.com/policing-political-protest-paradoxes-of-the-age-of-austerity/ (accessed March 2, 2013).

71. Alleen Brown, Will Parish, and Alice Speri. "Standing Rock Documents Expose Inner Workings of 'Surveillance-Industrial Complex.'" *The Intercept,* June 3, 2017; Alleen Brown, Will Parish, and Alice Speri, "Leaked Documents Reveal Counterterrorism Tactics Used at Standing Rock to 'Defeat Pipeline Insurgencies,'" *The Intercept,* May 27, 2017, https://theintercept.com/2017/05/27/leaked-documents-reveal-security-firms-counterterrorism-tactics-at-standing-rock-to-defeat-pipeline-insurgencies/ (accessed May 27, 2017).

72. John Porter, "Internal TigerSwan Situation Report," TigerSwan, October 16, 2016, https://theintercept.com/document/2017/06/03/internal-tigers wan-situation-report-2016-10-03/ (accessed May 27, 2017).

73. DAPL Security, "Security Operations Overview," TigerSwan, October 16, 2016, https://theintercept.com/document/2017/05/27/security-operations-over view-2016-10-16/ (accessed May 27, 2017); "Internal TigerSwan Situation Report," TigerSwan, September 7, 2017, https://theintercept.com/document/2017/05/27/internal-tigerswan-situation-report-2016-09-07 (accessed May 27, 2017); John Porter, "Internal TigerSwan Situation Report," TigerSwan, September 9, 2016, https://theintercept.com/document/2017/05/27/internal-tigers wan-situation-report-2016-09-22 (accessed May 27, 2017).

74. Alleen Brown, Will Parish, and Alice Speri, "Police Used Private Security Aircraft for Surveillance in Standing Rock 'No-Fly Zone,'" *The Intercept,* September 29, 2017 https://theintercept.com/2017/09/29/standing-rock-dakota-access-pipeline-dapl-no-fly-zone-drones-tigerswan (accessed September 27, 2017); Alleen Brown, "Arrests of Journalists at Standing Rock Test the Boundaries of the First Amendment," *The Intercept,* November 27, 2016, https://theintercept.com/2016/11/27/arrests-of-journalists-at-standing-rock-test-the-boundaries-of-the-first-amendment (accessed December 1, 2016).

75. Brendan McQuade, "Guns, Grenades, and Facebook," *Jacobin,* December, 5, 2016, https://www.jacobinmag.com/2016/12/standing-rock-sioux-dakota-access-dapl-obama-trump, (accessed December 5, 2016).

76. Will Parrish, "An Activist Stands Accused of Firing a Gun at Standing Rock. It Belonged to Her Lover—an FBI Informant," *The Intercept,* December 11, 2017, https://theintercept.com/2017/12/11/standing-rock-dakota-access-pipe line-fbi-informant-red-fawn-fallis/ (accessed December 11, 2017).

77. Joseph Bullington, "Standing Rock Felony Defendants Take Plea Deals, Still Face Years in Prison," *In These Times*, February 22, 2018, http://inthese times.com/rural-america/entry/20936/standing-rock-felony-defendants -dakota-access-pipeline-water-protectors (accessed March 11, 2018); Alleen Brown, Will Parish, and Alice Speri, "As Standing Rock Camps Cleared Out, TigerSwan Expanded Surveillance to Array of Progressive Causes.'" *The Intercept*, June 21, 2017, https://theintercept.com/2017/06/21/as-standing -rock-camps-cleared-out-tigerswan-expanded-surveillance-to-array-of-pro gressive-causes/ (accessed June 21, 2017).

78. Alleen Brown, Will Parish, and Alice Speri, TigerSwan Responded to Pipeline Vandalism by Launching Multistate Dragnet,'" *The Intercept*, August 26, 2017, https://theintercept.com/2017/08/26/dapl-security-firm-tigerswan-respon ded-to-pipeline-vandalism-by-launching-multistate-dragnet (accessed August 26, 2017).

79. John Porter, "Internal TigerSwan Situation Report," TigerSwan, February 2, 2017, https://theintercept.com/document/2017/06/21/internal -tigerswan-situation-report-2017-02-27 (accessed June 21, 2017).

80. Brown, Parish, and Speri, "Leaked Documents Reveal Counterterrorism Tactics Used at Standing Rock"; Porter, "Internal TigerSwan Situation Report," TigerSwan, October 16, 2016.

81. DHS Office of Intelligence Analysis, "TTPs Used in Recent US Pipeline Attacks by Suspected Environmental Rights Extremists, The Department of Homeland Security, May 2, 2017, https://theintercept.com/document/2017 /12/11/may-2017-field-analysis-report/ (accessed March 20, 2018).

82. Central Florida Information Exchange and North Dakota State and Local Intelligence Center, "Criminal Activities and Incidents Surrounding the Dakota Access Pipeline and Impact on the Sabal Trail Pipeline," April 2017. https://theintercept.com/document/2017/12/11/april-2017-joint-intelligence -bulletin (accessed March 20, 2018).

83. DHS Office of Intelligence Analysis, "Potential Domestic Intelligence Threats to Multi-State Diamond Pipeline Construction Project," The Department of Homeland Security, April 7, 2017, https://www.documentcloud. org/documents/4404359-DHS-Bulletin-Aug-9.html (accessed March 7, 2018).

84. Intelligence analyst, Recorded personal interview by author, February 27, 2013d.

85. "214 Indicted on Felony Riot Charges for Protesting Trump Inauguration," *Unicorn Riot*, March 15, 2017/ https://www.unicornriot.ninja /2017/214-indicted-felony-riot-charges-protesting-trump-inauguration/ (accessed March 15, 2017).

86. Sam Levin, "FBI Terrorism Taskforce Investigating Standing Rock Activists," *The Guardian*, February 10, 2017, https://www.theguardian.com /us-news/2017/feb/10/standing-rock-fbi-investigation-dakota-access (accessed February 10, 2017).

87. Federal Bureau of Investigation, "Black Identity Extremists Likely Motivated to Target Law Enforcement Officers," August 3, 2017, https://assets

.documentcloud.org/documents/4067711/BIE-Redacted.pdf, (accessed March 20, 2018).

88. Northern California Regional Intelligence Center, "Domestic Extremism Threat Update, California: Potential for Violence at Upcoming Rallies," Northern California Regional Intelligence Center, undated, https://www.docu mentcloud.org/documents/4404294-Parrish-Will-10-16-2017.html (accessed March 20, 2018).

89. DHS Office of Intelligence Analysis, "Domestic Terrorist Violence at Lawfully Permitted White Supremacists Rallies Likely to Continue," The Department of Homeland Security, August 9, 2017, https://www.document cloud.org/documents/4404359-DHS-Bulletin-Aug-9.html (accessed March 7, 2018); Will Parrish, "Police Targeted Anti-Racists in Charlottesville Ahead of 'Unite the Right' Rally, Documents Show," *Shadowproof*, March 7, 2018, https://shadowproof.com/2018/03/07/documents-reveal-police-targeting -anti-racists-charlottesville (accessed March 7, 2018).

90. Sam Levin, "California Police Worked with Neo-Nazis to Pursue 'Anti-racist' Activists, Documents Show," *The Guardian*, February 9, 2018. https:// www.theguardian.com/us-news/2017/feb/10/standing-rock-fbi-investigation -dakota-access (accessed March 7, 2018).

91. DHS Office of Intelligence Analysis, "White Supremacist Extremism Poses Persistent Threat of Lethal Violence," May 10, 2017, 104, https://www .documentcloud.org/documents/4404294-Parrish-Will-10-16-2017.html (accessed March 20, 2018).

92. DHS Office of Intelligence Analysis, "Domestic Extremists Movements Remain a Medium-Level Threat in Nevada," Department of Homeland Security, April 6, 2017, 141, https://www.documentcloud.org/documents /4404294-Parrish-Will-10-16-2017.html (accessed March 7, 2018).

93. The commitment to human rights compliant political policing is also evident in article coauthored by a former senior manager at the ROIC. The article condemns police monitoring of animal rights activists and advocates a shift away from "value-based decision-making" and toward "recognition-primed decision-making." Raymond Guidetti and Thomas Martinelli, "Intelligence-Led Policing—A Strategic Framework," *The Police Chief*, 76, no. 10, (2009), http://www .policechiefmagazine.org/magazine/index.cfm?fuseaction=display&article_id =1918&issue_id= 102009 (accessed, August 4, 2012).

94. German and Stanley, "What's Wrong with Fusion Centers."

95. Police administrator, NJ ROIC, Recorded personal interview by author, February 27, 2013b.

96. New Jersey Regional Operations Intelligence Center, Intelligence Analysis Crime Unit, "ROIC Daily Overview," January 7, 2014; New Jersey Regional Operations Intelligence Center, Intelligence Analysis Threat Unit, "ROIC Intelligence and Analysis Threat Unit Daily Overview," May 29, 2014.

97. Intelligence analyst, Recorded personal interview by author, February 27, 2013b.

98. Ibid.

99. Police administrator, NJ ROIC, Recorded personal interview by author, February 27, 2013b.

100. Emphasis added, DHS, "Domestic Terrorist Violence . . . Likely to Continue."

101. DHS Office of Intelligence and Analysis, "Right Wing Extremism: Current Economic and Political Climate Fueling a Resurgence in Radicalization and Recruitment," Department of Homeland Security, 2009, http://fas.org/irp/eprint/rightwing.pdf (accessed, August 20, 2012).

102. Daryl Johnson, *Right-Wing Resurgence: How a Domestic Terror Threat Is Being Ignored* (Lanham, MD: Rowman & Littlefield, 2012), 248–66.

103. Ibid., 274–84, 321–22.

104. DHS Office of Intelligence Analysis, "Sovereign Citizen Extremist Ideology Will Drive Violence at Home, During Travel, and at Government Facilities," February 5, 2015, https://d1ai9qtk9p41kl.cloudfront.net/media/pdf/Sovereign_Citizen_Extremist_Ideology_2-5-15.pdf (accessed March 20, 2018).

105. Ron Nixon, "Homeland Security Looked Past Antigovernment Movement, Ex-Analyst Says," *New York Times*, January 8, 2016, https://www.nytimes.com/2016/01/09/us/politics/homeland-security-looked-past-militia-movement-ex-analyst-says.html (accessed March 24, 2018).

106. Ron Nixon and Eileen Sullivan, "Revocation of Grants to Help Fight Hate under New Scrutiny after Charlottesville," *New York Times*, August 15, 2016, https://www.nytimes.com/2017/08/15/us/politics/right-wing-extremism-charlottesville.html (accessed March 24, 2018).

107. FBI Counterterrorism Division, "White Supremacist Infiltration of Law Enforcement," Federal Bureau of Investigation, October 17, 2006 https://s3.amazonaws.com/s3.documentcloud.org/documents/402521/doc-26-white-supremacist-infiltration.pdf (accessed March 20, 2018).

108. FBI Counterterrorism Division, "White Supremacist Infiltration of Law Enforcement," Federal Bureau of Investigation, October 17, 2006, https://s3.amazonaws.com/s3.documentcloud.org/documents/402521/doc-26-white-supremacist-infiltration.pdf (accessed June 20, 2018).

109. Alice Speri, "The FBI Has Quietly Investigated White Supremacist Infiltration of Law Enforcement." *The Intercept*, January 31, 2017. https://theintercept.com/2017/01/31/the-fbi-has-quietly-investigated-white-supremacist-infiltration-of-law-enforcement/ (accessed August 26, 2017);

110. Hunton and Williams, *Independent Review of the 2017 Protest Events in Charlottesville, Virginia* (Richmond, VA: Hunton and Williams, November 14, 2017), 70, 88, 98, 110–15, 152–53, http://ftpcontent.worldnow.com/wvir/documents/heaphy-reveiw-dec-1.pdf (accessed March 20, 2018).

CHAPTER 6. PACIFYING POVERTY

1. Karl Marx, *Capital, Vol. 1: A Critique of Political Economy* (New York: Penguin, 1992), 899.

2. Mark Neocleous, *The Fabrication of Social Order: Critical Theory of Police Power* (London: Pluto Press, 2000), 4, 13, 75–76.

3. George Rigakos, *Security/Capital: A General Theory of Pacification* (Edinburgh: Edinburgh University Press, 2016), 56.

4. Kristian Williams, *Our Enemies in Blue: Police and Power in America* (Cambridge, MA: South End Press, 2007), 41–46.

5. There are three distinct schools of police science:

> 1) mercantilism, which encouraged protectionist economic policy and whose general propensity was that of placing *capital in service of the state*; 2) cameralism, the closest German equivalent of mercantilism, which sought to create a science of *maximizing the collective welfare* of all through state regulation over, among other aspects, trade and commerce, and finally 3) liberalism, which advocated the individual over the collective and reversed the logics of mercantilism by policing the *state in the service of capital.*

George S. Rigakos, John L. McMullan, Joshua Johnson, and Gulden Özcan, *A General Police System: Political Economy and Security in the Age of Enlightenment* (Ottawa: Red Quill Books, 2009), 3, 5. Original emphasis.

6. Frances Fox Piven and Richard Cloward, *Regulating the Poor: The Functions of Public Welfare* (New York: Vintage, 2012), 11.

7. Mark Neocleous, "Social Police and the Mechanisms of Prevention," *British Journal of Criminology* 40, no. 4 (2000).

8. E.P. Thompson, "The Moral Economy of the English Crowd in the Eighteenth Century," *Past & Present* 50 (1971): 798.

9. George Karandinos, Laurie Kain Hart, Fernando Montero Castrillo, and Philippe Bourgois, "The Moral Economy of Violence in the US Inner City," *Current Anthropology* 55, no. 1 (2014): 10.

10. Elijah Anderson, *Code of the Street: Decency, Violence, and the Moral life of the Inner City* (New York: W.W. Norton & Company, 2000); Alice Goffman, *On the Run: Fugitive Life in an American City* (Chicago: University of Chicago Press, 2014); Cid Martinez, *The Neighborhood Has Its Own Rules: Latinos and African Americans in South Los Angeles* (New York: New York University Press, 2016); Susan A. Phillips, *Operation Fly Trap: LA Gangs, Drugs, and the Law* (Chicago: University of Chicago Press, 2012); Martín Sánchez-Jankowski, *Cracks in the Pavement: Social Change and Resilience in Poor Neighborhoods* (Berkeley: University of California Press, 2008).

11. Anderson, *Code of the Street*, 50, 121, 321.

12. Karandinos, Hart, Castrillo, and Bourgois. "The Moral Economy of Violence in the US Inner City," 10.

13. Rigakos, *Security/Capital*, 123.

14. Sandeep Chawla et al., *2005 World Drug Report* (New York: United Nations Office on Drugs and Crime, 2005), 16–19, http://www.unodc.org/unodc /en/data-and-analysis/WDR-2005.html (accessed August 4, 2014); Channing May, *Transnational Crime and Developing World* (Washington, DC: Global Financial Integrity, May 2017), 101–2, http://www.gfintegrity.org/wp-content /uploads/2017/03/Transnational_Crime-final.pdf (accessed June 20, 2018).

15. National Drug Intelligence Center, *New York-New Jersey High Intensity Drug Trafficking Area Drug Market Analysis, 2009* (Washington DC: US Department of Justice, April 2009), 11, http://www.justice.gov/archive /ndic/pubs32/32784/32784p.pdf (accessed August 3, 2013).

16. Executive Office of the President, *High Intensity Drug Trafficking Areas Program 2015 Report to Congress* (Washington, DC: Office of National Drug Control Policy, 2015), 83, 87, 116, https://obamawhitehouse.archives.gov /sites/default/files/ondcp/about-content/Congressional/hidta_program_2015 _report_to_congress.pdf (accessed May 24, 2018).

17. Matt Taibbi, "Apocalypse, New Jersey: A Dispatch from America's Most Desperate Town," *Rolling Stone*, December 11, 2013, http://www.rollingstone .com/culture/news/apocalypse-new-jersey-a-dispatch-from-americas-most -desperate-town-20131211 (accessed June 1, 2014); Police administrator, NJ ROIC, Recorded personal interview by author, April 24, 2013.

18. Philips, *Operation Fly Trap*, 15, 24, 61, 134.

19. Alfred W. McCoy *Policing America's Empire: The United States, the Philippines, and the Rise of the Surveillance State* (Madison: University of Wisconsin Press, 2009), 47–48, 50–51.

20. Alfred W. McCoy, *The Politics of Heroin: CIA Complicity in the Global Drug Trade* (Chicago: Lawrence Hill Books, 2003).

21. Division of Criminal Justice Services, *New York State 2010 Annual Report on Asset Forfeiture* (Albany, NY: Division of Criminal Justice Services, 2010), 2–3.

22. Police officer, County Police Department, Personal interview, City in Long Island, August 13, 2013; Police officer, Crime Analysis Center, County Police Department, Personal interview. August 13, 2013.

23. Mark Neocleous, *Administering Civil Society* (New York: Palgrave Macmillan, 1996), 89–90.

24. New York State Police, *Annual Report, 2009* (Albany: New York State Police, 2009), 109.

25. Intelligence analyst, Recorded personal interview by author, August 7, 2013.

26. Police officer, Municipal Police Department, Recorded personal interview by author, August 7, 2013a.

27. Division of Criminal Justice Services, *Operation IMPACT—Annual Report 2008* (Albany, NY: Division Criminal Justice Services, 2008), 13.

28. Police officer, Municipal Police Department, Recorded personal interview by author, March 13, 2013.

29. Police officer, ROIC Liaison, Municipal Police Department, Recorded personal interview by author, February 27, 2013.

30. Nick Clunn and Matthew McGrath, "High Rate of Gun Violence in Paterson Blamed on Cop Layoffs," *The Record*, March 14, 2012, http://www .northjersey.com/paterson/High_rate_of_gun_violence_in_Paterson _blamed _on_cop_layofs.htm (accessed, January 27, 2013).

31. Frank Davis and Rachel Goematt, "Operation Fourth Down Tackles Violent Blood Set in Paterson," Office of the Attorney General & New Jersey

State Police, Press Release, June 23, 2011, http://www.nj.gov/oag/news releases11 /pr20110623c.html (accessed January 27, 2013).

32. Peter Aseltine, "Forty-One Charged in Takedown of Major Drug Network with Ties to Latin Street Gangs That Distributed Heroin in Camden," Office of the Attorney General & Division of Criminal Justice. Press Release, May 30, 2012 (accessed August 4, 2014).

33. Peter Aseltine, "Ringleader and 14 Others Arrested in Takedown of Paterson Narcotics Supply Ring That Allegedly Distributed Millions of Dollars in Heroin," Office of the Attorney General & Division of Criminal Justice. Press Release, November 20, 2012 (accessed August 4, 2014).

34. Peter Aseltine, "Forty-Seven Charged in Takedown of Violent Drug Network That Distributed Millions of Dollars in Heroin and Cocaine in Camden," Office of the Attorney General and Division of Criminal Justice, Press Release, November 13, 2013 (accessed November 15, 2013).

35. Peter Aseltine, "Twenty-Eight Charged in Atlantic City Violent Crime Task Force Investigation 'Operation Blok Buster' Targeting Violent '800 Blok' Gang and Drug Dealing in Back Maryland Avenue Section of City," Office of the Attorney General & Division of Criminal Justice, Press Release, May 14, 2013 (accessed August 4, 2014).

36. Stephen Jones, Brian Polite, and Adam Grossman, "Troopers and Partners Dismantle Drug Network in 'Operation Smoke Screen,'" Office of the Attorney General & New Jersey State Police, Press Release, January 7, 2014 (accessed August 4, 2014).

37. Division of Criminal Justice Services, *Operation IMPACT—Annual Report 2009* (Albany, NY: Division of Criminal Justice Services, 2009), 33–34, http://www.criminaljustice.ny.gov/crimnet/ojsa/impact/2009annualreport.pdf (accessed April 3, 2013); P. David Soares, "Safe Homes–Safe Streets Initiative," Albany County District Attorney, undated.

38. "Zero Tolerance Lease," Albany County District Attorney, Undated.

39. Soares, "Safe Homes–Safe Streets Initiative."

40. Ibid.

41. "Safe Homes–Safe Streets Trespass Affidavit," Albany District Attorney, undated.

42. Albany Police Department, "Worksheet 2, Strategy for Part 1 and Firearm-Related Violent Crime: Targeting Firearm-Related Crime," Albany Police Department, 2010.

43. Division of Criminal Justice Services, *Operation IMPACT—Annual Report 2010* (Albany, NY: Division of Criminal Justice Services, 2010), 9, http://www.criminaljustice.ny.gov/crimnet/ojsa/impact/2010annualreport.pdf (accessed April 3, 2013).

44. Albany Police Department, "Worksheet 2, Strategy for Part 1 and Firearm-Related Violent Crime: Targeting Firearm-Related Crime," Albany Police Department, 2010.

45. Albany Police Department, "Operation IMPACT X: Agency Budget Narrative for the Period July 1, 2013 through June 30, 2014," Albany Police Department, 2014.

46. Albany Police Department. "Worksheet 2, Strategy for Part 1 and Firearm-Related Violent Crime: Targeting Firearm-Related Crime." Albany Police Department, 2010.

47. Reuben Jonathan Miller, and Forrest Stuart, "Carceral Citizenship: Race, Rights and Responsibility in the Age of Mass Supervision," *Theoretical Criminology* 21, no. 4 (2017): 533, 536.

48. Administrator, Municipal Police Department, Recorded personal interview by author, August 2, 2013.

49. Aaron Curtis, "Secondhand Dealers Face a Crackdown in Ontario County," *Monroe County Post*, April 30, 2015, www.monroecopost.com/article /20150430/news/150439983 (accessed June 20, 2018).

50. Police officer, Municipal Department, Recorded personal interview by author, City in Central New York, August 6, 2013.

51. David Lassman, "Onondaga County Exec Agrees to Veto Law after Hearing Merchants' Gripes," *Syracuse Post-Standard*, June 10, 2010, http:// www.syracuse.com/news/index.ssf/2010/06/onondaga_county_exec_agrees _to.html (accessed August 2, 2013).

52. Division of Criminal Justice Services, *Operation IMPACT—Annual Report 2009*, 52.

53. Police officer, Municipal Police Department, Recorded personal interview by author, August 6, 2013.

54. Jon Harris, "Syracuse Police Raid Seven Stores Receiving and Selling Stolen Property," *Syracuse Post-Standard*, December 13, 2013, http://www .syracuse.com/news/index.ssf/2013/12/syracuse_police_raid_seven_stores _receiving_and_selling_stolen_property.html (accessed August 10, 2014).

55. Sánchez-Jankowski, *Cracks in the Pavement*, 155–60.

56. Michael Jargowsky, *The Architecture of Segregation: Civil Unrest, Concentration of Poverty, and Public Policy* (New York: The Century Foundation, August 9, 2015), 8–12, https://s3-us-west-2.amazonaws.com/production.tcf.org /app/uploads/2015/08/07182514/Jargowsky_ArchitectureofSegregation-11.pdf. (accessed May 24, 2018).

57. Jim O'Hara, "Judge Finds Syracuse, Onondaga County Law Unconstitutional and a 'Ruse' to Sidestep Search Warrants," *Syracuse Post-Standard*, August 31, 2010, http://www.syracuse.com/news/index.ssf/2010/08 /city_county_secondhand_dealer.html (accessed August 10, 2014); People of the State of New York vs Gerald Workman (Onondaga County Court August 24, 2010).

58. Malcolm Burnley, "'Electronic Stop-and-Frisk' Is at the Fingertips of 3,000 Police Departments," *Next City*, https://nextcity.org/daily/entry /police-enlist-electronic-stop-and-frisk-to-patrol-pawnshops (accessed May 24, 2018).

59. Tim Knauss, "Onondaga County Legislature Tightens Scrutiny of Pawn Shops," *Syracuse Post-Standard*, April 2, 2013, http://www.syracuse.com/news /index.ssf/2013/04/onondaga_county_legislature_ti.html (accessed August 4, 2013); Tim Knauss, "It's Official: Sound Garden Freed from Syracuse Secondhand

Dealer Rules," *Syracuse Post-Standard,* June 10, 2013, http://www.syracuse .com/news/index.ssf/2013/06/its_official_sound_garden_free.html (accessed August 4, 2013); Lassman, "Onondaga County Exec Agrees to Veto Law."

60. Gabriela Mosquera and Celeste Riley, Assembly, No. 3925, March 13 2013, http://www.njleg.state.nj.us/2012/Bills/A4000/3925_I1.PDF (accessed August 4, 2014); James Beach, Senate, No. 2960, September 12, 2013, http:// www.njleg.state.nj.us/2012/Bills/S3000/2960_I1.PDF (accessed August 4, 2014).

61. New Jersey Regional Operations Intelligence Center Command, *NJ ROIC Annual Report* (Trenton: New Jersey State Police, 2012), 14.

62. Donna Weaver, "Ocean County Aims to Block Sale of Stolen Items to Pawn Shops in Atlantic City," *Press of Atlantic City*, August 26, 2014, https:// www.pressofatlanticcity.com/news/crime/technology/ocean-county-aims-to -block-sale-of-stolen-items-to/article_23279694-2d72-11e4-9461-0019bb 2963f4.html (accessed May 24, 2018).

63. Joseph Passantino, "Technology to Track Stolen Goods," *Hudson Reporter*, June 6, 2016, http://hudsonreporter.com/view/full_story/27032261/article -Technology-to-track-stolen-goods---Police-department-joins-burgeoning -online-database-cataloging-valuables---?instance=bayonne_top_story (accessed May 2018); Kelly Nicholaides, "South Bergen Police: RAPID Aids Agencies in Pawnshop Fencing Investigations," *South Bergnite*, July 7, 2016, https:// www.northjersey.com/story/news/bergen/2016/07/07/south-bergen-police -rapid-aids-agencies-in-pawnshop-fencing-investigations/94885792/ (accessed May 24, 2018).

64. Patricia Miller, "Ocean County Grand Jury Quickly Convicts Pawn Shop Owners of Receiving Stolen Property," *Berkley Patch*, July 15, 2016, https://patch.com/new-jersey/berkeley-nj/ocean-county-grand-jury-quickly -convicts-pawn-shop-owners-receiving-stolen.

CONCLUSION: THE CAMDEN MODEL AND THE CHICAGO CHALLENGE

1. Barack Obama, "Remarks by the President at the 122nd Annual IACP Conference," McCormick Center, Chicago, IL, October 27, 2015, https:// obamawhitehouse.archives.gov/the-press-office/2015/10/27/remarks-presi dent-122nd-annual-iacp-conference (accessed June 25, 2018); Barack Obama, "Remarks by the President on Community Policing," Salvation Army Ray and Joan Kroc Corps Community Center, Camden, NJ, May 28, 2015, https:// obamawhitehouse.archives.gov/the-press-office/2015/05/18/remarks-presi dent-community-policing (accessed June 25, 2018).

2. President's Task Force on 21st Century Policing, *Final Report of the President's Task Force on 21st Century Policing* (Washington, DC: Office of Community Oriented Policing Services, 2015), 1–4, https://ric-zai-inc.com /Publications/cops-p311-pub.pdf (accessed June 25, 2018).

3. Michael Fensom, "Scott Thomson: Bringing Community Back to Camden," *Inside New Jersey*, December 19, 2014, https://www.nj.com/inside

-jersey/index.ssf/2014/12/j_scott_thomson_bringing_community_back_to
_camden.html (accessed September 27, 2016).

4. Tom Jackman, "De-escalation Training to Reduce Police Shootings Facing Mixed Reviews at Launch," *Washington Post*, October 15, 2016; Chuck Wexler, "What It Will Take to Reduce Deadly Shootings by Police," *Washington Post*, January 19, 2018.

5. Joshua Burstein, "The Ex-Cop at the Center of Controversy over Crime Prediction Tech," *Bloomberg*, July 20, 2017, https://www.bloomberg.com/news/features/2017-07-10/the-ex-cop-at-the-center-of-controversy-over-crime-prediction-tech (accessed, June 28, 2018); Tod Newcombe, "Forecasting the Future for Technology and Policing," *Government Technology*, September 26, 2014, http://www.govtech.com/public-safety/Forecasting-the-Future-for-Technology-and-Policing.html (accessed September 27, 2016).

6. Jim Walsh, "Crime Numbers Plummet in Camden," *Courier-Post*, April 24, 2017, https://www.courierpostonline.com/story/news/crime/2017/04/24/camden-crime-statistics-improve/100845048/ (accessed June 28, 2018).

7. Community activist, Recorded personal interview by author, October 16, 2016a.

8. Michael Boren, "In Camden, Police Crackdown Clogs Court," *Philadelphia Inquirer*, December 8, 2014. http://articles.philly.com/2014-12-08/news/56807015_1_police-crackdown-north-philadelphia-tinted-car-windows (accessed September 28, 2016).

9. Community activist, Telephone interview by author, October 10, 2016a.

10. Michael Boren, "Complaints Rise under Camden Police," *Philadelphia Inquirer*, April 25, 2015, http://www.philly.com/philly/news/Excessive_force.html (accessed September 28, 2016).

11. Officer, Camden County Police, Recorded personal interview by author, Camden, NJ, October 17, 2016; Community activist, Telephone interview by author, Cortland, New York, October 10, 2016b.

12. Wesley Skogan, "The Promise of Community Policing," in *Police Innovation: Contrasting Perspectives*, edited by David Weisburd and Anthony A. Braga (New York: Cambridge University Press), 27–43.

13. Martin Innes, Laurence Abbott, Trudy Lowe, and Colin Roberts, "Seeing Like a Citizen: Field Experiments in 'Community Intelligence-Led Policing,'" *Police Practice and Research* 10, no. 2 (2009): 104.

14. Rebecca Everett, "Camden's 2017 murder rate was the lowest in decades. Will the trend continue?" NJ.com, January 9 2018. https://www.nj.com/camden/index.ssf/2018/01/camdens_2017_murder_rate_was_the_lowest_in_decades.html. (accessed June 28, 2018).

15. Community activist, Telephone interview by author, October 10, 2016.

16. Jim Walsh, "Homicides up in Camden, across Region," *Courier-Post*, January 23, 2017, https://www.courierpostonline.com/story/news/crime/2017/01/23/camden-crime-statistics-increase/96954166/ (accessed June 28, 2018).

17. Community activist, Telephone interview by author, Cortland, New York, October 10, 2016b.

18. Jim Walsh, "EDA approves $18.3M for Camden Hotel," *Courier-Post*, June 20, 2017, https://eu.courierpostonline.com/story/news/local/south-jersey /2017/06/16/eda-camden-hotel-norcross/403443001. (accessed July 1, 2017).

19. Rebecca Everett, "Camden Area Had the Highest Job Growth Rate Last Year?" NJ.com, April 24, 2017, https://www.nj.com/camden/index.ssf/2017/04 /camden_had_the_highest_job_growth_rate_last_year_h.html. (accessed June 28, 2018).

20. Community activist, Recorded personal interview by author, October 16, 2016a.

21. For a discussion of BLM in this context see: Keeanga-Yamahtta Taylor, *From #Blacklivesmatter to Black Liberation* (New York: Haymarket Books, 2016).

22. Jessica Lussenhop, "'Too Black, Too Strong': The Woodrow Wilson Tigers' National Anthem Protest," BBC, September 22, 2016. https://www.bbc .com/news/magazine-37423901 (accessed September 30, 2016).

23. Community activist, Recorded personal interview by author, Camden, New Jersey, October 16, 2016b.

24. Barbara Ransby, *Ella Baker and the Black Freedom Movement: A Radical Democratic Vision* (Chapel Hill: University of North Carolina Press, 2003); Taylor, *From #Blacklivesmatter to Black Liberation*, 164–73.

25. Quoted in Mariame Kaba, "Free Us All," *New Inquiry*, May 8, 2017 https://thenewinquiry.com/free-us-all/ (accessed June 28, 2017).

26. Community activist, Recorded personal interview by author, Camden, New Jersey, October 16, 2016b.

27. We Charge Genocide, *The Counter-CAPS Report: The Community Engagement Arm of the Police State* (Chicago: We Charge Genocide, October 28 2015), 3, 15, http://wechargegenocide.org/wp-content/uploads/2015/10/CAPS report-final.pdf (accessed October 28, 2015).

28. Jon Swaine, Lauren Gambino and Oliver Laughland, "Protesters Unveil Demands for Stricter US Policing Laws as Political Reach Grows," *The Guardian*, August 21, 2015, https://www.theguardian.com/us-news/2015/aug /21/protesters-unveil-police-policy-proposals (accessed June 28, 2018).

29. Noah Berlatsky, "At the United Nations, Chicago Activists Protest Police Brutality," *Atlantic Monthly*, November 17, 2014, https://www.theatlantic. com/national/archive/2014/11/we-charge-genocide-movement-chicago-un /382843/ (accessed June 28, 2018).

30. Terrence Laney and Janaé Bonsu, *Agenda to Keep Us Safe* (Chicago: Black Youth Project 100, September 30, 2014), http://agendatobuildblackfu tures.org/wp-content/uploads/2016/01/BYP100-Agenda-to-Keep-Us-Safe -AKTUS.pdf. (accessed July 28, 2018).

31. Black Youth Project 100, *Agenda to Build Black Futures* (Chicago: Black Youth Project 100, February 2016), http://agendatobuildblackfutures.org/wp -content/uploads/2016/01/BYP_AgendaBlackFutures_booklet_web.pdf (accessed July 28, 2018).

32. Flint Taylor, "How Activists Won Reparations for the Survivors of Chicago Police Department Torture," *In These Times*, June 26, 2015 http://inthes

etimes.com/article/18118/jon-burge-torture-reparations (accessed June 28, 2018).

33. Dan Berger, Mariame Kaba, and David Stein, "What Abolitionists Do," *Jacobin*, August 24, 2017, https://jacobinmag.com/2017/08/prison-abolition -reform-mass-incarceration (accessed August 24, 2017).

34. Movement for Black Lives, *A Vision for Black Lives: Policy Demands for Black Power, Freedom, and Justice* (The Movement for Black Lives, August 2016), https://policy.m4bl.org/wp-content/uploads/2016/07/20160726-m4bl -Vision-Booklet-V3.pdf (accessed September 1, 2016).

APPENDIX: RESEARCH AND THE WORLD OF OFFICIAL SECRETS

1. This story is true, but the name of the NYSIC's privacy officer has been fictionalized to "Lt. Veepings" for narrative effect. "Lt. Veepings" is an homage to Milton Mayer, a largely forgotten American essayists who often used the surname "Veepings" to refer to the anonymized and/or fictionalized bureaucrats in his essays. NYSIC Privacy/Security Officer, Email Message to Author, May 13, 2013.

2. Dana Priest and William Arkin, *Top Secret America: The Rise of The New American Security State* (New York: Little, Brown & Co., 2011), 67.

3. Brian Fung, "5.1 Million Americans Have Security Clearances. That's More Than the Entire Population of Norway," *Washington Post*, March 24, 2014 http://www.washingtonpost.com/blogs/the-switch/wp/2014/03/24/5 -1-million-americans-have-security-clearances-thats-more-than-the-entire -population-of-norway/ (accessed July 1, 2014)

4. Peter Galison, "Removing Knowledge," *Critical Inquiry* 31, no. 1 (2004): 230.

5. Joseph Collum, *The Black Dragon: Racial Profiling Exposed* (Ft. Lauderdale, FL: Gulf Stream Press, 2010).

6. Jerry Ratcliffe and Ray Guidetti, "State Police Investigative Structure and the Adoption of Intelligence-Led Policing., *Policing: An International Journal of Police Strategies & Management* 31, no. 1 (2008).

7. Joseph Fuentes, *Practical Guide to Intelligence-Led Policing* (Trenton: The New Jersey State Police, The Center for Policing Terrorism at the Manhattan Institute & Harbinger Technologies, September 2006), http://www.njsp.org /divorg /invest/pdf/njsp_ilpguide_010907.pdf (accessed August 4, 2012).

8. Renee Dianne Graphia, "An Exploratory Study of the Perceived Utility and Effectiveness of State Fusion Centers" (PhD diss., Rutgers, The State University of New Jersey, 2010); Carla Lewandowski, "Information Sharing Using a State Fusion Center: A Case Study of the New Jersey Regional Operations Intelligence Center" (PhD diss., University of Pennsylvania, 2012).

9. Kathy Charmaz, *Constructing Grounded Theory: A Practical Guide through Qualitative Analysis* (Thousand Oaks, CA: Sage, 2006), 5–6.

10. Terrence Hopkins, "World-Systems Analysis: Methodological Issues," in *World-Systems Analysis: Theory and Methodology*, ed. Terrence Hopkins and Immanuel Wallerstein (Thousand Oaks, CA: Sage, 1982), 148.

11. Patrick Biernacki and Dan Waldorf, "Snowball Sampling: Problems and Techniques of Chain Referral Sampling," *Sociological Methods & Research* 10, no. 2 (1981).

12. Charmaz, *Constructing Grounded Theory*, 5–6.

13. Brendan McQuade, "Police and the Post-9/11 Surveillance Surge: 'Technological Dramas' in 'the Bureaucratic Field,'" *Surveillance & Society* 14, no. 1 (2016); Brendan McQuade, "The Puzzle of Intelligence Expertise: Spaces of Intelligence Analysis and the Production of "Political" Knowledge," *Qualitative Sociology* 39, no. 3 (2016).

14. Brendan McQuade, "From the Carceral Leviathan to the Police State: Policing Decarceration in New York State," in *After Prisons? Freedom, Decarceration, and Justice Disinvestment*, ed. William Martin and Joshua Price (Lanham, MD: Lexington Books, 2016), 53–75; Rajiv Shah and Brendan McQuade, "Surveillance, Security, and Intelligence-Led Policing in Chicago," in *Neoliberal Chicago*, ed. Euan Hague, Larry Bennet, and Roberta Garner, 243–59 (Urbana: University of Illinois Press).

Works Cited

INTERVIEWS

Administrator, County Prosecutor's Office. Recorded telephone interview. July 2, 2013.

Administrator, County Prosecutors Office. Recorded telephone interview. June 9, 2013.

Community activist. Recorded personal interview. October 16, 2016a.

Community activist. Recorded personal interview. October 16, 2016b.

Community activist. Recorded telephone interview. October 10, 2016.

Federal official. Telephone interview. March 14, 2013.

Federal official. Recorded personal interview. August 8, 2013.

Federal official/Former State Administrator. Personal interview. September 27, 2013.

Field intelligence officer, Municipal Police Department. Telephone interview., June 3, 2014.

Intelligence analyst. Personal interview. April 30, 2013

Intelligence analyst. Personal interview. August 2, 2013.

Intelligence analyst. Recorded personal interview. January 28, 2013.

Intelligence analyst. Recorded personal interview. January 29, 2013.

Intelligence analyst. Recorded personal interview. February 27, 2013a.

Intelligence analyst. Recorded personal interview. February 27, 2013b.

Intelligence analyst. Recorded personal interview. February 27, 2013c.

Intelligence analyst. Recorded personal interview. February 27, 2013d.

Intelligence analyst. Recorded personal interview. February 27, 2013e.

Intelligence analyst. Recorded personal interview. May 14, 2013.

Intelligence analyst. Recorded personal interview. August 7, 2013.

Intelligence analyst. Telephone interview. March 10, 2014.

Intelligence analyst. Recorded telephone interview. July 1, 2013.

Intelligence analyst. Recorded telephone interview. July 27, 2013.

Parole officer. Recorded personal interview. April 24, 2013a.

Parole officer. Recorded personal interview. April 24, 2013b.

Police administrator, Municipal Police Department. Recorded telephone interview. June 27, 2013.

Police administrator, Crime Analysis Center. Recorded personal interview. July 15, 2013.

Police administrator, Municipal Police Department. Recorded personal interview. July 19, 2013.

Police administrator, Municipal Police Department. Recorded telephone interview. June 28, 2013.

Police administrator, Municipal Police Department. Recorded personal interview. August 2, 2013.

Police administrator, Municipal Police Department. Recorded personal interview. August 22, 2013.

Police administrator, NJ ROIC. Recorded personal interview. January 28, 2013a.

Police administrator, NJ ROIC. Recorded personal interview. January 28, 2013b.

Police administrator, NJ ROIC. Recorded personal interview. January 29, 2013.

Police administrator, NJ ROIC. Recorded personal interview. February 27, 2013a.

Police administrator, NJ ROIC. Recorded personal interview. February 27, 2013b.

Police administrator, NJ ROIC. Recorded personal interview. April 24, 2013.

Police administrator, NYSIC. Recorded personal interview. May 14. 2013a.

Police administrator, NYSIC. Recorded personal interview. May 14. 2013b.

Police administrator, NYSIC. Recorded personal interview. May 14, 2013c.

Police administrator, NYSIC. Recorded personal interview. May 14, 2013d.

Police administrator, NYSIC. Recorded personal interview. May 14, 2013e.

Police officer, Municipal Police Department. Personal interview. January 30, 2013.

Police officer, Municipal Police Department. Recorded personal interview. January 30, 2013.

Police officer, Municipal Police Department. Recorded personal interview. March 13, 2013.

Police officer, Municipal Police Department. Recorded telephone interview. June 11, 2013.

Police officer, Municipal Police Department. Recorded telephone interview. June 27, 2013.

Police officer, Municipal Police Department. Recorded personal interview. August 6, 2013.

Police officer, Municipal Police Department. Recorded personal interview. August 7, 2013a.

Police officer, Municipal Police Department. Recorded personal interview. August 7, 2013b.

Police officer, Municipal Police Department. Recorded personal interview. October 17, 2016.

Police officer, Municipal Police Department. Telephone interview. August 26, 2013.

Police officer, County Police Department. Telephone interview. June 12, 2014.

Police officer, County Police Department. Personal interview. August 13 2013

Police officer, County Prosecutor's Office. Recorded telephone interview. June 12, 2013.

Police officer, Crime Analysis Center, County Police Department. Personal interview. August 13 2013.

Police officer, ROIC Liaison, Municipal Police Department. Recorded personal interview. February 27, 2013.

Probation Officer, County Probation Department. Recorded personal interview. May 13, 2014.

Retired police administrator. Recorded personal interview. August 8, 2013.

Special agent, Federal Bureau of Investigation. Recorded personal interview. May 14. 2013.

State administrator, County Prosecutor's Office. Recorded telephone interview. June 9, 2013.

State administrator, New York Department of Criminal Justice Services, Office of Public Safety. Recorded personal interview. June 13, 2013.

State administrator. Email message to author. June 30, 2014.

State official, District Attorney's Office. Recorded telephone interview. June 26, 2013.

State official, Connecticut Intelligence Center. Recorded personal interview. August 22, 2012.

Systems administrator, NJ ROIC. Personal interview. January 29, 2013.

OTHER PRIMARY SOURCES (GOVERNMENT AND NGO
REPORTS, OPEN RECORDS REQUESTS, AND PUBLICLY
AVAILABLE DOCUMENTS)

Albany Police Department. "Operation IMPACT X: Agency Budget Narrative for the Period July 1, 2013 through June 30, 2014." Albany Police Department, 2014.

———. "Response IX (part B): Strategy for Addressing Firearm-Related Crimes." Albany Police Department, 2012.

———. "Worksheet 2, Strategy for Part 1 and Firearm-Related Violent Crime: Targeting Crime Hot Spots/Disrupting Drug Markets." Albany Police Department, 2010.

———. "Worksheet 2, Strategy for Part 1 and Firearm-Related Violent Crime: Targeting Firearm-Related Crime." Albany Police Department, 2010.

American Civil Liberties Union. "USA Patriot Act: Further Analysis." https://www.aclu.org/other/usa-patriot-act-further-analysis. Accessed March 4, 2018.

American Civil Liberties Union–Massachusetts and National Lawyers Guild–Massachusetts. *Policing Dissent: Police Surveillance of Lawful Political Activity in Boston.* Boston: American Civil Liberties Union–Massachusetts & National Lawyers Guild–Massachusetts, 2012. http://www.aclum.org/sites/all /files/policing_dissent_101812.pdf. Accessed October 15, 2012

Beach, James. Senate, No. 2960, September 12, 2013. http://www.njleg.state
.nj.us/2012/Bills/S3000/2960_I1.PDF. Accessed August 4, 2014.

Bergeron, Brenda, to Kenneth Krayeske. "RE: FOI Request 11-517." November
25, 2011.

Black Youth Project 100. *Agenda to Build Black Futures*. Chicago: Black Youth
Project 100, February 2016. http://agendatobuildblackfutures.org/wp-content
/uploads/2016/01/BYP_AgendaBlackFutures_booklet_web.pdf. Accessed
July 28, 2018.

BOTEC Analysis Corporation. *Assessment of the HIDTA Program: High
Intensity Drug Trafficking Areas*. Washington, DC: National Criminal
Justice Reference System, April 2002. https://www.ncjrs.gov/pdffiles1/nij
/grants/194118.pdf. Accessed August 17, 2014.

Burch, Andrea. "Arrest-Related Deaths, 2003–2009—Statistical Tables." The
Department of Justice, Bureau of Justice Statistics, November 2011. https://
www.bjs.gov/content/pub/pdf/ard0309st.pdf. Accessed March 25, 2012.

Bureau of Labor Statistics. "Preliminary 2016 Data on Employment Status by
State and Demographic Group." Bureau of Labor Statistics, January 27,
2017. https://www.bls.gov/lau/ptable14full2016.pdf. Accessed July 7, 2017.

Byers, Shala, to [redacted]. "Guidance Requested: Occupy Wall Street." October
17, 2011. http://www.justiceonline.org/docs/dhs-occupy-documents-4-pt1
.pdf. Accessed December 31, 2012.

Carson, E. Ann. "Prisoners in 2013." Department of Justice, Bureau of Justice
Statistics, September 30, 2014. https://www.bjs.gov/content/pub/pdf/p13
.pdf. Accessed June 23 2017.

———. "Prisoners in 2014." Department of Justice, Bureau of Justice Statistics,
September, 2015. https://www.bjs.gov/content/pub/pdf/p14.pdf. Accessed
June 23 2017.

Carson, E. Ann, and Elizabeth Anderson. "Prisoners in 2015." Department of
Justice, Bureau of Justice Statistics, December 2016. https://www.bjs.gov
/content/pub/pdf/p15.pdf. Accessed June 23 2017.

Carson, E. Ann, and Daniela Golinell. "Prisoners in 2011." US Department of
Justice, Bureau of Justice Statistics, December 2012. https://www.bjs.gov
/content/pub/pdf/p11.pdf. Accessed April 10, 2014.

———. "Prisoners in 2012." US Department of Justice, Bureau of Justice
Statistics, July 2013. https://www.bjs.gov/content/pub/pdf/p12ac.pdf
. Accessed April 10, 2014.

Central Florida Information Exchange and North Dakota State and Local
Intelligence Center. "Criminal Activities and Incidents Surrounding the
Dakota Access Pipeline and Impact on the Sabal Trail Pipeline." April 2017.
https://theintercept.com/document/2017/12/11/april-2017-joint-intelligence
-bulletin. Accessed March 20, 2018.

Chawla, Sandeep, Anja Korenblik, Suzanne Kunnen, Thibualt Le Pinchon,
Aruna Nathwani, Thomas Pietschmann, Wolfgang Romberg, Ali Saadeddin,
Johnny Thomas, and Melissa Tullis. *2005 World Drug Report*. New York:
United Nations Office on Drugs and Crime, 2005. http://www.unodc.org
/unodc/en/data-and-analysis/WDR-2005.html. Accessed August 4, 2014)

Civil Liberties and National Security Clinic, Yale Law School. *Trapped in Black Box: Growing Terrorism Watchlisting in Everyday Policing*. Washington, DC: The American Civil Liberties Union, April 2016. https://law.yale.edu /system/files/area/clinic/wirac_9-11_clinic_trapped_in_a_black_box.pdf . Accessed February 20, 2017.

Cooney, Daniel. Memorandum to Bart Johnson, October 24, 2004. "New York State Terrorism Tips Line."

DAPL Security. "Security Operations Overview." TigerSwan, October 16, 2016. https://theintercept.com/document/2017/05/27/security-operations-over view-2016-10-16/. Accessed May 27, 2017.

Davis, Robert, to Matthew Chandler. "Re: CBS News Media Request." November 16, 2011. http://www.justiceonline.org/docs/dhs-occupy-documents-1-398 .pdf. Accessed December 31, 2012.

DHS Office of Inspector General, *DHS' Role in State and Local Fusion Centers Is Evolving*. The Department of Homeland Security, OIG-9-2012, 2008. http://www.oig.dhs.gov/assets/Mgmt/OIG_09-12_Dec08.pdf. Accessed March 12, 2012.

DHS Office of Intelligence Analysis. "Domestic Extremists Movements Remain a Medium-Level Threat in Nevada." Department of Homeland Security, April 6, 2017. https://www.documentcloud.org/documents/4404359-DHS -Bulletin-Aug-9.html. Accessed March 7, 2018.

———. "Domestic Terrorist Violence at Lawfully Permitted White Supremacists Rallies Likely to Continue." Department of Homeland Security, August 9, 2017. https://www.documentcloud.org/documents/4404359-DHS-Bulletin -Aug-9.html. Accessed March 7, 2018.

———. "Potential Domestic Intelligence Threats to Multi-State Diamond Pipeline Construction Project." Department of Homeland Security, April 7, 2017. https://www.documentcloud.org/documents/4404359-DHS-Bulletin -Aug-9.html. Accessed March 7, 2018.

———. "Right Wing Extremism: Current Economic and Political Climate Fueling a Resurgence in Radicalization and Recruitment." Department of Homeland Security, 2009. http://fas.org/irp/eprint/rightwing.pdf. Accessed, August 20, 2012.

———. "Sovereign Citizen Extremist Ideology Will Drive Violence at Home, During Travel, and at Government Facilities." Department of Homeland Security, February 5, 2015. https://d1ai9qtk9p41kl.cloudfront.net/media /pdf/Sovereign_Citizen_Extremist_Ideology_2-5-15.pdf. Accessed March 20, 2018.

———. "TTPs Used in Recent US Pipeline Attacks by Suspected Environmental Rights Extremists. Department of Homeland Security, May 2, 2017. https:// theintercept.com/document/2017/12/11/may-2017-field-analysis-report/. Accessed March 20, 2018.

———. "White Supremacist Extremism Poses Persistent Threat of Lethal Violence." Department of Homeland Security, May 10, 2017. https://www .documentcloud.org/documents/4404294-Parrish-Will-10-16-2017.html. Accessed March 20, 2018.

Division of Criminal Justice Services. *New York State 2010 Annual Report on Asset Forfeiture.* Albany, NY: Division of Criminal Justice Services, 2010.

———. *Operation IMPACT—Annual Report 2008.* Albany, NY: Division Criminal Justice Services, 2008.

———. *Operation IMPACT—Annual Report 2009.* Albany, NY: Division of Criminal Justice Services, 2009.

———. *Operation IMPACT—Annual Report 2010.* Albany, NY: Division of Criminal Justice Services, 2010

———. *Operation IMPACT—Annual Report 2011.* Albany, NY: Division of Criminal Justice Services, 2011.

———. *Operation IMPACT—Annual Report 2012.* Albany, NY: Division of Criminal Justice Services, 2012:

———. *Operation IMPACT—Annual Report 2013.* Albany, NY: Division of Criminal Justice Services, 2013.

DSAC. *Liaison Information Report.* Washington, DC: Domestic Security Alliance Council, December 9, 2011. http://www.justiceonline.org/docs/fbi -occupy-documents-1.pdf. Accessed December 31 2012.

Eck, John E., and Ronald V. Clarke. *Intelligence Analysis for Problem Solvers.* Washington, DC: Office of Community Oriented Policing Services, Department of Justice, September 2013. https://popcenter.asu.edu/sites /default/files/library/reading/PDFs/Intell-Analysis-for-ProbSolvers.pdfpdf . Accessed June 14, 2014.

Electronic Privacy Information Center. "Spotlight on Surveillance: 'National Network' of Fusion Centers Raises Specter of COINTELPRO." EPIC, June 2007. https://www.epic.org/privacy/surveillance/spotlight/0607/default .html. Accessed March 4, 2014.

Executive Office of the President. *High Intensity Drug Trafficking Areas Program 2015 Report to Congress.* Washington, DC: Office of National Drug Control Policy, 2015. https://obamawhitehouse.archives.gov/sites /default/files/ondcp/about-content/Congressional/hidta_program_2015 _report_to_congress.pdf. Accessed May 24, 2018.

———. *High Intensity Drug Trafficking Areas (HIDTA) Program.* Washington, DC: US Office of the National Drug Control Policy, June 2011. https:// obamawhitehouse.archives.gov/sites/default/files/ondcp/policy-and -research/hidta_2011.pdf. Accessed August 17, 2014.

FBI Counterterrorism Division. "White Supremacist Infiltration of Law Enforcement." Federal Bureau of Investigation, October 17, 2006. https:// s3.amazonaws.com/s3.documentcloud.org/documents/402521/doc-26 -white-supremacist-infiltration.pdf. Accessed June 20, 2018.

Federal Bureau of Investigation. "Black Identity Extremists Likely Motivated to Target Law Enforcement Officers." August 3, 2017. https://assets.docu mentcloud.org/documents/4067711/BIE-Redacted.pdf. Accessed March 20, 2018.

———. "Crime in the United States 2012, Table 8, New Jersey, Offenses Known to Law Enforcement." 2012: https://ucr.fbi.gov/crime-in-the-u.s/2012

/crime-in-the-u.s.-2012/tables/8tabledatadecpdf/table-8-state-cuts/table
_8_offenses_known_to_law_enforcement_by_new_jersey_by_city_2012
.xls. Accessed June 1 2014.

———. "Joint Terrorism Task Forces." Undated. https://www.fbi.gov/investi
gate/terrorism/joint-terrorism-task-forces. Accessed March 4, 2018.

Felton, Preston. Memorandum to All Personnel, 12 March 2008. "New York
State Intelligence Center (NYSIC) Designation as State Fusion Center."

Fuentes, Joseph. "MOU Concerning the Establishment of the Real Time Crime
Center." Memorandum to A. Ponenti, April 21, 2016.

———. *Practical Guide to Intelligence-Led Policing.* Trenton: The New Jersey
State Police, The Center for Policing Terrorism at the Manhattan Institute
& Harbinger Technologies, September 2006. http://www.njsp.org/divorg
/invest/pdf/njsp_ilpguide_010907.pdf. Accessed August 4, 2012.

German, Mike, and Jay Stanley. *What's Wrong with Fusion Centers.*
Washington, DC: American Civil Liberties Union, December 2001. http://
www.aclu.org/files/pdfs/privacy/fusioncenter_20071212.pdf.   Accessed
January 3, 2012.

Government Accountability Office. *Information Sharing: Agencies Could
Better Coordinate to Reduce Overlap in Field-Based Activities.* Washington,
DC: Government Accountability Office, April 4, 2013. http://www.gao.gov
/products/GAO-13-471. Accessed April 14, 2013.

Greene, Judith, and Marc Mauer. *Downscaling Prisons: Lessons from Four
States.* Washington DC: The Sentencing Project, 2010. https://www.sen
tencingproject.org/wp-content/uploads/2016/01/Downscaling-Prisons
-Lessons-from-Four-States.pdf pdf. Accessed July 30, 2014.

Guardian. "The Counted: People Killed by Police in the US. *Guardian,* undated.
https://www.theguardian.com/us-news/ng-interactive/2015/jun/01/about
-the-counted. Accessed May 5, 2017.

Guerino, Paul, Paige M. Harrison, and William J. Sabol. "Prisoners in 2010."
Bureau of Justice Statistics, February 9, 2012. https://www.bjs.gov/content
/pub/pdf/p10.pdf. Accessed April 10, 2014.

Hunton and Williams. *Independent Review of the 2017 Protest Events in
Charlottesville, Virginia.* Richmond, VA: Hunton and Williams, November
14, 2017. http://ftpcontent.worldnow.com/wvir/documents/heaphy-review
-dec-1.pdf. Accessed March 20, 2018.

Institute for Economics and Peace. "Global Peace Index, 2016." In *Quantifying
Peace and Its Benefits.* Sydney: IEP, 2016, 8. http://economicsandpeace.org
/wp-content/uploads/2016/06/GPI-2016-Report_2.pdf. Accessed March 27,
2016.

"Internal TigerSwan Situation Report." TigerSwan, September 7, 2017. https://
theintercept.com/document/2017/05/27/internal-tigerswan-situation
-report-2016-09-07. Accessed May 27, 2017.

Jargowsky, Michael. *The Architecture of Segregation: Civil Unrest, Concentration
of Poverty, and Public Policy.* New York: The Century Foundation, August 9,
2015.   https://s3-us-west-2.amazonaws.com/production.tcf.org/app

/uploads/2015/08/07182514/Jargowsky_ArchitectureofSegregation-11.pdf. Accessed May 24, 2018.

Johnson, Bart. Memorandum to William DeBlock, February 14, 2007. "Information Sharing Environment Implementation Plan—Request for Correspondence from the Governor Designating the Upstate New York Regional Intelligence Center as New York State's Primary Center."

———. Memorandum to Preston Felton, March 26, 2007. "Upstate New York Regional Intelligence Center."

Kaeble, Danielle, and Mary Cowhig. "Correctional Populations in the United States, 2016." US Department of Justice, Bureau of Justice Statistics, April 2018. https://www.bjs.gov/content/pub/pdf/cpus16.pdf. Accessed May 17, 2018.

Kaeble, Danielle, and Lauren Glaze. "Correctional Populations in the United States, 2015." US Department of Justice, Bureau of Justice Statistics, December 2016. https://www.bjs.gov/content/pub/pdf/cpus15.pdf. Accessed March 22, 2016.

Karpel, Todd, to Mark Wiessman. "RE: Occupy Movements." November 26, 2011. http://s3.documentcloud.org/documents/1151739/surveillance-of -occupy-groups.pdf. Accessed May 22, 2014)

Laney, Terrence, and Janaé Bonsu. *Agenda to Keep Us Safe*. Chicago: Black Youth Project 100, September 30, 2014. http://agendatobuildblackfutures .org/wp-content/uploads/2016/01/BYP100-Agenda-to-Keep-Us-Safe -AKTUS.pdf. Accessed July 28, 2018.

Martorana, Rosemary, Dean Baratta, and Kimberly Brown. "Intelligence Reform at the State Level: Lessons Learned." State of New Jersey Office of Homeland Security and Preparedness. https://www.njhomelandsecurity .gov/media/webinar-intelligence-reform-at-the-state-level-lessons-learned . Accessed June 1, 2017.

Masse, Todd, Siobhan O'Neil, and John Rollins. *Fusion Centers: Issues and Options for Congress*. Washington, DC: Congressional Research Services, 2007. http://epic.org/privacy/fusion/crs_fusionrpt.pdf. Accessed March 12, 2012.

May, Channing. *Transnational Crime and Developing World*. Washington, DC: Global Financial Integrity, May 2017. http://www.gfintegrity.org/wp-content /uploads/2017/03/Transnational_Crime-final.pdf. Accessed May 24, 2018.

Mayer, Matt. "Consolidate Domestic Intelligence Entities Under the FBI." American Enterprise Institute. March 2016: https://www.aei.org/wp-content /uploads/2016/03/Fusion-Center.pdf. Accessed March 27, 2016.

Milgram, Anne. "Attorney General Law Enforcement Directive No. 2008-1: Submission and Analysis of Information Relating to Seized and Recovered Firearms." State of New Jersey, Office of Attorney General, Department of Law and Public Safety, March 17, 2008. http://www.nj.gov/oag/newsreleases08 /dir20080318.pdf. Accessed January 20, 2012.

Miller, Terry, Kenneth Kolosh, Kevin Fearn, and Kathleen Porretta. *Injury Facts, 2015 Edition*. National Safety Council, 2015. http://www.nsc.org

/Membership%20Site%20Document%20Library/2015%20Injury%20 Facts/NSC_InjuryFacts2015Ed.pdf. Accessed March 27, 2017.

Mosquera, Gabriela, and Celeste Riley. Assembly, No. 3925, 2013. http://www .njleg.state.nj.us/2012/Bills/A4000/fd3925_I1.PDF. Accessed August 4, 2014.

Movement for Black Lives. *A Vision for Black Lives: Policy Demands for Black Power, Freedom, and Justice.* N.p.: The Movement for Black Lives, August 2016. https://policy.m4bl.org/wp-content/uploads/2016/07/20160726 -m4bl-Vision-Booklet-V3.pdf. Accessed September 1, 2016.

National Commission on Terrorist Attacks upon the United States. *The 9/11 Commission Report: Final Report of the National Commission on Terrorist Attacks upon the United States.* New York: W.W. Norton & Company, 2004.

National Consortium for the Study of Terrorism and Responses to Terrorism. Global Terrorism Database. University of Maryland, 2017. https://www .start.umd.edu/gtd. Accessed March 28, 2017.

National Drug Intelligence Center. *New York–New Jersey High Intensity Drug Trafficking Area Drug Market Analysis, 2009.* Washington DC: US Department of Justice, April 2009. http://www.justice.gov/archive/ndic /pubs32/32784/32784p.pdf. Accessed August 3, 2013.

National Priorities Project. "U.S. Security Spending Since 9/11." May 26, 2011. https://www.nationalpriorities.org/analysis/2011/us-security-spending -since-911/. Accessed May 4, 2018.

New Jersey Building Authority. *New Jersey Building Authority Annual Report.* Trenton: New Jersey Building Authority, 2008. https://dspace.njstatelib.org /xmlui/handle/10929/15935. Accessed January 30, 2013.

New Jersey Regional Operations Intelligence Center. "Advisory: Occupy Wall Street March to Washington D.C.: Potential Impacts in New Jersey." November 9, 2011. http://www.documentcloud.org/documents/1094053 -occupy-docs-set-4.html. Accessed May 30, 2014.

———. "New Jersey SWEEP Report: Summer Warrant Effective Enforcement Program, 7/1/2010–9/1/2010." New Jersey Regional Operations Intelligence Center, September 15, 2010. http://www.nj.gov/oag/newsreleases10 /pr20100914a-Sweep-Stats.pdf. Accessed April 20, 2013.

———. "Situational Awareness Report: Attack on Afghan Resort Demonstrates Vulnerability of Hotels, June 26 2012." *Public Intelligence,* July 10, 2012. http://publicintelligence.net/njroic-kabul-hotel-bombing/. Accessed August 14, 2012.

New Jersey Regional Operations Intelligence Center Analysis Element to Anthony Tisdale. "Occupy Wall Street March to Washington D.C.: Potential Impacts in New Jersey." November 9, 2011. http://www.documentcloud. org/documents/1094053-occupy-docs-set-4.html. Accessed May 30, 2014.

New Jersey Regional Operations Intelligence Center Command. *NJ ROIC Annual Report.* Trenton: New Jersey State Police, 2012.

New Jersey Regional Operations Intelligence Center, Intelligence Analysis Threat Unit. "ROIC Intelligence and Analysis Threat Unit Daily Overview." New Jersey Regional Operations Intelligence Center, March 14, 2014.

————. "ROIC Intelligence and Analysis Threat Unit Daily Overview." The New Jersey Regional Operations Intelligence Center, July 25, 2014.

New York State Intelligence Center. "Current Assessment, 11/27/2012." In *Field Intelligence Office Guide Book*, 6–8. Albany: New York State Police, 2012.

————. "NYSIC Field Intelligence Officer." New York State Police (Undated).

————. "Threat Assessment: Major Terror Attacks against Hotels, 2002–2011, March 29, 2012." *Public Intelligence*, February 1, 2013. http://publicintelli gence.net/nysic-hotel-attacks. Accessed February 26, 2013.

New York State Police. *Annual Report, 2007.* Albany: New York State Police, 2007.

————. *Annual Report, 2008.* Albany: New York State Police, 2008.

————. *Annual Report, 2009.* Albany: New York State Police, 2009.

————. *Annual Report, 2010.* Albany: New York State Police, 2010.

————. "New York State Intelligence Center-2011." Albany: New York State Police, 2012.

————. "NYSP Office of Counter Terrorism-Prevention: The New York State Intelligence Center." Albany: New York State Police, 2013.

————. "SIS Budget 2012." New York State Police, 2012.

Northern California Regional Intelligence Center. "Domestic Extremism Threat Update, California: Potential for Violence at Upcoming Rallies." Northern California Regional Intelligence Center, undated. https://www .documentcloud.org/documents/4404294-Parrish-Will-10-16-2017.html. Accessed March 20, 2018.

Obama, Barack. "Remarks by the President at the 122nd Annual IACP Conference." McCormick Center, Chicago, IL, October 27, 2015. https://obamawhitehouse .archives.gov/the-press-office/2015/10/27/remarks-president-122nd-annual -iacp-conference. Accessed June 25, 2018.

————. "Remarks by the President on Community Policing." Salvation Army Ray and Joan Kroc Corps Community Center, Camden, NJ, May 28, 2015. https://obamawhitehouse.archives.gov/the-press-office/2015/05/18/remarks -president-community-policing. Accessed June 25, 2018.

Office of Inspector General. *Review of the Drug Enforcement Administration's El Paso Intelligence Center.* Washington, DC: Department of Justice, June 2010. http://www.justice.gov/oig/reports/DEA/a1005.pdf. Accessed May 25 2013.

Office of National Drug Control Policy. *National Drug Control Strategy: High Intensity Drug Trafficking Areas (HIDTA) Program, 2001 Annual Report.* Washington, DC: Office of National Drug Control Policy, 2001. https:// www.ncjrs.gov/ondcppubs/publications/enforce/hidta2001/hidta2001.pdf. Accessed August 17, 2014.

People of the State of New York vs Gerald Workman (Onondaga County Court August 24, 2010).

Porter, John. "Internal TigerSwan Situation Report." TigerSwan, February 2, 2017. https://theintercept.com/document/2017/06/21/internal-tigerswan -situation-report-2017-02-27. Accessed June 21, 2017.

———. "Internal TigerSwan Situation Report." TigerSwan, October 16, 2016. https://theintercept.com/document/2017/06/03/internal-tigerswan-situation -report-2016-10-03/. Accessed May 27, 2017.

———. "Internal TigerSwan Situation Report." TigerSwan, September 9, 2016. https://theintercept.com/document/2017/05/27/internal-tigerswan-situation -report-2016-09-22. Accessed May 27, 2017.

President's Task Force on 21st Century Policing. *Final Report of the President's Task Force on 21st Century Policing.* Washington, DC: Office of Community Oriented Policing Services, 2015. https://ric-zai-inc.com/Publications/cops -p311-pub.pdf. Accessed June 25, 2018.

Price, Michael. "National Security and Local Police." The Brennan Center for Justice, December 10, 2013: https://www.brennancenter.org/publication /national-security-local-police. Accessed December 15, 2013.

RNC Civil Disturbance Subcommittee. "Civil Disturbance Management Plan." August 14, 2008. https://www.stpaul.gov/DocumentCenter/View2/7395 .pdf. Accessed March 3, 2012.

Rollins, John. *Fusion Centers: Issues and Options for Congress.* Washington, DC: Congressional Research Service, 2008. http://www.dtic.mil/cgi-bin /GetTRDoc?AD=ADA482006. Accessed March 12, 2012.

Sakala, Leah. "Breaking Down Mass Incarceration in the 2010 Census: State-by-State Incarceration Rates by Race/Ethnicity." Prison Policy Initiative, May 24, 2014. http://www.prisonpolicy.org/reports/rates.html. Accessed July 10, 2014.

Smith, Terri. "Special Event Planning 2008 Republican National Convention." Homeland Security and Emergency Management, 2008. http://downloads .wikileaks-press.org/file/rnc-2008-homeland-security-planning.pdf. Accessed July 3, 2014.

Soares, David. "Safe Homes–Safe Streets Initiative." Albany County District Attorney, undated.

Upstate New York Regional Intelligence Center. "Field Intelligence Officers (FIO) Establishment Plan." New York State Police, 2005.

US Census Bureau. *Selected Economic Characteristics from the 2006–2010 American Community Survey 5-Year Estimates for Camden City.* Washington, DC: US Census Bureau, 2010. http://factfinder2.census.gov/faces/tableservices /jsf/pages/productview.xhtml?src=bkmk. Accessed June 1 2014.

US Department of Homeland Security. *Budget in Brief, Fiscal Year 2009.* Washington, DC: Department of Homeland Security, undated. https://www .dhs.gov/sites/default/files/publications/budget_bib-fy2009.pdf. Accessed May 1, 2017.

———. *Budget in Brief, Fiscal Year 2017.* Washington, DC: Department of Homeland Security, undated. https://www.dhs.gov/sites/default/files /publications/FY2017_BIB-MASTER.pdf. Accessed May 1, 2017.

———. *Funding Opportunity Announcement (FOA) FY 2014 Homeland Security Grant Program.* Washington, DC: Department of Homeland Security, 2014. http://www.fema.gov/media-library-data/1395161200285

-5b07ed0456056217175fbdee28d2b06e/FY_2014_HSGP_FOA_Final.pdf.
Accessed July 3, 2014.

US Department of Justice, Office of the Inspector General, Evaluation and Inspections Division. *The Department of Justice's Terrorism Task Forces.* Washington, DC: US Department of Justice, June 2005. https://oig.justice .gov/reports/plus/e0507/final.pdf. Accessed March 4, 2018.

US Department of Justice's Global Justice Information Sharing Initiative. *Baseline Capabilities for State and Major Urban Area Fusion Centers.* Washington, DC: Department of Justice and Department of Homeland Security, September 2008. https://www.fema.gov/pdf/government/grant /2010/fy10_hsgp_fusion.pdf. Accessed March 12, 2012.

———. *Common Competencies for State, Local, and Tribal Intelligence analyst.* Washington, DC: Department of Justice and Department of Homeland Security, June 2010. https://it.ojp.gov/documents/d/common%20competencies%20 state%20local%20and%20Tribal%20intelligence%20analysts.pdf. Accessed March 12, 2012.

———. *Fusion Center Guidelines Developing and Sharing Information and Intelligence in a New Era.* Washington, DC: Department of Justice and Department of Homeland Security, August 2006. https://www.fema.gov/pdf/ government/grant/2010/fy10_hsgp_fusion.pdf. Accessed March 12, 2012.

US House of Representatives, Committee on Homeland Security. *Majority Staff Report on the National Network of Fusion Centers*, July 2013. https:// www.archives.gov/files/isoo/oversight-groups/sltps-pac/staff-report-on -fusion-networks-2013.pdf. Accessed July 27, 2013.

US Senate, Permanent Subcommittee on Investigations. *Federal Support for and Involvement in State and Local Fusion Centers*, October 3, 2012. https://www.hsgac.senate.gov/imo/media/doc/10-3-2012%20PSI%20 STAFF%20REPORT%20re%20FUSION%20CENTERS.2.pdf. Accessed October 3, 2012.

Washington Post. "Fatal Force." *Washington Post*, undated. https://www.wash ingtonpost.com/policeshootings/?utm_term=.148246b81e5c. Accessed June 25, 2018.

Watson Institute for International Affairs. "Costs of War." Brown University, undated. http://watson.brown.edu/costsofwar/papers/summary. Accessed May 4, 2018.

We Charge Genocide. *The Counter-CAPS Report: The Community Engagement Arm of the Police State.* (Chicago: We Charge Genocide, October 28 2015. http://wechargegenocide.org/wp-content/uploads/2015/10/CAPSreport-final.pdf. Accessed October 28, 2015.

"Zero Tolerance Lease." Albany County District Attorney, Undated.

ALL OTHER SOURCES

"214 Indicted on Felony Riot Charges for Protesting Trump Inauguration." *Unicorn Riot*, March 15, 2017/ https://www.unicornriot.ninja/2017/214

-indicted-felony-riot-charges-protesting-trump-inauguration/. Accessed March 15, 2017)

Aaronson, Trevor. *The Terror Factory: Inside the FBI's Manufactured War on Terrorism*. Brooklyn, NY: Ig Publishing, 2013.

Aaronson, Trevor, and Margot Williams. "Trial Terror." *The Intercept*, August 30, 2018 (last update). https://trial-and-terror.theintercept.com/. Accessed October 2, 2018.

Abold, Justin Lewis, Ray Guidetti, and Douglas Keyer. "Strengthening the Value of the National Network of Fusion Centers by Leveraging Specialization: Defining" 'Centers of Analytical Excellence.'" *Homeland Security Affairs* 8, no. 1 (2012): 2–28.

Abramsky, Sasha. "Is This the End of the War on Crime?" *The Nation*, July 5, 2010. https://www.thenation.com/article/end-war-crime/. Accessed June 23, 2017.

Ackerman, Alissa R., Meghan Sacks, and Rich Furman. "The New Penology Revisited: The Criminalization of Immigration as a Pacification Strategy." *Justice Policy Journal* 11, no. 1 (2014): 1–20.

Adomaitis, Greg. "Camden County Warrant Sweep Nets 76 Arrests, Authorities Say." *South Jersey Times*, December 21, 2013. http://www.nj.com/camden/index.ssf/2013/12/camden_county_warrant_sweep_nets_76_arrests_authorities_say.html. Accessed April 20, 2014.

Alexander, Michelle. *The New Jim Crow: Mass Incarceration in the Age of Colorblindness*. New York: The New Press, 2012.

Allen, Theodore. *The Invention of the White Race, Vol. 2: The Origin of Racial Oppression in Anglo-America*. New York: Verso, 1997.

Anderson, Elijah. *Code of the Street: Decency, Violence, and the Moral life of the Inner City*. New York: W.W. Norton & Company, 2000.

Apuzzo, Matt, and Adam Goldman. *Enemies Within: Inside the NYPD's Secret Spying Unit and Bin Laden's Final Plot against America*. New York: Simon and Schuster, 2013.

Arrighi, Giovanni. *Adam Smith in Beijing: Lineages of the 21st Century*. New York: Verso, 2009.

———. *The Long 20th Century: Money, Power, and the Origins of our Times*. New York: Verso, 1994.

Arrighi, Giovanni, Terence K. Hopkins, and Immanuel Wallerstein. *Anti-Systemic Movements*. New York: Verso, 1989.

Arrighi, Giovanni, and Beverly Silver. "The End of the Long Twentieth Century." In *Business as Usual: The Roots of the Global Financial Meltdown*, edited by Craig Calhoun and Georgi Derluguian, 53–68. New York: New York University Press, 2011.

Aseltine, Peter. "Forty-One Charged in Takedown of Major Drug Network with Ties to Latin Street Gangs That Distributed Heroin in Camden." Office of the Attorney General & Division of Criminal Justice. Press Release, May 30, 2012. Accessed August 4, 2014.

———. "Forty-Seven Charged in Takedown of Violent Drug Network That Distributed Millions of Dollars in Heroin and Cocaine in Camden." Office of the Attorney General & Division of Criminal Justice. Press Release, November 13, 2013. Accessed November 15, 2013.

———. "Ringleader and 14 Others Arrested in Takedown of Paterson Narcotics Supply Ring that Allegedly Distributed Millions of Dollars in Heroin." Office of the Attorney General & Division of Criminal Justice. Press Release, November 20, 2012. Accessed August 4, 2014.

———. Twenty-Eight Charged in Atlantic City Violent Crime Task Force Investigation "Operation Blok Buster" Targeting Violent "800 Blok" Gang and Drug Dealing in Back Maryland Avenue Section of City." Office of the Attorney General & Division of Criminal Justice. Press Release, May 14, 2013. Accessed August 4, 2014.

Associated Press. "Mayors, Police Chiefs Talk Strategy on Protests." *Las Vegas Sun*, November 15, 2011. http://www.lasvegassun.com/news/2011/nov/15/us-occupy-cooperation/. Accessed December 28, 2011.

———. "U.S. Has Highest Rate of Imprisonment in World." *The New York Times*, January 7, 1991. http://www.nytimes.com/1991/01/07/us/us-has-highest-rate-of-imprisonment-in-world.html. Accessed May 12, 2017.

Balibar, Étienne. "Foucault and Marx: The Question of Nominalism." In *Foucault, Philosopher: Essays Translated from French and German*, edited by Timothy J. Armstrong, 38–56. New York: Routledge, 1992.

Baran, Madeleine. "Charges Dismissed against Three of RNC 8 Suspects." Minnesota Public Radio, September 16, 2010. http://www.mprnews.org/story/2010/09/16/rnc-charges-dismissed. Accessed March 3, 2012.

———. "Man Sentenced to 91 Days in RNC Protest Case." Minnesota Public Radio, August 27, 2010. http://www.mprnews.org/story/2010/08/27/rnc-plea. Accessed March 3, 2012.

Bennett, Hans. "The Black Panthers and the Assassination of Fred Hampton." *Journal of Pan African Studies* 3, no. 6 (2010): 215–22.

Berger, Dan, Mariame Kaba, and David Stein. "What Abolitionists Do." *Jacobin*, August 24, 2017. https://jacobinmag.com/2017/08/prison-abolition-reform-mass-incarceration. Accessed August 24, 2017.

Berlatsky, Noah. "At the United Nations, Chicago Activists Protest Police Brutality." *Atlantic Monthly*, November 17, 2014. https://www.theatlantic.com/national/archive/2014/11/we-charge-genocide-movement-chicago-un/382843/. Accessed June 28, 2018.

Biernacki, Patrick, and Dan Waldorf. "Snowball Sampling: Problems and Techniques of Chain Referral Sampling." *Sociological Methods & Research* 10, no. 2 (1981): 141–63.

Bleisch, Catherine. "Path to Freedom." YouTube video, 48:18. Posted by "The LRP." November 30, 2012. https://www.youtube.com/watch?v=vedfu-ulmbA. Accessed July 5, 2014.

Boggs, James. "Uprooting Racism and Racists in the United States." *The Black Scholar* 2, no. 2 (1970): 2–10.

Bolin, Göran. "The Forms of Value: Problems of Convertibility in Field Theory." *tripleC* 10, no. 1 (2012): 33–41.

Bond-Graham, Darwin. "Counter-Terrorism Officials Helped Track Black Lives Matter Protesters." *East Bay Express*, April 15, 2015. https://www.eastbay express.com/oakland/counter-terrorism-officials-helped-track-black-lives -matter-protesters/Content?oid=4247605. Accessed April 15, 2015.

Bonilla-Silva, Eduardo. "Color-Blind Racism." In *Race, Class, and Gender in the United States: An Integrated Study*, edited by Paula Rothenberg, 131–38. New York: Worth Publishers, 2007.

Boren, Michael. "Complaints Rise under Camden Police." *Philadelphia Inquirer*, April 25, 2015. http://www.philly.com/philly/news/Excessive _force.html. Accessed September 28, 2016.

———. "In Camden, Police Crackdown Clogs Court." *Philadelphia Inquirer*, December 8, 2014. http://articles.philly.com/2014-12-08/news/56807015_1 _police-crackdown-north-philadelphia-tinted-car-windows. Accessed September 28, 2016.

Boukalas, Christos. *Homeland Security, Its Law and Its State: A Design of Power for the 21st Century*. New York: Routledge, 2014.

Brown, Alleen. "Arrests of Journalists at Standing Rock Test the Boundaries of the First Amendment." *The Intercept*, November 27, 2016. https://theinter cept.com/2016/11/27/arrests-of-journalists-at-standing-rock-test-the -boundaries-of-the-first-amendment/. Accessed December 1, 2016.

Brown, Alleen, Will Parish, and Alice Speri. "As Standing Rock Camps Cleared Out, TigerSwan Expanded Surveillance to Array of Progressive Causes.'" *The Intercept*, June 21, 2017. https://theintercept.com/2017/06/21/as -standing-rock-camps-cleared-out-tigerswan-expanded-surveillance-to -array-of-progressive-causes/. Accessed June 21, 2017.

———. "Leaked Documents Reveal Counterterrorism Tactics Used at Standing Rock to 'Defeat Pipeline Insurgencies.'" *The Intercept*, May 27, 2017. https:// theintercept.com/2017/05/27/leaked-documents-reveal-security-firms -counterterrorism-tactics-at-standing-rock-to-defeat-pipeline-insurgencies/. Accessed May 27, 2017.

———. "Police Used Private Security Aircraft for Surveillance in Standing Rock 'No-Fly Zone.'" *The Intercept*, September 29, 2017. https://theintercept .com/2017/09/29/standing-rock-dakota-access-pipeline-dapl-no-fly-zone -drones-tigerswan. Accessed September 27, 2017.

———. "Standing Rock Documents Expose Inner Workings of 'Surveillance-Industrial Complex.'" *The Intercept*, June 3, 2017. https://theintercept .com/2017/06/03/standing-rock-documents-expose-inner-workings-of -surveillance-industrial-complex/. Accessed June 3, 2017.

———. "TigerSwan Responded to Pipeline Vandalism by Launching Multistate Dragnet.'" *The Intercept*, August 26, 2017. https://theintercept.com/2017 /08/26/dapl-security-firm-tigerswan-responded-to-pipeline-vandalism-by -launching-multistate-dragnet. Accessed August 26, 2017.

Brown, Elizabeth K. "Foreclosing on Incarceration? State Correctional Policy Enactments and the Great Recession." *Criminal Justice Policy Review* 24, no. 3 (2012): 317–37.

Brucato, Ben. "Fabricating the Color Line in a White Democracy: From Slave Catchers to Petty Sovereigns." *Theoria* 61, no. 141 (2014): 30–54.

Bullington, Joseph. "Standing Rock Felony Defendants Take Plea Deals, Still Face Years in Prison." *In These Times*, February 22, 2018. http://inthese times.com/rural-america/entry/20936/standing-rock-felony-defendants-dakota-access-pipeline-water-protectors. Accessed March 11, 2018.

Burnley, Malcolm. "'Electronic Stop-and-Frisk' Is at the Fingertips of 3,000 Police Departments." *Next City*, September 17, 2014. https://nextcity.org/daily/entry/police-enlist-electronic-stop-and-frisk-to-patrol-pawnshops. Accessed May 24, 2018.

Burstein, Joshua. "The Ex-Cop at the Center of Controversy Over Crime Prediction Tech." *Bloomberg*, July 20, 2017. https://www.bloomberg.com/news/features/2017-07-10/the-ex-cop-at-the-center-of-controversy-over-crime-prediction-tech. Accessed, June 28, 2018.

Bush, Roderick. *The End of White World Supremacy: Black Internationalism and the Problem of the Color Line.* Philadelphia: Temple University Press, 2009.

Camp, Jordan T. *Incarcerating the Crisis: Freedom Struggles and the Rise of the Neoliberal State.* Berkeley: University of California Press, 2016.

Carter, David L., and Jeremy G. Carter. "The Intelligence Fusion Process for State, Local, and Tribal Law Enforcement." *Criminal Justice and Behavior* 36, no. 12 (2009): 1323–39.

Charmaz, Kathy. *Constructing Grounded Theory: A Practical Guide through Qualitative Analysis.* Thousand Oaks, CA: Sage, 2006.

Churchill, Ward, and Jim Vander Wall. *The COINTELPRO Papers: Documents from the FBI's Secret Wars Against Dissent in the United States.* Boston: South End Press, 1990, 303.

Clunn, Nick, and Matthew McGrath. "High Rate of Gun Violence in Paterson Blamed on Cop Layoffs." *The Record*, March 14, 2012. http://www.northjer sey.com/paterson/High_rate_of_gun_violence_in_Paterson _blamed_on _cop_layofs.htm. Accessed, January 27, 2013.

Collum, Joseph. *The Black Dragon: Racial Profiling Exposed.* Ft. Lauderdale, FL: Gulf Stream Press, 2010.

Conte, Michaelangelo. "24 Netted by Hudson Sheriff's Office in Jersey City Warrant Sweep." *The Jersey Journal*, July 25, 2014. http://www.nj.com/hudson/index.ssf/2014/07/post_573.html. Accessed August 1, 2014.

———. "Hudson County Sheriff's Officers Nab 27 'Fugitives' in Sweep." *The Jersey Journal*, May 30, 2013. http://www.nj.com/hudson/index.ssf/2013/05/hudson_county_sheriffs_officer_6.html. Accessed August 1, 2014.

———. "Jersey City Cops, Other Law Enforcement Arrest 176 through Operation Summer Shield." *Jersey Journal*, June 4, 2011. http://www.nj.com/jjournal-news/index.ssf/2011/06/jersey_city_cops_other_law_enf.html. Accessed April 20, 2013.

Cooney, Mikaela, Jeff Rojek, and Robert J. Kaminski. "An Assessment of the Utility of a State Fusion Center by Law Enforcement Executives and Personnel." *Journal of Intelligence Analysis* 20, no. 1 (2011): 1–18.

Cope, Nina. "Intelligence Led Policing or Policing Led Intelligence: Integrating Crime Analysis into Policing." *British Journal of Criminology* 44, no. 2 (2004): 188–203

Cox, Oliver Cromwell. *Caste, Class, and Race: A Study in Social Dynamics.* New York: Monthly Review Press, 1948.

Craven, Krista, Torin Monahan, and Priscilla Regan. "Compromised Trust: DHS Fusion Centers' Policing of the Occupy Wall Street Movement." *Sociological Research Online* 20, no. 3 (2015): 1–14.

Cruz, Daniel. "Christie Marks Re-Opening of Mid-State Correctional Facility as Treatment Center." NJ TV News, April 10, 2017. http://www.njtvonline .org/news/video/christie-marks-re-opening-mid-state-correctional-facility -treatment-center/. Accessed June 23, 2017.

Cunningham, David, and Barb Browning. "The Emergence of Worthy Targets: Official Frames and Deviance Narratives within the FBI." *Sociological Forum* 19, no. 3 (2004): 351–52, 360–63.

Curtis, Aaron. "Secondhand Dealers Face a Crackdown in Ontario County." *Monroe County Post*, April 30, 2015. www.monroecopost.com/article/2015 0430/news/150439983. Accessed June 20, 2018.

Dannels, David, and Heather Smith. "Implementation Challenges of Intelligence Led Policing in a Quasi-Rural County." *Journal of Crime and Justice* 24 no. 2 (2001): 103–12.

Davis, Frank, and Rachel Goematt. "Operation Fourth Down Tackles Violent Blood Set in Paterson." Office of the Attorney General & New Jersey State Police. Press Release, June 23, 2011. http://www.nj.gov/oag/newsreleases11 /pr20110623c.html. Accessed January 27, 2013.

Davis, Mike. "The Urbanization of Empire: Megacities and the Laws of Chaos." *Social Text* 22, no. 4 (2004): 9–15

De Giorgi, Alessandro. *Re-thinking the Political Economy of Punishment: Perspectives on Post-Fordism and Penal Politics.* Burlington, VT: Ashgate, 2006.

Deflem, Mathieu. 2012. "Joint Terrorism Task Forces." In *Counterterrorism: From the Cold War to the War on Terror, Volume 1*, edited by Frank G. Shanty, 423–26. Santa Barbara, CA: Praeger/ABC-CLIO, 2012.

Demko, Paul. "Lawsuits Field Alleging Police Misconduct around RNC." *The Minnesota Independent*, February 27, 2009. http://minnesotaindependent. com/27788/lawsuits-filed-alleging-police-misconduct-around-rnc. Accessed March 2, 2012.

Donner, Frank J. *Protectors of Privilege: Red Squads and Police Repression in Urban America.* Berkeley: University of California Press, 1990.

Dries, Bill. "Tennessee Fusion Center Monitored July Protests in Memphis, Emails Reveal." *Memphis Daily News*, March 14, 2017. https://www.mem phisdailynews.com/news/2017/mar/14/tennessee-fusion-center-moni tored-july-protests-in-memphis-emails-reveal/. Accessed March 14, 2017.

Du Bois, W. E. B. *Black Reconstruction in America, 1860–1880.* New York: Free Press, 1999.

Dyer-Witheford, Nick. *Cyber-Marx: Cycles and Circuits of Struggle in High Technology Capitalism.* Urbana: University of Illinois Press, 1999.

Eason, John M. *Big House on the Prairie: Rise of the Rural Ghetto and Prison Proliferation.* Chicago: University of Chicago Press, 2017.

———. "Extending the Hyperghetto: Toward a Theory of Punishment, Race, and Rural Disadvantage." *Journal of Poverty* 16, no. 3 (2012): 274–95.

Eason, Stan. "Summer Shield Closes with 200 Arrests: Feds, States and Locals Join to End Drug Trade in City." City of Jersey City. Press Release, September 21, 2012. http://www.cityofjerseycity.com/uploadedFiles/Public_Notices/Press_Releases/majorOPreleasefinal1%5B1%5D.pdf. Accessed April 20, 2013.

Editorial Board. "Reducing Unjust Cocaine Sentences." *New York Times,* June 29, 2011. http://www.nytimes.com/2011/06/30/opinion/30thu3.html. Accessed June 23, 2017.

———. "Shrinking the Prison Population." *New York Times,* May 10, 2009. http://www.nytimes.com/2009/05/11/opinion/11mon2.html. Accessed June 23, 2017.

Elliott, Michael. "The Shoe Bomber's World." *Time,* February 16, 2002. http://content.time.com/time/world/article/0,8599,203478,00.html. Accessed June 12, 2014.

Ellis, Blake. "Counting the Homeless in America's Poorest City." *CNNMoney,* February 13, 2014. http://money.cnn.com/2014/02/12/pf/homeless-count/index.html. Accessed June 1 2014.

Epperson, Matthew, and Carrie Pettus-Davis, eds. *Smart Decarceration: Achieving Criminal Justice Transformation in the 21st Century.* New York: Oxford University Press, 2017.

Everett, Rebecca. "Camden Area Had the Highest Job Growth Rate Last Year?" NJ.com, April 24, 2017. https://www.nj.com/camden/index.ssf/2017/04/camden_had_the_highest_job_growth_rate_last_year_h.html. Accessed June 28, 2018.

———. "Camden's 2017 Murder Rate Was the Lowest in Decades. Will the Trend Continue?" NJ.com, January 9 2018. https://www.nj.com/camden/index.ssf/2018/01/camdens_2017_murder_rate_was_the_lowest_in_decades.html. Accessed June 28, 2018.

Fan, Mary D. "Street Diversion and Decarceration." *American Criminal Law Review* 50 (2013): 165–210.

Federici, Silvia. *Caliban and the Witch: Women, the Body, and Primitive Accumulation.* Brooklyn, NY: Autonomedia, 2004.

Fensom, Michael. "Scott Thomson: Bringing Community Back to Camden." *Inside New Jersey,* December 19, 2014. https://www.nj.com/inside-jersey/index.ssf/2014/12/j_scott_thomson_bringing_community_back_to_camden.html. Accessed September 27, 2016.

Fernandez, Luis. *Policing Dissent: Social Control and the Anti-Globalization Movement.* New Brunswick, NJ: Rutgers University Press, 2008.

Fitzgerald, Bryan. "Has Occupy Albany Movement Marched into History?" *Times Union,* October 20, 2012. http://www.timesunion.com/local/article

/Has-Occupy-Albany-movement-marched-into-history-3965918.php#src
=fb. Accessed July 14, 2014.

Forman James Jr. "Racial Critiques of Mass Incarceration: Beyond the New Jim Crow." *New York University Law Review* 87 (2012): 101–46.

Foucault, Michel. *The Birth of Biopolitics: Lectures at the Collège de France, 1978–1979.* New York: Macmillan, 2010.

———. *The Birth of the Clinic: The Archeology of Medical Perception.* New York: Routledge, 2012.

———. "Confessions of the Flesh." In *Power/Knowledge: Selected Interviews and Other Writings, 1972–1977,* edited by Colin Gordon, 194–228. New York: Pantheon 1980.

———. *Discipline and Punish: The Birth of the Prison.* New York: Vintage, 1995.

———. *Madness and Civilization: A History of Insanity in the Age of Reason.* New York: Vintage, 1988.

———. "Power and Strategies." In *Power/Knowledge: Selected Interviews and Other Writings, 1972–1977,* edited by Colin Gordon, 134–45. New York: Pantheon 1980.

Fung, Brian. "5.1 Million Americans Have Security Clearances. That's More Than the Entire Population of Norway." *Washington Post,* March 24 2014. http://www.washingtonpost.com/blogs/the-switch/wp/2014/03/24/5 -1-million-americans-have-security-clearances-thats-more-than-the -entire-population-of-norway/. Accessed July 1, 2014.

Galison, Peter. "Removing Knowledge." *Critical Inquiry* 31, no. 1 (2004): 229–43.

Garland, David. *The Culture of Control: Crime and Social order in Contemporary Society.* Chicago: University of Chicago Press, 2012

Gillette, Howard. *Camden after the Fall: Decline and Renewal in a Post-Industrial City.* Philadelphia: University of Pennsylvania Press, 2005.

Gilmore, Ruth. *Golden Gulag: Prisons, Surplus, Crisis, and Opposition in Globalizing California.* Berkeley: University of California Press, 2006.

Glick, Brian. *The War at Home: Covert Action against U.S. Activists and What We Can Do about It.* Boston: South End Press, 1989.

Goffman, Alice. *On the Run: Fugitive Life in an American City.* Chicago: University of Chicago Press, 2014.

Gosztola, Kevin. "The Risks Homeland Security Fusion Centers Pose to Americans' Civil Liberties." *Shadow Proof.* October 5, 2012. https://shadow proof.com/2012/10/05/the-risks-homeland-security-fusion-centers-pose -to-americans-civil-liberties/. Accessed March 4, 2014.

Gottschalk, Marie. *Caught: The Prison State and the Lockdown of American Politics.* Princeton, NJ: Princeton University Press, 2016.

———. *The Prison and the Gallows: The Politics of Mass Incarceration in America.* New York: Cambridge University Press, 2006.

Gramsci, Antonio. *Selections from the Prison Notebooks.* Edited by Quintin Hoare and Geoffrey Nowell Smith. New York: International Publishers Co., 1971.

Graphia, Renee Dianne. "An Exploratory Study of the Perceived Utility and Effectiveness of State Fusion Centers." PhD diss., Rutgers, The State University of New Jersey, 2010.

Graphia-Joyal, Renee. "Are Fusion Centers Achieving Their Intended Purposes? Findings from a Qualitative Study on the Internal Efficacy of State Fusion Centers." *Journal of Intelligence Analysis* 19, no. 1 (2010): 54–76.

———. "How Far Have We Come? Information Sharing, Interagency Collaboration, and Trust within the Law Enforcement Community." *Criminal Justice Studies* 25, no. 4 (2012): 357–70.

Greenberg, David. *Crime and Capitalism: Readings in Marxist Criminology.* Philadelphia: Temple University Press, 2010.

Greenberg, Ivan. *The Dangers of Dissent: The FBI and Civil Liberties since 1965.* Lanham, MD: Lexington Books, 2010.

Guha, Ranajit. "The Prose of Counterinsurgency." In *Culture/Power/History: A Reader in Contemporary Social Theory*, edited by Nicholas Dirks, Geoff Eley, and Sherry Ortner, 336–71. Princeton, NJ: Princeton University Press.

Guidetti, Raymond. "Local Policing: Expanding Reach with Limited Resources through Fusion Centers." *The Police Chief* 74, no. 2, (2012). http://www.policechiefmagazine.org/magazine/index.cfm?fuseaction=display&article_id=2599&issue_id=22012. Accessed August 4, 2012.

Guidetti, Raymond, and Thomas Martinelli. (2009) "Intelligence-Led Policing—A Strategic Framework." *The Police Chief* 76, no. 10, (2012). http://www.policechiefmagazine.org/magazine/index.cfm?fuseaction=display&article_id=1918&issue_id=102009. Accessed, August 4, 2012.

Guidetti, Raymond, and James Morentz. "Geospatial Statistical Modeling for Intelligence-Led Policing." *The Police Chief* 77, no. 8 (2010). http://www.policechiefmagazine.org/magazine/index.cfm?fuseaction=display_arch&article_id=2152&issue_id=82010. Accessed, August 4, 2012.

Gurnon, Emily. "Last 'RNC 8' Protesters Admit Guilt—but Remain Defiant." *St. Paul Pioneer Press*, October 20, 2010. http://www.twincities.com/news/ci_16382084. Accessed March 2, 2012.

Guy, Shoshana, America's 'Invincible' City Brought to Its Knees by Poverty, Violence." NBC News, March 7, 2013. http://www.nbcnews.com/feature/in-plain-sight/americas-invincible-city-brought-its-knees-poverty-violence-v17225824.

Hall, Stuart, Chas Critcher, Tony Jefferson, John Clarke, and Brian Roberts. *Policing the Crisis: Mugging, the State and Law and Order.* New York: Palgrave Macmillan, 2013.

Handler, Joel F. *Social Citizenship and Workfare in the United States and Western Europe: The Paradox of Inclusion.* New York: Cambridge University Press, 2004.

Harcourt, Bernard. *Illusion of Order: The False Promise of Broken Windows Policing.* Cambridge, MA: Harvard University Press, 2009.

———. "Neoliberal Penality: A Brief Genealogy." *Theoretical Criminology* 14, no. 1 (2010): 74–92.

Harring, Sidney. *Policing Class Society: The Experience of American Cities, 1865–1915*. New Brunswick, NJ: Rutgers University Press, 1983.

Harris, Jon. "Syracuse Police Raid Seven Stores Receiving and Selling Stolen Property." *Syracuse Post-Standard*, December 13, 2013. http://www.syracuse.com/news/index.ssf/2013/12/syracuse_police_raid_seven_stores_receiving_and_selling_stolen_property.html. Accessed August 10, 2014.

Harvey David. *A Brief History of Neoliberalism*. New York: Oxford University Press, 2005.

———. *The Enigma of Capital and the Crises of Capitalism*. London: Profile Books, 2011.

Henry, Aaron. "The Perpetual Object of Regulation: Privacy as Pacification." *Socialist Studies/Études Socialistes* 9, no. 2 (2013): 94–110.

Herman, Susan N. "Collapsing Spheres: Joint Terrorism Task Forces, Federalism, and the War on Terror." *Willamette Law Review* 41 (2005): 941–70.

Hinton, Elizabeth. *From the War on Poverty to the War on Crime: The Making of Mass Incarceration in America*. Cambridge, MA: Harvard University Press, 2016.

Hodai, Beau. *Dissent or Terror: How the Nation's Counter Terrorism Apparatus, in Partnership with Corporate America, Turned on Occupy Wall Street."* Madison, WI: Center for Media and Democracy and BDA Press, May 2013. http://www.prwatch.org/files/Dissent%20or%20Terror%20FINAL.pdf. Accessed May 20, 2013.

Hopkins, Terrence. "World-Systems Analysis: Methodological Issues." In *World-Systems Analysis: Theory and Methodology*, edited by Terrence Hopkins and Immanuel Wallerstein, 134–58. Thousand Oaks, CA: Sage, 1982.

Horvitz, Paul, and *Inquirer* Trenton Bureau. "N.J. Gun Law: A Question of Fairness." *Philadelphia Inquirer*, July 25, 1986. http://articles.philly.com/1986-07-25/news/26099338_1_sentencing-judge-gun-law-excessive-sentences. Accessed August 4, 2014.

Hylton, Hilary. "Fusion Centers: Giving Cops Too Much Information?" *Time*, March 9, 2009. https://content.time.com/time/nation/article/0,8599,1883101,00.html. Accessed March 13, 2012.

"'If You See Something, Say Something™' Campaign." Department of Homeland Security. http://www.dhs.gov/if-you-see-something-say-something%E2%84%A2-campaign. Accessed August 1, 2014.

Ignatiev, Noel. *How the Irish Became White*. New York: Routledge, 2009.

Innes, Martin, Laurence Abbott, Trudy Lowe, and Colin Roberts. "Seeing Like a Citizen: Field Experiments in 'Community Intelligence-Led Policing.'" *Police Practice and Research* 10, no. 2 (2009): 99–114.

Isacson, Adam and Sarah Kinosian. "Which Central American Military and Police Units Get the Most U.S. Aid?" *WOLA: Advocacy for Human Rights in the Americas*, April 16, 2016. https://www.wola.org/analysis/which-central-american-military-and-police-units-get-the-most-u-s-aid/. Accessed December 7, 2016.

Isikoff, Michael. "Unaware of Tsarnaev Warnings, Boston Counterterror Unit Tracked Protester." NBC News, May 9, 2013. http://investigations.nbcnews.com/_news/2013/05/09/18152849-unaware-of-tsarnaev-warnings-boston-counterterror-unit-tracked-protesters. Accessed November 5, 2013.

Jackman, Tom. "De-escalation Training to Reduce Police Shootings Facing Mixed Reviews at Launch." *Washington Post,* October 15, 2016.

Jackson, Arrick, and Michael Brown. "Ensuring Efficiency, Interagency Cooperation, and Protection of Civil Liberties: Shifting from a Traditional Model of Policing to an Intelligence-Led Policing (ILP) Paradigm." *Criminal Justice Studies* 20, no. 2 (2007): 111–29.

Jackson, Richard. *Writing the War on Terrorism: Language, Politics and Counter-terrorism.* Manchester, UK: Manchester University Press, 2005.

Jackson, Will, Joanna Gilmore, and Helen Monk. "Policing Unacceptable Protest in England and Wales: A Case Study of the Policing of Anti-fracking Protests." *Critical Social Policy* (2018): 0261018317753087.

Jackson, Will, Helen Monk, and Joanna Gilmore. "Pacifying Disruptive Subjects: Police Violence and Anti-fracking Protests." *Contention* 3, no. 2 (2015): 81–93.

Jarvis, Lee. *Times of Terror: Discourse, Temporality and the War on Terror.* New York: Springer, 2009.

Jessop, Bob. "Constituting Another Foucault Effect: Foucault on States and Statecraft." In *Governmentality: Current Issues and Future Challenges,* edited by Ulrich Bröckling, Susanne Krasmann, and Thomas Lemke, 56–73. New York: Routledge, 2010.

———. *The Future of the Capitalist State.* Malden, MA: Polity, 2002.

———. "Pouvoir et stratégies chez Poulantzas et Foucault." *Actuel Marx* 36 (2007): 89–107; English translation available at https://www.researchgate.net/publication/312506809_Poulantzas_and_Foucault_on_Power_and_Strategy_Pouvoir_et_strategies_chez_Poulantzas_et_Foucault. Accessed January 4, 2018.

———. "Putting Neoliberalism in Its Time and Place: A Response to the Debate." *Social Anthropology* 21, no. 1 (2013): 65–74.

———. *State Power: A Strategic-Relational Approach.* Cambridge: Polity, 2008.

Jessop, Bob, and Ngai-Ling Sum. *Beyond the Regulation Approach: Putting Capitalist Economies in Their Place.* Northampton, UK: Edward Elgar Publishing, 2006.

Johnson, Bart, and Shelagh Dorn. "Fusion Centers: New York State Strategy Unifies Law Enforcement." *The Police Chief* 75, no. 2 (2007). www.policechiefmagazine.org/magazine/index.cfm?fuseaction=display_arch&article_id=1419&issue_id=22008. Accessed January 4, 2012.

Johnson, Daryl. *Right-Wing Resurgence: How a Domestic Terror Threat Is Being Ignored.* Lanham, MD: Rowman & Littlefield, 2012.

Johnson, L.K., 2015. *A Season of Inquiry Revisited: The Church Committee Confronts America's Spy Agencies.* University Press of Kansas.

Jones, Stephen, Brian Polite, and Adam Grossman. "Troopers and Partners Dismantle Drug Network in 'Operation Smoke Screen.'" Office of the Attorney General and New Jersey State Police. Press Release, January 7, 2014. Accessed August 4, 2014.

Joseph, George. "Exclusive: Feds Regularly Monitored Black Lives Matter since Ferguson." *The Intercept*, July 24, 2015. https://theintercept.com/2015/07/24/documents-show-department-homeland-security-monitoring-black-lives-matter-since-ferguson/. Accessed July 24, 2015.

———. "NYPD Officers Accessed Black Lives Matter Activists' Texts, Documents Show." *The Guardian*, April 4, 2017. https://www.theguardian.com/us-news/2017/apr/04/nypd-police-black-lives-matter-surveillance-undercover. Accessed April 4, 2017.

———. "Undercover Police Have Regularly Spied on Black Lives Matter Activists in New York." *The Guardian*, August 18, 2015. https://theintercept.com/2015/08/18/undercover-police-spied-on-ny-black-lives-matter/. Accessed August 18, 2015.

Joseph, George, and Murtaza Hussain. "FBI Tracked an Activist Involved with Black Lives Matter as They Travelled across the U.S., Documents Show." *The Intercept*, March 19, 2018. https://theintercept.com/2018/03/19/black-lives-matter-fbi-surveillance/. Accessed March 19, 2018.

Jung, Moon-Kie, and Yaejoon Kwon. "Theorizing the US Racial State: Sociology since Racial Formation." *Sociology Compass* 7, no. 11 (2013): 927–40.

Kaba, Mariame. "Free Us All." *New Inquiry*, May 8, 2017. https://thenewinquiry.com/free-us-all/. Accessed June 28, 2017.

Kalyvas, Andreas. "Stateless Theory: Poulantzas's Challenge to Postmodernism." In *Paradigm Lost: State Theory Reconsidered*, edited by Stanley Aronowitz and Peter Bratsis, 105–42. Minneapolis: University of Minnesota Press, 2002.

Karandinos, George, Laurie Kain Hart, Fernando Montero Castrillo, and Philippe Bourgois. "The Moral Economy of Violence in the US Inner City." *Current Anthropology* 55, no. 1 (2014): 1–22.

Katz, Matt. "Camden Recovery Aids Some." *Philadelphia Inquirer*, November 10, 2009. http://www.philly.com/philly/news/special_packages/inquirer/2009 1110_Recovery_aids_some_areas.html. Accessed June 1, 2014.

———. "Camden's Waterfront—and Its Woes." *Philadelphia Inquirer*, November 9, 2009. http://articles.philly.com/2009-11-09/news/24987966_1_municipal-rehabilitation-poorest-city-aquarium. Accessed June, 1, 2014.

Katznelson, Ira. *When Affirmative Action was White: An Untold History of Racial Inequality in Twentieth-Century America*. New York: WW Norton and Company, 2005.

Kava, Janine. "Crime Fighting Efforts in Western New York Get a Boost." Division of Criminal Justice Services. Press Release, July 7, 2008. http://www.criminaljustice.ny.gov/pio/press_releases/2008-0707a_pressrelease.html. Accessed April 3, 2013.

Kienscherf, Markus. "Beyond Militarization and Repression: Liberal Social Control as Pacification." *Critical Sociology* 42, nos. 7–8 (2016): 1179–94.

Kilgannon, Corey, and Michael S. Schmidt. "Vendors Who Alerted Police Called Heroes." *New York Times*, May 2, 2010. http://www.nytimes.com/2010 /05/03/nyregion/03vendor.html. Accessed June 12, 2014.

Kilgore, James. "Mass Incarceration: Examining and Moving beyond the New Jim Crow." *Critical Sociology* 41, no. 2 (2015): 283–95.

———. *Understanding Mass Incarceration: A People's Guide to the Key Civil Rights Struggle of Our Time.* New York: The New Press, 2015.

Knauss, Tim. "It's Official: Sound Garden Freed from Syracuse Secondhand Dealer Rules." *Syracuse Post-Standard*, June 10, 2013. http://www.syracuse .com/news/index.ssf/2013/06/its_official_sound_garden_free.html. Accessed August 4, 2013.

———. "Onondaga County Legislature Tightens Scrutiny of Pawn Shops." *Syracuse Post-Standard*, April 2, 2013. http://www.syracuse.com/news /index.ssf/2013/04/onondaga_county_legislature_ti.html. Accessed August 4, 2013.

Kohler-Hausmann, Julilly. "'The Attila the Hun Law': New York's Rockefeller Drug Laws and the Making of a Punitive State." *Journal of Social History* 44, no. 1 (2010): 71–95.

———. "Guns and Butter: The Welfare State, the Carceral State, and the Politics of Exclusion in the Postwar United States." *Journal of American History* 102, no. 1 (2015): 87–99.

Korzeniewicz, Roberto Patricio, and Timothy Patrick Moran. *Unveiling Inequality: A World-Historical Perspective.* New York: Russell Sage Foundation, 2009.

Kramer, Mattea, and Chris Hellman. "'Homeland Security': The Trillion-Dollar Concept That No One Can Define." *TomDispatch.com*, February 28, 2013. http://www.tomdispatch.com/post/175655/. Accessed March 1, 2013.

Kroll, Andy. "Mayors and Cops Traded Strategies for Dealing with Occupy Protesters." *Mother Jones*, November 16, 2011. http://www.motherjones .com/mojo/2011/11/occupy-protest-coordinate-crackdown-wall-street . Accessed November 16, 2011.

Laday, Jason. "Camden County Towns to Study Possible Merger of Police Departments." *South Jersey Times*, July 23, 2013. http://www.nj.com/cam den/index.ssf/2013/07/camden_county_municipalities_to_study_merger _at_police_departments.html#incart_river. Accessed February 14, 2018.

———. "Camden Police Security at July 2012 Concert Cost $77K in Overtime: Documents." *South Jersey Times*, January 14, 2016. http://www.nj.com /camden/index.ssf/2014/01/camden_police_security_at_july_2012_concert _cost_77k_in_overtime_documents.html. Accessed October 24, 2016.

Lassman, David. "Onondaga County Exec Agrees to Veto Law after Hearing Merchants' Gripes." *Syracuse Post-Standard*, June 10, 2010. http://www .syracuse.com/news/index.ssf/2010/06/onondaga_county _exec_agrees _to.html. Accessed August 2, 2013.

Levin, Sam. "California Police Worked with Neo-Nazis to Pursue 'Anti-racist' Activists, Documents Show." *The Guardian*, February 9, 2018. https://www

.theguardian.com/us-news/2017/feb/10/standing-rock-fbi-investigation -dakota-access. Accessed March 7, 2018.

———. "FBI Terrorism Taskforce Investigating Standing Rock Activists." *The Guardian*, February 10, 2017. https://www.theguardian.com/us-news/2017 /feb/10/standing-rock-fbi-investigation-dakota-access. Accessed February 10, 2017.

Lewandowski, Carla. "Information Sharing Using a State Fusion Center: A Case Study of the New Jersey Regional Operations Intelligence Center." PhD diss., University of Pennsylvania, 2012.

Linder, Urs T. "State, Domination, and Politics: On the Relationship between Poulantzas and Foucault." In *Reading Poulantzas*, edited by Alexander Gallas, Lars Bretthauer, John Kannankulam, and Ingo Stützle, 138–52. Pontypool, UK: Merlin Press, 2011.

Lindorff, Dave. "Did the White House Direct the Police Crackdown on Occupy?" *Counterpunch*, May 14, 2012. http://www.counterpunch.org/2012/05/14 /did-the-white-house-direct-the-police-crackdown-on-occupy/. Accessed May 20, 2012)

———. "Evidence Homeland Security Coordinated Occupy Crackdown." *Counterpunch*, March 23, 2012, Weekend Edition. http://www.counterpunch .org/2012/03/23/evidence-homeland-security-coordinated-occupy-crack down/. Accessed March 30, 2012.

Linnemann, Travis. *Meth Wars: Police, Media, Power*. New York: New York University Press, 2016.

Lorique, Paul, Peter Aseltine, and Brian Polite. "Attorney General Announces Two-Pronged Strategy to Combat Rising Gun Violence in Trenton." Office of Attorney General and New Jersey State Police. Press Release, August 15, 2013. http://nj.gov/oag/newsreleases13/pr20130815b.html. Accessed August 4, 2014.

Lussenhop, Jessica. "'Too Black, Too Strong': The Woodrow Wilson Tigers' National Anthem Protest." BBC, September 22, 2016. https://www.bbc.com /news/magazine-37423901. Accessed September 30, 2016.

Luxemburg, Rosa. *The Accumulation of Capital*. New York: Routledge, 2003.

Mandel, Ernest. Introduction to *Capital, Vol. 1: A Critique of Political Economy*, by Karl Marx, 11–86. New York: Penguin, 1992.

Manza, Jeff, and Christopher Uggen, *Locked Out: Felon Disenfranchisement and American Democracy*. New York: Oxford University Press, 2006.

Martin, William. "Decarceration and Justice Disinvestment: Evidence from New York State." *Punishment & Society* 18, no. 4 (2016): 479–504.

———. "From Mass Imprisonment to Decarceration and Justice Disinvestment." In *After Prisons? Freedom, Decarceration, and Justice Disinvestment*, edited by William Martin and Joshua Price, 1–14. Lanham, MD: Lexington Books, 2016.

Martin, William, and Joshua Price, eds. *After Prisons? Freedom, Decarceration and Justice Disinvestment*. Lanham, MD: Lexington Books, 2016.

Martinez, Cid. *The Neighborhood Has Its Own Rules: Latinos and African Americans in South Los Angeles*. New York: NYU Press, 2016.

Marx, Karl. *Capital, Vol. 1: A Critique of Political Economy*. New York: Penguin, 1992.

———. "On the Jewish Question." *Marxist.org*, September 2009. https://www.marxists.org/archive/marx/works/1844/jewish-question/. Accessed August 1, 2017.

Marx, Karl, and Friedrich Engels. "The Manifesto of the Communist Party." In *The Marx-Engels Reader, Second Edition*, edited by Robert Tucker, 469–500. New York: W.W. Norton, 1978.

Maslauskas Dunn, Brendan. "New Evidence Shows U.S. Government Spied on Wobblies, Activists." *Industrial Worker*, April 2014. https://libcom.org/library/new-evidence-shows-us-government-spied-wobblies-activists. Accessed June 5, 2014.

Mauer, Marc. "Can We Wait 88 Years to End Mass Incarceration?" *Huffington Post*, February 19, 2014. http://www.huffingtonpost.com/marc-mauer/88-years-mass-incarceration_b_4474132.html. Accessed June 23, 2017.

———. *Race to Incarcerate*. New York: The New Press, 2006.

McCartin, Joseph A. *Collision Course: Ronald Reagan, the Air Traffic Controllers, and the Strike That Changed America*. New York: Oxford University Press, 2011.

McCoy, Alfred W. *Policing America's Empire: The United States, the Philippines, and the Rise of the Surveillance State*. Madison: University of Wisconsin Press, 2009.

———. *The Politics of Heroin: CIA Complicity in the Global Drug Trade*. Chicago: Lawrence Hill Books, 2003.

McLeod, Allegra M. "Decarceration Courts: Possibilities and Perils of a Shifting Criminal Law." *Georgetown. Law Journal* 100 (2011): 1587–674.

McMichael, Christopher. "Urban Pacification and "Blitzes" In Contemporary Johannesburg." *Antipode* 47, no. 5 (2015): 1261–78.

McMichael, Philip. "Incorporating Comparison within a World-Historical Perspective: An Alternative Comparative Method." *American Sociological Review* (1990): 385–97.

McNeill, Fergus, and Kristel Beyens, eds. *Offender Supervision in Europe*. New York: Palgrave Macmillan, 2013.

McQuade, Brendan. "A Critical View of Counterinsurgency: World Relational State (De)formation." *Yonsei Journal of International Studies* 4, no. 1 (2012): 67–90.

———. "Cognitive Capitalism and Contemporary Politics: A World Historical Perspective." *Science & Society* 79, no. 3 (2015): 363–87.

———. "Demilitarization Ruse." *Jacobin*, May 24, 2015. https://www.jacobinmag.com/2015/05/camden-obama-police-brutality-black-lives-matter/. Accessed May 24, 2015.

———. "From the Carceral Leviathan to the Police State: Policing Decarceration in New York State." In *After Prisons? Freedom, Decarceration, and Justice Disinvestment*, edited by William Martin and Joshua Price, 53–75. Lanham, MD: Lexington Books, 2016.

———. "Guns, Grenades, and Facebook." *Jacobin*, December, 5, 2016. https://www.jacobinmag.com/2016/12/standing-rock-sioux-dakota-access-dapl-obama-trump. Accessed December 5, 2016.

———. "Police and the Post-9/11 Surveillance Surge: 'Technological Dramas' in 'the Bureaucratic Field.'" *Surveillance & Society* 14, no. 1 (2016): 1–19.

———. "The Prose of Police Power: Pacification, Critical Theory and Socialist Strategy." *Social Justice*, forthcoming. Brooklyn, NY: Verso, forthcoming 2020.

———. "The Puzzle of Intelligence Expertise: Spaces of Intelligence Analysis and the Production of 'Political" Knowledge.' *Qualitative Sociology* 39, no. 3 (2016): 247–65.

———. "*Windows into the Soul* or the Clouded Glass of Surveillance Studies." *Critical Sociology* 44, nos. 4–5 (2018): 815–24.

Medsger, Betty. *The Burglary: The Discovery of J. Edgar Hoover's Secret FBI*. New York: Knopf, 2014.

Mies, Maria. *Patriarchy and Accumulation on a World Scale: Women in the International Division of Labour*. New York: Palgrave Macmillan, 1998.

Milkis, Sidney, and Jerome M. Mileur. *The Great Society and the High Tide of Liberalism*. Amherst: University of Massachusetts Press, 2005.

Miller, Judith. "Intelligent Policing Comes to New Jersey." *City Journal* 18, no. 3 (2008). http://www.city-journal.org/2008/18_3_snd-new_jersey_policing.html. Accessed October 24, 2012.

Miller, Patricia. "Ocean County Grand Jury Quickly Convicts Pawn Shop Owners of Receiving Stolen Property." *Berkley Patch*, July 15, 2016. https://patch.com/new-jersey/berkeley-nj/ocean-county-grand-jury-quickly-convicts-pawn-shop-owners-receiving-stolen.

Miller, Reuben Jonathan. "Devolving the Carceral State: Race, Prisoner Reentry, and the Micro-Politics of Urban Poverty Management." *Punishment & Society* 16, no. 3 (2014): 305–35.

Miller, Reuben Jonathan, and Amanda Alexander. "The Price of Carceral Citizenship: Punishment, Surveillance, and Social Welfare Policy in an Age of Carceral Expansion." *Michigan Journal Race & Law* 21 (2015): 291–314.

Miller, Reuben Jonathan, and Forrest Stuart. "Carceral Citizenship: Race, Rights and Responsibility in the Age of Mass Supervision." *Theoretical Criminology* 21, no. 4 (2017): 532–48.

Mills, C. Wright. *The Sociological Imagination*. New York: Oxford University Press, 2000.

Monaghan, Jeff, and Kevin Walby. "Making Up 'Terror Identities': Security Intelligence, Canada's Integrated Threat Assessment Centre and Social Movement Suppression." *Policing and Society* 22, no. 2 (2012): 133–51.

Monahan, Torin. "The Future of Security? Surveillance Operations at Homeland Security Fusion Centers." *Social Justice* 37, nos. 2–3 (2010/2011): 84–98.

———. "The Murky World of 'Fusion Centres.'" *Justice Matters* 75 no. 1 (2009): 20–21.

Monahan, Torin, and Neal A. Palmer. "The Emerging Politics of DHS Fusion Centers." *Security Dialogue* 40, no. 6 (2009): 617–36.

Monahan, Torin, and Priscilla Regan. "Zones of Opacity: Data Fusion in Post-9/11 Security Organizations." *Canadian Journal of Law and Society* 27, no. 3 (2013): 301–17.

Morgan, Scott, Kathleen O'Leary-Morgan, and Rachel Boba Santos. *City Crime Rankings 2014*. Thousand Oaks, CA: CQ Press, 2014.

Moynihan, Colin. "Officials Cast Wide Net in Monitoring Occupy Protests." *New York Times*, May 22, 2014. https://www.nytimes.com/2014/05/23/us/officials-cast-wide-net-in-monitoring-occupy-protests.html. Accessed May 22, 2014.

Muhammad, Khalil Gibran. *The Condemnation of Blackness: Race, Crime and the Making of Modern Urban America*. Cambridge, MA: Harvard University Press, 2010.

Murakawa, Naomi. *The First Civil Right: How Liberals Built Prison America*. New York: Oxford University Press, 2014.

Murray, Lucas. "535 Arrested in Camden Drug Sweeps." *Courier-Post*, November 7, 2012. http://archive.courierpostonline.com/article/20121008/CRIME/310070036/535-arrested-Camden-drug-sweeps. Accessed June 1, 2014.

Nelson, Bruce. *Divided We Stand: American Workers and the Struggle for Black Equality*. Princeton, NJ: Princeton University Press, 2002.

Neocleous, Mark. "'A Brighter and Nicer New Life': Security as Pacification." *Social & Legal Studies* 20, no 2 (2011): 191–208.

———. *Administering Civil Society*. New York: Palgrave Macmillan, 1996.

———. *Critique of Security*. Edinburgh: Edinburgh University Press, 2008.

———. "The Dream of Pacification: Accumulation, Class War, and the Hunt." *Socialist Studies/Études Socialistes* 9, no. 2 (2013): 14–17.

———. *The Fabrication of Social Order: Critical Theory of Police Power*. London: Pluto Press, 2000.

———. "From Social to National Security: On the Fabrication of Economic Order." *Security Dialogue* 37, no. 3 (2006): 363–84.

———. "Privacy, Secrecy, Idiocy." *Social Research* 69, no. 1 (2002): 85–110.

Neocleous, Mark. "Security as Pacification." In *Anti-Security*, edited by Mark Neocleous and George Rigakos, 23–56. Ottawa: Red Quill Books, 2011.

———. "Security, Liberty and the Myth of Balance: Towards a Critique of Security Politics." *Contemporary Political Theory* 6, no. 2 (2007): 131–49.

———. "Social Police and the Mechanisms of Prevention." *British Journal of Criminology* 40, no. 4 (2000): 710–26.

———. *The Universal Adversary: Security, Capital and "the Enemies of All Mankind."* New York: Routledge, 2016.

———. *War Power, Police Power*. Edinburgh: Edinburgh University Press, 2014.

Newcombe, Tod. "Forecasting the Future for Technology and Policing." *Government Technology*, September 26, 2014. http://www.govtech.com

/public-safety/Forecasting-the-Future-for-Technology-and-Policing.html. Accessed September 27, 2016.

Newkirk, Anthony. "The Rise of the Fusion-Intelligence Complex: A Critique of Political Surveillance after 9/11." *Surveillance & Society*, 8 no. 1 (2010): 43–60.

Nicholaides, Kelly. "South Bergen Police: RAPID Aids Agencies in Pawnshop Fencing Investigations." *South Bergnite*, July 7, 2016. https://www.north jersey.com/story/news/bergen/2016/07/07/south-bergen-police-rapid -aids-agencies-in-pawnshop-fencing-investigations/94885792/. Accessed May 24, 2018.

Nickerson, Jeff. "Occupy Providence to Vacate Burnside Park after Reaching Agreement with the City." *Greater City Providence*. Accessed July 31, 2014. http://www.gcpvd.org/2012/01/24/occupy-providence-to-vacate-burnside -park-after-reaching-agreement-with-the-city/. Accessed July 14, 2014.

Nixon, Ron. "Homeland Security Looked Past Antigovernment Movement, Ex-Analyst Says." *New York Times*, January 8, 2016. https://www.nytimes .com/2016/01/09/us/politics/homeland-security-looked-past-militia -movement-ex-analyst-says.html. Accessed March 24, 2018.

Nixon, Ron, and Eileen Sullivan. "Revocation of Grants to Help Fight Hate under New Scrutiny after Charlottesville." *New York Times*, August 15, 2016. https://www.nytimes.com/2017/08/15/us/politics/right-wing -extremism-charlottesville.html. Accessed March 24, 2018.

O'Brien, John, and Jim O'Hara. "Onondaga County DA: Syracuse Police Violations of Suspects' Rights 'Shocking.'" *Syracuse Post-Standard*, January 11, 2013. http://www.syracuse.com/news/index.ssf/2013/01/onondaga _county_da_syracuse_po.html. Accessed June 20, 2013.

O'Connor, Anahad, and Eric Schmitt. "Terror Attempt Seen as Man Tries to Ignite Device on Jet." *New York Times*, December 26, 2009, sec. US. http:// www.nytimes.com/2009/12/26/us/26plane.html. Accessed June 12, 2014.

O'Hara, Jim. "Judge Finds Syracuse, Onondaga County Law Unconstitutional and a 'Ruse' to Sidestep Search Warrants." *Syracuse Post-Standard*, August 31, 2010. http://www.syracuse.com/news/index.ssf/2010/08/city_county _secondhand_dealer.html. Accessed August 10, 2013)

———. "New Program Targets Chronic Criminals." *Syracuse Post-Standard*, May 6, 2008. http://www.syracuse.com/news/index.ssf/2008/05/new _program_targets_chronic_cr.html. Accessed August 3, 2013.

O'Harrow, Robert. "DHS 'Fusion Centers' Portrayed as Pools of Ineptitude and Civil Liberties Intrusions." *Washington Post*, October 2, 2012. https://www .washingtonpost.com/investigations/dhs-fusion-centers-portrayed-as -pools-of-ineptitude-and-civil-liberties-intrusions/2012/10/02/10014440 -ocb1-11e2-bd1a-b868e65d57eb_story.html. Accessed October 2, 2012.

Occupy Arrests. June 24, 2014. http://occupyarrests.moonfruit.com/. Accessed July 7, 2014.

Office of Attorney General, The State of New Jersey. "Violent Crime Initiative Captures over 150 Fugitives throughout the State." Office of Attorney

General, Press Release, January 25, 2017. http://www.nj.gov/oag/news releases17/pr20170125c.html. Accessed June 10, 2018.

Office of Governor Andrew Cuomo, Press Room. "Governor Cuomo Announces New Crime Analysis Center in Niagara County, Newest of Seven Supported by New York State." Press Release, February 29, 2016. https://www.gover nor.ny.gov/news/governor-cuomo-announces-new-crime-analysis-center -niagara-county-newest-seven-supported-new. Accessed June 1, 2017.

———. "Governor Cuomo Announces Expansion of New York's Crime Analysis Center Network to the Hudson Valley Region." Press Release, June 13, 2018. http://www.criminaljustice.ny.gov/pio/press_releases/2018-6-13 _pressrelease.html. Accessed June 26, 2018.

———. "Newest of Seven Centers Supported by $5.5 Million from New York State to Help Police and Prosecutors More Effectively Solve, Reduce and Prevent Crime." Office of Governor Andrew Cuomo. Press Release, October 12, 2016. https://www.governor.ny.gov/news/governor-cuomo-announces -new-north-country-crime-analysis-center. Accessed June 1, 2017.

Office of Public Affairs. "Multi-Agency Fugitive Sweeps Put 55 Wanted Persons in Jail." New Jersey State Police, Press Release, June 24, 2015. http:// www.nj.gov/lps/njsp/news/2015/20150624.shtml. Accessed July 14, 2017.

———. "Multi-Agency Fugitive Sweeps Put 55 Wanted Persons in Jail." New Jersey State Police. Press Release, June 24, 2015. http://www.nj.gov/lps /njsp////////news/2015/20150624.shtml. Accessed July 14, 2017.

Office of Senator Charles Schumer, Press Room. "Schumer Announces, after His Push, New Crime Fighting Resources Coming to Niagara County with Designation of County as 'High Intensity Drug Trafficking Area.'" Press Release, October 13, 2016. https://www.schumer.senate.gov/newsroom/press -releases/schumer-announces-after-his-push-new-crime-fighting-resources -coming-to-niagara-county-with-designation-of-county-as-high-intensity -drug-trafficking-area_designation-will-now-mean-additional-resources-to -fight-scourge-and-help-disrupt-trafficking. Accessed June 1, 2017.

Olmsted, Kathryn S. *Challenging the Secret Government: The Post-Watergate Investigations of the CIA and FBI.* Chapel Hill: University of North Carolina Press, 2000.

Olson, Joel. *The Abolition of White Democracy.* Minneapolis: University of Minnesota Press, 2004.

Osborne, James. "Nearly 40 People Arrested in North Camden Drug Sweep." *Philadelphia Inquirer,* August 19, 2012. http://articles.philly.com/2012-08 -19/news/33262050_1_open-air-drug-markets-drug-trade-police-sweep. Accessed June 1 2014.

Özcan, Gulden, and George Rigakos. Pacification. In *The Wiley-Blackwell Encyclopedia of Globalization,* edited by George Ritzer, 1–4. Hoboken, NJ: Wiley-Blackwell, 2014. https://onlinelibrary.wiley.com/doi/10.1002/9780 470670590.wbeog621

Parenti, Christian. *Lockdown America: Police and Prisons in the Age of Crisis.* New York: Verso, 2000.

Parrish, Will. "An Activist Stands Accused of Firing a Gun at Standing Rock. It Belonged to Her Lover—an FBI Informant." *The Intercept*, December 11, 2017. https://theintercept.com/2017/12/11/standing-rock-dakota-access -pipeline-fbi-informant-red-fawn-fallis/. Accessed December 11, 2017.

———. "Police Targeted Anti-Racists in Charlottesville Ahead of 'Unite The Right' Rally, Documents Show." *Shadowproof*, March 7, 2018. https:// shadowproof.com/2018/03/07/documents-reveal-police-targeting-anti -racists-charlottesville. Accessed March 7, 2018.

Passantino, Joseph. "Technology to Track Stolen Goods." *Hudson Reporter*, June 6, 2016. http://hudsonreporter.com/view/full_story/27032261/article -Technology-to-track-stolen-goods---Police-department-joins-burgeoning -online-database-cataloging-valuables---?instance=bayonne_top_story. Accessed May 2018.

Patburg, Zach. "Paterson Layoff of 125 Police officers Draws Protests." *The Record*, April 18, 2011. http://www.northjersey.com/news/041811_Paterson _layoff_of_125_police_officers_draws_protests.html. Accessed January 20, 2012.

Peck, Jamie. "Workfare: A Geopolitical Etymology." *Environment and Planning D: Society and Space* 16, no. 2 (1998): 133–61.

———. *Workfare States*. New York: Guilford Press.

Perez, Evan. "Secret Court Attracts Scrutiny." *Wall Street Journal*, June 9, 2013.

Peteritas, Brian. "Fusion Centers Struggle to Find Their Place in the Post-9/11 World." *Governing*, June 2013. http://www.governing.com/topics/public -justice-safety/gov-fusion-centers-post-911-world.html. Accessed July 7, 2013.

Petersilia, Joan. "Beyond the Prison Bubble." *Wilson Quarterly* 35, no. 1 (2011): 50–55.

———. "California Prison Downsizing and Its Impact on Local Criminal Justice Systems." *Harvard Law & Policy Review* 8 (2014): 327–57.

Pfeifer, Joseph. "Network Fusion: Information and Intelligence Sharing for a Networked World." *Homeland Security Affairs* 8 (2012): 1–20.

Phelps, Michelle S. "Mass Probation: Toward a More Robust Theory of State Variation in Punishment." *Punishment & Society* 19, no. 1 (2017): 53–73.

Phillips, Susan A. *Operation Fly Trap: LA Gangs, Drugs, and the Law*. Chicago: University of Chicago Press, 2012.

Picketty, Thomas. *Capital in the Twenty-First Century*. Cambridge, MA: Belknap, 2014.

Piven, Frances Fox, and Richard Cloward. *Regulating the Poor: The Functions of Public Welfare*. New York: Vintage, 2012.

Platt, Tony, Jon Frappier, Ray Gerda, Richard Schauffler, Larry Trujillo, Lynn Cooper, Elliot Currie, and Sidney Harring. *The Iron Fist and the Velvet Glove: An Analysis of the US Police*. San Francisco: Synthesis Publications, 1982.

Portnoy, Jenna. "Christie: Trenton Should Copy Camden's Regional Police Force." *Star Ledger*, August 21, 2013. http://www.nj.com/politics/index .ssf/2013/08/christie_in_camden_education.html. Accessed June 10, 2104.

Potter, Will. *Green Is the New Red: An Insider's Account of a Social Movement Under Siege*. San Francisco: City Lights Publishers, 2011.

Poulantzas, Nicos. *Political Power and Social Classes*. London: Verso, 1978.

———. *State, Power, Socialism*. New York: Verso, 1978.

Powell, Jonathan. *Terrorists at the Table: Why Negotiating Is the Only Way to Peace*. New York: St. Martin's Press, 2015.

Pragacz, Andrew. "Is This What Decarceration Looks Like? Rising Jail Incarceration in Upstate New York." In *After Prisons? Freedom, Decarceration, and Justice Disinvestment*, edited by William G. Martin and Joshua M. Price, 99–214. Lanham, MD: Lexington Books, 2016.

Price, Joshua M. "Serving Two Masters? Reentry Task Forces and Justice Disinvestment." In *After Prisons? Freedom, Decarceration, and Justice Disinvestment*, edited by William G. Martin and Joshua M. Price, 77–98. Lanham, MD: Lexington Books, 2016.

Priest, Dana, and William Arkin. *Top Secret America: The Rise of the New American Security State*. New York: Little, Brown & Co. 2011.

Quijano, Aníbal. "Coloniality of Power and Eurocentrism in Latin America." *Nepantla: Views from South* 1, no. 3 (2000): 533–80.

Quijano, Aníbal, and Immanuel Wallerstein. "Americanity as a Concept; or, The Americas in the Modern World." *International Social Science Journal* 44, no. 4 (1992): 549–57.

Ransby, Barbara. *Ella Baker and the Black Freedom Movement: A Radical Democratic Vision*. Chapel Hill: University of North Carolina Press, 2003.

Ratcliffe, Jerry. *Intelligence-Led Policing*. Cullompton, UK: Willan Publishing, 2008.

Ratcliffe, Jerry H., Evan T. Sorg, and James W. Rose. "Intelligence-Led Policing in Honduras: Applying Sleipnir and Social Psychology to Understand Gang Proliferation." *Journal of Police and Criminal Psychology* 30, no. 2 (2015): 112–23.

Ratcliffe, Jerry, and Ray Guidetti. "State Police Investigative Structure and the Adoption of Intelligence-Led Policing." *Policing: An International Journal of Police Strategies & Management* 31, no. 1 (2008): 109–28.

Ratcliffe, Jerry, and Kyle Walden. "State Police and the Intelligence Center: A Study of Intelligence Flow to and from the Street." *Journal of Intelligence and Analysis* 19, no. 1 (2010): 1–19.

Ray, Penny. "AG Announces Greater Police Presence on Trenton Streets." *Trentonian*, May 14, 2014. http://www.trentonian.com/general-news/2014 0514/ag-announces-greater-police-presence-on-trenton-streets. Accessed August 4, 2014.

Reeves, Joshua. "If You See Something, Say Something: Lateral Surveillance and the Uses of Responsibility." *Surveillance & Society* 10, nos. 3–4 (2012): 235–48.

Regan, Priscilla, and Torin Monahan. "Fusion Center Accountability and Intergovernmental Information Sharing." *Publius: The Journal of Federalism*. (2014). doi: 10.1093/publius/pju016.

————. "Beyond Counterterrorism: Data Sharing, Privacy and Organizational Histories of DHS Fusion Centers." *International Journal of E-Politics* 4, no. 3 (2013): 1–14.

Regan, Priscilla, Torin Monahan, and Krista Craven. "Constructing the Suspicious: Data Production, Circulation, and Interpretation by DHS Fusion Centers." *Administration and Society* (2013). doi: 0095399713513141.

Rigakos, George. *Security/Capital: A General Theory of Pacification*. Edinburgh: Edinburgh University Press, 2016.

————. "'To Extend the Scope of Productive Labour': Pacification as Police Project." In *Anti-Security*, edited by Mark Neocleous and George Rigakos, 57–84. Ottawa: Red Quill Books, 2011.

Rigakos, George, and Aysegul Ergul. "Policing the Industrial Reserve Army: An International Study." *Crime, Law and Social Change* 56, no. 4 (2011): 329–71.

————. "The Pacification of the American Working Class: A Time Series Analysis." *Socialist Studies/Études Socialistes* 9, no. 2 (2013): 167–98.

Rigakos, George S., John L. McMullan, Joshua Johnson, and Gulden Özcan. *A General Police System: Political Economy and Security in the Age of Enlightenment*. Ottawa: Red Quill Books, 2009.

Risen, James. "Inquiry Cites Flaws in Counterterrorism Offices." *New York Times*, October 2, 2012. http://www.nytimes.com/2012/10/03/us/inquiry-cites-flaws-in-regional-counterterrorism-offices.html. Accessed October 2, 2012.

Roberts, Michael. *The Long Depression: How It Happened, Why It Happened, and What Happens Next*. Chicago: Haymarket Books, 2016.

Robinson, Cedric J. *Black Marxism: The Making of the Black Radical Tradition*. Chapel Hill: University of North Carolina Press, 1983.

Roediger, David R. *The Wages of Whiteness: Race and the Making of the American Working Class*. New York: Verso, 2007.

Rogers, Donna. "Missing Link: A New Link Chart Capability Adds Functionality to RISSNet Criminal Intelligence Reports." *Law Enforcement Technology* 31, no. 7 (2004): 20–22.

Rogers, Simon. "Occupy Protests around the World: Full List Visualised." *The Guardian*, November 14, 2011. http://www.theguardian.com/news/data blog/2011/oct/17/occupy-protests-world-list-map. Accessed July 7, 2014.

Rothman, David. "Perfecting the Prison: The United States, 1789–1865." In *The Oxford History of the Prison: The Practice of Punishment in Western Society*, edited by Norval Morris and David J. Rothman, 100–116. New York: Oxford University Press, 1995.

Roy, Ananya, Stuart Schrader, and Emma Shaw Crane. "'The Anti-Poverty Hoax': Development, Pacification, and the Making of Community in the Global 1960s." *Cities* 44 (2015): 139–45.

Rudolf, John. "Chris Christie Pushes Camden Police Force to Disband, Despite Questions over New Plan's Finances." *Huffington Post*, November 19, 2012. http://www.huffingtonpost.com/2012/11/19/chris-christie-camden-police_n_2025372.html. Accessed June 1 2014.

Sampson, Robert J., and Charles Loeffler. "Punishment's Place: The Local Concentration of Mass Incarceration." *Daedalus* 139, no. 3 (2010): 20–31.

Sánchez-Jankowski, Martín. *Cracks in the Pavement: Social Change and Resilience in Poor Neighborhoods.* Berkeley: University of California Press, 2008.

Santiago-Valles, Kelvin. "The Fin de Siècles of Great Britain and the United States: Comparing Two Declining Phases of Global Capitalist Hegemony." In *Endless Empire: Spain's Retreat, Europe's Eclipse, America's Decline,* edited by Alfred W. McCoy, Josep M. Fradera, and Stephen Jacobson, 182–90. Madison: University of Wisconsin Press, 2012.

———. "'Race,' Labor, 'Women's Proper Place,' and the Birth of Nations: Notes on Historicizing the Coloniality of Power." *CR: The New Centennial Review* 3, no. 3 (2003): 47–69.

Sassen, Saskia. *Expulsions: Brutality and Complexity in the Global Economy.* Cambridge, MA: Harvard University Press, 2014.

———. "A Savage Sorting of Winners and Losers: Contemporary Versions of Primitive Accumulation." *Globalizations* 7, nos. 1–2 (2010): 23–50.

Schrader, Stuart. "Policing Political Protest: Paradoxes of the Age of Austerity." *Periscope: Social Text Collective,* December 9, 2012. http://what-democracy-looks-like.com/policing-political-protest-paradoxes-of-the-age-of-austerity/. Accessed March 2, 2013.

———. "To Secure the Global Great Society: Participation in Pacification." *Humanity: An International Journal of Human Rights, Humanitarianism, and Development* 7, no. 2 (2016): 225–53.

Schultz, Christian A. "The Homeland Security Ecosystem: An Analysis of Hierarchical and Ecosystem Models and Their Influence on Decision Makers." MA thesis, Naval Postgraduate School, 2012.

Schulz, G.W. "Assessing RNC Police Tactics: Missteps, Poor Judgments and Inappropriate Detention." *MinnPost,* September 1, 2009. http://www.minnpost.com/politics-policy/2009/09/assessing-rnc-police-tactics-missteps-poor-judgments-and-inappropriate-deten/. Accessed March 2, 2012.

Scott, James. *Domination and the Arts of Resistance: Hidden Transcripts.* New Haven, CT: Yale University Press, 1992.

———. *Weapons of the Weak: Everyday Forms of Peasant Resistance.* New Haven, CT: Yale University Press, 1987.

Seaton, Matt. "Naomi Wolf: Reception, Responses, Critics." *The Guardian,* November 28, 2011. http://www.theguardian.com/commentisfree/cifamerica/2011/nov/28/naomi-wolf-reception-responses-critics. Accessed November 30, 2011.

Seigel, Micol. "Objects of Police History." *Journal of American History* 102, no. 1 (2015): 152–61.

Shabazz, Rashad. *Spatializing Blackness: Architectures of Confinement and Black Masculinity in Chicago.* Urbana: University of Illinois Press, 2015.

Shah, Rajiv, and Brendan McQuade. "Surveillance, Security, and Intelligence-Led Policing in Chicago." In *Neoliberal Chicago,* edited by Euan Hague, Larry Bennet, and Roberta Garner, 243–59. Urbana: University of Illinois Press.

Shelley, Kevin. "Survey: Nearly 15 percent of Camden Properties Abandoned." *Courier-Post*, August 14, 2014. http://www.courierpostonline.com/story /news/local/south-jersey/2014/08/14/survey-nearly-percent-camden -properties-abandoned/14059361/. Accessed July 14, 2017.

Siman, Maíra, and Victória Santos. "Interrogating the Security-Development Nexus in Brazil's Domestic and Foreign Pacification Engagements." *Conflict, Security & Development* 18, no. 1 (2018): 61–83.

Simon, Darran. "Christie Sends Troopers into Camden amid Crime Surge." *Philadelphia Inquirer*, December 12, 2011. http://articles.philly.com/2011 -12-12/news/30507131_1_state-troopers-police-force-law-enforcement.

Simon, Jonathan. *Governing through Crime: How the War on Crime Transformed American Democracy and Created a Culture of Fear*. New York: Oxford University Press, 2007.

Singh, Nikhil Pal. *Race and America's Long War*. Berkeley: University of California Press, 2017.

Skocpol, Theda. "Political Response to Capitalist Crisis: Neo-Marxist Theories of the State and the Case of the New Deal." *Politics & Society* 10, no. 2 (1980): 155–201.

Skogan, Wesley. "The Promise of Community Policing." In *Police Innovation: Contrasting Perspectives*, edited by David Weisburd and Anthony A. Braga, 27–43. New York: Cambridge University Press, 2006.

Skoufalos, Matt. "3 from Collingswood Collared in Camden Drug Bust." *Collingswood Patch*, September 12, 2012. http://collingswood.patch.com /groups/police-and-fire/p/3-from-collingswood-collared-in-camden-drug -bust. Accessed June 1 2014.

Speri, Alice. "The FBI Has Quietly Investigated White Supremacist Infiltration of Law Enforcement." *The Intercept*, January 31, 2017. https://theintercept .com/2017/01/31/the-fbi-has-quietly-investigated-white-supremacist -infiltration-of-law-enforcement/. Accessed August 26, 2017.

Spoto, MaryAnn. "Plan to Close Riverfront State Prison in Camden Draws Controversy." *NJ Advance Media for NJ.com*, March 9, 2009. http://www .nj.com/news/index.ssf/2009/03/plans_to_close_riverfront_stat.html . Accessed June 23, 2017.

Stampnitzky, Lisa. *Disciplining Terror: How Experts Invented "Terrorism."* New York: Cambridge University Press, 2013.

Stiglitz, Joseph, and Linda J. Bilmes. "The True Cost of the Iraq War: $3 Trillion and Beyond." *Washington Post*, September 5, 2010. http://www.washing tonpost.com/wp-dyn/content/article/2010/09/03/AR2010090302200.html. Accessed June 24, 2018.

Stoker, Sam. "Framing the 'RNC 8." *In These Times*, October 8, 2008. http:// inthesetimes.com/article/3962/framing_the_rnc_8. Accessed March 2, 2012.

Stützle, Ingo. "The Order of Knowledge: The State as a Knowledge Apparatus." In *Reading Poulantzas* edited by Alexander Gallas, Lars Bretthauer, John Kannankulam, and Ingo Stützle, 170–85. Pontypool, UK: Merlin Press, 2011.

Sullivan, S.P. "Christie Will Shut Down 250-Inmate N.J. Prison Unit." *NJ Advance Media for NJ.com*, February 28, 2017. http://www.nj.com/politics /index.ssf/2017/02/christie_will_shut_down_250-inmate_nj_prison_unit .html. Accessed June 23, 2016.

Swaine, Jon, Lauren Gambino, and Oliver Laughland. "Protesters Unveil Demands for Stricter US Policing Laws as Political Reach Grows." *The Guardian*, August 21, 2015. https://www.theguardian.com/us-news/2015 /aug/21/protesters-unveil-police-policy-proposals. Accessed June 28, 2018.

Taibbi, Matt. "Apocalypse, New Jersey: A Dispatch from America's Most Desperate Town." *Rolling Stone*, December 11, 2013. http://www.rolling stone.com/culture/news/apocalypse-new-jersey-a-dispatch-from-americas -most-desperate-town-20131211. Accessed June 1, 2014.

Takei, Carl. "From Mass Incarceration to Mass Control, and Back Again: How Bipartisan Criminal Justice Reform May Lead to a For-Profit Nightmare." *University of Pennsylvania Journal of Law and Social Change* 20, no. 2 (2017): 125–83.

Taylor, Flint. "How Activists Won Reparations for the Survivors of Chicago Police Department Torture." *In These Times*, June 26, 2015. http://inthesetimes.com /article/18118/jon-burge-torture-reparations. Accessed June 28, 2018.

Taylor, Keeanga-Yamahtta. *From #Blacklivesmatter to Black Liberation*. New York: Haymarket Books, 2016.

Thompson, E.P. "The Moral Economy of the English Crowd in the Eighteenth Century." *Past & Present* 50 (1971): 76–136.

Vargas, Claudia. "Camden Tax Collection Inches Up." *Philadelphia Inquirer*, July 10, 2013. http://articles.philly.com/2013-07-10/news/40471880_1 _county-force-collection-rate-city-money. Accessed June 1 2014.

Vickery, Kenneth P. "'Herrenvolk' Democracy and Egalitarianism in South Africa and the US South." *Comparative Studies in Society and History* 16, no. 3 (1974): 309–28.

Vis, Barbara. "States of Welfare or States of Workfare? Welfare State Restructuring in 16 Capitalist Democracies, 1985–2002." *Policy & Politics* 35, no. 1 (2007): 105–22.

Visser, Jelle. "Union Membership Statistics in 24 Countries." *Monthly Labor Review* 129, no. 1 (2006): 38–49.

Vitale, Alex. "The Command and Control and Miami Models at the 2004 Republican National Convention: New Forms of Policing Protests." *Mobilization: An International Quarterly* 12, no. 4 (2007): 403–15.

———. *City of Disorder: How the Quality of Life Campaign Transformed New York Politics*. New York: New York University Press, 2008.

Wacquant, Loïc. *Deadly Symbiosis: Race and the Rise of the Penal State*. Malden, MA: Polity, 2009.

———. *Punishing the Poor: The Neoliberal Government of Social Insecurity*. Durham, NC: Duke University Press Books, 2009.

Waitzkin, Howard, and Ida Hellander. "Obamacare: The Neoliberal Model Comes Home to Roost in the United States—If We Let It." *Monthly Review* 68, no. 1

(2016). https://monthlyreview.org/2016/05/01/obamacare/. Accessed July 4, 2017.

Wall, Tyler. "Unmanning the Police Manhunt: Vertical Security as Pacification." *Socialist Studies/Études Socialistes* 9, no. 2 (2013): 32–56.

Wall, Tyler, Parastou Saberi, and Will Jackson, eds. *Destroy, Build, Secure: Readings on Pacification*. Ottawa: Red Quill Books, 2017.

Walsh, Jim. "Crime Numbers Plummet in Camden." *Courier-Post*, April 24, 2017. https://www.courierpostonline.com/story/news/crime/2017/04/24 /camden-crime-statistics-improve/100845048/. Accessed June 28, 2018.

———. "EDA approves $18.3M for Camden Hotel." *Courier-Post*, June 20, 2017. https://eu.courierpostonline.com/story/news/local/south-jersey/2017 /06/16/eda-camden-hotel-norcross/403443001. Accessed June 28, 2018.

———. "Homicides up in Camden, across Region." *Courier-Post*, January 23, 2017. https://www.courierpostonline.com/story/news/crime/2017/01/23 /camden-crime-statistics-increase/96954166/. Accessed June 28, 2018.

Walsh, William F., and Gennaro F. Vito. "The Meaning of Compstat Analysis and Response." *Journal of Contemporary Criminal Justice* 20, no. 1 (2004): 51–69.

Weaver, Donna. "Ocean County Aims to Block Sale of Stolen Items to Pawn Shops in Atlantic City." *Press of Atlantic City*, August 26, 2014. https:// www.pressofatlanticcity.com/news/crime/technology/ocean-county-aims -to-block-sale-of-stolen-items-to/article_23279694-2d72-11e4-9461 -0019bb2963f4.html. Accessed May 24, 2018.

Weiner, Tim. *Enemies: A History of the FBI*. New York: Random House, 2013.

Western, Bruce. *Punishment and Inequality in America*. New York: Russell Sage Foundation, 2006.

Wexler, Chuck. "What It Will Take to Reduce Deadly Shootings by Police." *The Washington Post*, January 19, 2018.

Whittin, Jon. "New Jersey Is 7th Worst State for Income Inequality." New Jersey Policy Perspective, December 15, 2016. https://www.njpp.org/budget/new -jersey-is-7th-worst-state-for-income-inequality. Accessed January 17, 2017.

Williams, Kristian. *Our Enemies in Blue: Police and Power in America*. Cambridge: South End Press, 2007.

Wolf, Naomi. "The Crackdown on Occupy Controversy: A Rebuttal." *The Guardian*, December 2, 2011. http://www.theguardian.com/commentisfree /cifamerica/2011/dec/02/crackdown-occupy-controversy-rebuttal-naomi -wolf?commentpage=1. Accessed December 2, 2012.

———. "Revealed: How the FBI Coordinated the Crackdown on Occupy." *The Guardian*, December 29, 2012. http://www.theguardian.com/commentis free/2012/dec/29/fbi-coordinated-crackdown-occupy. Accessed December 28, 2012.

———. "The Shocking Truth about the Crackdown on Occupy." *The Guardian*, November 25, 2011. http://www.theguardian.com/commentisfree/cifam erica/2011/nov/25/shocking-truth-about-crackdown-occupy. Accessed November 25, 2011.

Zaitchik, Alexander. "Meet Alex Jones." *Rolling Stone*, March 2, 2011. http://
www.rollingstone.com/politics/news/talk-radios-alex-jones-the-most-para
noid-man-in-america-20110302?print=true. Accessed July 12, 2014.
Zdan, Alex. "Trenton Sees 19 Homicides, Sharp Increase in Shootings in First
6 Months of the Year." *Times of Trenton*, July 7, 2013. http://www.nj.com
/mercer/index.ssf/2013/07/trenton_sees_spikes_in_homicides_shootings
_in_first_six_months_of_2013.html. Accessed August 4, 2014.

Index

Aaronson, Trevor, 32
abolitionist campaigns, 169–70
Abramsky, Sasha, 89
Accurnit, 2
ACLU (American Civil Liberties
Union), 3, 22, 23, 39–40, 134
administrative power, 27–30
African Americans: Black Freedom
Movement, 167–72; black poverty as
pathology, 62–63; Black Power
movement, 45–46, 113; Camden, NJ
census data, 6; COINTELPRO
activities against, 113, 117, 127;
colorblind racism, drug laws and, 64,
66; criminalized populations, mass
supervision of, 93, 95; *herrenvolk*-
welfare state, 17, 49–50, 57–60;
incarceration rates, 46, 47–48;
political policing of, 120, 128, 132,
137; racial and class oppression,
history of, 55–56; racial profiling,
New Jersey, 178; slave patrol, South
Carolina, 142–43; Syracuse, NY
hyperghettoes, 157–58, 158*fig*;
unemployment rates for, 105. *See
also* Black Lives Matter (BLM)
movement; race and racism
agency reports. *See* data collection and
use
AIDs Coalition to Unleash Power, 117
air traffic controller strike (1981), 65

Albany County Crime Analysis
Center (ACAC), 101–2, 153–55
Alexander, Michelle, 48
American Civil Liberties Union
(ACLU), 3, 22, 23, 39–40, 134
American Enterprise Institute, 23
American Legion, 58
American Legislative Exchange
Council (ALEC), 126
anarchists, policing of, 120–21, 122,
133, 135
Anderson, Elijah, 144–45
Animal Enterprise Protection Act
(1992), 118
Animal Liberation Front (ALF), 118,
119
Anti-Drug Abuse Act (1986), 66
anti-globalization movement, 120,
122–23
Arizona Counter Terrorism
Information Center (ACTIC), 126
Arizona Senate Bill (SB) 1070, 126
asset forfeiture, 19, 140, 148–49, 152
Attica Prison rebellion, 63–64
authoritarian statism, 50, 78
automated license plate readers, 21, 22,
79, 93, 163

Bacon's Rebellion (1676), 56
Berger, Dan, 169–70
Bilmes, Linda, 26